S0-BJZ-827

FUNDAMENTALISM in American Religion 1880 - 1950

A forty-five-volume facsimile series reproducing often extremely rare material documenting the development of one of the major religious movements of our time

■ *Edited by*
Joel A. Carpenter
Billy Graham Center, Wheaton College
■ *Advisory Editors*
Donald W. Dayton,
Northern Baptist Theological Seminary
George M. Marsden,
Duke University
Mark A. Noll,
Wheaton College
Grant Wacker,
University of North Carolina

A GARLAND SERIES

■ Volume 1

Second Coming of Christ: Premillennial Essays of the Prophetic Conference held in the Church of the Holy Trinity, New York City [1878]
[Includes an introduction to the set]

■ Volume 2

Prophetic Studies of the International Prophetic Conference, Chicago, November, 1886
bound with
Addresses on the Second Coming of the Lord, Delivered at the Prophetic Conference, Allegheny, Pa., December 3-6, 1895

■ Volume 3

Addresses of the International Prophetic Conference, held December 10-15, 1901, in the Clarendon Street Baptist Church, Boston, Mass.
bound with
The Coming and Kingdom of Christ, a Stenographic Report of the Prophetic Bible Conference held at the Moody Bible Institute of Chicago, February 24-27, 1914.

■ Volume 4

Light on Prophecy, A Coordinated, Constructive Teaching, being the Proceedings and Addresses at the Philadelphia Prophetic Conference, May 28-30, 1918
bound with
Christ and Glory, Addresses Delivered at the New York Prophetic Conference, Carnegie Hall, November 25-28, 1918

■ The Prophecy Conference Movement

Volume 4

Edited by
Donald W. Dayton

Garland Publishing, Inc.
New York & London 1988

For a list of titles in this series, see the final pages of this volume.

These facsimiles have been made from copies in the Billy Graham Center of Wheaton College.

Library of Congress Cataloging in Publication Data

The Prophecy conference movement/edited with an introduction by Donald W. Dayton.
p. cm. — (Fundamentalism in American religion, 1880-1950)
Reprint of works originally published 1879-1918.
Contents: v. 1. Second Coming of Christ: premillennial essays of the Prophetic Conference held in the Church of the Holy Trinity, New York City — v. 2. Prophetic Studies of the International Prophetic Conference. Chicago, November, 1886. Addresses on the Second Coming of the Lord, delievered at the Prophetic Conference, Allegheny, Pa., December 3-6, 1895 — v. 3. Addresses of the International Prophetic Conference held December 10-15, 1901, in the Clarendon Street Baptist Church, Boston, Mass. The Coming and Kingdom of Christ: a stenographic report of the Prophetic Bible Conference held at the Moody Bible Institute of Chicago, February 24-27, 1914 — v. 4. Light on prophecy: a coordinated, constructive teaching being the proceedings and addresses at the Philadelphia Conference, May 28-30, 1918. Christ and glory: addresses delivered at the New York Prophetic Conference, Carnegie Hall, November 25-28, 1918/edited by Arno C. Gaebelein.
ISBN 0-8240-5007-X (alk. paper)
1. Eschatology—Congresses. 2. Millenium—Congresses. 3. Second Advent—Congresses. 4. Bible—Prophecies—Congresses. I. Dayton, Donald W. II. Series.
BT21.P76 1988
236'.9—dc19 88-24301

Design by Valerie Mergentime
Printed on acid-free, 250-year-life paper
Manufactured in the United States of America

CONTENTS

■ *Light on Prophecy*
A Coordinated, Constructive Teaching being the Proceedings and Addresses at the Philadelphia Prophetic Conference, May 28-30, 1918

■ *Christ and Glory*
Addresses delivered at the New York Prophetic Conference, Carnegie Hall, November 25-28, 1918

Edited by Arno Gaebelein

LIGHT ON PROPHECY

A Coordinated, Constructive Teaching

BEING

THE PROCEEDINGS AND ADDRESSES
at the PHILADELPHIA PROPHETIC CONFERENCE

May 28-30, 1918

NEW YORK
THE CHRISTIAN HERALD
BIBLE HOUSE

Printed by *The Christian Herald* for the Executive Committee of the Philadelphia Conference on the Return of Our Lord, the Committee having revised and approved the same for publication.

PREFATORY NOTE

"Is it possible I am in the wrong place? Is *this* the *Bible* Conference on the Return of Our Lord?"

A woman who had just climbed to the *fourth* gallery of the Academy of Music in Philadelphia asked this question. Evidently she had just arrived from a distance, as she deposited her bags on the floor by her seat, patting a boy for lugging them up the precipitous stairways for her.

She had taken a glance at the crowded galleries and floor below, and then at the stage. The latter did have rather a theatrical appearance. The speakers and Conference leaders were grouped in the center, surrounded by a white-clad choir of three or four hundred women singers, with a sprinkling of men singers.

"Yes, Madam, this *is* the Bible Conference," said a gentleman on one side of her, while another, on the other side, remarked, "The Lord has a whole lot of people who love His appearing."

With arms akimbo she stood gazing at the crowd and exclaimed, "Well, I do declare!"

The visiting woman had not expected a Korean revival crowd. Indeed she was fortunate to get in at all that day. The seating capacity of the Academy of Music is 3300, and on the first evening and the second and third *afternoon and evening* the Academy *overflowed*. On the third evening the overflow filled two floors of a church, the Chambers-Wylie Memorial, and in turn the *overflow overflowed* into the Witherspoon Hall.

The attendance and enthusiasm at the Bible Conference on the Return of our Lord, held in Philadelphia, Tuesday, Wednesday and Thursday, May 28, 29 and 30, 1918, passed far beyond the expectations of the management of the Conference.

A Philadelphia business man was so impressed by the great Advent meetings held in London in the autumn of 1917 that he was led to confer informally with a few earnest fellow Christians, and, with their prayerful approval, call together a larger group of ministers and laymen of Philadelphia to consider holding a widely representative Conference on the Return of the Lord. Accordingly, on January 19, 1918, thirty-seven ministers and laymen met for prayer and counsel, and unanimously decided to issue a Call for such a Conference. The following Executive Committee was appointed:

Charles L. Huston, Chairman; Vice-President and General Manager of the Lukens Steel Co., at Coatesville, Pa., and Chairman of the General Assembly's Committee on Evangelism of the Presbyterian Church, U. S. A.

Roger B. Whittlesey, Recording Secretary; Secretary-Treasurer of the China Inland Mission, whose headquarters for North America are 235 W. School Lane, Germantown, Pa.

John L. Steele, Treasurer; William Steele & Sons Company, Philadelphia, Engineers and Contractors.

Rev. John R. Davies, D.D., Pastor of Bethlehem Presbyterian Church, corner Broad and Diamond Streets, Philadelphia.

Robert B. Haines, Jr.; Haines Gauge Company, and Secretary of the American Branch of the Scripture Gift Mission, 119 South Fourth Street, Philadelphia.

Dr. Frank W. Lange; General Secretary of the Philadelphia School of the Bible, 1720 Arch Street, Philadelphia.

Rev. L. W. Munhall, D.D.; Editor of the "Eastern Methodist," and well known as a successful evangelist.

Ormond Rambo, of Rambo, Rambo & Mair, Attorneys at Law.

Max I. Reich, President of the Philadelphia Local Branch, Hebrew Christian Alliance of America.

T. Edward Ross, of Lybrand, Ross Brothers & Montgomery, Certified Public Accountants.

W. W. Rugh, of the Philadelphia Branch of the National Bible Institute, 200 North Fifteenth Street, Philadelphia.

Rev. J. R. Schaffer, Pastor of the Spruce Street Baptist Church, Philadelphia.

Joseph M. Steele, of William Steele & Sons Company, Engineers and Contractors, Philadelphia.

Rev. Benjamin Stern, Pastor of Emanuel Reformed Church, Philadelphia.

Allan Sutherland, Manager of Sunday School and Church Supply Department, Presbyterian Board of Publication and Sabbath School Work.

Rev. H. S. Tillis, Pastor of Weston Memorial Baptist Church, Philadelphia.

Charles Gallaudet Trumbull, Editor of the *Sunday School Times*, 1031 Walnut Street, Philadelphia.

Bishop Robert L. Rudolph, Bishop of the New York and Philadelphia Synod, Reformed Episcopal Church.

J. Davis Adams, Printing, 119 South Fourth Street, Philadelphia.

The overwhelming interest in the Conference justified the most sanguine expectations of the committee.

The addresses published in this volume are presented to the Christian public both in the nature of a Report of the Conference proceedings and as a "constructive, coordinated teaching of just what the Word of God does say about the return of our Lord."

With the hope that the reading of this book may provoke a careful, systematic study of God's Word itself the Committee prayerfully commends it to your consideration.

Signed: Rev. William L. Pettingill
Rev. J. R. Schaffer
J. D. Adams } *Editorial Committee.*

CONTENTS

LIGHT ON PROPHECY

A CALL FOR A BIBLE CONFERENCE ON THE RETURN OF OUR LORD

In the shadow of the tragedy of world-wide war Christians everywhere have been burdened in spirit and bewildered in mind by the complex conditions of the hour. But with an eagerness springing from a sense of personal need and a newly awakened desire to know the purposes of God as revealed in His Word, many are turning with intense interest, and many indeed with restful assurance, to the prophetic utterances of the Word of God for light.

Among all the questionings in the hearts of God's people none seem to press so urgently for a clear answer as those concerning the personal return of the Lord Jesus. Many Christians have never until now sought to know what the Scriptures really teach about "the blessed hope," and others have been diverted from such study by the confusion of voices on this theme, even though it occupies such a pivotal place of importance in the Bible.

Moved, therefore, by the hope that a Bible Conference on the return of our Lord and related events, such as the regathering of Israel and the fulfilment of prophecy concerning the end of the age, may be used by the Holy Spirit for the enlightenment of many believers and for the salvation of the lost, the undersigned invite all who "love his appearing" or who are earnestly seeking light on this subject to meet in the Academy of Music, Philadelphia, on May 28th, 29th and 30th, 1918, with eminently safe and sane pastors and Bible teachers of different denominations, to consider prayerfully the teachings of Scripture as to the Lord's return.

We believe that great personal blessing and a widely extended testimony may result from fellowship and study at a Conference in which eager hearts turn to the unerring Word of God, to learn in unhurried, prayerful study what that Word plainly teaches about the personal return of the Lord Jesus, and the practical bearing of this truth upon our duty as Christians to-day.

In view of the world-wide desire for clear light on this theme, we rejoice in the statement of truths concerning our Lord's return and a call to the churches recently issued by a notable group of British brethren, and the unusual response to that call on the part of the churches; and in numerous signs of interest from the home churches, the mission field, the army camps, and from trained and untrained students of the Bible everywhere. It is to unite in securing and in giving light on this theme and to present an unhesitating Scriptural testimony that all interested are earnestly invited to this conference, the details of which will be announced later.

WILLIAM D. B. AINEY
R. V. BINGHAM
JOHN R. DAVIES
FREDERIC W. FARR
H. W. GRIFFITH-THOMAS
HARRIS H. GREGG
ROBERT B. HAINES, JR.
CHARLES L. HUSTON
FRED KELKER
L. W. MUNHALL
W. J. MONTGOMERY
THOMPSON W. McKINNEY
MARK A. MATTHEWS
CORTLAND MYERS
GEORGE F. PENTECOST
P. W. PHILPOTT
JAMES M. GRAY
HERBERT MACKENZIE
WILLIAM L. PETTINGILL
WM. B. RILEY
MAX I. REICH
WM. H. RIDGWAY
EDWARD RONDTHALER
ROBERT M. RUSSELL
T. EDWARD ROSS
ROBERT L. RUDOLPH
JOHN L. STEELE
C. I. SCOFIELD
GEORGE C. SHANE
D. M. STEARNS
JOSEPH M. STEELE
R. A. TORREY
CHARLES GALLAUDET TRUMBULL
C. F. WIMBERLY
A. E. THOMPSON

Conference Headquarters
1310 Morris Building
Philadelphia

GREETING BY THE CHAIRMAN

Charles L. Huston, Chairman of the Conference Committee, Vice-President and General Manager of the Lukens Steel Co. at Coatesville, Pa., and Chairman of the General Assembly's Committee on Evangelism of the Presbyterian Church, U. S. A., presiding, Tuesday morning session of the Conference, introduced Rev. Orson R. Palmer, Pastor Berachah Church, Philadelphia, Home Director, Africa Inland Mission for North America, who conducted the devotional period, assisted by Rev. Harry D. Tillis, Rev. W. W. Rugh, Rev. Wm. B. Riley, and Rev. P. W. Philpott.

Mr. Huston, in opening the conference, said:

CHAIRMAN HUSTON'S OPENING ADDRESS

Our beloved friends and brothers and sisters in Christ: I take it that it is not out of place for those who have issued the call for this conference, to give such a greeting to you who have so splendidly responded. To you who have come in response to the call, at the very outset we want to say that the attitude of the conference committee, of the speakers, and, we trust and believe, of all those who are here, is that of absolute patriotism, absolute loyalty to the "powers that be." Our Lord has commanded us in His Word to "render to Caesar the things that are Caesar's and to God the things that are God's." Paul, in the 13th chapter of his Epistle to the Romans, tells us that "the powers that be are ordained of God. Whosoever therefore resisteth the power, resisteth the ordinance of God." Again, the apostle exhorts believers to be subject to the powers "not only for wrath, but also for conscience sake. For for this cause pay ye tribute also," recognizing the civil authorities and rendering obedience unto them because they are ordained of God.

It seems particularly fitting that at this time the program notices of the different days of the conference should be given. The keynote for the first day is "Humiliation"; the second day, "Exaltation of Christ"; and the third, and closing day, "Praise." This program is one that recognizes the need of absolute dependence upon God and of humiliation before him. We are also to bear in mind the proclamation that has just been issued by President Wilson, calling upon the people of the United States to spend, not only one day, but the entire week, in humiliation and prayer before Almighty God, confessing our sins and placing ourselves in the right attitude before Him, in order that His blessing may be upon us in this time of stress and strain and conflict; praying that our leaders may be guided, that we all may be guided, and that God will bless our nation and our allies. We trust that the especial blessing of God will be upon the sessions of this conference, because of the light that shall be thrown upon present conditions from the Scriptures. We are seeking to find out what the Scriptures have for us; what saith the Lord; not to fit a private or pet theory, but to learn what God hath spoken. In Deut. 29:29, we read: "The secret things belong unto the Lord our God: but those things which are revealed belong to us and to our children for ever, that we may do all the words of this law"; so the things that are revealed belong to us. It behooves us to seek the illumination of the Holy Spirit upon the revelation of God through the Spirit in His blessed Word, that we may know what He has given us; and we are here for this purpose. The call that was issued by thirty-five Christian men inviting you to this Bible Conference on the Return of Our Lord, is before us, and it seems proper that it should be read at this time.

A CALL FOR A WORLD CONFERENCE

This Bible Conference on the Return of Our Lord, held at Philadelphia this May 28th, 29th and 30th, 1918, adopts the following statement of belief:

First: We believe that the Bible is the inerrant, one and final Word of God; and, therefore, is our only authority.

Second: We believe in the Deity of our Lord Jesus Christ; that He is very God; and in His substitutionary death, as an atonement for sin; in His bodily resurrection and ascension and the certainty of His second appearance "without sin unto salvation."

Third: We believe that our Lord's prophetic Word is at this moment finding remarkable fulfilment; and that it does indicate the nearness of the close of this age, and of the coming of our Lord Jesus Christ.

Fourth: We believe that the completed church will be translated to be forever with the Lord.

Fifth: We believe that there will be a gathering of Israel to her land in unbelief, and she will be afterward converted by the appearance of Christ on her behalf.

Sixth: We believe that all human schemes of reconstruction must be subsidiary to the coming of our Lord Jesus Christ, because all nations will be subject to His rule.

Seventh: We believe that under the reign of

Christ there will be a further great effusion of the Holy Spirit upon all flesh.

Eighth: We believe that the truths embodied in this statement are of the utmost importance in determining Christian character and action in reference to the pressing problems of the hour.

And Resolves, if our Lord tarry, that a great world Bible Conference be held at Philadelphia May 27th to June 1st, 1919.

It might be well also to give an outline of the program of the conference. You will notice that on Tuesday the general topic will be, "Teachings Fundamental to the Return of Our Lord," in order to establish the basis of the whole conference. As stated before, the keynote of the first day's conference is "Humiliation"; on the second day, to-morrow, the general topic will be, "The Return of Our Lord as Related to Present Conditions," and all the teachings will bear upon that part of the whole subject. The keynote of to-morrow is "Exaltation of Christ." On Thursday, the closing day, the general topic assigned is "The Return of Our Lord in the Program of Prophecy," and the keynote of that day is "Praise." The doctrine of the return of our Lord will be taught from the Word of prophecy, coupled with the question, "What Manner of Persons Ought We to Be?" What application has the doctrine to our conduct and to our daily activities?

We are to have the pleasure of hearing from Rev. Harris H. Gregg, formerly pastor of the First Presbyterian Church of St. Louis, where Dr.

James H. Brookes, that valiant servant of God and teacher of God's Word, formerly ministered. Mr. Gregg is now the pastor of the Elim Chapel, Winnipeg, Canada, and he will address us on the subject, "Hath God spoken?" in order to start off with the foundation of God's own Word for the entire basis of all our teachings and all our conclusions.

HATH GOD SPOKEN?

Rev. Harris H. Gregg, D.D.

Pastor of Winnipeg, Canada, Presbyterian Church, and former pastor of Dr. James H. Brookes' Church at St. Louis, Mo.

Our Lord Jesus Christ and the Scriptures are our theme this morning, in reply to the question of the topic "Hath God Spoken?" The subject, of course, is the inspiration of the Word of God. Our Lord Jesus Christ fills the eye of God, fills the lips of the Holy Ghost, He fills the mouth of the Word of God; He fills the heart of His church. Our Lord is the only thing that the church is in God's sight, He is its only righteousness, its only holiness, its only redemption, its only foundation, its only way to God. He is all the truth of God. He is our dwelling place, our food, and our blessed hope. Christ is all.

The attention is called, in the first place, to the fact that

OUR LORD JESUS CHRIST IS THE THEME OF THE SCRIPTURES

He is the Lord and Seed of the woman in Genesis, the Lord and Seed of Abraham, Isaac, Jacob and

Judah. When the Holy Spirit is telling us of the first man, He has our Lord in mind as the Last Man. When He is telling us of the substitute, He has Christ in mind as our Substitute. When He is telling us of Noah, who, on the basis of that sacrifice which pointed to Calvary, takes possession of the renewed earth, He has in mind our Lord Jesus Christ, who, on the basis of His sacrifice for sin, some day is going to take possession of the new earth. When He is telling us of Abraham, the stranger coming from a far country and living a life of faith and having nothing but a grave there, He has in mind a greater Stranger, coming from a farther country, and living a life of faith in this Word in that same land, and getting nothing but a cross. When He is telling us of the miraculous birth of Isaac, his being laid on the altar, and on the third day rising, is a figure of speech; He is thinking of the virgin birth of our Lord Jesus, and the story of His Calvary and His resurrection on the third day. When He is telling us of Israel, a prince of peace with God and man, He is thinking of our Lord. When He is telling us of Jesus, that great Sufferer of the Old Testament, who through suffering entered into His glory again, He is thinking of "the sufferings of Christ, and the glories that should follow." Our Lord is the Lamb of God in Exodus; the High Priest of Leviticus; the Star out of Jacob in Numbers; the Prophet like unto Moses in Deuteronomy; the Captain of the host of the Lord in Joshua; the Messenger of Jehovah in Judges; our Kinsman in Ruth; the Lord and Seed of David in Samuel; the King of kings and Lord of lords in Kings and Chronicles; the Lord of heaven and earth in Ezra and Nehemiah; our Mordecai sitting on the throne in Esther. In Job, He is our risen Redeemer. In the Psalms, He is just about everything. He is the happy Man of the first Psalm; the Son of God of the second; the Son of man of the eighth, under whose feet some day all of creation shall be placed; the risen Man of the 16th Psalm; the persecuted Man of the 22d; the Shepherd of the 23d; the King of glory of the 24th; our Saviour in the 51st; the King of the 72d; our great High Priest after the order of Melchizedek, of the 110th; the One who leads everything that hath breath in praising God in the 150th Psalm. He is the suffering and then the glorified One in Isaiah; He is the Lord our righteousness in Jeremiah; the Man of sorrows in Lamentations; the Messiah who comes and is cut off in Daniel, getting nothing, and coming the second time as the Son of man in the clouds of heaven and getting everything then. He is our risen Saviour and Son of God in Hosea. He fills each one of the minor prophets. He is the King of the Jews, rejected but risen, in Matthew; the Servant in Mark; the Lord and Seed of the woman in Luke; the Son of God in John; our ascended Lord and Christ in Acts; our Righteousness in Romans; the Firstfruits from the dead in Corinthians; the Authority and Theme of Paul's apostleship in Galatians. He is the Head of the church and Head over all things to the church in Ephesians; our Lord Jesus Christ in Philippians; the fulness of the Godhead in Colossians; our great High Priest who is passed into the heavens, in Hebrews; and in the Book of Revelation He is the Throne-sitter, now upon a throne of grace, later a throne of judgment, and then the throne of his glory. "In the volume of the book it is written of me," He says, in the 40th Psalm and in the 10th chapter of Hebrews. How familiar our Lord was with the Scripture! When his ministry is recorded in the Gospels, He speaks of creation and of marriage, and refers to Satan in the beginning as we have recorded in the third chapter of Genesis. He speaks of Abel in the 4th chapter of Genesis, He speaks of Noah, He speaks of Abraham, He speaks of Moses, He speaks of David and Elijah, and Elisha, and of John, and of Daniel the prophet. How constantly He used the Scriptures, and always as being the words of God!

Our Lord is not only the Theme of the Scriptures. In the second place, your attention is called to the fact that

OUR LORD JESUS CHRIST IS THE PERFECT EXAMPLE OF ITS PERFECT STANDARD

In other words, he lived the Word of God, and His life was as true as that Word of God. That Word of God molded in Him and produced the only perfect, sinless life that there is any record of in the Word of God. He lived it. Were it possible for Him to have lived a lie, it were possible for that not to be the Word of God. It is impossible for it to be anything but the absolute and eternal Word of God.

In the third place, your attention is called to the fact that

OUR LORD JESUS CHRIST IS THE VIEWPOINT OF THE WORD OF GOD

Let us get our bearings. This book is largely the history of two men. In God's sight, only two men have ever done anything—the first man and the Last Man. We read that in the beginning God created the heaven and earth, and the last thing he created was man; that man became a chaos, and turned his dominion into a chaos through sin. But before God created the heaven and the earth, He purposed that a man should be over his work. and not an angel; but He purposed that His Sor should be that Man. So when this first man went to pieces through sin, and death marked his entire being—spirit, soul, and body—God did not have to change an iota of His purpose. For His purpose and counsels all centered in His Son, who should be the Last Man.

He did not send His Son into this world immediately upon this first man's sinning. He waited a long time, until the fulness of time, in order to allow this first man to show what he became when he became a sinner; and all human history, from the sin of Adam in the Garden of

Eden unto the cross of Jesus Christ, is but the story of what that man became when he became a sinner. That man, through sin, brought death upon himself, and upon his whole race. He murdered the whole human race; he became like Satan—a murderer and a liar—upon his becoming a sinner. That man started this war—not the Kaiser. That man started all your sin and all your suffering, and dug all of your graves. When he had fully shown himself to be nothing but dead in trespasses and sins, from which God could get nothing for himself, nor for man, God sent His Son, born of a virgin, and growing up through thirty years of obscurity. And when He showed Himself and the first man met him, through his Jewish and Gentile seed, the first man put Him to death. He could not stand the holiness of the Son of God, for he was a sinner. He could not stand His humiliation, for Satan promised to make him as God. He could not stand His unselfishness, for he is the embodiment of self. So he crucified Him; but, on the third day, God raised Him from the dead, and, raised from the dead, He becomes the beginning of the new creation of God, and the Last Man in reference to that man. The first man was made a living soul; the Last Man, a quickening spirit; and He breathed His own eternal, risen, saving life in the upper room the day of His resurrection upon those who had received Him. Now He is seated at God's right hand, continuing His work of new creation; forming His church, every member of which is a new creature in Christ Jesus. After He completes His church, He will return and establish the kingdom of His father David; that will be a part of the new creation. After that, there will be the new heaven and the new earth, and the former heaven and earth shall be remembered no more for ever; and Satan, sin, and death can never stain with the distant touch a portion of the new creation in Christ Jesus. Out of the side of the Adam, God took Eve, and from Eve a race has been born. Out of the wounded side of God, a new creation—a race—is formed, that is nearer and dearer to God than all the principalities and powers that worship around that burning throne at this moment.

This Book is the viewpoint of this Last Man, (pointing upward), and every other book that has ever been written is the book and viewpoint of this man (pointing downward). All other books are the books of the dead. This Book alone is the Book of the Living One. Satan played this trick on mother. He intruded his lie (placing man's book between eye and Bible) between God's Word and our mother, and got her to look at God's Word, which said, "In the day that thou eatest, thou shalt surely die." He persuaded her to look at this book through his lie, and she gave *this* up (God's Word), and became like Satan and gave birth to her firstborn, a murderer and a liar. This is the method of God. Through this Book (holding Bible between eye and man's book), look at every other book that has ever been written and you will give this book (man's book) up. The Pharisees (placing man's book between eye and Bible), through their schoolbooks, looked at Christ in His Word, and crucified Him. The Sadducees, through Greek learning and Babylonian culture, looked at Christ and Moses and the Prophets, and joined in crucifying Him. Those who received Him simply as Christ and the Word of God, looked at all else and received Him and proclaimed Him to be the Son of God. When the church in Rome, listening to Babylonian culture, locked this Book up and only looked at it through what it had formed through Babylonian culture, they came to the point where they would not allow this Book to be even read. But all that God gave to Luther was just to bring this Book out, this way (bringing the Bible out from under man's book and placing it as the glass through which to see every other book), and look at the church of Rome and of Reformation again.

All unbelief is but one method from the Garden of Eden till Satan shall be put in the pit. It is just this. It does not matter what form of Hindooism, or Pantheism or science, if you permit anything to intrude itself between the Word of that living and enthroned Last Man, you will give Him up and be lost. But if, through Him and His Book, you look down into the tomb of that first man, you will live for evermore. That man got himself into a fix when he sinned; he got himself into a box, and that was his casket, and we were all born in his casket. He has built universities around his head in Babylonia, in Egypt, in Greece, in Germany, in England, and in New England, and throughout Canada, but he cannot think himself out of being dead in trespasses and sins. He has marvelous hands, and he has wrought inventions beyond human description. Arts have been created and lost, so numerous have been all the works of his hand, but he has never worked himself out of that casket. He has built cities, and civilizations, and eras around those feet, but he has never walked out of that casket. No one ever comes out of that casket, but by the words of the Son of God. "The hour is coming, and now is," He says, "when the dead shall hear the voice of the Son of God, and they that hear shall live," and when He takes us out of that casket, he never shoves us back.

The blood washes sin away. Sin cannot wash blood away. How did God plan this new creation of His? By having His Son become the Son of man, to fall in this old sin-and-death-stricken creation as a grain of wheat falls into the ground and dies; and out of the death of Jesus Christ, out of His tomb, He takes you and He takes me, He takes His church; He takes all the titles that he possesses as a man; He takes His high priesthood; He takes His kingdom; He takes His right as a Man to sit on God's throne, before which angels stoop and veil their faces and worship. Out of that tomb He has taken his church; out of it He has taken, already in title, the kingdom of His father David; out of it He has taken the new heaven and the new earth. And so we have this

Book as the viewpoint of the Lord Jesus Christ. But, more than that,

THE LORD JESUS CHRIST IS THE ARCHETYPE OF THIS BOOK

Creation is His written Word. The Bible is His written Word, and He Himself is the living Word. The unwritten Word of God in creation runs into the written Word for its fulfilment, for the interpretation of its parables and types and teachings, as the Old Testament runs into the New Testament for its fulfilment and interpretation of the promises, types and parables; and both center in the Lord Jesus Christ. Therefore, He points to creation as familiarly as He pointed to the tabernacle, as he tells His own story. Pointing to the sun, He says, "I am the Light of the world." You know Him as the Rock of ages. You know Him as the Hyssop. You know Him as the Seer. You know Him last as the Lamb. You know Him as the Lion of the tribe of Judah. You know Him as the Last Man, of which the first man Adam was a type. He made all creation turn its face toward Himself and tell the story of His coming, His person, and His work.

The Lord Jesus Christ was born of a virgin by the Holy Ghost, representing life from the dead. God, in creation, in history, and in redemption, has always shown Himself to be life from the dead—the resurrection of life. He put Adam to sleep, and Eve, and all the human race; and He never looks into the face of a human being, but He is reminded that, when He created the human race, He showed Himself to be the God of resurrection. When he gave Isaac Sarah, who never had a son, He represented life from the dead; and He never looks into the face of a Jew without remembering that, as God of the covenant of Abraham and Jacob, He showed Himself to be the God of resurrection. When He sent His only Son into the world, He must needs again show Himself to be the God of resurrection and was virgin-born. Later, on the third day, He was raised from the dead, and He has provided a like redemption for all who receive Him for their Saviour and their Lord. Eve spoke of God as her Saviour, knowing herself in her nature to be a sinful woman, and produced a sinless Christ; and the same Holy Spirit is able to take forty fallible men, sinful men, and produce a sinless Word of God. And the divine and the human in Christ is but the archetype of the divine and human, and, though human, sinless and errorless—the verbally inspired words of a living God.

The highest reach of man's intellect in all the centuries of things has been this, that God must be, and God therefore is.

The human intellect cannot reach the bottom of that revelation by a billion centuries of life, traveling at one hundred and eighty-six thousand miles a second. Our Lord Jesus Christ, being God, often speaks of Himself in a threefold manner, for God is One in Three and Three in One. He says, "I am the way, the truth, and the life." He also speaks of Himself, in Revelation, as the One that was, and is, and is to come, and this is the only Book capable of treating all subjects, that speaks of that threefold manner in which Christ Himself is the Archetype of the past, and the present, and the future. That is the only Book that will tell you of man's past, his origin; that will explain man to-day to himself, and tell man's future. That is the only Book that will tell you of the past of sin, the present fear and power of sin, and the future of sin. It is alone the Book that will tell you of the past of salvation, its origin; its present aspect, and its future destiny. That is the only Book that will tell you of the past of Satan, how he became the devil; his present sphere and place, and his future destiny. That is the only Book that will tell you of the past of Israel, its origin; why Israel is wandering among the nations apart from Christ Jesus, and the future of Israel. That is the only Book that will tell you of the past of the church, explain the present condition of the church as well as of Christendom, and tell you of the future destiny of the church. That is the only Book that will tell you of the past of creation, explain the present chaotic condition of creation, and tell you of the new heavens and the new earth. It is the only Book that will tell you of your past, that will give you any light upon your present, and that will calmly foretell your future. The past, the present, and the future of our Lord as the Archetype of that threefold aspect in which all subjects are treated in a completeness that only God can speak on any and all of these themes.

THEN OUR LORD JESUS CHRIST IS THE MESSAGE OF THIS BOOK

When this first man became a sinner, he became a sin problem and a death problem; and if he cannot settle his sin problem and his death problem, he is incapacitated for eternity, and for settling any of the other problems that grow out of the consequences of sin and death. But there is a Man who has settled the sin question and the death question, and who has been ordained of God to likewise settle every other problem for this man who is perfectly helpless in his box to settle anything for himself, in time or eternity. All of God's expectations for the human race, for salvation, for labor and capital, for commerce, for education, for government, lie in that Man (pointing above), and never in this man (pointing beneath). "My soul, wait thou only upon God, for my expectation is from Him." Therefore, God's message is a message concerning His Son, and He wants the world to know what He has done for the world, even the world that crucified His Son, even the world that loves darkness rather than light. The Lord Jesus Christ is the message of that Book; He is the message of God to our hearts, and "satisfies our longing as nothing else can do."

He is not only the message of this Book, but, in the next place,

THE LORD JESUS CHRIST IS THE LIFE OF THIS BOOK

Isn't it wonderful that he not only was controlled by this Book, that it molded and formed His life, but that He is the very Life of this Book to-day? Through the Holy Spirit, He sent this Book to be sown as seed from Jerusalem unto the uttermost parts of the earth; and wherever it is sown in a human heart, Jewish or Gentile, from Jerusalem to the uttermost parts of the earth, and where it is received, Christ Jesus acts upon that heart and life. That is great sowing, is it not? He could not come up in the life of those that hear this Word, unless He is the Life of that Word. You cannot sow Shakespeare from Jerusalem and get even a Shakespearette, but you can sow that book in 556 languages and dialects, and each one will get Christ coming up in the heart, where He is received. He is the Life of this Word, and He is reproducing Himself, though absent from this earth, in all who receive Him.

He is, in the next place,

THE SUPREME WITNESS OF GOD TO THE FACT THAT THE BIBLE IS THE WORD OF GOD

In His message to the Laodicean church, the seventh church in the Book of Revelation, our Lord Jesus Christ is spoken of to those Laodicean

Christians as being the Faithful and True Witness —the One who knows. Lincoln and Douglas used to debate in Illinois before Lincoln sat in the President's chair, and one time in a debate, Lincoln took as his subject that a kingdom divided against itself cannot stand. He argued that this government could not stand with slavery in the south and freedom in the north, and when he got through, Mr. Douglas debated that it could stand. When he had a chance to reply to Mr. Douglas, Mr. Lincoln, rising to speak for the second time, said, "Mr. Douglas has taken this debate out of my hands, and it is no longer between Mr. Douglas and myself. It is between Mr. Douglas and a Man who spake as never man spake before, who said that a kingdom divided against itself cannot stand. If Mr. Douglas says it can stand, the debate is between him and that Man who spake as never man spake."

Mr. Higher Critic, the Lord Jesus Christ says the Scriptures cannot be broken. If you say that they can, we have no time to debate with you. We will just sit down and watch the debate through with you in your casket and that Man on the cross; and, Mr. Higher Critic, the debate will be finished at the judgment of the great white throne. The One who said on the cross, "It is finished!" meant not only atonement for sin, but He meant also that that first man is finished—all his thinking and all his works. In God's sight, the human came to an end at the cross of Jesus Christ. "It is finished!" "Heaven and earth shall pass away, (kisses Bible) but My Word shall not pass away."

In the last place,

THE LORD JESUS CHRIST IS THE WEARER OF THE CROWN FOR THIS BOOK

In the Garden of Eden the Lord showed Himself to be a Prophet. He told Satan that He was going to become the Seed of the woman, and as such would bruise his head. When He became the Seed of the virgin at the place of the skull, He bruised the head of the serpent, thus showing Himself to be a Prophet. Then He showed Himself to be a Priest. He killed the sacrifices, shedding blood, and with the skins of the animals clothed father and mother with the garments of salvation, telling typically the story that when He became the Seed of the woman and shed His blood, He Himself would become the righteousness, sanctification and redemption of all who received Him. We are accepted in the Beloved; we are in glory in the Person of God's Son. Then He showed Himself to be a King—the first Prophet, the first Priest, and the first King. Opening the door of the Garden of Eden, the King ushered our parents out and said, "In My Kingdom, sin and death cannot remain. I am Alpha and Omega." When He became the Seed of the woman, He was a Prophet; now in the glory He is our great High Priest; and when He comes again, he will be King of kings and Lord of lords. All other prophets are between His first prophetic office and His last. All ordained priests of God are but priests of God until He comes. All other kings are but kings until He becomes the King; and He wears all the titles and all the crowns of this Book, because He has worn the crown of thorns of that old creation. He wears all the titles and crowns of the new creation. The Lord Jesus Christ is the center, and the circumference, and the crown of glory of the living Word of God. Let us pray.

(PRAYER)

Our Father, which art in heaven. In our Lord, we are before Thee in the glory this morning, accepted in the Beloved, and, though here in these bodies of humiliation, living in a world that still rejects thee, we thank Thee, Lord Jesus, that Thou art living Thy life in our hearts and in our lives. Be it unto each one of us in this conference according to the word of Thy salvation; be it unto each one of us according to Thy word of sanctification; be it unto each one of us according to Thy word of perfect redemption; be to us, Lord Jesus, all Thou wouldst be to those whom Thou hast loved and redeemed with Thy precious blood. Be all in us that Thou wouldst be, and through us until we shall look into Thy face and be like Thee. For we shall see Thee face to face; and, our Father, we thank Thee for it. In Christ Jesus' name.

The chairman of the afternoon of session said:

Dr. Scofield, having suffered a physical breakdown, though holding out to the last minute, hoping and praying for sufficient strength, found himself unable to come to the conference and sent the following telegram:

[COPY]

Ashuelot, New Hampshire,
May 25, 1918.

To the Philadelphia Conference on the Return of Our Lord, Greeting:

I pray that God may guide all your proceedings, especially in the putting forth of a fearless warning that we are in the awful end of the Times of the Gentiles, with no hope for humanity except in the personal return of the Lord in glory; and also a statement of the fundamentals of Christian belief, which may form a clear basis for Christian fellowship in a day of apostasy.

C. I. Scofield.

Mr. Charles G. Trumbull, Editor of "The Sunday School Times" of Philadelphia, presented the following Resolution of regret and sympathy:

[COPY]
Dr. C. I. Scofield,
Ashuelot, N. H.

The following Resolution was unanimously

adopted by the Conference to be telegraphed to you this afternoon:

To our beloved friend and teacher in the fellowship of our Lord Jesus Christ, Dr. Scofield:

We thank our God upon all our remembrance of you, always in every supplication of ours on behalf of you making our supplication with joy, for your fellowship in furtherance of the gospel from the first day until now; being confident of this very thing, that He who began a good work in you will perfect it until the day of Jesus Christ: even as it is right for us to be thus minded on behalf of you, because we have you in our heart.

We who have met together in Christ at the Philadelphia Bible Conference on the Return of Our Lord unite in sending to you our heartfelt love, and want you to know of our real sorrow in not having your personal presence and fellowship and messages at this time. Thousands had counted joyfully upon seeing you and hearing you, and the fact that the loving heavenly Father has, in His providence, not seen best to permit this, does not alter the sense of deep personal loss through your absence, while at the same time we confidently count upon the Father to provide all things in your absence.

We are praising God at this time for having, through His grace in the Lord Jesus Christ, called you many years ago, first to believe on Jesus, then to break the Bread of Life and minister His blessings freely, through his Word, to the whole world.

We praise God that you were willing thus to be made an ambassador of Christ, and willing to devote your life to the study of God's Word, to the gathering together of the fruits of the study of others in that Word, and then to bring together the results of this rich study in the edition of the English Bible which God is now distributing throughout the world, to the eternal blessing of multitudes.

Because of this ministry into which God called you, and because of your response, we not only love the Lord, but we also love you. God has given you a place in our hearts' love that it is difficult to describe and express. A great warmth of tenderness and affection springs up in our hearts as we think of you, and as we turn the pages of the Reference Bible, and as we remember you in prayer, asking God to more than make up to you and to us the losses of this temporary separation.

While looking eagerly, with you, for the coming again of our Lord, to receive us unto Himself, that where He is, there we may be also, at the same time we rejoice that, however near or far may be our Lord's coming, your ministry in His name in the opening up of the riches of His Word will go right on, uninterrupted and increasingly as we believe, until He come. We therefore pray God's special and increasing blessing upon all the results, past, present, and future, of your personal ministry; and we count confidently upon your prayers that God bless and use the testimony of this present Conference on the Return of Our Lord to the salvation of many, and to the consecration and purifying and empowering of still more.

Beloved, we pray that in all things thou mayest prosper and be in health, even as thy soul prospereth. And the God of peace Himself sanctify you wholly, and may your spirit and soul and body be preserved entire, without blame at the coming of our Lord Jesus Christ. Faithful is He that calleth you, who will also do it. Looking for that blessed hope and glorious appearing of the great God and our Saviour Jesus Christ, we are,

Affectionately your friends in Him,

The Philadelphia Bible Conference on the Return of Our Lord.

The Committee, being advised of Dr. Scofield's physical condition and having in mind their obligation to the Conference as well as the teaching structure of the program, at the last moment invited Dr. John M. MacInnis, of Syracuse, N. Y., to prepare two of the addresses assigned to Dr. Scofield. At considerable inconvenience to himself Dr. MacInnis very graciously consented to serve us.

WHAT IS PROPHECY AND WHY STUDY IT?

By Rev. John M. MacInnis, B.D., Ph.D.

Pastor of South Presbyterian Church, Syracuse, N. Y.

I wish you might bear in mind that this subject was only given to me late last week, and that I was requested to stick to my text, as the program aims to be a constructive program, presenting a constructive idea of the truth connected with the Lord's second coming. We should also remember that the work aims to be of a teaching and constructive nature rather for inspirational purposes.

Having this in mind, we shall approach the subject, not so much from the point of view familiar to most of us who hold the premillennarian view of the coming of the Lord as from the point of view of the difficulties which present themselves to candid minds who are not yet able to see their way to accept this truth.

Jesus Christ is the greatest—incomparably the greatest—of the prophets, and the supreme and final authority in all things pertaining to prophecy. The nearer we get to Him in our definition of prophecy, the richer, fuller, and more comprehensive will our definition be. While our Lord was on earth, few men got as close to Him as Peter. He was one of the three who formed the inner circle. We know that they often talked about the prophets and prophecies. It is most reasonable to assume that Peter asked our Lord many questions regarding the prophecies of the Old Testament and how they came. It is reasonable to assume that Peter's definition of prophecy was influenced by these conversations with our Lord. He says that "men spake from God, being moved by the Holy Spirit," or, literally, "being carried along by the Holy Spirit." This definition has in it three things worthy of our attention.

First: He says, "Men spake from God." These men were real men, with real relationships, ambitions, aspirations, and affections. They were men with real interests in the things with which they came in contact: men, for example, like Isaiah, who was one of the greatest of the Old Testament prophets. He was a husband, a father, a citizen, and a true patriot. He was a man of his own day, a citizen of the Jewish nation, loving it and deeply interested in the things that concerned it. He was in every way a true, strong, robust, clearheaded, enthusiastic patriot, and a warm friend of the king who played the greatest part in the great crisis in which Isaiah prophesied to the nation. It was that kind of a man that God laid hold on when He wanted to speak to the people. It is important in our study of prophecy to remember this fact. We must also remember that these men, when they spoke from God, spoke primarily concerning the problems with which they were face to face at that time, and spoke in the language and forms of speech that the people could understand. It is important that we should emphasize this particular fact, because it is generally stated that those who accept the premillennarian point of view forget the human element in the prophecies of the Bible. If we do, it is very unfortunate, because it is only as we understand the circumstances under which these messages were given that we can fully appreciate the permanent value and universal message which they contain.

In the second place, Peter tells us that these real men, speaking to a real situation and facing real and immediate problems, spake "from God." The idea is that they spake not only from God but for God. They did not speculate about God and God's universe primarily, but they spoke a message for God to the people. There is a fundamental difference between speaking from God and for God, and speculating about God and His universe. The one is giving men God's truth, the other is expressing one's opinion about God. That is the difference between the ordinary man and a real prophet. In a great crisis like the present world-crisis, it makes all the difference in the world as to whether a man speaks about the President of the United States and his policies, or for the President, declaring his policies. The one is mere opinion—the other is a message of authority and fundamental importance. These men, while they were real men with earth relations and viewpoints, spoke from and for God. It is not, for the present, a question as to how they came to find God's message, but simply a recognition of the fact that they did speak from God. In all probability, Peter learned that fact from Jesus Christ.

So, in the third place, he emphasizes the fact that they did not originate their message. They "spake as they were carried along by the Holy Spirit," the Holy Spirit inspiring them so that they could know what God wanted them to say. This was essential to their speaking from God and for God. They could not speak for God if they did not know God's mind and God's message. This statement does not say how the Holy Spirit imparted that information to them. It is not a discussion of the psychology of revelation, but simply the declaration of a fact. The important thing is that God could make His mind known to these men. The only way in which He could secure that was through their thinking faculties. There is no other way to get into human personality. You hear what I have to say at this time. I am not able to take the words that I am uttering and transfer them from myself and put them into your brain, but I am doing something that is stimulating you as thinking beings to think the things that I am saying; and, while you may not have all the content of the words I utter, nor the full world-consciousness from which I am speaking, yet with all our limitations we feel that we are making a reasonable success in conveying to you the thought that I have in mind. But which one of you can explain the psychology and mystery of personality and personal relationships that make that possible? If we, then, with all our limitations, and weaknesses, and our ignorance regarding personality and its possibilities, are able to communicate one with the other in such a way as to feel reasonably sure that we understand one another, we should not think it impossible that God could so stimulate human minds as to give them the exact message that He wanted given to the people. Peter said that He did and, therefore, the prophets were able to speak from God and for God. These men were so stimulated and carried along by the Holy Spirit that they found the mind of God and were able to speak, knowing that they were speaking the mind of God. Therefore, in many of the great crises when they spoke, they prefaced their message with a "Thus saith the Lord." In some instances they were not able to fully understand the manner of the times spoken of in the message, and they made their own message a subject of searching investigation and study, in order that they might fully understand the significance of it. Primarily, then, prophecy is the message of men who spoke from and for God.

The next question that naturally arises is, "What did these men talk about?" It is only necessary for us to let our minds run casually through the subject matter of the Old and New

Testaments to realize that they talked about the things that were of immediate and fundamental interest to the people that were living in their day and involved their relations with God and with one another.

Hence, the messages of men like Abraham, and Moses, and Elijah, and Amos, and Isaiah, and Jeremiah, and John the Baptist were primarily messages to the people of their own day about what they ought to do in order that they might be true to God, to their fellows, and to themselves. In speaking to them about these relationships and these responsibilities, they naturally had to speak about the outlook of the individual and the nation in their world relations, for these prophets always emphasized that what they were and what they did in their life-time influenced the generations to follow. Not only that, but they also emphasized that what was to follow ought to have a stimulating influence upon them in the performance of their task in their day. It was not possible for them to get a right perspective of their own task and their own generation without some idea of the goal toward which their life was moving. Hence, as the Holy Spirit carried these men along, He gave them a vision of the goal of history and God told them what was going to come to pass in the latter days. It is this that gives us the predictive element in prophecy. The tendency in our day has been to ignore this phase of prophecy. Men have thought because they discovered the historical element, which we have already emphasized, there was no longer any room for the predictive element. This is especially true with those who have been endeavoring to get rid of the supernatural in the Bible and have tried to explain it as a natural product like the religious literatures of other religious peoples. However, it is absolutely impossible to make a strictly scientific and historical study of the Bible, both Old and New Testaments, and not see that in it we have more than mere human insight. In the vision of the future that is given by the prophets, we have a revelation that no human insight could have given to man.

This brings us to another question which naturally suggests itself at this point: "Is there anything in prophecy as we find it that would suggest that Peter's definition is a correct definition?" "Is there anything in it that would indicate that these men actually spoke as they were moved by the Holy Spirit and were able to give insights that indicated that they had the mind of God concerning the things of which they spoke?" There are many lines along which we could answer this question, giving detail incidents of how these men, speaking hundreds of years before Christ came, gave particular facts concerning Him that were fulfilled in minute detail. We could also point out how prophecy concerning nations like Babylon, and Assyria, and Egypt were fulfilled in minute detail. Thus, all you who were here this morning heard many suggestions as to how this Book is simply throbbing with lines of activities and interests that dovetail in a constructive unfolding of a great plan. In the Old Testament we have the seed; in the New we have the bloom.

There are two things I wish to call your attention to at this time, and I have only time to just refer to them, in order to suggest that the insight of these men must have been something more than the mere insight of human intelligence. A particular scientific study of these things is to my mind a conclusive demonstration of the fact that these "men spake as they were carried along by the Holy Spirit."

The first is the dream and the ambition of the people of Israel. That is one of the most interesting phenomena of all history. Beginning away down with the time of Abraham, this obscure people began to think of themselves as a peculiar people, who were to become a great nation and prove a blessing to all the nations of the earth. In the face of failure, opposition, and persecution, they persisted in not only dreaming this, but in enlarging the conception and adding little details to it that made the fulfilment increasingly difficult. In fact, by the time we come to the prophets of the Babylonian crisis, the prospects of a detailed fulfilment became exceedingly remote and improbable. Yet in the face of the calamities and failures which came to the people, they persisted in their dream, and their hope became centered in a Messiah who could finally lead them into the realization of this dream. It is impossible to take these dreams in their historical setting and see in them a probability of fulfilment, but the fact of history is that they have been largely fulfilled; and even if nothing else were to come of the people of Israel than what has already been fulfilled, what seems like a human impossibility has already been accomplished. This little, insignificant, weak, struggling nation, that only seemed like Poland among the nations of to-day, among the great nations of antiquity, has actually come to be a blessing to all the nations of the earth through Jesus of Nazareth, who is the fulfilment of her prophecies and hope, and the nations of the earth have already come to dwell in the tents of Shem.

Now, the question is, How did they come to dream that, and, having dreamed that, how did they come to insist on dreaming that which seemed like a human improbability if not impossibility? Peter's definition of prophecy would explain it, but I do not know of any other explanation that satisfies all the facts in the case. There is one explanation that is reasonable, one explanation that is adequate, and it is this, "Men spake from God, being moved, or carried along, by the Holy Ghost."

In the second place, we have in the Old Testament a wonderfully interesting outline of world history that was given thousands of years ago. Here it stands as it was given before Alexander had conquered the world or Rome had come to her glory. Beginning with Babylon the Great, it says that there would be four great world-empires, and then the world would continue in small kingdoms until the end, when the kingdom of the Son of Man or the Ancient of Days would be set up.

Hegel, the great German philosopher, in giving us a philosophy of history from the point of view of the philosopher, without any reference to the Book of Daniel at all, gives us practically the same divisions of history that Daniel gave us to the present time. Some of the most ambitious and greatest characters of history have tried to make this outline different. They have been ambitious to establish a fifth world-empire to correspond with that of Alexander's or Caesar's. Charlemagne and Napoleon failed to establish such an empire, and he who is now baptizing the world with blood and fire shall not succeed in establishing it, because this Word says that there shall be no fifth world-empire until Jesus shall set up His kingdom and "reign where'er the sun doth his successive journeys run."

Taking it from the point of human probability or political insight based upon a study of history, no one in the day of Daniel could have given such an outline as this, yet here the outline stands. How did this man happen to get this insight? There is one reasonable and adequate explanation that I know of, and it is the explanation given us by Peter: "Godly men spake as they were carried along by the Holy Spirit."

Now a word regarding the last part of our subject—"Why study prophecy?" We are told to-day that it is a waste of time, and that we become visionary and impractical when we give our time to a study of prophecy. Some insist that the study of prophecy leads to paralysis in real constructive Christian work. This being the case, it is proper that we should answer this question—"Why study prophecy?" We should be able to give a reason for coming to a place like this and giving several days to the consideration of these subjects, when the world is calling for the most real and vital kind of service. It is a day when we are being challenged to great and real things, and a day in which men ought to live at their best and give the best that is in them to the real interests of the world.

Let me suggest two or three reasons why the study of prophecy enables us to do this very thing. First, we ought to study it in order that we may know the mind of God. If God has spoken, it is our duty to know what He hath said. If He has spoken, it makes all the difference in the world concerning the things about which He has spoken. If He has given any indication as to what He is now doing, or what His purpose in history is, it is of superlative importance that we should find it out; believing that this Book is the message of men who spoke from God and for God, it is our duty to study it in order that we may find out what God has said concerning the coming days.

In the second place, we should study prophecy in order that we may have a right perspective of history and that we may be enabled to understand our times, the meaning of the movements of our day, and the significance of the crisis through which we are passing.

You may be surprised to have me mention this—that those of us who hold the idea of the second coming of Christ are accused of ignoring the plain teaching of history. On the contrary, I am convinced as never before that it is impossible for a man to get the right perspective of history apart from a true appreciation of the significance and meaning of the truth of the coming of Christ.

We are accused of bringing the truth into disrepute and turning the minds of careful and scientific scholars against the study of the Bible and especially of the last things, because of the narrow arbitrary way in which we present this truth. One of the main objections is that we are so materialistic and literal in our interpretations, that we deny that God can accomplish His great moral purpose through spiritual means, and that we dishonor God in suggesting that He is not able to accomplish His ends through spiritual means. Now, a thorough study of prophecy and all the prophets would have made such a statement absurd. If modern scholars had lived in the days of Micah or of Isaiah and could have heard them speak about God giving us a Son, and of a Child born, and of a suffering Servant coming, and of a Saviour being wounded and dying for the sin of the world, they would have rebuked these prophets, giving them to understand that to suggest that God would have to do these things in order to accomplish the redemption of the race was to dishonor Him, because it was to deny that He was able to consummate His great ends in a spiritual way. However, the question is not as to what God could do, but as to what He did do. The prophets prophesied that God would come into our life and in Jesus Christ would redeem us, and in the fulness of time Jesus came. The Babe was born; Jesus walked, a Man among men, in Galilee and Judea; He was crucified on the cross; He was laid in the tomb, and on the third day He rose again. That was very materialistic, but, nevertheless, no one can deny that in that material form God accomplished the thing that is essential to the redemption of the race. That is not theory, it is fact. If God chose to accomplish that part of redemption in that way, why should it be a dishonor to Him to choose to consummate it by a new revelation of Jesus Christ, this time apart from sin unto salvation? The fact of the matter is, so far as our opinions are concerned, they are mere opinions. The only way that we can find out as to how God is going to consummate this age, or any other age, is by revelation. Of course, we know that any revelation that is given us will not be inconsistent with the justice and righteousness of God, which is another way of saying that it cannot be inconsistent with the moral nature of the universe. Jesus has revealed to us that this age is to be consummated by His coming again, and the New

Testament makes it very clear that that coming will be in like manner as the disciples saw Him ascend into heaven. How that could be inconsistent with the morality, the righteousness, or spirituality of God is more than I can understand. A modern writer contends that such a consummation would be a contradiction of established scientific knowledge; for example, the evolutionary theory. As His coming is the consummation of activities, instead of its being a break with the real progress of history, it is the consummation of this progress. We are not opposed to a real evolution; that is, a progress that is carrying out the intelligent plan that is moving to a definite consummation. We are against an evolutionary theory that would limit God in His own universe, and that would contradict what God has revealed in His Son Jesus Christ.

The thing that is clear from a study of the world that we are now in, and from the study of prophecy, is that things are not as they were, and that things are not going to continue as they are, but there is change on every hand, and the only thing that is unchangeable is the will and the purpose of God, which are being carried out through all change and moving toward a consummation.

Jesus says that the consummation of this particular age is going to be precipitated by His coming again, and until that time comes He tells us that there will be wars and rumors of war; nation rising against nation, and kingdom against kingdom, and that wheat and tares shall grow together until the great day of adjustment. Men said that there could never be a war like this again, but the fact is that there is a war like this. Men said that if a war like this ever came, it could never last very long, but the fact is that it has lasted over three years; and the strange and interesting thing about it is that it has lasted because man took the simplest instruments known to him and brought the great machines of destruction to confusion by digging himself into the earth and defying the genius of the twentieth century.

So these inferences of men have been defeated because our world is a world of active beings who have the power of choice, and consequently we cannot know just exactly what they are going to do, excepting as it may be revealed to us by someone who knows the future. We may come to general conclusions, but no one can speak emphatically regarding these conclusions. What happens depends not on a closed machine but on the choice made by intelligence.

Christ, who has lived the only perfect life that has been lived, and who alone can speak as knowing the mind of God perfectly, says that He is coming again, and that God is going to consummate this age in that way. Whose word shall we accept? Christ's word or the critics' word?

One more word in conclusion. We ought to study prophecy in these days, not only in order to get the exact mind of God regarding these things, but that they may become great convictions with us through experiencing them, so that we may be prophets to our day. I do not say prophets in the sense that we shall do the exact kind of work that Isaiah and Jeremiah did when they wrote down their messages, but prophets in the sense that we speak for God and from God to our day as they spoke to their day. You remember that Jesus said that "as the Father sent Me into the world, so I send you into the world." Unquestionably the thing that He had in mind was that, as He was here to speak for the Father and from the Father, so His disciples are in the world to speak for Him and from Him.

We are living in a day when men speculate about God, and tell us what they think about God, and what He ought to do, and the way in which He ought to accomplish the tasks undertaken. In this crisis men are not looking for our opinions; they are asking as to whether God has spoken or not. If God has spoken, they want to hear what He has said. If we have a word from God, this is the word to utter. In order to speak the message of this Book, we must first experience it, for it is not God's message for us until first of all we have accepted it as such and experienced it in our own lives; but, having experienced it, God asks us to go out to the world and speak it for Him and from Him. This is the thing that will bring back the note of authority into preaching and will make our messages living and vital. But we should be very careful that we do not elevate our own interpretation into the place of God's Word. The facts of God's Word are one thing; our interpretations of these facts are quite another thing. The supreme need in this moment is men and women who have the courage to respond to the challenge of the divine truth as revealed by the prophets, and who speak it as a living reality to the bleeding heart of a perishing world.

I believe that a careful, intelligent, serious study of prophecy under the guidance of the Holy Spirit will make it possible for men to thus speak for God and from God. It will also enable them to brace their minds as Peter literally says, giving them a clear, comprehensive outlook on history that will enable them to be calm and confident in the midst of falling and crumbling nations, and in the throes of all human conflicts as the shadows deepen and the darkness gathers, and men's hearts fail them because of fear. They who are true students of the prophets will stand confident and strong, knowing that God is in all these things moving toward the great consummation in which Jesus shall come, fulfilling the dream of prophets and realizing the hope of all true prophecy.

Charles L. Huston, Chairman, in introducing Dr. Matthews, said:

The next on our program will be an address by Dr. Mark A. Matthews, D.D., Pastor of the First Presbyterian Church of Seattle, Washington, and former Moderator of the General Assembly of the Presbyterian Church, U. S. A. Dr.

Matthews, has, I think it is said, the largest Presbyterian congregation in the United States in that far Western city. He has come on here from his attendance at the General Assembly in Columbus, in order to help us in this program, and we shall be glad to hear from him. He is affectionately known in the West as the "Tall Pine of the Sierras," and we are glad to welcome Dr. Matthews with us. His subject will be "The Doctrine of Our Lord's Return—Is It Safe and Sane, Does It Appeal to Scholars or Only to the Uninformed?"

THE DOCTRINE OF OUR LORD'S RETURN

REV. MARK MATTHEWS, D.D.

Pastor of the First Presbyterian Church of Seattle, Washington. Former Moderator of the General Assembly of the Presbyterian Church in the United States of America

My place on this program is to announce and prove from Scripture the doctrine of the second advent of Jesus Christ. You will notice from the program that I am not privileged to discuss the two phases, features, times, and instances of the second advent of Jesus Christ; but to present to you, based upon Scriptural authority, the fact of His coming. Those of us who have been asked to take part in this program understand that this is to be a teaching program, rather than an inspirational program, because what is said here is to be reported to the world. What we say therefore ought to stand, if it is supported by the Word of God, or it ought to fall if it fails to receive the support of the divine, infallible Word. It is said, by the critics of this doctrine, that it is a theory formulated by a certain coterie of people. If it is, then I have no place on this program, but if it is a doctrine taught by God's infallible Word, then I not only have a right on this program but have authority to say what I shall attempt to say.

In order that we may get the whole picture of what I shall undertake to teach, let us begin where the Scriptures say the beginning should be; Christ was, Christ is, Christ shall be, for ever and for ever. He was with God. The Word which was with God before the beginning became flesh and dwelt among us. That same Word shall in the form in which it ascended dwell among us again. That is a general statement of the doctrine. It is true or it is false. If it is true, it is true because God's Word states it. If it is false, it is false because its origin is no higher than human intellect or human reasoning. When Jesus Christ came into this world, the Incarnate Son of God, His incarnation guaranteed and made absolutely certain every other step he took and is yet to take. It was impossible for Jesus Christ to take upon Himself human form and remain in that form. Therefore, the incarnation guaranteed and forced the crucifixion. Sometimes men talk as if they doubted the virgin birth of Christ, and at the same time admit that He was crucified on Calvary. If He was crucified on Calvary, then He was, by the Holy Ghost, conceived in the womb of the virgin. He could not have been crucified had He been born of human parents. The incarnation of Jesus Christ guaranteed and forced the crucifixion upon Calvary. Clothed upon, He had to be unclothed. The crucifixion of Christ guaranteed His resurrection. His resurrection guaranteed His ascension. He said in John 14:3, "If I go and prepare a place for you, *I will come again.*" Is that not sufficient? The angels said He would come again. Acts 1:11: "This same Jesus, which is taken up from you into heaven, *shall so come in like manner as ye have seen Him go into heaven.*" The Holy Ghost said that, and I believe every word Jesus Christ said, and every word Jesus Christ and the Holy Ghost have written.

First: Jesus Christ was. He came the first time according to prophecy—why not the second time according to prophecy? If prophecy was correct the first time and was infallible the first time, and was to the most minute detail fulfilled the first time, why not the second time? If prophecy was worthy of literal construction and absolute belief when it spoke of the first advent of Jesus Christ, why is it not now to be literally construed, and why is it not worthy of absolute belief when it speaks of the second advent? If I may, let me talk to my fellow lawyers (as I am a member of the bar of this country), I appeal to you, if the evidence and the witnesses are unimpeached in the first part of the case, how are you going to impeach the same witnesses in the second part of the case? When you have accepted their credibility and admitted their infallibility, and when both have been proven to be true in the first statement, how are you going to discredit them when they speak of the second event in the life of the same person about whom they are testifying? Let us study the prophecy of the first coming:

Isaiah 7:14—"Behold, a virgin shall conceive, and bear a Son, and shall call His name Immanuel." Micah 5:2—"At Bethlehem." All these prophecies I am going to mention are speaking about the movements of Jesus Christ up to and after His first advent. Jeremiah 31:15 speaks of the "children being killed." Hosea 11:1—"Called out of Egypt." Zechariah 9:9 speaks of His entering into Jerusalem. Psalms 41:9 and 55:12-14 speak of the betrayal. Zechariah 13:7 speaks of His being forsaken by His disciples. Zechariah 11:12 speaks of His being sold for thirty pieces of silver; Zechariah 11:13—the potter's field bought; Isaiah 50:6—that He would be spit upon and scourged; Exodus 12:46 and Psalm 34:20—that not a bone should be broken; Psalm 69:12—that gall and vinegar should be given Him; Psalm 22—that His hands and feet should be pierced and His garments parted. Isaiah 52 told of His sufferings, His rejection, His patience and His death. All these prophecies fortelling the first coming of Christ were fulfilled to the letter. I am talking about the doctrine based upon the infallibility of God's Word, which infallibility foretold the first coming. Why not believe it when it tells of His premillennial second advent?

Now, if you do not believe the second coming doctrine as taught in the Scriptures, then tear out the passages that tell of the first coming. You must take the Bible as a whole and believe it, or you must be like the Satanic cults and agents of the country—tear it up. Let us apply this rule.

HE IS—Where is Jesus Christ now? A while ago, in describing this program, I said that the crucifixion guaranteed the resurrection, the resurrection guaranteed the ascension, and I left Him in your minds as ascended. Where is the resurrected Son of God now? First John 2:6—"We have an advocate with the Father, Jesus Christ the righteous." Where is Christ? He is at the right hand of God, making intercession for you and for me. The Bible tells me where He is. I believed the Bible when it told me that He would come the first time; I believe the Bible when it tells me where He is *now*, and what He is doing now; and I believe the Bible when it tells me what He is going to do, namely, that He is coming for me.

Second: He is coming. He said, "I will come again and receive you unto myself, that where I am, there ye may be also." The Scriptures teach that Jesus Christ is coming. Let me bring the doctrine a little closer, if I may, in the following passages: Luke 1:31-33, inclusive, makes a very strong case. Let us see. The 31st verse says: "And, behold, thou shalt conceive in thy womb, and bring forth a Son, and shall call His name Jesus." 32nd: "He shall be great, and shall be called the Son of the Highest: and the Lord God shall *give unto Him the throne of His father David.*" I believe the 31st and 32nd verses. What I want to know is, why some very learned people reject the 33rd verse. Listen! *"And He shall reign over the house of Jacob for ever; and of His kingdom there shall be no end."*

Now, if verses 31 and 32, foretelling the first advent, are accepted, why not the 33rd, foretelling the second advent, and what will take place? Why not accept *all three as true?* Let us take another step. From the 40th chapter, beginning with the 10th verse, of Isaiah, through chapter 63 to verse 4, you will find Christ's second return foretold. In these chapters it is stated He will come to execute judgment upon the nations and restore Israel, and they also show the glory that will follow in the Davidic kingdom.

Now, my friends, there are not two Isaiahs. You know some people get in a condition where they see double. When they get in that condition, if you are talking about worldly people walking the streets, you say they are intoxicated. *So,* if there are ministers of the gospel who say they see two Isaiahs, I say they have been *inoculated* by that infamous virus, German rationalism and German theology, which was prepared by the devil himself. Why? Because I challenge the real scholarship of the world to produce two Isaiahs. When that scholarship becomes fair and honest and sincere and sees the true divisions of this Book, it will say, the first forty chapters deal with the judgments to come upon Jerusalem and Judah and the nations; and the last chapters mentioned deal with Christ returning to Israel, restoring the kingdom, and establishing His power for ever, bringing judgment to the nations and bringing glory to the house of Jacob. That is the correct division, and every Hebrew scholar knows it. Isaiah 42:1—"He shall bring forth judgment to the Gentiles." First Corinthians, 1st chapter, the 7th verse, says, "waiting for the coming of our Lord Jesus Christ"—"parousia," a personal presence. In Malachi 3:1—"Behold, I will send my messenger, and he shall prepare the way before me." Now, that part of the verse refers to John the Baptist and is quoted in the New Testament—Matthew 11:10—in reference to John the Baptist, but that is not all the verse. The second part of the verse reads: "And the Lord, whom ye seek, shall suddenly come to His temple, even the messenger of the covenant, whom ye delight in; behold, *He shall come, saith the Lord of hosts.*" This part is nowhere quoted in the New Testament and *refers to the second coming of Christ,* because Malachi in his vision of the advents of Christ speaks of both the first and second advents of Christ in the same general prophecy, using the same general terms as he does in this verse. He refers to the first advent in the first part and to the second advent of Christ in the last part of the verse. In Zechariah 12th to 14th chapters inclusive, you find one prophecy the general theme of which is the return of our Lord, and the establishment of His kingdom. Study Isaiah 59:20 for the time of the coming. Study Matthew 24, beginning with the 3rd verse, for the description of His coming. Study the three aspects of His return in Matthew 25, which shows that there will be a testing of profession and of service, and a testing of a Gentile nation. Matthew, my friends, was written to the Jews and is a *kingdom* book. Remember that, when you are dealing with it. Jesus Christ said in John 14:2, 3, and in John 14:28—"I will come again." In John 14:16—"I will see you again." There is another great fact—*this doctrine is our hope.* I speak of the church. It is our hope. Hebrews 9:28 says: "Unto them that look for Him shall *He appear the second time* without sin unto salvation." He is not coming back to re-enact Calvary, but He is coming back to bring the judgments of Calvary to the nations, and the glory of His atonement to Himself and to His church. His work is not finished yet. First Corinthians 1:7 says, "waiting for the coming of our Lord Jesus Christ"; Titus 2:13, "looking for the blessed hope." But somebody is going to say, "These Scriptures you mention tell of the coming of Christ, but Christ has come, and Christ comes every time one is saved, and Christ comes every time a man confesses Him." I am not talking about the vicarious atonement of Jesus as it is applied by the Holy Ghost to the soul of the repentant. I am talking about the second coming, the visible, personal appearance of Christ. That is what the Scriptures I have quoted are talking about. First Thessalonians 4:16—"The Lord Himself shall descend from heaven with a shout." Why did they say "The Lord himself"? Put that little sentence out, if you do not believe the doctrine; but you cannot put it out. It is impossible. First Thessalonians 4:16—"The dead in Christ shall rise first." First Corinthians 15:22-23—"They that are Christ's at His coming." First Thessalonians 4:15—"We which are alive and remain unto the coming of the Lord shall not prevent them which are asleep."

My friends, Christianity rests its entire claim upon the resurrection of Jesus Christ. You must put out of history the resurrection of Jesus if you would destroy Christianity. The whole world is challenged to destroy Christianity if it can. In order to do it, it must destroy the resurrection of Jesus Christ. Is Christianity supernatural? I point you to the empty tomb. Is Christianity sufficient? I point you to the *empty cup*. Is Christianity effective? I point you to the empty tomb. Is Christianity destined to rule the world? I point you to the empty tomb; for the last enemy that shall be destroyed is death, and He who arose from the dead and became the firstfruit guaranteed that you and I shall arise and shall share in that resurrection and its power. Now, if Christ arose, and no man can deny it, I again challenge the critics who understand handling evidence, and say to them that there is no fact in history more scientifically and legally and divinely established than the resurrection of Jesus Christ. If I did not have the empty tomb and its history, which is infallible evidence, I have the living evidence of men who have been saved because He arose, and who testify to that fact. Are there Christians in this room? Are there men who know experimentally that they have been born again? Are there men who know experimentally Jesus Christ, the Son of God? If there are, then they are infallible, living witnesses of the fact that Jesus Christ arose. There is no fact in history more perfectly proven than the resurrection of Christ (1 Cor. 15:12-26). His resurrection made compulsory His ascension. His ascension is an absolute guarantee of His second advent, for He said, "If I go, I will come again." Christianity is supernatural and infallible, because Jesus Christ, very God of very God, rose from the dead, ascended to the Father, and is seated at the right hand of God.

The resurrection and ascension guarantee the second coming of Jesus Christ. He came to present to the world the love of God and to establish His Father's kingdom. God has never been defeated. He came. They rejected both the King and the kingdom—didn't they? God Almighty has never been defeated. They went further; they said, "We will destroy this man who assumes to rule over Caesar, and who calls Himself God," and they, so far as they were concerned, crucified Him. God has never been defeated. They buried Him. They sealed the tomb with the power of the imperial government of Rome. They put a guard at its door. Jesus Christ arose, He was up before the angel announced the fact. The angel did not roll back the stone and *let* Jesus arise. He was up before the angel rolled back the stone and told the story. They rejected the kingdom, and Jesus Christ arose from the dead and ascended to the Father. Was He going to leave Himself without a witness in this world? No! What did He do? He said, "I will send a second paraclete," the third Person of the Trinity, the Holy Ghost, to convince the world of sin, of righteousness and judgment. What else? He came to testify to the things Christ came to do for those who love and accept Him. What else? To have in charge the work of regeneration, to take the blood of Christ and create a new creation; and to build His body, the church. Then on the day of Pentecost the body of Christ began formation, and on that same day the body of the Antichrist began formation; and the two have been growing together like the tares and the wheat, and will continue so to grow until Christ destroys the tares. What else? Jesus Christ left the church in the world. The kingdom of God is not in the world now. "Lord, teach us to pray." (To whom did Christ teach that prayer? To some Jews who had been converted.) "Thy kingdom come, Thy will be done." That prayer will be prayed in the distant future, and every line will be answered. To-day the church of Jesus Christ is in the world, presenting to man the gospel of Christ as a savour of life to those who believe and savour of death to those who do not believe. Christ must come back to finish the work He began. The kingdom is not here, but these passages that I have quoted, and passages all through the Bible, say the kingdom of God *shall be* established.

Now, there is one point on which we all agree. The man who does not believe on the coming of Christ talks about the kingdom of God being established, and the kingdom of God *shall be established*, but Christ has fixed the time. It cannot be established now. It cannot be established until the King comes back to establish the kingdom (Dan. 2:44-45). Who is Christ now? He is the High Priest, making the advocate's plea for me. When will Christ be King of kings and Lord of lords, reigning in absolute sovereignty over the world? *When He comes.* All of that is based upon the resurrection of Jesus Christ. He came, He was crucified, He was buried, He arose, He ascended. He will come; and the kingdom will be established. By whom? It will be established *at the return of Christ, and by Christ when He returns,* and not by the preaching of the gospel.

Jesus arose from the dead and sitteth at the right hand of God. The resurrection and ascension guarantee His return. Acts 1:11—"This same Jesus shall so come in like manner as *ye have seen Him go into the heavens.*"

Zechariah 14:4—"And His feet shall stand in *that day* upon the Mount of Olives." Read Matthew 24:29-30, Mark 13:26, Luke 21:27. Mark 14:64, Matthew 26:64—"We shall see the Son of Man sitting on the right hand of power, and coming in the clouds of heaven." Is that enough?

Zechariah 12:10—"And they shall look upon Him whom they have pierced." Listen! Zechariah 14:5—"And the Lord my God shall come, and *all the saints with Him.*" First Thessalonians 3:12 —"The coming of our Lord Jesus Christ, with all His saints."

Third: This hope. The premillennial return of our Lord Jesus Christ is the stabilizing doctrine of the Bible. It produces watchfulness (Matt. 24:42-44). It assures sobriety, seriousness and piety (1 Thess. 5:2-6). It presents consolation, hope and joy (1 Thess. 4:14-18, inclusive). In Titus 2:13 we are taught that, "looking for that blessed hope," we are to grow in grace.

My friends, this doctrine is the stabilizing doctrine of the church and ought to be preached by everyone. I have recited history to prove the historical points mentioned, and the Scriptures just cited reveal the fact of the stabilizing, evangelizing effect of this doctrine. Wherever the church of Jesus Christ has been true to His infallible Word, His vicarious atonement and His return, and has unfolded all the steps He has taken and is yet to take, souls have been born and have been daily added to the church. I appeal to the history of the church to prove that whenever she has been true to the gospel of Christ and to His infallible Word, she has always prospered. I appeal to your experience. Wherever ministers of the gospel have preached Christ and Him crucified, *and have indoctrinated the people,* their pews have been filled and their ministry has been honored of God. Wherever they have preached philosophy and a "social program," made by Pharisees and unregenerate parasites, they have found death in the pews and cobwebs in their church buildings. No minister nor church can prosper when God and His infallible Word, the deity of His Son, the vicarious atonement and His blessed return have been left out of the preaching. History proves the truthfulness of that statement.

Christianity is the life of Christ revealed in the life of the redeemed, under the control and direction of the Holy Ghost. Men ask, "Can you explain how men are born, regenerated, saved and join the church at every service?" Certainly! That is the purpose of the preaching of the gospel of Jesus Christ; that is the reason the church doors are opened and the gospel is preached. The minister is fishing for souls. I have often wondered why some preachers preach. They do not seem to be fishing for souls. Some preachers amuse me very much. Generally speaking, the best people on the earth are the ministers. They are the least appreciated, the most underpaid, and the most over-educated crowd on earth. (You laugh at that. I was sincere.) But I have often wondered why men stand up and preach a nice little essay they have made, and then (did you ever watch them?) they close the Bible and say, "Let us sing"; and after a short prayer and benediction they go out quietly to their homes. Did you ever see a service like that? My friends, it is a crime against the unsaved man in the pew for you to close your sermon, if you preach a gospel sermon, without making an appeal for men to accept Christ.

It is a crime against the unsaved man for you to close your service without making an appeal for him to accept Christ as his personal Saviour and confess Him before men. "Oh," some ministers say, "we open the doors of the church at communion service once in every three months." In other words, you are fishing twice a day every Sunday and after you have caught a few minnows they must dangle on the hook until next communion day. Why aren't you just as fair as you are with the fish when you are really fishing out here in the creek? You waste too much time with worms and not enough with the gospel. If you caught a trout you would take him off your hook, wouldn't you? You aren't fishing for the science and pleasure of reeling in the cord, are you? You are fishing to catch fish. Jesus Christ said, "I put you in the world to preach the gospel." What is the gospel? *Christ.* Not your theory of Christ, but Christ. There is too much sermonizing and not enough Bible-izing. Preach Christ and Him crucified. It will produce conviction, and conversion, and regeneration at every service. He put the church in the world to do the evangelizing until He comes to establish the kingdom.

His second coming is a stabilizing doctrine. This doctrine produces watchfulness. It produces sacrifice. It produces love and consolation. Is there a truth in all this world that hangs over the battlefield of Europe with such consolation as this truth? I heard Sir George Adam Smith, one of the great Hebrew scholars of the world, say: "We have gone astray, and some of us very far, but since the war the resurrection of Jesus Christ is nearer and dearer to us than ever before, and the field of carnage is illumined by the light that comes streaming from God's Word because He arose from the dead." Friends, Christ said He would come; and that the dead in Christ shall rise first. Come, Lord Jesus, and bring the redeemed dead to life again! The casualty lists will come. Remember to go to your Word, to the unfailing Word of God, to the empty tomb, and to this blessed hope, for He will bring your boy safely back on the morning of the resurrection, *if he was a Christian,* a resurrected and glorified saint to meet the Lord in the air.

I am asked to speak of the types. In the Old Testament from Eden to Calvary we had the altar. The altar unfolded three infallible facts—three! First: Every time a sacrifice was made, it testified to the depravity of man. Second: Every time a sacrifice was made, it testified to the inefficiency and to the weakness and failure of law to save. Third: Every time a sacrifice was made, it pointed to *the* sacrifice *to be made on Calvary.* Now, that is what the altar taught in the Old Testament. In the New Testament Jesus Christ from Calvary to the kingdom established a communion table. First Corinthians 11:26 says—

"For as often as ye eat this bread and drink this cup ye do show the Lord's death *till He come.*" It makes me happy to serve the communion. He left the communion table as an infallible evidence of His certain, physical, personal, visible, tangible return. He is coming in person. He is coming in bodily form. He is coming in glory. He is coming for His saints. He is coming with His saints to establish the kingdom. Does the communion table say: "Do this in remembrance of Me until the whole world is converted?" No. Till everybody who belongs to the church has wings? No. But, "*Till I come and raise the dead and change the living and catch them up to meet* the Lord in the air."

We shall see Him, know Him, and dwell with Him *here* and *hereafter,* and in the *new heavens, for ever and for ever.*

Address of Hon. Henry B. F. Macfarland

In a leaflet of the pre-Conference literature, "The Testimony of the Centuries to the Coming of Christ," there appeared a quotation from the old philosopher Plato, who twenty-five hundred years ago said: "It is necessary that a Lawgiver be sent from heaven to instruct. Oh, how greatly do I desire to see that man, and who he is." That the ancient heathen philosopher has many successors to-day, uninstructed in our "more sure

Word of prophecy," was evident from the statement of Hon. Henry B. F. Macfarland, of Washington, D. C., who presided at the Tuesday evening session of the Conference.

The statement is significant, coming from one of the ablest secular journalists of the country. Mr. Macfarland spent many of the earlier years of his career in the Senate and House press galleries in the nation's capitol, and there were few men on the floors below him enacting the nation's laws, who would not have admitted that he was the peer of the ablest of them. He was honored of the famous Gridiron Club, and was perhaps the dean of the National Press Club when he retired from journalism to practice law at the Washington bar, and to become a Commissioner of the District of Columbia. He is at present president of the Red Cross in Washington.

Mr. Macfarland said, in part: "Because I am a layman and know what many laymen are now thinking, may I say that the war has changed the thought of the whole world. When the war came, the intelligent world thought that it was going ahead in a constant improvement which would bring in its own millennium, a word which most people used without the slightest idea of where it came from or what it meant. Under the leadership of men of science and philosophy, and, in most cases, of men in Germany, somehow or other, by a process of education, of evolution, we were to have a constantly improving world in which presently peace would reign. There were those who thought that it would be necessary to provide for the judicious settlement of international disputes, and others who thought that it must be done by a federation or a league of nations that would enforce peace. Unquestionably the working theory of many intelligent public men in this and in all countries was that we should go on and on and on in a constant process of improvement to make the world better, and to finally bring about a state of universal peace, education, enlightenment and justice. Now all that has been shattered. Men of that type are now endeavoring to form a new theory, to readjust their minds to the startling facts which reveal the absolute falsity of that old theory, facts that disclose the real character of Germany, which was regarded by some of them as the leader in this process of civilization. Now they are all seeking, more or less distinctly and consciously, for a new working theory of life.

"Many of them are not religious men. They are not men whom we, who belong to the church, would consider as being Christians, but they are serious minded patriots; world minded patriots; looking and inquiring, as men were looking and inquiring in Rome and Greece when Jesus came the first time to the world. Though there may be a veil before their faces, though they may not read what is written in the Word, there is unquestionably in the minds of many of them, as it is revealed in private conversation, a hope that out of all this terrible storm may come a new order, which shall be better than anything they have dreamed; and it is very significant that many of them are looking to an appearing of God, as the only One who can help—mankind being at the end of its power—coming as the only One who can drive away the storm, make peace in the world, reconstruct the world's society and bring good out of overwhelming evil. Now, what is that, my dear friends, but the very thought which we consciously hold, the blessed hope of the glorious appearing of our Lord and Saviour, Jesus Christ? John R. Mott confirmed my own experience and impressions when, returning from one of his recent journeys to Europe, he said to me: 'There is no hope in man; our only hope is in a miracle. It is a very significant thing that, while so little is being said in the pulpits, so much is being said in the pews, in the offices and in dinner conversations by laymen and laywomen, of their hope that the Lord Himself may return to set all things right.'

"But in whatever way men and women are thinking of this great teaching about the future—as fundamentally important as the first coming, the death and resurrection of Jesus Christ—certainly it is the most important subject before the American people and the world today."

Rev. George H. Dowkontt conducted the devotional services, at the close of which the Chairman introduced Dr. William B. Riley.

THE GREATEST QUESTION CHRIST EVER ASKED

REV. WM. B. RILEY, D.D.

Pastor of the First Baptist Church of Minneapolis, Minn., and President of the Northwest Bible School, Bible teacher and lecturer

Mr. Chairman, Brethren and Sisters: I am very happy to address this audience, and to bring to you the theme announced for the evening. I want, however, preliminary to its discussion, to remind you of the context as well as the text suggested by this subject, and you will permit me to read some verses from the 16th chapter of the Gospel according to Matthew, verses 13 to 20.

"When Jesus came into the coasts of Cæsarea Philippi, He asked His disciples, saying, Whom do men say that I the Son of man am? And they said, Some say that Thou art John the Baptist; some, Elias; and others, Jeremias, or one of the prophets. He saith unto them, But whom say ye that I am? And Simon Peter answered and said, Thou art the Christ, the Son of the living God. And Jesus answered and said unto him, Blessed art thou, Simon Bar-jona: for flesh and blood hath not revealed it unto thee, but My Father which is in heaven. And I say also unto thee, That thou art Peter, and upon this rock I will build my church; and the gates of hell shall not prevail against it. And I will give unto thee the keys of the kingdom of heaven: and whatsoever thou shalt bind on earth shall be bound in heaven: and whatsoever thou shalt loose on earth shall be loosed in heaven. Then charged He His disciples that they should tell no man that He was Jesus the Christ."

It was as Jesus approached Cæsarea Philippi that He, with His little company, halted; probably to rest a few minutes from a weary journey, and, possibly, to receive and take the next meal. While waiting, He snatched the opportunity for some further instruction of those first students in the true "Christ's College."

Like all great teachers, He questioned; and, like the wise teacher, He prepared His questions with reference to their progress in study and understanding. The time of His decease at Jerusalem was not far away, and that it might be properly understood and sanely interpreted, they must properly understand Him and sanely interpret Him. Hence the question, "Whom do men say that I the Son of man am?"

Beyond controversy, this is the greatest question Christ ever asked. The question, with Peter's reply and Jesus' remarks, involves the three central facts of the New Testament Scriptures. These facts might take the form of themes, and be expressed in three phrases, around which every word uttered, from Matthew 1:1 to Rev. 22:21, clusters and circulates. They would be these: the Christ of God, the church of God, and the kingdom of God. The order of their statement is the order of their appearance in Scripture, and suggests also the program inspiration follows in the development of the themes themselves.

THE CHRIST OF GOD

He was the occasion of this question of the centuries. "Whom do men say that I the Son of man am?" Before that question all others pale; even the most important ones seem insignificant indeed.

To that question, there are three answers that claim attention, at least upon the ground of age: the answer of natural reason, the answer of scientific research, and the answer of divine revelation.

THE ANSWER OF NATURAL REASON!

Possibly the most ancient exponent of this was Satan himself. Whether he actually doubted the Deity of Christ, not recognizing Him when first he saw Him in the flesh, we do not know; but certain it is that in the wilderness, following our Lord's baptism, he called into question every essential feature of His deity.

He questioned His power to work miracles, and proffered Him a stone to be turned into bread as a test, he questioned His captaincy of the angelic host, and dared Him to cast himself down and give proof of their allegiance in the swiftness of their descent from heaven to suspend Him in mid-air, and he questioned his inheritance of the earth—or his final lordship, in the same, and asserted a self ownership.

The leading modern exponent of this reply was Strauss. In the last century that great skeptic gave to the world his mythical theory of Jesus, contending that no such person, as pictured in the New Testament, ever lived, save in the minds of the imaginative apostolate. Matthew, Mark, Luke and John, Peter, Paul and others "materialized Him out of the star dust of their Messianic hopes and training." As one expresses the Strauss conception, by that infatuation which sometimes befalls men, as a result of an inordinate affection for a natural leader, they magnified a plain peasant into a god of all grace and power, and, by a process of corporate scheming, palmed Him off on the world as a supernatural being.

The weakness of the modern mind, and the intellectual incapacity of some modern ministers, was never more clearly demonstrated than by the fact that Strauss' irrational explanation has been so widely received.

The time came, however, when the more thoughtful doubters reached the logical conclusion that the disciples of Jesus were no more able to invent such a character as the Christ of the Gospels, than they were to create the character itself. Beyond dispute, one colossal figure has crossed the centuries, and that figure is Christ. Who is He? This fact gave rise to the second reply.

IT IS THE ANSWER OF SCIENTIFIC RESEARCH!

That answer is in line with what some said, even in Jesus' time. Peter reports their opinion of Jesus after this manner: "He is John the Baptist, or Elias, or Jeremias, or one of the prophets." They had seen too much of Him; they had studied Him too carefully; they had examined His conduct and character too scientifically, to join in the Strauss-skeptic reply.

The true scientist tries conscientiously never to ignore facts! Even so long ago as Christ's time, honest students saw that, while He looked like a man, and behaved like a man, He was both in appearance and accomplishment more than the ordinary man. They deemed that He was at least such as John, or even Elias, or Jeremias. How modern that sounds! How much in line with the clerical skeptic of this day!

A modern religious leader consents that Jesus was not an ordinary man, but seeks to explain Him by saying, "He is only a man; yet He is the only Man." That paradox, however, while seeking a way of escape, puts its author into much more perplexing questions still. We cannot overlook its utter lack of logic. The poet says,

"If Christ were a man,
And only a man, I say,
That, of all mankind, I would cleave to Him,
And to Him would I cleave alway!"

If Christ was a man and only a man, He is a dead man; and those who lean on Him lean on one who long since failed. If Christ was a man and only a man, He was a deceiving man, for He said, "I and My Father are one," and the deceiver is always an insufficient support. If Christ was a man and only a man, He is unworthy of worship and to cleave to Him always is a violation of the first commandment.

The skeptical scientist of the present moment likes to style himself an advanced thinker. He makes the same answer now that the scribe and Pharisee (the learned men of two millenniums ago) made then. His answer involves Mary in harlotry, Joseph in fornication, makes Jesus a bastard, leaves the church without an explanation and the kingdom of God without promise or prospect.

But that Christ was not content with such a reply is evident in the fact that He pressed His disciples for yet another answer, and by Peter's lips it was voiced.

THAT WAS THE ANSWER OF DIVINE REVELATION

Simon Peter said, "Thou art the Christ, the Son of the living God." Jesus told him that that was the greatest thought he had ever had since his birth. It was not the flash of wit; it was not the expression of genius; it was not the speech of the clever; it was a revelation from God. Like all other good and perfect gifts, that knowledge came down from above. Peter was at his best when he made that reply. But the human voice is only at its best when it expresses the divine mind.

Someone says, "How do we know this is the divine mind?" Our reply is, Because in accord with the divine Word; in accord with the prophecy, "The Seed of the woman shall bruise the serpent's head"; in accord with the statement, "Behold, a virgin shall conceive, and bear a Son, and shall call His name Immanuel"; in accord with the announcement of Gabriel, "Fear not, Mary: for thou hast found favor with God. And, behold, thou shalt conceive in thy womb, and bring forth a Son, and shalt call His name Jesus;" in accord with the angel's statement to Joseph, "Fear not to take unto thee Mary thy wife: for that which is conceived in her is of the Holy Ghost"; in accord with the divine voice to Mary, "The Holy Ghost shall come upon thee, and the power of the Highest shall overshadow thee: therefore also that holy thing which shall be born of thee shall be called the Son of God"; in accord with the life He lived, the death He died, the resurrection He accomplished, the ascension that occurred before the eyes of hundreds.

Ah, Peter, God made to you the revelation of the ages! He was—He is "the Christ, the Son of the living God!" To deny that is to leave His birth, His life, His death, His ascension without explanation! To deny that is to dispute the history of the rise and growth and power of the

Christian church, and to deny that is to put one's self in opposition to the promised kingdom to come, with this Prince of Peace in the place of power.

Certainly, one day, men who still believe in the authority of the sacred Scripture, will cease from denying the virgin birth, the attested miracles, the matchless words, the sacrificial death, the certain resurrection, the glorious ascension, and even the promised second coming of the Christ, for if the Scriptures have any weight, any value, they testify to all these as they testify to Peter's declaration that He was "the Son of God."

So much, then, for the first portion of the text, the Christ of God. Let us turn now to the second portion of the text.

THE CHURCH OF GOD

"I say also unto thee, That thou art Peter, and upon this rock I will build my church; and the gates of hell shall not prevail against it."

The church of God rests upon the divine Christ. It was not Peter upon whom the church was built, or it would have crumbled when they crucified Him. It was not even Peter's confession, "Thou art the Christ, the Son of the living God"; for a mere statement is not sufficient for a foundation stone. It was the fact to which Peter replied, namely, that Jesus was the Christ, the Son of the living God; for facts are sufficient and stable. Upon that foundation-fact—the deity of Christ—

the church stands, and upon that the church will for ever stand. You cannot build a church upon any other basis! You can construct a house and call it a church; you can gather the people into some sort of an assembly, and call it a church; you can get the newspapers to say it is a church; but you do injustice to the biblical term. A house and an assembly do not necessarily mean a church. Where Christ is not honored as God, there can be no church. The Millennial Dawnites cannot build a church; they deny that Jesus is the equal of the Father, calling Him "creature" instead of "Creator." Christian Scientists can never build a church; they deny that Christ is God, and call Him either that "Great Teacher" or "Truth." Unitarians can never build a church; they have left out of their airy fabric the only adequate foundation Stone. These, and others that might be mentioned, construct houses and call them churches; but they rest upon the sand, and are destined to go down in that distressing storm which will surely sweep the earth, and illustrate for us the fact that "other foundation can no man lay than that is laid, which is Jesus Christ." One has said, "When Milton speaks of the 'earth's base as built on stubble,' he describes the attempt of those who set Christ, the very Son of God, aside, and then seek to build a church."

Superficial and thoughtless men are always liable to be deceived by appearances. One passes a street and sees a house built in churchly form, and folks entering it with demure mien, and, standing up together, they read the Scriptures, and render songs, and pass out, at its close, in perfect decorum; and he says, "That is a church!" Not if it rests on any other foundation than Christ, the Son of God. It may have the form of a church, but it is without the power of it; it may have the lines of a church, but it is without its life!

Dr. Jefferson has said, "The difference between a pool and a spring is that a spring is fed from within, while a pool is fed from without." That is the very difference between the true church and the counterfeit. Every counterfeit church lives as a parasite lives, by sucking its very existence from the life of another body; it takes in, and continues its existence as a pool does; it never overflows and refreshes the world as a spring does. Where did the Millennial Dawn movement get its membership? Whence do Christian Science churches bring their recruits? How does Unitarianism manage to live at all? None of them make converts from the world, by seeing men and women regenerated—saved from sin; they draw upon other churches as a pool draws upon a fountain; and they have their existence only because the church that has accepted Jesus Christ as the Son of God has power to make converts, power to overflow as a spring overflows, power to contribute to every piece of low ground about it as a spring makes contribution, power to fill up the pools and save them from utter and even foul stagnation, by pouring fresh streams into them. It ought not to be difficult, then, for one to tell whether he is connected with a church of Christ, or with an institution that has stolen the livery of heaven to serve the devil in.

But mark the second fact here stated concerning the church:

THE GATES OF HELL SHALL NOT PREVAIL AGAINST IT.

Death has claimed the bodies of the saints for centuries; it is claiming them now with every tick of the clock; it comes as a demon, determined to depopulate the church; it gathers to its rapacious maw the minister to-day; it strikes down the deacon to-morrow; on the third day it will lay low the noblest woman who ever graced the membership of the local body of believers; and the day after it will throttle the life of the child who confessed Christ but yesterday; and one who looks upon this devilish, devastating work might imagine that the church of Jesus Christ would, at least, perish before this persistent enemy! But no! The birth-rate of those begotten by the Spirit has forever exceeded the death-rate of the redeemed; and we have the sure promise of the Son of God that it will for ever remain so.

Tertullian was one day addressing the Roman officials, and he voiced that fact when he said, "We are but of yesterday; and yet we have filled every place belonging to you; cities, islands, castles, towns, assemblies, your very camps, your tribes, companies, palace, senate, forum; we leave you your temples only." Truly, of Christ, the Head of the church, it has been written, "He walks down the centuries with the tread of the Conqueror, and, though nineteen hundred years have passed since He died on the cross, in all these centuries He has been lifting empires off their hinges, and turning the stream of history into new channels." Emerson was right, therefore, when he said, "His name is ploughed into the world." Renan was right when he remarked, "His life has been made a corner-stone in the building of the race." Lecky was right when he declared, "The simple record of three short years of His active life has done more to regenerate and to soften mankind than all the disquisitions of philosophers, and all the exhortations of moralists." He who conquered in the regions of the sea of Galilee, and called to Himself the thousands upon the great Mediterranean, is still calling to Himself thousands by the great Atlantic and on the shores of the great Pacific; and His influence is felt in every continent of the world, and His conquests increase with every passing day. It must be evident even to the unthinking that He is making good to His church His word, "The gates of hell shall not prevail against thee." I pity the men who have linked their fortunes to a failing enterprise! I find a justifiable pride and an unspeakable pleasure in the fact that I linked my life to Jesus Christ, and allied my fortunes with that of an institution, the success of which is as sure as the Word of God, and the sweep of which is as wide as the world itself

Premillennialists have been charged with a declaration of the failure of the church. It is a false indictment! In the divine program the church has had a place; and it is filling it, and will not fail. But that place was not the final place in the divine scheme of the world's redemption. That belonged, rather, to

THE KINGDOM OF GOD

Is not the progress marked in this Scripture both marvelous and suggestive—the Christ of God, first; the church of God, second; the kingdom of God, last. Listen! "I will give unto thee the keys of the kingdom of heaven: and whatsoever thou shalt bind on earth shall be bound in heaven, and whatsoever thou shalt loose on earth shall be loosed in heaven. Then charged He His disciples that they should tell no man that He was Jesus the Christ."

From the concluding Scripture, three suggestions:

Christ has authority in the kingdom of God. Christ, who is "Head over all" to the church by divine appointment, is also Lord of the kingdom. As the man who carries all the keys to the house, is master of the same, so Jesus of Nazareth—God manifest in the flesh—is to be natural Master in that kingdom where all potentates shall fall before Him, and all nations shall serve Him.

As one reflects upon this text, he wonders if there is not this further suggestion here. You will remember that Paul teaches that "flesh and blood cannot inherit the kingdom of God" (1 Cor. 15:50), and immediately explains by reminding us that when the kingdom comes it will be made up of "incorruptible" and "immortal" men—men who, through His reappearance, have conquered against death, and have been changed in a moment from mortal to immortal, and men who, though dead, by the same event shall have been brought back in body, changed from the corruptible to the incorruptible (1 Cor. 15:51-57). Christ Himself is the King that brings men from the bondage of mortality to the freedom of immortality, and from beyond the bars of death to the liberty of an everlasting life; and He fits them alike for place, privilege and power in the kingdom. Is not that the very significance of what John saw in the Patmos vision? On the part of Christian believers there is universal agreement that he had a vision of Jesus in His glory, and when he saw Him, he looked upon "One like unto the Son of man, clothed with a garment down to the foot, and girt about the paps with a golden girdle. His head and His hairs were white like wool, as white as snow; and His eyes were as a flame of fire; and His feet like unto fine brass, as if they burned in a furnace; and His voice as the sound of many waters. And he had in His right hand seven stars: and out of His mouth went a sharp twoedged sword: and

His countenance was as the sun shineth in his strength. And when I saw Him, I fell at His feet as dead. And he laid His right hand upon me, saying unto me, Fear not; I am the first and the last: I am He that liveth, and was dead; and, behold, I am alive for evermore, Amen; and have the keys of hell and death" (Rev. 1:12-18).

"I have the keys of *hell*"—the word means "hades" or "the grave—the place of the dead" —"and of death." Yes, He holds the keys to both! He can bring the Elijahs out of the prison house of mortality; and He can bring the Lazaruses from beyond the bars of corruption; and when these types have been multiplied in the last living, or buried, believer, the kingdom of heaven will have come; not to be inherited by flesh and blood, as the church of God is constituted, but to be made up of the "immortal" and the "incorruptible," as God has ordained from the first, and as His ruling Son shall finally order.

In that kingdom He will share office with the saints. To Peter, at first, He said, "I will give unto thee the keys of the kingdom of heaven; and whatsoever thou shalt bind on earth shall be bound in heaven"; but at that moment He was speaking to Peter as a representative only; to Peter as a spokesman for the disciples. Turn but a single page in your New Testament and Jesus is speaking to His disciples, and to the whole company of them he said, "Verily I say unto you, Whatsoever ye shall bind on earth shall be bound in heaven: and whatsoever ye shall loose on earth shall be loosed in heaven" (Matt. 18:18). Dr. John Monroe Gibson, commenting in the Expositor's Bible upon this passage, says, "When the Master's voice shall be silent, the voice of the rock disciple shall have the same authority to bind and to loose, to regulate church offices, as if He Himself were with them." But, unfortunately for such a comment, it misses the main point of both prophecy and history. Historically, Peter had no such power, else Paul would not have successfully withstood him concerning his mistake; and from the Scripture standpoint, let it be understood that this was never spoken at all with reference to the church. When the statement was made to Peter, the kingdom was the subject of discussion; and when the promise was made to all the disciples, the kingdom still remained the subject of which the Master was speaking. Scripture has a marvelous habit of harmonizing with Scripture, and in these sacred pages you will never find the church and the kingdom confused. Peter was given no special power in the church; the Papacy, therefore, have missed the whole point of the Master's promise; and, in imagining that the keys of the church were hung at the girdle of Peter, they have indulged in a monstrous assumption, involving at least two mistakes. The first is, that this promise was ever restricted to Peter; it was first spoken to him, but only a little later to all the disciples (Matt. 18:18). Among his brethren, Christ is no respecter of persons. The second mistake is to apply it to *the church* when it was promised for *the kingdom.* Having gotten the correct perspective, behold how the Scriptures harmonize! Even the Old Testament prophets declare that, in the day of the Lord, saviours and judges should come upon Mount Zion; the New Testament tells us how this will be fulfilled, for Christ promised those who were to follow Him in the regeneration that they should reign with Him, and His apostolic company enjoyed special promise in this matter. To them Jesus said, "Ye are they which have continued with Me in My temptations. And I appoint unto you a kingdom, as My Father hath appointed unto Me; that ye may eat and drink at My table in My kingdom, and sit on thrones judging the twelve tribes of Israel" (Luke 22:28-30).

This Scripture provides no basis whatever for papal priesthood; and none whatever for the Catholic confessional! It relates to that day when judgment will have come to the world, and when the saints shall share with Jesus in determining whose sins are remitted, and whose are retained; and who shall be bound and consigned to everlasting punishment, and who shall be received into eternal life (Matt. 25:46). The Biblical distinction between the church period and the kingdom period brings to instructed believers a blessed suggestion. Concerning the church, no believer has a right to be discouraged: "the gates of hell shall not prevail against it." But, anticipating the kingdom, every instructed believer should be buoyant with the assurance that it will prevail against death and hades, for when the kingdom shall come, death will have no more dominion over God's people, and the believer's grave will be instantly robbed of its last inmate; and the immortal and the incorruptible, robed in the glory of new life, shall shine forth as the sun in the kingdom of their father. "Who hath ears to hear, let him hear" (Matt. 13:43).

It is a remarkable speech with which this sentence is followed and this study is closed: "Then charged He His disciples that they should tell no man that He was Jesus the Christ."

The kingdom, consummated, Christ will efface His official self. Here we have a suggestion that becomes a symbol, a statement that takes on the proportions of a type! Run through your New Testament and see how often it is recorded that Christ wrought a great work and then effaced Himself from the public scrutiny. He wanted the glory to be given to God, His Father. His whole plan is that that should be the final effect of His ministry. In the fifteenth chapter of First Corinthians, Paul, writing by the pen of inspiration, tells us that when He has rendered the last service He came to perform, namely, that of having put down "all rule and all authority and power," and having abolished death itself, which is the last enemy—that when all things shall be subjected to Him; when all saints, and all angels, will be ready to break forth in praises beyond anything He has heard or known in the eternity of the past; at that very time, He will efface Himself again, having turned all over to God the Father, "that God may be all in all."

When I contemplate Christ's character in the light of Christ's conduct, past and future; when I look upon the church and remember that it is but the expression of His love; when I anticipate the kingdom and remember it will be all by His power and by His will; when I see Him at last Conqueror over the whole world, standing before God, angels, men, and devils, resplendent, glorious, triumphant; and then, while I look, he suddenly effaces Himself, that His Father may have all the honor, He looms so large that I cannot refrain my lips, and I marvel not that believers break forth, from time to time, in singing:

"All hail the power of Jesus's name!
Let angels prostrate fall!
Bring forth the royal diadem,
And crown Him Lord of all.

"Crown Him, ye morning stars of light,
Who fixed this earthly ball!
Now hail the strength of Israel's might,
And crown Him Lord of all.

"Ye chosen seed of Israel's race,
Ye ransomed from the fall;
Hail Him who saves you by His grace,
And crown Him Lord of all.

"Sinners, whose love can ne'er forget
The wormwood and the gall,
Go spread your trophies at His feet,
And crown Him Lord of all.

"Let every kindred, every tribe,
On this terrestrial ball,
To Him all majesty ascribe,
And crown Him Lord of all.

"Oh, that with yonder sacred throng
We at His feet may fall!
We'll join the everlasting song,
And crown Him Lord of all."

Ah, Peter, you were right! He is the Christ, the Son of the living God!

DID THE CROSS OF CHRIST FULFIL ALL THE PROMISES?

PASTOR WILLIAM L. PETTINGILL

Dean of the Philadelphia School of the Bible; pastor of North Church at Wilmington, Delaware; author of "Simple Studies in Romans," "Simple Studies in the Revelation," etc.

In the 8th and the 9th verses of the 15th chapter of the Epistle to the Romans it is written: "Now I say that Jesus Christ was a minister of the circumcision for the truth of God, to confirm the promises made unto the fathers: and that the Gentiles might glorify God for His mercy." Our Lord's purpose in coming to the world is here shown to be threefold:

First, He came for the truth of God.

Second, He came to confirm the promises made unto the fathers.

Third, He came in order that the Gentiles might glorify God for His mercy.

I. Our Lord Jesus Christ came, first of all, for the truth of God. The word "truth" here might better be read, "truthfulness." He came to demonstrate the truthfulness and righteousness of His Father; He came to show that God was "not a man that He should lie." He came to manifest that all that God had said should be done, and that all God's ways are right ways. It was needful that the Lord Jesus Christ should come to the earth for that purpose, even if there had been no other purpose. If no one was to live on the earth after the cross had been set up and the blood of the Son of God had been shed, it was still needful that that cross should be set up and that that blood should be shed.

In Romans 3:25 it is written that the Lord Jesus Christ came in order to show the righteousness of God "in the passing over of sins done aforetime, in the forbearance of God." For thousands of years there had been going on what seemed to be a continual scandal, with reference to God's forgiveness of sins. God was apparently forgiving sins on inadequate grounds, and for unrighteous reasons. The blood of bulls and goats cannot take away sins, and yet God seemed to be forgiving sins on account of the blood of bulls and goats. Now, as a matter of fact, the blood of bulls and goats never took away sins; the blood of bulls and goats never furnished God with a righteous reason for forgiving a single sin. It is not true that men were forgiven in olden times by reason of the blood of lambs, and rams, and bullocks. It seemed to be true, but it was not. The seeming of it to be true made God seem to be unrighteous. The Lord Jesus Christ was ordained from before the foundation of the world to die on a certain day on the brow of Calvary in order that God might righteously forgive sins; and in olden times God was passing over sins, not on account of the blood of bulls and goats, but on account of the blood to which the blood of bulls and goats pointed, the blood typified by the blood of bulls and goats. God was forgiving sins because, in His reckoning from before the foundation of the world, the Lamb of God was already slain; and it was needful, in order that the righteousness of God might be manifested in the passing over of sins done aforetime, that Jesus should come and die on the cross of Calvary.

The same thing is stated again in Hebrews 9, where, in verse 15, it is shown that our Lord Jesus' death was, in part at least, "for the redemption of transgressions that were under the old testament." He died then for Adam and Eve, and the rest of the Old Testament folks, as well as for you, and for me, and for "whosoever will." He was "the propitiation for our sins, and not for ours only, but also for the sins of the whole world" (1 Jno. 2:2). Our Lord Jesus, when He died on the cross, did a work that reached away back into the past even to Eden, and also reached away down into the future, even to the last man that shall live in the world. He died for all, and in God's reckoning, therefore, all died; and He died for all, that they which live should not henceforth live unto themselves, but unto Him who died for them and rose again (2 Cor. 5:15).

Our Lord Jesus Christ was a Minister of the circumcision for the truth of God—for the truthfulness of God. It was therefore necessary, as we have seen, that he should die on the cross of Calvary in order to manifest the truthfulness and righteousness of His Father.

II. Our Lord Jesus Christ came down from heaven to confirm the promises made unto the fathers. The text says that He was a Minister of the circumcision: that is to say, His ministry had to do primarily with the circumcised nation, His people Israel. Certain great and wonderful promises had been made to Israel, and our Lord Jesus came, as the text shows, to confirm those promises. Most of the promises made unto the fathers were made unto fathers in Israel. It is true that there were promises made even before the days of Israel; but most of the promises were made to that nation after that nation had come into existence. The question is asked to-night, whether, by His death on the cross, our Lord Jesus fulfilled all the promises. He did not. But He did, by His death on the cross and by his testimony while here upon earth, confirm all the promises. In 2 Peter 1:19 we read that "we have also a more sure Word of prophecy." Or, as the Revision has it, "we have the Word of prophecy made more sure"; that is, confirmed. The word of prophecy has been "made more sure," or confirmed, in two ways: first, by the fulfilment of much of it, and, second, by our Lord's testimony as to the ultimate fulfilment of the remainder of it. Now, the Word of prophecy includes " the promises made unto the fathers" which our Lord came to confirm. He confirmed them, first, by fulfilling many of them; and He confirmed them, in the second place, by reiterating all of them.

In Luke 24:44, our Lord Jesus declared that all things which were written in the Law, and in the Prophets, and in the Psalms, concerning Him, must be fulfilled. When He made use of that expression, "the Law and the Prophets and the Psalms," He was referring, as all His hearers knew, to the whole of the Old Testament, which Old Testament was made up then, as it is made up now, of thirty-nine books, precisely the same thirty-nine books as we now have in the Old Testament. They were arranged in different order, but they were the same thirty-nine books, without any change whatever. In that passage, Luke 24:44, as well as in the 27th verse of the same chapter, our Lord Jesus Christ signed His name to the whole of the Old Testament, as the Word of God; and the endorsement of Jesus Christ is worth more to us than the endorsement of all the men in the wide world beside. We believe God.

He fulfilled many of the promises. And He fulfilled them in a certain way. He always fulfilled them literally. And the fact that He so fulfilled them gives us an unmistakable clue to promises yet remaining unfulfilled. People are having much controversy in these days about the matter of interpretation of prophecy. There are those who say that prophecy is not to be taken literally and that we are not to look for its literal fulfilment; but the fact is that very much prophecy has already been fulfilled, and that not one word of prophecy has ever been fulfilled otherwise than with absolute literalness. For an example, let us look at a passage in the 3rd chapter of Hosea, the 4th and 5th verses of that chapter, concerning the people of Israel. Part of that passage has been fulfilled, and part of it remains unfulfilled. All the fulfilment has been with exact literalness; and so, of course, we expect the rest of the prophecy to be fulfilled literally. Let us look at that Word of that prophecy to-night. It has to do with the circumcision, with the children of Israel. Hosea lived and preached about the same time as Isaiah. He tells us in the opening of his book that he prophesied during the reigns of Uzziah, Jotham, Ahaz and Hezekiah, kings of Judah, the very same kings named by Isaiah in his prophecy. This was nearly 800 years before Christ, when the words that Hosea uttered were very improbable, very incredible, absolutely unbelievable, from a human standpoint. Listen to what he says:

1. "For the children of Israel shall abide many days without a king." You remember how they lusted after a king, how they desired a king. Well, almost anybody can have a king who wants one. Even a band of gypsies can have a king. And when a nation wants a king so badly that it fights against God until He gives it a king in His wrath, and then afterward gives it a king of His own

choosing; when to this king of His own choosing God has promised a seed that shall never come to an end; and when this king of God's own choosing has been succeeded by a line of kings which still occupies the throne after the lapse of centuries, it seems most unreasonable, most incredible, that there should come a time when this people should "abide many days without a king." But what has happened? For 2,500 years Israel has had no king of her own. And yet Israel is a nation, a great and powerful nation, to-day. Without a land, driven out of her own land. She has a land, indeed, given to her by God, with a title that no man can finally set aside, but men have driven her out of her land; and for 1,900 years not even a remnant of Israel was allowed in that land. I say, Israel is a great and numerous people, but it has already dwelt "many days without a king."

2. The preacher did not stop there. He went on and said that during this time, during the "many days" referred to, this nation should also be "without a prince." You would suppose that if the nation did not have a king, it would then have a prince, under the sovereignty of some king. And, indeed, so it was for a little time with this nation; but that time long since has passed and the nation now for "many days" has been "without a prince."

3. Hosea goes further. He says that during this time he is talking about the children of Israel should be "without a sacrifice." You know that this nation began with a sacrifice. You know

that the Passover was the fundamental thing with this nation. You know that it was on the night of the Passover that this nation sprang into being, and you know that God established the Passover, and said that it should go on and on and that the people must not depart from it. Well, you say, they are celebrating the Passover every year. That is true, but the text does not say they should not have a Passover; the text says they should be "without a sacrifice." A Passover without a sacrifice seems an impossible anomaly, worse by far than "Hamlet with Hamlet left out," and yet Orthodox Jewry the world over celebrates the Passover every year "without a sacrifice," and has been doing that for centuries together. "The Scriptures cannot be broken."

4. The man of God also declared that, during the "many days" of which he spoke, the children of Israel should be "without an ephod." The ephod was the most prominent thing in the investiture of the high priest; it was the place in his robe where the breastplate was located. Therefore, because of its prominence, the word "ephod" came to be used as a synonym for the priesthood itself. What the prophet is saying is that they should have no priesthood. And so it has been even to this day for centuries together. They have been separated from their land and from their city, where only their priests could officiate according to their law. Therefore they have had no priesthood.

5. And then the prophet says that they should

be "without an image." This means that during the long period referred to they should not be image worshipers. You remember, do you not, that this was a national sin in Israel—to worship idols—and the prophets were raised up betimes to warn them against the sin of idolatry. If Hosea had been left to his own wits about it, he would never have been foolish enough to make a prophecy like this. It was contrary to reason. And yet God took this people to the very cesspool of idol-worship, he took them to Babylon, and left them there for seventy years, and they were cured of their idolatry for ever and ever. I do not know whether you would call that homeopathy, "like cures like," but I do not doubt that it certainly cured idolatry in that case; and to-day you cannot find a Jew, anywhere in the world, bowing down to worship an idol. Jews do not make good Roman Catholics. And the Russian Jew, particularly, hates the sight of a church spire, because the thing called Christianity in Russia is nothing but a system of ikon worship, and they will have nothing to do with images.

6. Hosea then declares, further, that during this long interim the children of Israel should be "without teraphim." You know about the teraphim, do you not? They were the household gods, the images they worshiped in their homes. You remember that when Jacob slipped away from Laban, with his wives and families and servants and cattle and all the rest, Rachel stole the teraphim from her father's house. When Laban came

rushing after the caravan, what he was disturbed about was the disappearance of the teraphim; but though the caravan was searched, the teraphim were not found, for Rachel was sitting on them. "Wherefore hast thou stolen my gods?" said Laban. Poor gods! they could neither prevent a woman from stealing them, nor reveal their whereabouts when search was made for them! You know where this thing happened. You know how Laban came up, and how he and Jacob thrashed the thing out; and then how, after a search of the caravan failed to locate the missing teraphim, they finally established "the Mizpah benediction"! They set a heap of stones between them, and said, "The Lord watch between me and thee while we are absent one from another!" That means, "The Lord keep His eye on you while I can't!" We call that a benediction, but it was rather a malediction. The teraphim were a thorn in the flesh to Israel in the Land. Why, we read, even in the history of David, that on the night when he ran away from the face of Saul, his wife Michal put a teraph into his bed, and then showed the bed to those who were searching the house and said that David was sick and this was David in the bed. I wonder where she got that teraph. The teraphim must have grown since Rachel's time, for in Rachel's day you could have put a dozen in your vestpocket and they would not have been any trouble at all.

Well, now, here is some prophecy which has been fulfilled, and fulfilled literally. Humanly considered, it was unbelievable, it was incredible, it was contrary to reason and it was contrary to common sense; but it has come to pass. Everything that God does is above reason, human reason. I met a man the other day who said he would not believe anything in the Bible that was contrary to reason. I said, "Whose reason?" and he said, "Mine!" Well, of course, according to that man we all ought to bow down and worship his reason, for his reason is different from mine, different from yours; and if his reason is the final appeal in these matters, his reason is greater than God, and we ought to worship his reason, instead of God. Listen to me: Do you call it reasonable that God should come into the world in the form of a little baby, without a human father; that He should grow up in the world to be a man; that He should take upon Himself the form of a servant; that He should humble Himself; that He should become obedient to death, even the death of the cross, in order to save you and me? I say to you that this is above all reason; and yet I believe it with all my heart; I revel in it with all my soul; I rejoice in it with all my being. Let reason stand aside and give place to faith in the revelation of God.

I do not know all about it, I cannot reason it all out, I cannot explain it all, but I believe God. And He has helped me to believe Him; and God knows I need help to believe Him, for I am a sinful creature and I find it very difficult to believe God. Unbelief is my besetting sin, and yours, and yours; but God has come to our assistance here and given us an aid to faith by fulfilling through the centuries a most improbable, unbelievable, incredible Scripture.

But, beloved, the preacher did not stop there. The prophet went on and said this:

7. "Afterwards shall the children of Israel return and seek the Lord their God, and David their king; and shall fear the Lord and His goodness in the latter days." They say that the Jew has no future. They say that the Jew has frittered away all his opportunities. They say that the Jew has so sinned against God that God has set him aside. Well, beloved, if sin could set aside the promises of God, the unconditional promises of God, if man's unfaithfulness could negative, or vitiate, or make null and void an unconditional promise of God, then, for one, I want to say that I never could love God, and I never could worship God. My love and worship must be directed toward a God who tells the truth, and who stands by His promises, and whose faithfulness cannot be affected by the unfaithfulness of men. Though we be faithless, He abideth faithful, for He cannot deny Himself. Thanks be to God; He has no wish to avoid His promises. He has reiterated His promises to Israel and the promises are just as true to-day as when Isaiah 27:6 was written: "He shall cause them that come of Jacob to take root: Israel shall blossom and bud, and fill the face of the world with fruit." The future of the world depends

upon God's promises to Israel, for it has pleased God to promise to bring the universal blessing to this race through the despised and dispersed people called the Jews. God has said, in the 8th chapter of Zechariah, "As ye were a curse among the nations, O house of Judah, and house of Israel; so will I save you, and ye shall be a blessing: fear not, but let your hands be strong. . . . In those days it shall come to pass, that ten men shall take hold out of all languages of the nations, even shall take hold of the skirt of him that is a Jew, saying, We will go with you: for we have heard that God is with you."

People do not generally love the Jew, and it may be admitted that the Jew is not always lovely or lovable. But, however black he may be painted, God will yet be glorified in this people. He will yet save them and make them a blessing. The day will surely come when not one of them shall say to his neighbor or his brother, Know the Lord, for they shall all know Him, from the least of them unto the greatest of them, for this is Jehovah's covenant unto them (Jer. 31:31-34). There is a promise to be fulfilled, a promise which God will fulfil as surely as God is God, because His mouth has spoken it.

Sometimes the two lines of Messianic prophecy in the Old Testament converge in one passage of Scripture, these two lines having to do with "the sufferings of Christ and the glory that should follow" (1 Pet. 1:11). For example, in Isa. 9:6, 7, it is written, "Unto us a child is born, unto us a

Son is given." So much has been fulfilled with great exactness. The child has been born, and the Son has been given. It could not have been put the other way. For the Son as such was not born; the Son was given, while the child was born. Observe the change in the tense in that passage. It says, "Unto us a child *is* born, unto us a Son *is* given, and the government *shall be* upon his shoulder." The child was born and the Son was given; the government is not yet upon His shoulder, but it is bound to be, as sure as God is God. "The government shall be upon His shoulder, and He shall be called Wonderful, Counsellor, the Mighty God, the Father of the Ages, the Prince of Peace. Of the increase of His government and peace there shall be no end, upon the throne of David, and upon His kingdom, to order it, and to establish it with judgment and with justice from henceforth even for ever. The zeal of the Lord of hosts shall perform this." Even that is not too great a task for the zeal of the Lord of hosts.

Just before our Lord was to be born of the virgin, that virgin was visited by Gabriel, and Gabriel said, in the words recorded in Luke 1:31-33: "Behold, thou shalt conceive in thy womb, and bring forth a Son, and shalt call His name Jesus. He shall be great, and shall be called the Son of the Highest." So far, the prophecy has been fulfilled with absolute literalness. It is contrary to reason, perfectly so; it is contrary to reason for a virgin to have a son, when that son has no human father. Nothing reasonable about that. Yet God came down and did this thing. We call it a miracle. I suspect that the Lord has to smile at our gulping about miracles. We say, "O what a miracle!" and He smiles. Why, what we call miracles are perfectly easy things with Him, and when we get up there we shall see how foolish it was for us to bother our heads about the impossibility of miracles. Nothing is impossible with God. So far, I say, the promise is fulfilled, but Gabriel does not stop there. He says: "And the Lord God shall give unto Him the throne of His father David, and He shall reign over the house of Jacob for ever; and of His kingdom there shall be no end." I submit to you, friends, that if human language is a vehicle for thought, then there is no possibility of misunderstanding the meaning of these words. This woman did bring forth a Son, she did call Him Jesus. He was great; He was called the Son of the Highest, and the Lord God shall give unto Him the throne of his father David, and He shall reign, not only over the house of Jacob according to this particular promise, but over all the nations of the world beside, for it is written in Zechariah 14:9, that "the Lord shall be King over all the earth; in that day shall there be one Lord, and His name one. In this day there are too many lords, "war lords," and each one is trying to decide who is lord. I am not able to predict how the present struggle is to end temporarily, but I know that one day there will be only one kingdom and one King in the earth, for the mouth of the Lord has spoken it. May God bring it to pass in His own time and way.

III. Our Lord Jesus Christ came down from heaven, not only to demonstrate the truthfulness and righteousness of God, and to confirm the promises made unto the fathers, but also "that the Gentiles might glorify God for His mercy." The Gentiles had no promises. If salvation was to come to them, it must come as a matter of pure mercy. I do not deny that salvation is always a matter of pure mercy, but after a promise is made, its fulfilment is primarily a matter of simple righteousness. Therefore, a righteous God who had made promises to Israel was required by His own righteousness to fulfil them. But, since no promises had been made to the Gentiles, there was no such righteous requirement for God to save them, or even to offer salvation to them. In offering salvation to Gentiles, therefore, He acted in mercy; and the Gentiles have special reason to "glorify God for His mercy."

Promises are now made even to Gentiles. And our righteous Father will surely fulfil every one of them. "Whosoever will may come." "Him that cometh I will in no wise cast out." In the gospel is "the righteousness of God revealed from faith to faith . . . even the righteousness of God which is by faith of Christ Jesus unto all and upon all them that believe; for there is no difference: for all have sinned, and come short of the glory of God; being justified freely by His grace through the redemption that is in Christ Jesus: whom God hath set forth to be a propitiation through faith in His blood, to declare His righteousness for the remission of sins that are past, through the forbearance of God; to declare, I say, at this time His righteousness: that He might be just, and the justifier of him that believeth in Jesus" (Rom. 1:17; 3:22-26).

"Thanks be unto God for His unspeakable gift!"

William H. Ridgway, of Coatesville, Pa., author of the "Busy Men's Corner" in the *Sunday School Times;* teacher of the "Iron Rose" Bible Classes, presided at the Wednesday morning session and said in part: "Mr. Huston and I come from the greatest steel place in the whole United States, a place upon which the eyes of the Government are now fixed, for we make plates for the ships. We make steel at Coatesville, and the quality of our steel depends upon what we put into it. If we put nickel in our steel we have a tremendously strong product; and if we put vanadium in our steel, we have a still stronger product. The premillennial view of the Lord Jesus Christ is the vanadium which, when put into the Christian life, will make it strong to endure."

Mr. Ridgway introduced Dr. Herbert W. Bieber, of Tyrone, Pa., who conducted the opening exercises.

Commenting on Paul's triumphant testimony in First Corinthians 15:50-58, Dr. Herbert W. Bieber of Tyrone, Pa., said: "I should like to say here that we are told in this passage that the premillennial doctrine does not paralyze, it energizes." Reading further in First Thess. 4:13-18, Dr. Bieber commented upon the passage "wherefore comfort one another with these words" as follows: "That word comfort does not mean the saying of nice words; it means strength. There is nothing in these tempestuous days that gives me so much strength as the knowledge that I may hear the shout of the Lord at any moment."

Dr. Bieber introduced Dr. D. M. Stearns, asking him to lead in prayer. "Just a word before I lead you in prayer," said Dr. D. M. Stearns; "a brief comment upon a remark my brother made, that the doctrine of the coming of our Lord does not paralyze but energizes. I have seen it for forty years; and unless any of you brethren have been talking the coming of Christ for forty years, you can hardly tell what an inspiration it is to see what is going on here at this Conference. For thirty-eight years a pastor of a church and for several years an evangelist, it has been my inspiration, my life, to tell of the coming of Him who alone can make the earth a fit place to live in; to tell of Him who alone can bring peace on earth. And He will; and while we submit cheerfully to the powers that be, and do what we are asked to do, we look higher than men—we cease from men and look to Him alone who can do these things. The premillennial coming of Christ to set up His kingdom on earth really does energize, and never paralyzes. For example, I have been a pastor in Germantown for twenty-five and a half years, previously in Scranton and in Boston, and in a little church of 250 people this is what I have seen within the last year or two. For many years that little company has given over $10,000 a year for missions; current expenses about $3000 or $4000. Two years ago they gave $17,000 to missions; last year they gave $25,000 to missions, and this year they have already given over $12,000 to missions. From a company of 250 people with no missionary committee, and no missionary organization! God does it all. Now, these are facts, dear friends, and if any of your churches are lacking in missionary zeal, there is only one reason why; they do not understand the coming of Jesus Christ. We are not here to win the world to Christ, it is not in the plan. We are here to get a bride for God's Son. We are here to get an Eve for the last Adam, and when the last Adam shall receive His Eve and the marriage of the Lamb shall take place, then He will come in His glory to set up His kingdom."

After Dr. Stearns led in prayer, Mr. Ridgway said:

"I am very sorry to have to announce that, owing to serious illness, Dr. Scofield has not been able to be with us. We will now be addressed by Dr. John MacInnis upon the topic, 'Where is Christ Now, and What is He doing?'"

WHERE IS JESUS NOW, AND WHAT IS HE DOING?

REV. JOHN M. MACINNIS, B.D., PH.D.

Pastor of South Presbyterian Church, Syracuse, N. Y.

"The day is in the morning" and after a good night's rest our minds are fresh and we can get down to a quiet, earnest study of one of the most important subjects before the church of God.

The topic we are asked to consider is, "Where is Jesus Now, and What is He Doing?" What I conceive to be the answer to that question is one of the greatest challenges before the church at the present time; and if our gathering together in this conference does not strengthen us to meet this challenge, our coming together has been in vain, for we must constantly hold in mind that a conference like this is not only a privilege, but also a tremendous responsibility. If the things that we specially profess to accept be true, there rests upon us the greatest responsibility resting upon any people in the world at the present time. This responsibility is indicated in a comprehensive answer to our question—"Where is Christ Now, and What is He Doing?"

On the authority of His own word, Jesus is

here now. He said, "Wherever two or three are gathered in My name, there am I in the midst of them." He also said, "Lo, I am with you all the days, even unto the consummation of the age." That means the bright days and the dark days; the days of peace and the days of conflict; all the days until the purpose of the age is consummated. We are gathered in His name, and therefore have a right to believe that He is One in our midst. He is closer to us than we are one to another, and no one is more interested in all that we think, and do, and say, than He is. But He is not here in the sense that He was with the disciples when He spoke to them in the upper room. We do not see him with our natural eyes. He said to them, "I go away," and He did go away. He is not here in the sense in which He will be here when He comes again. We are told that every eye shall see Him in a sense in which we do not see Him now, but there is no contradiction between the two statements. If we accept the one, it is not necessary that we should think that we ought to reject the other. Jesus spoke in the common people's language, and He used the ordinary vehicle of expression, and the disciples understood thoroughly what He said. We believe He said what He meant and He meant what He said, otherwise it is hopeless for us to find His mind. We, with all our boasted learning, and science, and accuracy of thought and expression, do not speak other than the Lord spoke. We speak about going away and still continuing with people while we are away; we speak of coming back again and having been with the people all the time that we were away, and the people understand perfectly what we mean. There is a sense in which we are with people while we were absent from them in body. Therefore, we can very easily see that Jesus literally meant what He said when He told His disciples that He was going away and still that He would continue with them and that He would come again to them. He is with us in a sense that we cannot be in a place from which our body is absent, by the presence of His Holy Spirit. In this presence He can touch our lives, inspire us, comfort and guide us, so that we may constantly feel that presence. That is one of the most comforting truths in all God's Word, and we yield to no man of any school of thought in our allegiance to, and appreciation of, the fact of the actual presence of Jesus Christ in the life of His people and church, and in the life of the world to-day. At the same time we recognize that Jesus is not here in the sense that He is going to be here when He comes again.

Where is He in that sense at present? He said, "I go to the Father." The writer of the Hebrews says that He appears before the face of God, so that we know that He is with the Father, at His right hand. We are told that while the disciples stood on Mt. Olivet they saw Him ascend, and a cloud received Him out of their sight. Then we are told that a little while later Stephen, while he was being stoned, lifted up his eyes and saw

Jesus standing at the right hand of God. A few days after that, we are told that Paul, while on his way to Damascus, heard the voice of Jesus speaking to him, and in his first letter to the Corinthians he tells us that he saw the Lord. Whatever the right hand of power may mean, it evidently does not put Jesus so far away that He cannot talk to people that are upon earth. The fact that these people said these things in this plain, common sense way, does not necessarily mean that they believed in "a flat earth" and all the other things so often associated with crude ideas of science. If we were to see what they saw at that time to-day, and were to write down an explanation of what we did see, should we not use the same kind of language as they used? With all our profound and comprehensive knowledge of science, we still talk about things that are going up from the face of the earth, as ascending into heaven, and even if we were to call a professor of science to describe the thing that the disciples saw, I feel confident that he would describe it in pretty much the same language that they used to describe it. The people of that day understood what they meant, and if we accept their words in the simple way in which they used them, there is no reason why we should have any difficulty in understanding what they described. It makes very little difference to us as to the real location of heaven. It is impossible for us to think of these things without having a location in mind. When we say heaven is above us, we are no more defining a place than the man who says that God is everywhere. "Everywhere" is somewhere. There is no trouble along these lines if we will only use the sanctified common sense that God has given to us. It is really pathetic to read a lot of the stuff that is written in the name of scholarship, trying to mix people up on these simple statements that were written for the common people who heard Jesus and His disciples gladly.

Jesus, then, being at the right hand of God the Father, our next question is, "What is He doing?" Of course, it is unthinkable that He is inactive. We are told that He is making intercession for His people, and as such we are told that He is our High Priest after the order of Melchizedek. That's a commonplace of Christian thought, and I have always accepted it in the ordinary way. I have always rejoiced to know that I have a High Priest who is touched with all the feelings of my infirmities, because He has been tempted in all points like as I am, yet without sin; but when I was asked to speak on this subject this time, I felt that I must look a little closer into the subject, and find out just exactly what the significance of this fact is. I immediately turned to the great book of the high priesthood of Jesus Christ, the Book of Hebrews. The evening that I consented to speak on the subject, I read it through before I went to bed, I got up early the next morning and read it over again, and again, and still again, and I have been reading it ever since. It is a wonderful book. The heart of the message is the high priesthood of Jesus Christ, and it shows that it is one of the most tremendously significant and fundamental things in all the Word of God. In fact, the significance of that priesthood is the heart of the gospel.

Let us get it in its historical setting. In order to do this, we shall have to go away back and briefly review the story that leads up to the declaration of that book. Going back as far as Isaiah, the greatest of the Hebrew prophets, we find that his hope for Israel and for the world centered in a Messiah. With this message he was commanded to comfort the people of Jehovah. He told them that the way of the Lord would be prepared by one who would come and be as a voice crying in the wilderness. We are also told that, when the hearts of the people would turn toward Him in response to this preparation, the glory of God would be revealed and all flesh should see it. When we come over to the New Testament, we find that, when the forerunner of Jesus was announced, the very words of Isaiah are used to describe his ministry, and furthermore, we are told that he was to come in the spirit and power of Elijah. His great message was, "Repent, for the kingdom of heaven is at hand." He meant what he said. The kingdom of heaven was near, within the grasp of that generation, and everything that he did seemed to indicate that there was a great crisis which had a fundamental significance in the development of God's program concerning the world. God was moving in a special way, and doing something very particular and something that tremendously affected the whole life of the world. Therefore, he pleaded with the people to repent and to turn unto God. When the disciples were coming down from the Mount of Transfiguration, where they saw Jesus in communication with Moses and Elijah, they asked Jesus, Why is it that people say that Elijah should come before the end of the age? and you remember Jesus said, Indeed, Elijah has already come, and the disciples evidently understood that He had reference to John the Baptist. But Jesus explains what he meant, for He said, in speaking of John and the people's attitude toward him, "If ye will receive him, this is Elijah which is to come"; but the important thing is that they did not receive him. Elijah was to be sent in order that he might "turn the heart of the fathers to the children, and the heart of the children to their fathers, lest the coming of God might be a smiting of the earth with a curse."

Now the people did not respond to the ministry of John, and, consequently, God could not carry out His program in the sense in which he could have carried it out had they responded. We must remember that there is a living option in every promise that God gives. This is made very clear in the promises that He gave to the people of Israel through Moses. He made it very clear that if they followed the course that He indicated, it would mean to them a blessing and they would be made a blessing. On the other hand, He indicated that if they disobeyed, then a different thing would come to them. But the thing that is very clear at this point is that God was ready to do a very definite thing, provided the people repented and turned unto Him. When Jesus began His ministry, He took up this same message and preached this same gospel, saying, "Repent, for the kingdom is at hand," and here again we need to realize that Jesus meant just exactly what He said. The kingdom was near, within reach. A little later in His ministry, He spoke of the kingdom being in their midst. That unquestionably had reference to the fact that, in the person of the King who was realizing the life made possible by absolute submission to God, the very life and power of the kingdom were in the midst of the people. Not only that, but He could say to the disciples, There are some of you who are standing here who will see a glimpse of the power and glory of this kingdom before you die; and nine days after, He took them up to the mount where He was transfigured, and they saw the outshining of the very power and glory that were residing in Him, and that made possible the work that He accomplished, as well as the life that He lived. In Jesus Christ God came into a new and fundamentally significant relationship with the human race, and, in the recognition of this fact, it seems to me, we are to find the explanation of a great many things that are embarrassing the people of

God at this time in connection with some of the sayings of Jesus and His apostles regarding the coming of the Lord. The fact that Jesus came, and that He offered Himself in the sacrifice of the cross, and that He rose again, and has been accepted at the right hand of God and has sent the Holy Spirit into the world, has made a fundamental change in the universe, and things are not what they were before this sublime stoop and glorious ascent on the part of our Lord.

With this in mind, let us look for a minute at what Peter said to the people on the day of Pentecost. Having recounted these facts that I have already mentioned, he said that God declared this Jesus whom the people of Jerusalem had crucified, to be Lord and Christ. He has accepted Him as His King, and Peter definitely says that He has so declared Him. In speaking to them a little later, he said to them, You have rejected and crucified Him, but now repent, that is change your mind, and turn toward God, that He may send seasons of refreshing from the presence of the Lord, and that He may send the Christ, whom the heaven must receive until the times of restoration of all things whereof God spoke by the mouth of His holy prophets. We must believe that that was a real offer and contained a living option. Had the people repented and turned at that time, there would have been "times of refreshing from the presence of the Lord" such as would have made possible the coming of Jesus Christ. But again the people refused, again they rejected, and, consequently, God did not see fit to send Christ, and presumably for the same reason as indicated by Malachi when he said, "lest he smite the earth with a curse." For Peter suggests this same thing in his second Epistle, when he said that the long suffering of God and the seeming delay of the return of Christ were explained by the fact that it is not His desire that any should perish. On the contrary, His heart is set on the redemption of the world.

With this in mind, let us now come to the book of the high priesthood of Jesus, and let us try to follow the arguments as they are presented. I sometimes fear that the real point of the Epistle has been lost in the interest given to details. The thesis of the Epistle is stated at the very beginning: "God, having of old time spoken unto the fathers in the prophets by divers portions and in divers manners, hath at the end of these days spoken unto us in his Son." So that is the thesis: "God has spoken to us in His Son." Now he suggests certain things about this Son: He is "appointed Heir of all things, through whom also He made the ages" (or dispensations); He is also "the effulgence of the divine glory and the very image of the substance of Deity and upholds all things by the word of His power." But the main thing here spoken of is that this One who is all this, when He had made purification of sins, sat down on the right hand of the Majesty on high. Now note that it was when He made purification of sins that He assumed the place in which He now appears as our High Priest. The writer goes on to show that this One is greater than the angels, and that His throne is for ever, and the sceptre of righteousness is the sceptre of His kingdom. So He is recognized as both Lord and Christ, while the angels are simply "ministering spirits sent forth to do service for the sake of them that shall inherit salvation." In the light of this fact, we are warned to take earnest heed to the things that are said, lest we drift away. This word has brought us to a new order, and it is very clear that to drift from this new order to the old order would be a calamity. Hence, we are warned over and over again lest we lose sight of this fact; and the great question in connection with it, "How shall we escape if we neglect so great salvation?" Evidently, the salvation here spoken of is a salvation made possible through Him who made purification for sin, and who is our High Priest at the right hand of the Majesty on high.

In the 8th chapter we are told that this is the chief point in all that has been said. Literally this is the pith of what we have been saying. We have such a High Priest, who sat down on the right hand of the throne of the Majesty in the heavens. By reason of the sacrifice that He has offered and the place that He occupies, He is able to "save to the uttermost them that draw near unto God through Him," and we are told that we have the right to come into the very presence of

God with boldness because He has opened up a new and living way.

In the light of this fact, we are told not to cast away our boldness, which hath great recompense of reward, and that we have need of patience, knowing that if the will of God is done we may receive the promise, and that promise is associated with the coming of Him who is to come and shall not tarry; and we are urged to have the faith that is unto the saving of the soul.

In the 11th chapter we are told what faith is, and what it has done in the past. But those who have triumphed through faith in the past have not yet "received the promise, God having provided some better thing concerning us, that apart from us they should not be made perfect." Therefore, we are challenged to "lay aside every weight, and the sin that doth so easily beset us," and to "run with patience the race that is set before us, looking unto Jesus the Author and Perfecter of our faith," who has brought us not unto a mount that cannot be touched, but has brought us "unto mount Zion, and unto the city of the living God, the heavenly Jerusalem, and to innumerable hosts of angels, to the general assembly and church of the firstborn who are enrolled in heaven, and to God the Judge of all, and to the spirits of just men made perfect, and to Jesus the Mediator of the new covenant, and to the blood of sprinkling, that speaketh better things than that of Abel." This all involves a relation that makes the powers of the kingdom of God available to those who avail themselves of all that Jesus is by reason of His place at the right hand of God as our High Priest.

Jesus, our High Priest, who is declared to be both Lord and Christ, is waiting until He can come a second time "apart from sin unto salvation" unto them that wait for Him. His sacrifice has been accepted of God; He is able to save to the uttermost; He is able to establish the new heaven and the new earth; and now He is waiting for His people to accomplish the task that has been entrusted to them, a task that can only be carried out through a recognition of the power that is set at our disposal by reason of the thing that Jesus has already done. This power is the power that was manifested in his own life, and the very power by which he was raised from the dead, and the power that was manifested in the life of the disciples as they proclaimed Him as Saviour, Lord, and Christ, on the day of Pentecost. Our message to the world is a message of repentance, a message that declares that Jesus is appointed King and it is His right to reign, and a challenge to the people of the world to accept Him as their Lord and King. He is God's accepted and appointed King, and He alone can save men. No man can believe this great fact and accept what is involved in the high priesthood of Jesus and not be a missionary. If we know He is God's appointed King, and if we know He is waiting to come and consummate His great program of redemption, which means "a new heaven and a new earth wherein dwelleth righteousness," how can we rest day or night until the last nation and man has heard this fact!

Men are gathering from all parts of this nation and other nations to consider a peace program. Those of us who understand the Scriptures and the truth involved in the high priesthood of Jesus Christ know that there can be no peace in earth until He is recognized as Lord and King. We know that we cannot have peace until He comes. We also know that He has entrusted a task to us. The task is to make the fact of His coming, first, for sin, and secondly, apart from sin unto salvation, known to all the world. He delays, not because He is not interested and not because He is not touched with the sorrows and tragedy of earth, but because He has set His heart on the redemption of the world and it is not His will that any should perish; and, therefore, He wants His coming to be a blessing and not a curse.

We may speak of the work that we have entrusted to us, as finishing the church, His bride; but that is to be done by the proclamation of the gospel of grace and the gospel of His kingdom, for it is impossible to preach His grace comprehensively without relating it to the gospel of His kingdom. The gospel of the kingdom is the gospel that shows the goal toward which He is moving. The church is to be completed, but it is to be completed for a purpose, and the great purpose upon which Christ has set His heart is that indicated by the prayer that He has taught

His people—"Thy kingdom come, Thy will be done in earth as it is in heaven."

Are we big enough and great enough to get that vision? Have we got sufficient faith in Jesus Christ and the word that He has spoken, to believe with all our souls that that is not only His purpose, but that He is able to carry out His program, and that He will respond whenever His people are ready to do the thing that He has entrusted them to do in this age? He has brought us into touch with reality, He has opened up the new and living way, He has put the powers of the eternal kingdom at the disposal of His people, and He has given us a divine task to accomplish. and He is waiting for us to accomplish that task. Shall we obey Him?

I want to tell you that if we who are here can fully realize that one fact associated with the high priesthood of Jesus Christ we shall go out from this prophetic conference on fire, witnessing morning, noon and night concerning our divine Lord and the hope of His coming. I believe that the great hour has come. Christ is waiting. He is the only hope of the world. Can He depend upon us to make the message known in all the earth? Jesus is at the right hand of the Majesty on high, making intercession for His people, and waiting for the moment when He can consummate His program of world redemption. He is waiting for us. He has entrusted us with a task, and He is waiting for us to accomplish that task. Christians have but one task—one all-important task,

—and that is, to make our High Priest and the power of His life known in the world. That means more than talking—it means living the Christ life. The power to live that life is only possible by coming into touch with reality through the priestly offering and intercession of Jesus. He is there to make this life a reality to every one that believes. Let us therefore come with boldness to the throne of grace, where God and the eternal realities are made real in us, that we may be true witnesses of Christ, who alone is the hope of the world.

GOD'S PLAN IN THIS DISPENSATION

REV. JAMES M. GRAY, D.D.

I am asked to speak on "God's Plan in This Dispensation," and I commence by reading the words of James, the brother of our Lord, as recorded in the 15th chapter of the Acts, beginning at the 13th verse: "Men and brethren, hearken unto me: Simeon hath declared how God at the first did visit the Gentiles, to take out of them a people for His name. And to this agree the words of the prophets; as it is written, After this I will return, and will build again the tabernacle of David, which is fallen down; and I will build again the ruins thereof, and I will set it up: that the residue of men might seek after the Lord, and all the Gentiles, upon whom My name is called, saith the Lord, who doeth all these things. Known unto God are all His works from the beginning of the world.'

To understand these words, and to place them where they belong in the divine program, we need to go back for nearly a thousand years before they were spoken. David is seated upon the throne of Israel, and God has given him rest from all his enemies around about. Jerusalem is his capital. It has become the city of David, and he would make it the city of God. The ark has been brought up there, and now he would build a house for the ark; but God will not permit him to do so, and sends to him His prophet Nathan to inform him of that fact.

The words of Nathan are recorded in the 7th chapter of 2 Samuel, where God, through him, says to David: "I will appoint a place for My people Israel, and will plant them, that they may dwell in a place of their own, and move no more; neither shall the children of wickedness afflict them any more, as beforetime. . . . Also the Lord telleth thee that He will make thee an house. And when thy days be fulfilled, and thou shalt sleep with thy fathers, I will set up thy seed after thee, which shall proceed out of thy bowels, and I will establish His kingdom. He shall build an house for My name, and I will stablish the throne of His kingdom for ever. I will be his Father, and he shall be My son."

Notice that God is here speaking of a period in the history of Israel which has not yet been seen upon this earth, for He says, "I will appoint a place for My people Israel, and will plant them, that they may dwell in a place of their own, and move no more." They were in a place of their own at the time these words were spoken, for they were in Canaan; but they were called upon to move some centuries afterwards, and although some of them returned again, once more were they called upon to move, and they have been kept moving from that day until now. But a time is coming, when they will be planted in a place of their own and move no more.

In that day also shall the children of wickedness afflict them no more. The children of wickedness, that is, the Gentile powers of the earth, have been afflicting them in all the centuries, but God's Word is true and the affliction will some day end. The day it will end is indicated in the words, "Also the Lord telleth thee that He will make thee an house;" not a material house of wood or stone, not even a spiritual house, as though one were to take these words symbolically as indicating the church of Christ; but a house in a sense of a dynasty, a kingdom upon this earth. Thus He adds, "When thy days be fulfilled, and thou shalt sleep with thy fathers, I will set up thy seed after thee, which shall proceed out of thy bowels, and I will establish his kingdom."

Some might say, this means Solomon, but a greater than Solomon is here, for the next verse declares that God "will stablish the throne of his kingdom for ever." This was not true of Solomon, but, to settle it beyond a peradventure, he adds, "I will be his Father, and he shall be My son." This passage is quoted in the New Testament and applied definitely to our Lord and Saviour, Jesus Christ. You will find it in the first chapter of the epistle to the Hebrews, where the writer is showing the superiority of Christ over the angels, and says in the course of his argument, "Unto which of the angels said He at any time, Thou art My Son, this day have I begotten

Thee? And again, I will be to Him a Father, and He shall be to Me a Son?" The inference is that He said this not to any angel, but to Him alone who is described in that same chapter, as "the brightness of His glory and the express image of His person."

Here, then, we have a prophecy that Israel is one day to be returned to her own land, to be removed no more, and to be afflicted no more, and that in that day the kingdom of David shall be set up, over which his Son shall reign, that Son being none other than Jesus Christ, our Lord and Saviour.

THE LAPSE OF CENTURIES

Hundreds of years have now elapsed since David's death. Solomon has succeeded him. Solomon has died and Rehoboam has succeeded him. Iniquity and idolatry have entered the nation, and in chastisement God has divided them. Ten tribes have seceded under Jeroboam and are known as the kingdom of Israel, and only two tribes have remained loyal to the House of David and are called the kingdom of Judah.

Iniquity and idolatry increase in Israel, and she is carried into captivity by the Assyrians, never to return again as a distinct nation to her own land. The kingdom of Judah remains in her territory a century and a half longer, but at length, and for the same reason, Babylon comes down against her and carries her into captivity.

But the Lord had promised that Judah would return after seventy years, which was fulfilled, although the nation thereafter remains a vassal, first to Persia, then Greece and then to Rome.

One day, when the nation has thus been returned, a great event takes place, as recorded in the first chapter of Luke. The angel of God came into a city of Galilee, named Nazareth, to a virgin espoused to a man whose name was Joseph, of the house of David, and the virgin's name was Mary. And the angel said, "Hail, thou that art highly favoured, the Lord is with thee: blessed art thou among women. . . . And the angel said unto her, Fear not, Mary: for thou hast found favour with God. And, behold, thou shalt conceive in thy womb, and bring forth a Son, and shalt call His name Jesus. He shall be great, and shall be called the Son of the Highest: and the Lord God shall give unto Him the throne of his father David: and He shall reign over the house of Jacob for ever; and of His kingdom there shall be no end."

Surely the time has at last come when God is to fulfil His prophecy to David! But, alas, we are mistaken. The Son has been born, and He is great, and He is called the Son of the Highest, but the Lord God has not yet given unto Him the throne of His father David, and He does not as yet reign over the house of Jacob for ever. And why? You know the answer. "He came unto His own, and His own received Him not." They hid, as it were, their faces from Him. He was "despised and rejected of men." "We will not have this man to reign over us," they said. They crucified Him; He died and was buried.

But, glory be to God, it was not possible that He should be holden of death, and so on the third day He rose again from the dead, and showed Himself alive by many infallible proofs, as we read in the first chapter of the Acts, being seen of His disciples for forty days, and "speaking of the things pertaining to the kingdom of God."

And one day when they were thus assembled together with Him, they asked of Him, saying, "Lord, wilt Thou at *this* time restore again the kingdom to Israel?" It was as though they had said, "We expected Thee to have done that prior to Thy crucifixion and Thy death. We were disappointed then, but now that Thou hast risen from the dead, is it not Thy purpose to do so now?"

How significant that Jesus does not correct any supposed misunderstanding on their part about the kingdom. He does not say, as some interpreters of the Bible would have had Him say, "The kingdom will never be set up." He does not say, "Thou art mistaken, the Old Testament prophecies are null and void." He does not say, "The church which I have come into the world to redeem and to build up is to take the place of the kingdom." Nothing of the kind! He says, in effect, the kingdom will be restored, but "it is not for you to know the times or the seasons, which the Father hath put in His own power. But ye shall receive power, after that the Holy Ghost is come upon you: and ye shall be witnesses unto Me both in Jerusalem, and in all Judæa, and in Samaria, and unto the uttermost part of the earth. And when He had spoken these things, while they beheld, He was taken up; and a cloud received Him out of their sight. And while they looked stedfastly toward heaven as He went up, behold, two men stood by them in white apparel; which also said, Ye men of Galilee, why stand ye gazing up into heaven? this same Jesus, which is taken up from you into heaven, shall so come in like manner as ye have seen Him go into heaven. Then returned they unto Jerusalem from the mount called Olivet," and after Pentecost began their witnessing.

THE MYSTERY OF THE GENTILES

This witnessing was done in Judæa and Samaria, and then at length one of them under the guidance of the Holy Spirit began to witness to the Gentiles. First, it is Peter before Cornelius and his household at Cæsarea, and later it is Paul and Barnabas at Antioch.

What can this mean? The church composed entirely of Jews and located in Jerusalem is astounded at these things. Is it possible that the Gentile is to receive the same blessings in Christ as the Jew? Is he to come into all the privileges of the elect people without becoming one of them in fact? It can not be. And so they call a council of the church, the first in its history, to consider this thing.

This council is being held in Jerusalem, and James, the brother of our Lord, is presiding over it. Peter gives his testimony as to what took place in the house of Cornelius, and Paul and Barnabas give their testimony as to Antioch. And now a critical moment has arrived in the great assembly, and the Spirit of God makes His presence known in an unusual way. James arises, and says: "Men and brethren, hearken unto me: Simeon (Peter) hath declared how God at the first did visit the Gentiles, to take out of them a people for His name. And to this agree the words of the prophets; as it is written, After this (*i.e.*, after I have taken out from among the Gentiles this people for My name), I will return, and will build again the tabernacle of David, which is fallen down; and I will build again the ruins thereof, and I will set it up; that the residue of men might seek after the Lord, and all the Gentiles, upon whom My name is called, saith the Lord, who doeth all these things."

THE AGE OF THE OUT-GATHERING

That is God's purpose in this dispensation. He is not now converting the world, nor setting up His kingdom. He is now taking out from among the Gentiles a people for His name. The witnessing is still going on unto the uttermost part of the earth, individuals from among all peoples, and nations, and tongues, are being called out in response to the gospel message. They are believing on the Lord Jesus Christ and confessing His name. They are being baptized by His Spirit into the body of which He is the Head, and at last, when this out-gathering shall have been brought to an end, the body of Christ, which is His church, having been completed, He "Himself shall descend from heaven with a shout, with the voice of the archangel, and with the trump of God: and the dead in Christ shall rise first: then we which are alive and remain shall be caught up together with them in the clouds, to meet the Lord in the air: and so shall we ever be with the Lord."

This, my beloved brethren, is not the age of the ingathering, that age is to follow; this is the age of the out-gathering, the out-gathering of an elect people to be united with Christ in glory in that day when He shall come to reign, as the appointed King over the millennial earth.

And so we read that "after this," after the out-gathering has taken place, after the church age is completed, and the body of Christ is united with the Head, and glorified as He is glorified, "after this I will return, and will build again the tabernacle (*i.e.*, the kingdom) of David which is fallen down; and I will build again the ruins thereof, and I will set it up." As surely as God has spoken these words, so surely shall they be fulfilled upon this earth. And the object or the result in mind is one for which our hearts may well praise God, namely, "that the residue of men might seek after the Lord, and all the Gentiles, upon whom My name is called, saith the Lord, who doeth all these things."

As was stated this morning, His glory shall yet fill the earth. The knowledge of the Lord shall cover the earth as the waters cover the sea. This world is to be converted to God and to His Son. All the nations of the world shall yet submit themselves to Him. "The kingdoms of this world shall become the kingdom of our God and of His Christ," but God is not using the church today to bring that great blessing about. He is using the church for another purpose; and when that purpose has been fulfilled, Christ shall come with his glorified church in order that Israel may take up her work again upon this earth, and through her testimony unto Him bring the nations to His feet.

Oh, my brethren, if we only understood the Word of God! If we would only read and study it in order that we might understand it, how differently we should look upon the awful carnage at the present time, and what peace we should have in the midst of it all, and with how much more satisfaction, and joy, and power should we be co-operating with God, in carrying out his purpose on the earth! Nine-tenths of the trouble and worry in the visible church to-day is explained by the fact that to a great extent we are working in opposition to God, instead of co-operating with Him.

THE CALLING OF THE CHURCH

Now, as a closing word, let me call your attention to the vocation or calling of the church as indicated in the fourth chapter of Ephesians.

Paul in that epistle, as you know, is speaking of the church as the body of Christ, and at verse eight of chapter four, he says of our ascended Lord, that "he gave gifts unto men. . . . And He gave some, apostles; and some, prophets; and some, evangelists; and some, pastors and teachers."

Why did He bestow these gifts upon the church? Remember, it is He who *does* bestow them. Colleges and universities, and seminaries and Bible institutes cannot bestow them. They may have a part in the preparation of them, but except a man is given to the church as a prophet, or an evangelist, or a pastor, or a preacher, he can not become such in the heavenly sense.

But why are these gifts bestowed? For a single reason only. They have just one thing to do. They are "for the perfecting of the saints." But, the saints being perfected, what are they to do? The text explains that they are to engage in "the work of ministering for the edifying (the building up) of the body of Christ."

Shall they always, and for ever, be engaged in that work? No, only until "we all come in the unity of the faith, and of the knowledge of the Son of God, unto a perfect man, unto the measure of the stature of the fulness of Christ. That "perfect man," my brethren, is not the individual man; it does not mean you nor me, as such; the "perfect man" is that mystical man of whom I have been speaking, that man conceived of in the thought of Christ as the Head and the church as the members of His body.

The day is coming when we all shall come in the unity of the faith and the knowledge of the Son of God unto this perfect man. That will be the day when there shall be manifested the measure of the stature of the fulness of Christ. When that day comes, then "Christ, who is our life, shall appear, and we also shall appear with Him in glory."

AFTERNOON SESSION

Robert B. Haines, of the Haines Gauge Company, and Secretary of the American Branch of the Scripture Gift Mission, Philadelphia, presided during the afternoon session. After urging attendants upon the Conference to carry back home the inspiring messages they were hearing, Mr. Haines went on to say:

"The plan of this conference is a progressive. teaching program, based upon the Bible—the words of Jesus Christ, the Son of the living God, not on visionary speculation; but we must have the illumination of the Holy Spirit to guide us as we study, so that our understanding may be opened, and we have the assurance that our understanding will be opened, and we have the promise that He will give the Holy Spirit to those who truly desire and ask Him (Luke 11:13).

"The first day of the conference was for prayer and humiliation before God, the only attitude in which to approach our Lord. The lessons were teachings fundamental to our Lord's return—the Bible in its entirety as the inerrant Word of God, the deity, the virgin birth, the incarnation of Jesus Christ; His humiliation, His ministry, His atoning death.

"There is no salvation and no hope for the future apart from the blood. All who are saved must come under it just as surely as the Israelites of old came under it when it was sprinkled upon the doorposts of their houses in Egypt, and whoever did not come under it was cut off.

"The lessons of the second day—to-day—are teachings relating to the age in which we live. The present high-priestly work of Christ; the purposes of God in this age; the capture of Jerusalem; the regathering of Israel, etc. All these teachings are illuminating and are to exalt Him.

"Oh, let us honor and fall prostrate before Him who has done so much for us, for 'He alone shall be exalted in that day.'

"To-morrow the theme is, 'The Return of Our Lord and Saviour in Prophecy,' and deals with our resurrection and rapture—His coming for us, His body, His bride, the church; the judgment of our works; and His coming again later with His saints to bring in the millennial age. Our hearts should be filled with praise and rejoicing at this approaching event.

"It may not be out of place to say a word concerning the origin of this great conference. Last fall, when we heard of the capture of Jerusalem by the English, under General Allenby, after so many centuries of Turkish misrule, our hearts were filled with thankfulness to our wonder-working God, as we felt that this was one indication that the Times of the Gentiles were surely nearing the end, and this afternoon the speaker, Dr. Thompson, who has lived for many years in Jerusalem, will tell us the story of the capture of the city. Immediately after the report of this momentous event was flashed around the world, great advent and prophetic conferences were held in London and Dublin for praise and thanksgiving that Jerusalem at last was freed from the Turks.

"The reports of these meetings which came over to America in the *London Christian* and other papers were most inspiring, and a few of us in Philadelphia felt that the time was opportune to hold a similar advent testimony meeting, in sympathy with our brethren across the sea, for the study of the prophetic Word. A small group met by agreement one bitter cold day last winter, and after consultation and prayer, fifty invitations were sent to various laymen and ministers to meet together on a Saturday afternoon for further conference. Thirty-nine busy men responded to this call, and those who could not attend sent messages of approval and encouragement. Who can say that such a movement as this was not God's doing? We feel that this conference is of God, and not of man. It has involved a great amount of work in a short time, as you can understand, and I wish to thank our most efficient secretary, Mr.

J. Davis Adams, for the work he has done, and it has not been easy; also all the members of our committee, who have worked together harmoniously and without friction. I wish to thank our large office staff—mostly voluntary—for their cheerfulness, efficiency, and kindness, and for their labor and manifest results.

"One of our speakers, Dr. William B. Riley, has a vision of holding great conferences similar to this one in different parts of the country, from the Atlantic to the Pacific Coast, and we hope this one may be a forerunner of others.

"The eyes of people have been closed long enough to the great truth of our Lord's return, the prophetic Word, and the closing end of the age in which we now live; and it rests upon us who appreciate this great fact, to speak forth the truth in these days, for 'the truth shall set you free.' "

Mr. Haines then introduced the Rev. Dr. A. E. Thompson, for fifteen years pastor of the American Church at Jerusalem, and who was finally driven out by the Turks at the outbreak of the war.

THE CAPTURE OF JERUSALEM

REV. A. E. THOMPSON

Pastor of the American Church at Jerusalem (driven by the Turk from the Holy City at the outbreak of the World War). He is at present Field Secretary for the American Committee for Armenian and Syrian Relief

The capture of Jerusalem is one of those events to which students of prophecy have been looking forward for many years. Even before Great Britain took possession of Egypt, there were keen-sighted seers who foresaw the day when God would use the Anglo-Saxon peoples to restore Jerusalem. When the war broke out, there were some of us who were convinced that it would never end until Turkish tyranny was for ever a thing of the past in the Holy City. When the city was captured, we felt very confident we could put one hand upon this great event which had stirred the heart of the whole Christian world, and, laying open our Bible at many places in the Prophets, say as confidently as Peter on the day of Pentecost, "This is that which was spoken by the prophets."

The capture of Jerusalem is more than a prophetic event, it is a pivot in prophecy. The Germans might enter Paris and we would weep; but, desperate as that event would be, it would only be an incident in the great panorama of the ages. The flags we love might be carried into Berlin, and how we would rejoice! But even that would only be an incident. The Hun might again sack Rome, but not one of us could with any assurance put our finger upon any text of Scripture and say it was so written. Constantinople might fall, and a babel of voices would be heard among our prophets. But when Jerusalem was captured, we all said with one consent, "This is the climax of the ages." We have entered a prophetic era. We are looking upon the things which Moses, and the prophets, and Christ Himself have foretold.

The capture of Jerusalem is not the end, but the beginning. There are several things I want to call your attention to, of which it is but the beginning.

First of all, it is the beginning of the downfall of Mohammedanism. In the year 636 A.D., Caliph Omar conquered Jerusalem. Ever since, with the exception of a few decades when a Christian crusader king ruled the Holy City, it has lain under Mohammedan oppression, an oppression that no one can comprehend unless he has lived under it and tried to preach the gospel of Jesus Christ. But when General Allenby entered the city quietly, unostentatiously, on foot, with bared head, not claiming any honor to himself, but as a Christian gentleman, as a believer in the King of kings and Lord of lords, feeling that he had the high privilege of doing the thing to which the ages had looked, the doom of Mohammedanism was sealed. All through those centuries Jerusalem has been one of the three holy cities of the Mohammedan world. The Arab still calls it El Kuds es Shereef—the Exalted Holy Place. Ask a villager how far it is to Jerusalem, and you will get no answer; but ask him how far it is to El Kuds, and he will say, "Two or three hours"; meaning that you can get there on a donkey, if it is willing to go, in that length of time. Jerusalem, the Holy City. Holy it was to the Jew, holy it is to the Christian, holy it has been to the Mohammedan. When the flag of Islam gave place to a Christian flag, it meant more than the capture of a city. It meant the triumph of the cross. The entry of Turkey into the war was celebrated by bringing the green banner of the prophet, that is seldom unfurled, all the way from Medina to Jerusalem, where with stately pomp it was carried into the city, Jew and Christian and Mohammedan uniting, some with true heart and some with hypocrisy, in doing it honor; but that green flag of Mahomet will never fly over the Holy City again.

From the minarets of Jerusalem for centuries there has been heard the cry, "La Allah ila Allah wa Mahomet rasool Allah," "There is no God but God, and Mahomet is His prophet." But there was once in Jerusalem a Prophet who spake as never man spake. The day is soon coming when men will no longer honor the prophet of Mecca, for the Prophet of the Highest will be acknowledged unto the uttermost parts of the earth. Not Mahomet, but Christ; not the crescent, but the cross; not Mohammedanism, but Christianity; were triumphant when the British flag was planted upon the tower of David.

In the second place, the capture of Jerusalem was the beginning of the defeat of age-long Turkish tyranny. I am not unmindful that for a century the process of disintegration has been going on, but I still say that not the freeing of Greece, not the signing of the treaty of Berlin, not the wresting of Montenegro, of Bulgaria, of Bosnia and Herzegovina from their oppressors, not the liberation of Roumania, but the deliverance of Jerusalem was the crisis in the history of Turkey. In the fifteenth century, hordes of Turks began to pour out of the heart of Asia. Wave after wave swept into Asia Minor. Finally, the great Osman led his tribesmen into this territory, and, uniting the tribes, swept on from land to land in a mighty tide of conquest. They captured Constantinople. They did something far more significant. They took possession of the Holy City, and the rule of the Saracen, which after all had much in its favor, gave place to what we can not call government, nor even misrule, but only "the murderous tyranny of the Turk." The Turk knows not how to govern. He only knows how to maltreat. Jerusalem has been groaning for these centuries under his oppression.

When the war broke out, the Turks were offered

a great thing. What that offer was, was revealed to one of our missionaries one day. A young Effendi, friendly to Christians, called with three strangers, and lured them on to reveal the hopes and aspirations of the Mohammedans in this war. They were playing for a great stake. The Empire was to be greater than Osman ever dreamed. Whatever the cost, it was well worth the battle. Constantinople, Bagdad, Cairo, and Jerusalem were again to be great centers. They would last, how long? Until the Kaiser had accomplished his purpose. That was the part of the program which Berlin did not tell Constantinople. We all know it to-day. The wise in Turkey knew it then. The Turks played the game. They staked all, and when they lost Jerusalem, their doom was sealed.

I left Jerusalem on the day before Christmas, 1914, an exile, driven from home, from the work I loved, leaving our mission, leaving three American women, who could remain when we Canadians were hunted from the land, leaving the fruitage of the best years of my life; ordered to be aboard that train—and God only knows what would have happened had I refused or failed. As we hurried down the street, I looked up to the tower of David, and there I saw this flag. Look at it! What a flag! A blood-red field with "the horned moon and one lone star within its nether tip." Emblem of death! Emblem of night! For centuries it has been flying over Jerusalem. It gave promise that one day there would be moonlight, that some day the sun would rise; but it has floated over Jerusalem for all these centuries, and it is still a star and crescent on a blood-red field. Never so bloody has it been as in these dark and desperate days. As I looked at that flag upon that old tower, I said, "Thank God, when I come back again, not that rag, but 'the flag that has braved a thousand years, the battle and the breeze,' will be flying there"; for I knew that God had set England at the gates of Palestine to do His will; and, though England might have sinned, and though she might be paying for her sin with blood, God had a purpose, and by His grace she would work it out.

In Cairo we met the Colonials, fifty thousand strong, from Australia and New Zealand, the most splendid body of men I have ever seen. They were praying for the opportunity to carry this flag into Jerusalem. We knew there were only four ragged regiments of untrained Syrian peasants in the city, and that the ten thousand New Zealanders alone could plant this flag where I had seen the Star and Crescent waving. How they cheered when, at the dedication of a Y. M. C. A. tent, I told them so, and said, "Boys, I'm sorry I shall not be there to welcome you, but I expect to be there to say good-bye"! A few weeks later, those brave fellows leaped from the boats into the water at Gallipoli, stormed the heights and cleared the way for the landing of the army; and though their bones are strewn on that peninsula, when shall their glory fade?

Their comrades formed a part of Murray's contingent which conquered the desert and set the standard of their country in South Palestine. It was the Anzac cavalry that captured Beersheba. They were in the thick of it at Gaza. They cleared the way on the rapid advance up the plains. They rode into Jaffa. They were side by side with the Highlanders, the Welshmen, the Londoners and the Ghurkas when the fastnesses of the Judean hills were captured.

The capture of Jerusalem was a surprise. We who thought we knew said those wadies leading into the hills were impregnable. Evidently the Germans and Turks thought so, too. Just before it was accomplished, I met our beloved American consul for the first time since that memorable day when, by his Christian grace and wisdom, he saved us from the Turk when we had been twice butted from the Jaffa wharf by Turkish rifles. He told me, as a father would tell his boy, of those years of the military preparations; of the seventy thousand troops, the flower of the Turkish army, who guarded those hills when he left; of the triple line of trenches as fine as anything in France, and added, "Allenby will never try to storm those hills and capture the city; he will pursue them up the plain and cut them off from the north." So said we all. Yet it was but a day or two till we read that the British were on the hills. There was but one road by which the artillery could be transported. It passed through the Bab el Wad, that is, the Gate of the Valley, which is a veritable death-trap. "In that straight pass a thousand could well be checked by three." The Turks knew it. The British knew it. Our consul knew it. But Allenby went through that pass without losing a gun. He threw a line of khaki up on the crest of the hill along which Jesus walked to Emmaus with two disciples. That line held for a week against desperate attacks till roads were built, till the Southern army marched through Hebron and past Bethlehem and all was ready to close in for a united attack on the Holy City. Then, down the boulder-strewn mountain sides, where there was scarcely a bridle-path, and up the equally rocky ascent to the city, poured the infantry, recking nothing of the batteries planted against the city walls, where they knew the British would not silence them lest they destroy the sacred city, fearing not the machine guns hidden in the Jewish houses. The southern flank had captured the Jericho road, and was cutting off the retreat. The northern wing was astride the Damascus road leading north. Once again it seemed that the streets of Jerusalem would run red with blood.

Two days before, the civilians had been given notice to leave. The day before, they were ordered to be ready at daybreak to quit the city. One of our teachers, seeking an explanation why no further order came, went down to the Jaffa gate. She arrived just in time to see the officials hand out a white flag to a foreign officer whom she thought was an Austrian, who bore it out the

Jaffa road. She did not understand what it meant till she saw the Kilties, the Anzacs and the Londoners marching in, unopposed, while the city went wild with joy as this old British flag was unfurled. Jerusalem had been taken, and not a drop of blood had been spilt in the city.

That was God. God forbid that I should deny to my countrymen the honor due to them for their strategy and courage! But General Allenby entering the city, not in gorgeous triumph but on foot, gave the glory to the Lord of battles. The clock had struck the hour. The time appointed for the Turk to go had come, and he went at God's command.

Now, if the hour of the passing of the Turk from Palestine has come, it means great things to the Promised Land. It marks the beginning of the end of the desolation. Have you ever noticed Isaiah's message to Israel? It was given to him when, with breaking heart at the declension and death of his great king, the young prophet betook himself to the Temple. His heart broke indeed when he received that message—a message that blindness of eyes, deafness of ears, and hardness of heart would be visited upon Israel until their houses should be left without a man, their cities without inhabitants, and their land be utterly desolate (Isa. 6:9-13). It was that vision of desolation that broke the heart of Jesus as He was riding in triumph into Jerusalem. We who have lived there have seen it fulfilled. Yes, and we have seen more. We have seen a little garden in a valley, watered by one of those few mountain springs; a terraced hillside here and there; the Jewish colonies, forty of them, turning the wilderness into a very garden of the Lord. Now these colonies are being restored. The fellah is again holding his plow with one hand and prodding his oxen with the other. Starving survivors are earning bread on roads and reconstruction. I have been denied the privilege of being one of that party of Americans who are probably landing to-day. They have gone with the equipment of language, of knowledge, of money, of material, and with well-considered plans for the relief of the people and the re-habilitation of the Land. The chief engineer of the party said, when leaving New York, "You men need not fear that you will shake with Syrian fever. There will never be any more fever there. We will make Jerusalem the healthiest city in the world." The Jews are pouring in their millions, and will soon pour in their men. The Allied governments are behind it all. Surely the capture of the City of the Great King means that the end of the desolation is at hand. "Jerusalem shall be trodden down of the Gentiles, UNTIL THE TIMES OF THE GENTILES BE FULFILLED" (Luke 21:24).

It means also the beginning of the end of the dispersion. There are, it seems to me, three stages in the regathering of Israel. The first is the *one-by-one* regathering (Isa. 27:12). That has been going on. It began before you and I had any interest in the Jew, when some of us were self-satisfied unbelievers in the literal fulfilment of prophecy. The Russian pogroms kept it going. For thirty-five years the Jews have been returning like doves to their windows, while the Syrians have been leaving the Land on every ship.

The capture of Jerusalem prepared the way for the second stage. There will be a national movement, backed by international power. There are many prophecies of such a regathering. Isaiah says, in one of his climacteric passages: "It shall come to pass in that day, that the Lord shall set His hand *the second* time to recover the remnant of His people, that shall remain, from Assyria, and from Egypt, and from Pathros, and from Cush, and from Elam, and from Shinar, and from Hamath, and from the islands of the sea. And He shall set up an ensign for the nations, and shall assemble the outcasts of Israel, and gather together the dispersed of Judah from the four corners of the earth" (Isa. 11:11-12). How carefully the Spirit of God directed the prophet! This does not predict the return from Babylon, but a *second* restoration from the four corners of the earth. In the latter part of the passage he speaks of a highway from Assyria for their return. In another place he says, "In that day shall there be a highway out of Egypt to Assyria" (Isa. 19:23). The Germans, Turks and British have been fulfilling these predictions. "All aboard for Bagdad!" will be heard in the Cairo depot after the war.

Last night, as I was leaving the meeting, a burly man accosted me with, "Well, what do you think of that kind of interpretation of prophecy?" "To what do you refer?" I replied. "Well, that passage in Hosea about Israel." "I suppose you mean the part which says that they will return and seek the Lord their God and David their king in the latter days." "Yes, and everybody knows that was fulfilled," he responded. "Then will you tell me when?" I inquired. "Why, after the Babylonish captivity," said our friend. "You mean that the Jews had kings of the line of David?" I asked. "Certainly," said this corrector of teachers. "Will you kindly name them?" I asked quite innocently. Just then a friend greeted him and ended the interview. If he is here to-day I hope he will tell me the names of those Jewish kings that sat on David's throne after the captivity.

We all know who that King will be. "Great David's greater Son" will fulfil that prophecy. That will be the third stage in the second return—the Messianic regathering, I like to call it. "The Lord God shall give unto Him the throne of His father David: and He shall reign over the house of Jacob for ever; and of His kingdom there shall be no end" (Luke 1:32-33).

Again, the capture of Jerusalem indicates that we are at **the beginning of the end of the declaration of the gospel.** One of the prophets says that, when Israel forsook Jehovah, she built temples. When the church began to forsake the

Lord, they erected costly cathedrals and great buildings which we call churches. Nowadays, we build institutional churches. Jesus gave his church just one command: "Go ye into all the world, and preach the gospel to every creature" (Mark 16:15). Speaking of the end of the age, he said, "This gospel of the kingdom shall be preached in all the world for a witness unto all nations; and then shall the end come" (Matt. 24:14). I am not here to break a lance in the arena of conflicting interpretations of this great declaration, but I am here to say that Jesus Christ gave us a thing to do and we have not done it. What has happened in Jerusalem, what is happening in Israel, what is manifest among the nations, shows that the great political and national events are culminating in the predicted end-time drama. Yet we loiter. Some, thank God, are about our Master's business. Yonder on the heights of Ecuador a little band are looking over the Andes into the heart of South America where millions of Indians are utterly unevangelized. From the French Soudan and the French Congo comes the cheering word that the door is open to enter the heart of unreached Africa. Anam is opening to our missionaries. Our outposts have entered the borders of Tibet. And now the capture of Jerusalem gives promise that the Mohammedan world is no longer closed against us; but that

"Arabia's desert ranger to Him shall bow the knee."

It is a clarion call to preach the gospel to every creature, such as the church has never before heard.

At such an hour it is not for us to fold our arms and look up, to sigh over conditions around us, to pray to be caught away out of the wreck of this sin-cursed world. I am asking Him to give me strength, to give me renewed purpose, to give me men at my back to carry this gospel a little further and so to bring back our King. If this conference fails in this, it fails of His will. I would not cross the street to talk to a crowd of premillennialists about the coming of the Lord unless they were looking for and hastening His coming by sending forth the gospel. There are premillennialists who are so taken up with theories, that they have no thought for missions. They have never sacrificed anything to send the gospel to the regions beyond. They have never suffered for the completion of the task which He is waiting up yonder for us to finish. That is my message to this convention.

The capture of Jerusalem also meant **the defeat of German design.** It is not the overthrow of German autocracy, but it is God's token that the process has begun. "Mittel Europa" is a phrase to us. It is a destiny to the Germans. But what use is "Mittel Europa" without Jerusalem? What avail is "Berlin to Bagdad" while old England holds the Gates of Hercules, the Suez Canal, Colombo and Hong Kong? This is the world's highway, and nobody knows it half so well as the

Kaiser. That is what he means by "the freedom of the seas." Freedom, forsooth! Why, wherever that old British ensign flies on the four seas there is freedom. It is the guarantee that any nation can send its ships into any port on peaceful errand. But if they come for war, for aggression, for destruction, that flag defies them. Its stands for the freedom of the seas, not for one Empire, but for all nations, small or great. Germany thought to control the freedom of the seas by capturing the Suez Canal, and was defeated. She sought to conquer the Egyptian desert, and was defeated. She clung to Beersheba and Gaza, and again she was defeated. Her feet were planted within thy walls, O Jerusalem, but, thank God, she was driven out. That defeat was the handwriting on the wall. "Insignificant," the Germans say. God says it is significant. For it will be in Palestine that Germany will finally meet her judgment. No, not in this war, but in a bloodier struggle.

There is a section of the prophet Ezekiel which covers the events of which I am speaking. The thirty-fifth chapter is the doom of Edom. The Mohammedans are the religious, and the Turkish power, the political, successors of ancient Edom. What is said in that chapter is being fulfilled in Turkey and in Mohammedanism. Isaiah's burden of Dumah is the cry of a man in the darkness of Islam to the watchman in the watchtower of missions. We heard it before the war. We shall hear it yet again when the war is over. God cannot fully judge him till we have offered him the gospel. The thirty-sixth and thirty-seventh chapters are the promise of the final restoration of Israel to their Land, to their covenant position, and to their Messiah. The thirty-eighth and thirty-ninth chapters are THE DOOM OF GERMANY.

That may be challenged. It is long since that students recognized Russia in this prophecy. It includes Russia. But, if I rightly understand the described territory, it lies north of the Rhine, the Danube, the Black Sea, the mountains of Armenia and the Persian Gulf, with a large section of Africa, south of Egypt. It is not "Mittel Europa," but a great Northern Empire. As Ezekiel describes it, it includes the then known world except the region ruled by the four successive world-empires of Daniel's vision.

Before the war, some of us saw these prophetic forecasts. When war burst upon us, we said it would result in a Russo-Germanic alliance. With intensest interest we watch the rapid unfolding of Ezekiel's vision. It would seem as if God had chained these nations to those fiery wheels and was whirling them on to their destiny.

It is strange that otherwise sane interpreters forget that there can be no war without two powers. Many of our would-be prophets have been so transfixed by the image and the Beasts in Daniel that they have failed to see the King of the North of the eleventh chapter who will come against the King of the South like a whirlwind, and shall enter into the glorious Land.

This is exactly what Ezekiel presents in detail. He even declares that he is the one of whom the earlier prophets spoke, that is, the Assyrian. Ezekiel does not describe the human power which will contend against him. It is manifest, however, that it is the mighty power that will hold protectorate over the restored Jews.

With the end of the war, Germany and Russia, with other nations in alliance, will be in a sore plight. Loaded down with debt, they will, says Ezekiel, look on the land of unwalled villages, devise an evil device "to take a spoil, and to take a prey; to turn their hand against the waste places that are now inhabited, and against the people that are gathered out of the nations, that have gotten cattle and goods, that dwell in the middle of the earth." That is it. They want the riches of restored Israel. They want the central city of the earth. They lost it in 1917. They will never rest till they besiege it again.

Now God is not the Author of evil. He never tempts any man or nation. But when a man or a nation sets his heart to do an evil thing, God says, as he did to Judas, "Come on, get this thing done quickly, for thy time of judgment has come." So shall it be with Germany. She has set her heart to win empire at any cost. She has derided God's Holy Scriptures, denied the supernatural and exalted the superman. She has denied the fulfilment of prophecy and has exalted the god of forces. She has cast mercy and honor to the winds. Like Israel of old, her prophets are profane, and her priests teach for reward, and her people love to have it so. God seems to care not. He lets her curse and blast mankind. Yet not for ever. Ezekiel says that God will call the beasts and birds to a sacrifice upon His holy mountains. He will put hooks in her jaws and hasten her to the conflict. With proud confidence she will sweep into Palestine. It seems to be unprepared, as was Belgium. God will meet them with every device they have invented. Pestilence, sword, fire, brimstone, all her own devilish weapons will overwhelm her. Of her mighty millions, only one-sixth will survive the carnage. The inhabitants of the Land will be seven months in burying the bodies which the beasts and birds have not devoured. That is the end of Germany.

And finally, **the capture of Jerusalem marked the beginning of the end of all imperialism.** The book of Daniel is the history of the rise, course and fall of imperialism. Before Neo-Babylonia there was no world power. Assyria was God's battleaxe to judge many nations; but the Assyrians had not the genius for empire. Germany will be the heart of a great northern confederacy, but it wili be only one arm of a world "balance of power." We have seen the tragic end of her career portrayed so graphically by Ezekiel. Daniel pictured the four world-empires. They have come and gone. Out of the ruins of Rome rose modern nations, represented by the feet of the image, made of a mixture of iron and clay.

It is the prophet's vision of the conglomerate principles of modern government, with the contending forces of autocracy and democracy. Out of it will come a confederacy represented by the ten toes of the image and the ten horns of the fourth Beast. Who can now doubt that the President's policy of "a league of nations strong enough to make war impossible" will be the outcome of the war? If that league includes essentially the territory of the old Roman Empire and the lands which have been colonized from that region, and if the northern confederacy is also formed, we shall know assuredly that we have come to the climax of this age.

Out of that group of ten kingdoms will arise a little horn, thrusting out three and dominating the others. Drunk with the lust for empire, he will lift up his hand against the holy people, blaspheme against high heaven, and finally proclaim himself God in the Temple at Jerusalem. The Jews will pass through the throes of the Time of Jacob's Trouble. Armageddon will be fought. The blood will flow to the horses' bridles on that great two-hundred-mile battle-line. The very heavens will answer pang for pang to this stricken world, while the earth will be shaken to its center. Mankind, terror-stricken, will cry to the rocks to fall on them. Then, out of the opening heavens, will come our Christ. The brightness of His appearing will paralyze Antichrist. His feet shall stand where He said farewell to His disciples. The remnant of the Jews shall shout, "Hosannah! Blessed be He that cometh in the name of the Lord!" Then one, drawing near, shall cry, "What are these wounds in His hands?" Then shall they "look upon Him whom they have pierced, and mourn for Him." Oh, what mourning it will be! The father will rush to his bedchamber, and the mother to her solitary kitchen, unable to share their grief for their long rejection of Jesus the Crucified One. But the days of their mourning will end when they behold in their Messiah the fountain opened unto the house of David and to the inhabitants of Jerusalem for sin and for uncleanness. Their Light has come, and the glory of Jehovah has risen upon them. King of kings and Lord of lords, He shall rule from sea to sea, and from the rivers unto the ends of the earth. Then the Massey-Harris Company with gather up the shells they shipped to Europe to plow it into fields of blood, beat them into plows and harvesters, and send them back to the sunny fields of France. The songs of the reaper will be heard where now the shrieks of the slaughtered are drowned in the roar of battle; and the nations shall learn war no more. Then shall Jerusalem be holy in very deed, and the earth shall be filled with the glory of God as the waters cover the sea. Captive daughter of Zion, thine hour of deliverance is at hand!

THE RE-GATHERING OF ISRAEL IN UNBELIEF

REV. JAMES M. GRAY, D.D.

Dean of the Moody Bible Institute of Chicago; author of "Synthetic Bible Studies," "Great Epochs of Sacred History," "The Christian Workers' Commentary," "How to Master the English Bible," etc.

I commence this address by laying down a definition of the Bible, which is, the history of the redemption of the human race on this earth. I emphasize the last phrase, "on this earth." There are some who seem to think that the Bible is taken up chiefly with heaven, but it says very little about heaven. It is dealing chiefly with the earth and the people that are upon it. God loves the earth and its people, notwithstanding all that the people are doing at the present time to contradict that statement. As was said this morning, His glory shall fill the earth, and the knowledge of the Lord shall cover the earth as the waters cover the sea.

Keeping in mind, therefore, that the Bible is the history of the redemption of the human race on this earth, I ask you to note, in the second place, that God is using two instruments, or two servants, in the carrying out of His purpose of redemption. One instrument, the primary one, of course, is "His only begotten and well-beloved Son," the Seed of the woman who should bruise the serpent's head, the Seed of Abraham in whom all the families of the earth shall be blessed, the Son of David whose kingdom shall be established for ever, "the Lamb of God which taketh away the sin of the world," whose "own self bare our sins in His own body on the tree." But God is pleased to reveal a secondary instrument, in the nation of Israel. The human race had been some time on the earth before He made that truth known. It is first revealed to us in the call of Abram to be the father of that nation as indicated in the 12th chapter of Genesis.

GOD'S PURPOSE IN ISRAEL

Now what had, or what has God in mind, in the use of Israel as His servant? Three things: (1) He desired Israel to be a depository for His truth in the earth, and unto Israel was committed the sacred oracles. The writer of every book of the Bible was a Jew, and the Jews kept the Bible intact for the world until the coming of Christ and the establishment of the Christian church. (2) He desired Israel to be a channel for the incoming of the personal Redeemer to the earth, and, as you know, Israel has given to the world its only Saviour, though she crucified Him when He came. (3) He desired Israel to be a national witness to

Himself before the other nations of the earth, in order that those nations in response to that witness, beholding Him as the only and true God in His attributes of justice, power, holiness, truth and love, might be brought into loving and cheerful submission to His holy will.

Israel has fulfilled the first two purposes, but has not as yet fulfilled the third. She has never borne a faithful and true witness to God, and the result is seen in the conflict of the nations in the present war. This war can be traced directly to the unfaithfulness of Israel as a witness to God, in consequence of which there is not a Christian nation upon the face of the earth. In every nation there are many Christians, but there is not a Christian nation as such, and there never has been. Moreover, so far as Israel is concerned, she, too, is suffering the punishment of her unfaithfulness in being scattered among these nations, persecuted, "sifted as corn is sifted in a sieve," and yet not one grain shall fall to the earth, is the testimony of God. In other words, it is God's purpose, as all of the prophets witness, to bring Israel back to her land, first indeed in unbelief, but afterwards she shall look upon Him whom she pierced, and shall mourn because of Him, and in that day she shall cry in the language of Isaiah, "Lo, this is our God, we have waited for Him, we will rejoice and be glad in His salvation!" Then it is that Israel shall again take up the broken threads of her testimony for God, and through which the Gentiles shall be brought to know Him and the kingdoms of the world at length shall become "the kingdom of our Lord and of His Christ."

THE ABUNDANCE OF PROOF

The proof of the regathering of Israel is embarrassing in its riches. Where shall one begin in the Bible to talk about it? Genesis is filled with it, Leviticus, Numbers, Deuteronomy. You cannot understand the book of Psalms until you have this great truth as its key. It is the beginning and the ending of the so-called prophetic books from Isaiah to Malachi. Matthew is rich in this teaching, Luke possesses it, the Acts, Romans, and when we come to the book of Revelation—what is that book without it?

It is the warp and woof of the whole Bible, but for the sake of brevity and convenience I am limiting your attention to a single chapter, the 30th of Deuteronomy.

The situation is this: Moses is soon to climb Mt. Pizgah to view the promised land which he was not permitted to enter, and then to take his flight into the presence of God; and before he goes, he is leaving this last word and testament with Israel—a word of warning, instruction, and hope. He is setting before his people in chapters 27 to 30, the blessings and the cursings which will come on them in either case as they obey or disobey their God, and at the close of his rendition of the cursings we read these words:

"And it shall come to pass, when all these

things are come upon thee, the blessing and the curse, which I have set before thee, and thou shalt call them to mind among all the nations, whither the Lord thy God hath driven thee, and shalt return unto the Lord thy God, and shalt obey His voice according to all that I command thee this day . . . with all thine heart, and with all thy soul, that then the Lord thy God will turn thy captivity, and have compassion upon thee, and will return and gather thee from all the nations, whither the Lord thy God hath scattered thee.

"And the Lord thy God will bring thee into the land which thy fathers possessed, and thou shalt possess it and He will do thee good, and multiply thee above thy fathers.

"And the Lord thy God will circumcise thine heart, and the heart of thy seed, to love the Lord thy God with all thine heart, and with all thy soul, that thou mayest live.

"And the Lord thy God will put all these curses upon thine enemies, and on them that hate thee, which persecuted thee.

"And the Lord thy God will make thee plenteous in every work of thine hand, in the fruit of thy body, and in the fruit of thy cattle, and in the fruit of thy land, for good; for the Lord will again rejoice over thee for good, as He rejoiced over thy fathers: if thou shalt hearken unto the voice of the Lord thy God, to keep his commandments and His statutes which are written in this book of the law, and if thou turn unto the Lord thy God with all thine heart, and with all thy soul."

SEVEN PROMISES OF GOD

Here are seven promises for Israel, each of them beginning with the letter "R," which will enable us to recall them easier.

(1) We have a promise of *remembrance:* "It shall come to pass, when all these things are come upon thee . . . and thou shalt call them to mind among all the nations, whither the Lord thy God hath driven thee." Israel has not called these things to mind as yet, but the time is coming when she shall do so, for the mouth of the Lord hath spoken it. (2) The promise of remembrance is followed by a promise of *repentance:* "And shalt return unto the Lord thy God, and shalt obey His voice according to all that I command thee this day, thou and thy children, with all thine heart, and with all thy soul." (3) The promise of repentance is followed by the promise of *regathering:* "Then the Lord thy God will turn thy captivity, and have compassion upon thee, and will return and gather thee from all the nations, whither the Lord thy God hath scattered thee." (4) The promise of regathering is followed by the promise of *restoration* to the land: "The Lord thy God will bring thee into the land which thy fathers possessed, and thou shalt possess it; and He will do thee good, and multiply thee above thy fathers." (5) The promise of the restoration is followed by that of their *regeneration,* for although they are going back at first in unbelief, yet it is written: "The Lord thy God will circumcise

thine heart, and the heart of thy seed, to love the Lord thy God with all thine heart, and with all thy soul, that thou mayest live." (6) The promise of regeneration is followed by one of *retribution* upon their Gentile enemies: "And the Lord thy God will put all these curses upon thine enemies, and on them that hate thee, which persecuted them." (7) And finally, the promise of retribution is followed by one of *replenishment* in the land: "And the Lord thy God will make thee plenteous in every work of thine hand, in the fruit of thy body, and in the fruit of thy cattle, and in the fruit of thy land, for good; for the Lord will again rejoice over thee for good, as He rejoiced over thy fathers: if thou shalt hearken unto the voice of the Lord thy God, to keep His commandments and His statutes which are written in this book of the law."

But someone may say, "What about that 'if'?" Let it not divert your thought from the fulfilment of these promises for a moment. It is a good deal like the "if" of the inspired apostle Paul used more than once in the New Testament. When he says to the church at Colosse, "If ye then be risen with Christ, seek those things which are above, where Christ sitteth on the right hand of God," he does not use "if" in the sense of a condition, or a contingency. It is axiomatic with Paul, and he is using it declaratively. It were as though he said, "*Inasmuch* as," or, "*Seeing that* ye are risen with Christ, set your mind on things above."

I do not say that the "if" in this instance is axiomatic, as in the case of Paul, but I do say that there is no condition, no contingency in it; it is a declaration of fact. We learn that as we come to compare this word by Moses with the same word by the lips and pens of all the holy prophets that have spoken since the world began. It is God's decree, and God will see that it is carried out.

ISRAEL'S UNBELIEF

But our theme is the re-gathering of Israel in *unbelief,* and their re-gathering at first is of such a character. As a matter of fact, Israel has been in process of re-gathering to her own land for decades and generations, and always she is gathering there in unbelief, so far as her Messiah is concerned. Zionism is only one of the many agencies for bringing her back. There are other organizations engaged in the colonization of Palestine with the Jew, and after this war is over the Jew will go back in numbers beyond anything that most of us have conceived of.

The Gentile nations feel an obligation to send the Jew back to Palestine which they cannot possibly avoid. For example, the Turk is gradually being driven out of the Holy Land, never to return. But who will have control of that so very important part of the earth when the Turk is gone? Shall Russia have control of it? That would mean the pre-eminence of the Greek church, and the Roman Catholic nations never would permit it. Shall France or Austria have control of it? That would mean the pre-eminence of the Roman Catholic church, and Russia would not permit it. Do not think for a moment that Russia shall continue in her present dilapidated condition for very long. The prophets tell us that Russia has a future, a future of national and worldly greatness and power, a mighty strength that she has never realized in the history of the past. But no Protestant country could have control of Palestine, for then the Roman Catholic nations, and those in which the Greek church is in the ascendency, would unite in protest and opposition. Therefore, there is only one people from a national point of view that can be permitted to re-people Palestine—the people to whom Palestine by right belongs for ever.

Speaking further of their return in unbelief, I quote a paragraph or two from John Wilkinson's "Israel, My Glory." He remarks that many Christians, in ignorance of the purpose of God in thus restoring them, have contended that to restore the Jews in unbelief would tend to confirm them in their unbelief. And, as the rejection of Christ was one of the causes of their national rejection, why should they be thus restored to Palestine before repenting of their sin, and before acknowledging Him as their Messiah and Lord? He replies that it obviates the difficulty when we remember that the Jews are not to be restored for immediate blessing, but that, between their national restoration and their national blessing, they are to experience that Time of Jacob's Trouble, of which the prophets speak. God levies chastisement upon Israel in Palestine, in the very place where the national sins were committed which caused the national rejection.

Listen to the words of Jeremiah: "Thus saith the Lord; we have heard a voice of trembling, of fear, and not of peace. Ask ye now, and see whether a man doth travail with child? wherefore do I see every man with his hands on his loins, as a woman in travail, and all faces are turned into paleness? Alas! for that day is great, so that none is like it: it is even the time of Jacob's trouble; but he shall be saved out of it."

Listen to these words of Daniel: "And at that time shall Michael stand up, the great prince which standeth for the children of thy people: and there shall be a time of trouble, such as never was since there was a nation even to that same time: and at that time thy people shall be delivered."

Listen to the words of Jesus in the 24th of Matthew, where he says: "Then shall be great tribulation, such as was not since the beginning of the world until now; no, nor ever shall be."

Let us remember, dear friends and brethren, that Jacob's Trouble will reach its climax in the culmination of the power of the Antichrist. Just prior to his destruction by the personal advent of the Lord Jesus, he will make a desperate, though unsuccessful effort to destroy the Jewish nation. When we are now referring to the personal advent of the Lord Jesus, it is not to His coming in the air, where His church will be caught up to meet Him. So far as I know, there is nothing to interfere with that coming, and I am looking for Him every day. But the coming now referred to with reference to the deliverance of Israel is that second aspect of His Second Coming when He comes with His church, and "His holy angels in flaming fire, taking vengeance on them that know not God, and obey not the gospel of our Lord Jesus Christ."

The Antichrist will in that day, as already stated, make a desperate, though unsuccessful effort to destroy the Jewish nation, because that nation is the most powerful of the living witnesses to the existence of the one only and true God, and to the inspiration of the Bible as the Word of God. No wonder that the Antichrist should seek by one supreme effort to wipe it from the face of the earth. In that day, the language of Israel's ancient enemies will be repeated, when they said, "Come and let us cut them off from being a nation." But just at the moment of Israel's extremity, when the Antichrist seems to have complete success, the clouds part asunder over the Mount of Olives and Christ returns, the Jews are delivered, and the Antichrist is destroyed.

At the Wednesday evening session the chair was occupied by Dr. Howard A. Kelly of Baltimore, Md. Dr. Kelly holds a position almost unique in his profession. With academic, professional, and honorary degrees from the Universities of Pennsylvania, Washington and Lee,

Aberdeen, and Edinburgh, his rank as a scholar is clearly recognized. His published works have caused him to be reckoned the most eminent of all authorities in his own field.

Dr. Kelly remarked upon the large attendance and great enthusiasm in connection with the present Conference. "I was talking to one of my good friends yesterday noon, in another large city," said he, "about this very matter we now have under consideration. He is one of the leading Bible teachers of the world, and one of the noblest and best men I have ever known; but he has fought shy of this matter. He said: 'I have not taken hold of it, because the churches are all against it. I have not seen it quite clearly, and I do not want to antagonize the churches I am trying to bring together.' Now, from the appearance of this splendid audience this evening, one might think the churches are, after all, getting together on this great subject."

The devotional services introducing the evening program were conducted by the Rev. Dean A. C. Peck of Denver, Colo. He said: "Upon returning to my hotel this evening, I met a man from New Jersey, whom I knew long ago. He had seen the crowds in front of this building, and commented upon the great interest manifested in these meetings. He asked me, 'Just what do you people stand for over there, and what are you doing?' I told him the distinctive doctrines of our faith." Dean Peck commented on Phil. 2:5-11.

WAR ON GERMAN THEOLOGY

REV. CORTLAND MYERS, D.D.

Pastor of Tremont Baptist Temple, Boston, Mass.

Mr. Chairman, Ladies and Gentlemen: The abomination of abominations in the modern religious world is that ripe, rank, rampant, rotten new theology made in Germany. Martin Luther in the great Reformation gave to the German people an open Bible, and with that open Bible in their hands they became a very prosperous and powerful people. In these last forty years of their history, they have reversed the conditions, having taken that open Bible and torn it in shreds and trampled it beneath their feet like mere scraps of paper, thus substituting for real Christianity and the principles of the gospel of the Son of God, the law of the survival of the fittest, with the result now manifest in our world-tidal wave of barbarism, savagery, and immorality. For they have secured by this process in recent years, a nation of agnostics and atheists, and it is not a long way from infidelity to immorality. For they have secured by this the other. We see the harvest fields being reaped from these seeds of German rationalism and false philosophy. All this is unquestionably true, and it is a grave question to-night whether this war would be burdening our world with its curse if it had not been for the new theology started in Germany some years ago and permeating and poisoning our theological seminaries as well as our other institutions, and some of our pulpits, and even reaching the hearts of many Christian people.

You will make the discovery, if you will read history—the religious history of the world—that the Person of Christ has always been the center of the battlefield; and it has been no different in this instance. You have heard that before; the world has often heard it; but we have failed to learn the lesson. I know of a boy who went to school and who always had difficulty with his grammar. He could manage arithmetic, history, spelling, and most of the other subjects, but he had great difficulty with grammar. This one subject he was unable to master and apply He would always say this—"I have went." The teacher became wearied with her efforts to cure him of that apparently fatal disease, and said: "I am going to correct you of this. I shall keep you after school, and you will write this sentence, 'I have gone,' one hundred times." The boy sat down on that hard bench in front of the desk, heaved a heavy sigh and sobbed a moment, and then wrote one hundred sentences all in a row, "I have gone," and counted backwards every time he wrote, to be sure that he did not write one too many. When he had finished the last line, he sighed once more, and then wrote this sentence at the bottom of the page, "I have written this one hundred times, and I have went home."

We have been pointing in other directions sometimes without remembering the fact concerning theology and the discussion of the centuries and the real center of all the difficulties. It is pre-eminently the Person of Christ; and the one question to ask, in the face of this tidal wave of German theology, is, Who is this Christ? Who is He? That is the interrogation that ought to find its way into the heart of humanity at this hour, and so fasten itself there with its divine answer that we never can be shaken from it. Who is He? First of all, He is the supreme Authority in religion. We always demand an authority in religion. The world always has. It must always demand this. Philosophy doesn't demand it; science does not demand it. But when we come to religion, the human heart always demands some real authority. Some men have said that it was in the individual soul; that the personal consciousness of the man was sufficient for his authority in religion. I grant you that he has an aptness for worship and the recognition of God; that he has a conscience that dictates to him something about the path of right; but he cannot find in his own heart the authority that will satisfy himself and satisfy his fellow-man. There must be something other than that which comes from a man's own consciousness and his individual soul for his authority. Some other people have said, We must have authority, so we will have a vice-gerent of God on earth, and we will establish a Pope in Rome. I grant you that that gentleman is not too far away and he is sufficiently easy of access, but his infallibility has depended upon a long line of Popes, good and bad—mostly bad.

Where are we going to have our real authority in religion? Some people tell us that we have it in the Bible. Some tell us that we have it in Christ. I do not know how you can separate the two. I think they are married and cannot be divorced. The Bible centers in Christ. My authority must be in the Book of Christ and in the Christ of the Book, and I never can be satisfied with anything less. The preacher who does not have this as his authority is in a very strange position. Who can listen to him? If it is his personal consciousness that is going to transact this business, or if his individual soul is his authority, then he comes before his fellowmen with nothing whatever to bring to them as a message. He must have something outside of himself.

When the ambassador went to the Court of St. James's, he went with the authority and the word of the United States Government back of him. Yes, but that did not satisfy. Something had to be added. He went into the Court of St. James's, but he did not represent this country in reality until he went into his pocket and drew out a sealed document and then he was accredited representative of this Government at the court of St. James's. A man might say that he was God's messenger—and God has the right and authority to send His messengers—nevertheless he is not God's ambassador unless he comes with this Book as his signed and sealed authority, sealed by the Holy Ghost. When he presents that, he is God's representative to this world and he can preach with authority. He is a fakir if he tries anything else. We have had a large amount of difficulty in America from foreign immigration. We have had a large amount of blessings—perhaps most of our ancestors came across the seas; perhaps some of you came across the seas—but we have had our perils; and we have never realized them quite as much as we do to-night. We are conscious now that there is so much of traitorism, hidden traitorism; and it ought to be hunted down to the last single man or woman, and just as quickly as possible.

I grant you that we ought to give our level best to our country at this time. I have only one son. I love him better than I do my own soul. He has already given one year to France. When this war first broke out, he left his college course to go to France. He is in the United States army now. I will give him. I will give my money. I will give my strength. I will go the limit, and I would to God I was a younger man and I would go in the trenches myself. I will not take second place with any single one of you for patriotism.

I say we ought to fight this battle against barbarism, and militarism, and the rest of the devil's catalog, and, God helping us, we will.

But I also say to you that we ought to make war, and strenuous war, and fight to a finish, against foreign innovation or immigration into our religious world. If the churches of Great Britain, America, and France, fifty years ago had fought this iniquity, this infamous thing, there never would have been any war in the world now. Go back to fountainhead and you will find that your crimson stream has its source in the rank German theology that has been forcing its way into the veins and arteries of all our religious life. We ought to fight it to the finish. I know an Italian man who had a boy that was obstreperous. Finally he ran away from home. His father afterwards found him and brought him before the court. The judge questioned him and said, "Don't you know that your father has the right to whip you?" He said, "No, sir; he is a foreigner, and no foreigner can lick me. I am an American." Well, by the grace of God, no foreigner can transact this unholy business with me. No, sir! we will have none of it—absolutely none of it. The authority for our message and mission on this old sin-cursed earth is in the Christ of that Book and the Book of the Christ, and we stand behind it and believe it against all earth and hell. We will have no Pope infallible or otherwise, for our authority. We will have no German rationalism for our authority. We will have only the Christ of the Book for our authority. I hate this traitorous stuff. Yes, I hate it! I have seen too much of it. I see the abominable curse working its way now into the churches and in the hearts of my fellow ministers. I see it damning our theological seminaries. I hate it! I hate it! I hate the new theology as I hate hell, from which it came!

WHO IS JESUS CHRIST?

Who is He? is our question. He is the supreme Authority in religion. Who is He? He is God in human flesh, nothing less. How do I know it? I know it, first of all, because He was the embodiment of truth and could never speak falsehood; and He said so. I believe Him. He said, "He that hath seen Me hath seen the Father." "No man cometh unto the Father but by Me. Before Abraham was, I am. I and My Father are one." When He heard from the lips of other men the statement that He was God, He never rebuked them, He never objected to it. When Peter said, "Thou art the Christ, the Son of the living God," our Lord commended it as the greatest of all truths. "On this rock," He said, "I will build my church; and the gates of hell shall not prevail against it." When Thomas, after the resurrection morning, looked into His face once more, and said, "My Lord and my God," Jesus accepted it. I am not giving any foolish nor false interpretation to Scripture. I am reading it, and I am believing it with more emphasis than I believe anything else.

I was down in North Carolina a week or two ago, and an old colored educator down there told me that the scripture expositions of some of the negro preachers were very, very strange. He said that a friend of his in that town saw a negro minister reprimanding a lot of little negro boys who were out in the street, playing marbles. He walked up and said, "What is the matter?" "I was just telling these boys about their sins—trying to keep them from committing sin." "Why, boys have got to have exercise," he told him, "and play—you don't think there is any harm in playing marbles, do you?" The colored preacher replied, "You don't understand the Scriptures. Don't the Bible say, 'Marble (marvel) not?' "

Some of my new theology friends have given Scripture exposition just as ridiculous interpretation as that, taking the simplest statements from the lips of Jesus, and the simplest statements in the Book, and misstating them, and misrepresenting them, and trying to read them out or read something into them that is not there—instead of reading them in a commonsense fashion and believing them. I believe what Christ said about Himself, and He said that He was God in human flesh. I believe it because He said to some other people, and He is saying to us, If ye cannot believe My words, "believe Me for the very works' sake"; and that life of His was covered with manifestations of the supernatural.

In 1832, Charles Darwin made that famous trip of his around the world in the ship *Beagle.* He stopped, or tried to stop, on the coast of Terra del Fuego. In his record of that visit, he said that that was the most savage spot his eyes had ever rested on, and that he could not put the practices of those barbarians and cannibals in writing. It was impossible to describe what he saw with his own eyes. The British Admiralty ordered that no ship should ever stop there again. One morning—early morning—by the side of a bridge in England, at one of the abutments, they found a baby wrapped only in newspaper—no father, no mother, as known. It was St. Thomas' Day, so they called the baby Thomas, and as they found him by a bridge, they called him Bridges. He was Thomas Bridges. They put him in the almshouse. He stayed in the almshouse all through his boyhood and young manhood, and under that kind of environment he was educated and brought up. The years passed, and one day, one wonderful day, this same Christ—God in human flesh—came into those almhouse yards, reached down His pierced hand, took hold of that (it is almost unbelievable), took hold of that pauper's hand, made him kingly and touched him with the divine. Then that regenerated soul made his application to the English Missionary Society, and they sent him to Charles Darwin's cannibal-savage land. Christianity is always heroic, and never afraid. The scientist Darwin had said he would never again put foot on that savage territory. Even the British Admiralty said, Don't venture on that soil; but the missionary said, I am going to bring Christ even to the savages. He struggled on, with the help of the Spirit of God; it was most heroic, miraculous. He gave them a language, and before he passed into glory, he had given them the entire Bible in that language that he first gave them. There is no longer a cannibal in that part of the world; the whole of Terra del Fuego was revolutionized. Charles Darwin contributed to the Missionary Society in recognition of this miracle. I challenge you to answer, and I challenge the world to answer, What is the explanation of that miracle—multiplied by ten thousand more that my Lord has transacted on this old earth—if He was not God in human flesh? I know He was divine, because of what He did. I know He was the Son of God—God in human flesh—because of personal experience. Oh, memory sometimes is sweet! But alas, alas, there are bitter drops in the cup. I had to stand with a man in New York City by his wife's bedside when she was passing away from this life and home, leaving him in his young manhood, leaving that beautiful home and two beautiful little girls. And she was a picture—a perfect picture—a beauty in form, and feature, and character. I stood by his side and held his one hand as she was breathing out the last remnant of life. There were red flushes on her cheeks after the last breath was gone; her cheeks seemed red in the casket. You could not believe she was dead. I saw him reach up his other hand and say, "Lord Jesus, Lord Jesus, I love you just the same"; and I saw Christ reach down and take hold of that smitten man's hand and hold him up by His divine grace. It was wonderful. Six weeks after that, he was crossing the great prairie at midnight, out West, on a sleeper. Unable, in his agony, to sleep, the moon shining through the window on to his berth, there he lay on his back. Twelve o'clock, one o'clock, two o'clock; no sleep. On that shining mirrored berth above him in the moonlight, this happened. Tears rolling down like bubbles on a mountain stream, he reached up that same hand and asked Christ once more to take hold of it, and he saw the reflection—he saw the reflection of his own hand coming down and meeting his as he reached it up. It seemed as real to him as that. He dropped back on his pillow, and, within sixty seconds, as he afterwards told me, he was sleeping like a babe on its mother's bosom. Jesus Christ reached down His pierced hand and took hold of my friend's hand that night on the Western prairie, and put him to sleep like a mother puts her baby to sleep. Don't talk to me about that being merely human! He is God in human flesh, and we know it by experience. I have reached out my hand, too, through the darkness and He has clasped it with loving pressure, and I know it. No man can take that from me.

I am here; you know I am here. My friends are here. I touch them and I know them; yes, I know that. I am here—I am absolutely sure of it. But I will tell you something else. There is Another here, and His presence is just as real as my own. He is here on this platform. I know He is here; and some glorious day—oh, how I wish I would never get back to Boston! I wish He would come to-night—yes, He is some day coming—coming in that same bodily presence that the disciples saw on the resurrection morning—and with a thousand times more joy than they had, I shall meet Him and I shall be with Him for ever, and then I shall be like Him.

I should like to get this right. I should like to get it right once more for my own sake, and for yours. I think it is the most important thing that we can think about, for if we are going to talk about the poison of German theology, then we need renewed emphasis and conviction, and I say once more that He is the supreme Authority in religion. He is God in human flesh, and He is the world's only Redeemer. When the *Tuscania* went down in North British waters, she was being convoyed by the British fleet. I am sorry it was so, for that British fleet has done such wonders for her own transports, and done such wonders in other directions, that I am sorry they had that mishap with our own American boys. Let me ask you if you know or realize what we here in America owe to that British Navy? If it had not been for that navy, you would know more about this war than you know now. Amongst other things, first of all, the British Navy has saved the rest of this world up to to-night. When that *Tuscania* went down, do you know what happened? If you do, I will repeat it to you, for it is one of the most remarkable things ever known on the seas of this earth. Your American soldier boys were there from Wisconsin and from New England, and from North Carolina. When that ship was struck, the Birkenhead order was given, and those soldiers all lined up in their places on deck and awaited further orders, and their turns with life-boats and life-savers, if there were any. Every single soldier lined up and took his place, and when that ship went down, it still had nearly two hundred of our American boys standing in line. They went down still standing in line, and they were singing "The Star-Spangled Banner." I will fight German theology till the crack of doom, and if I go down, I'll go down with my colors flying and I'll go down singing,

> "In the cross of Christ I glory,
> Towering o'er the wrecks of time,
> All the light of sacred story
> Gathers round His head sublime."

There are some things about which we may differ — merely secondary things — matters of opinion are secondary things. We are coming closer together—thank God for that!—we are coming nearer together, and this convention is an evidence of it.

There are some things without which there is no Christianity, any more than you can have the human body without a heart pumping the blood through the veins and arteries, even to the finger tips. The heart is absolutely essential. The other things may be secondary. My little finger is off, but that is not essential. It is like some of the differences in denominational life. I might get along without this arm. My son over in France saw at the beginning of this war a young Frenchman in perfect condition and yet without any arms, and with both legs off at the body. He still retained that which was essential to the make-up and life of the human body. Now there are some things, I declare to you, without which there is no Christianity. There is no Christianity without the deity of Jesus Christ, the virgin birth of Christ (under the touch of God), the atonement of Christ on Calvary, His bodily resurrection, and His second coming. You can take that Book and throw it away for ever—throw it to the rubbish, and have no more use for it—if that is not true. It is absolutely essential. And by that, to-night, to-morrow, for the rest of life, I shall stand, and must stand, believing that Jesus Christ is this world's only hope, its only Redeemer; through His atonement for sin on Calvary. Yes, I must stand on that. That was a wonderful thing that General Foch did at the battle of the Marne. Recently, someone asked the general how he had come forth from the battle. He said immediately, "A miracle." When this war is written in history, that may be the decisive battle. He said, "A miracle." Then he pointed up dramatically and said, "The good God. For," he said, "the flower of the German army—sixteen deep—an iron wall—stood against poorly prepared Frenchmen only four deep at the Marne." And do you remember what happened? I don't wonder that Foch was made commanding general. At the Battle of the Marne, General Joffre sent word to General French to advance. General French, with that splendid British Army, sent word back, "I am sorely pressed and must have support." When Foch received Joffre's order, he sent word immediately back, "My right has been turned; my left is rolled up; my center is smashed. I have ordered an advance all along the line." That advance all along the line pushed the Germans back, and farther back into the swamps, and at last the run was on for the coast. From Belgium to Switzerland that line was stretched, and it has been bent, but, blessed be God, it has not been broken, and it never will be. Our religious line in the battle against German theology may be bent, but the Christian world needs to stand up heroically—"advance all along the line"—and, by God's grace, it shall never, never, never be broken.

Who is He? I have been to hundreds of conventions. I have had the privilege and blessing of preaching the gospel of the Son of God to more than thirteen millions of people in every part of the world, but this is the finest audience at a convention that I ever saw in my life. Now—listen! Who is He? He is the One who went out into the Garden of God, picked a bouquet of the most beautiful flowers, and threw them down on this planet as a special token of His love. In all the valleys, and on the mountain sides, and in the gardens and the fence corners they blossomed—the fragrant tulips and lilacs and primroses, and thousands of others. He is the One who walked up to an angel artist's easel, picked up the brush, and, with one sweep of His mighty hand, circled the storm-cloud with a rainbow as if He was running a many-colored ribbon through the garments of the storm. He was the One who, in the morning, with those same hands, pushed the gates open, without a creak, on their hinges, while the king of Day, with his royal retinue, drove Darkness back into its hiding, and turned glory over this planet, and gave us a new day. He is the One—He is the One—who took the notes of seraphs and covered them with feathers, and filled the forest with a chorus of ten thousand singers, while the angel messengers paused on their holy errands to listen to the music from another world; and then they picked up the notes and carried them back home. He is the One—He is the One—who will sweep with His royal chariot across every battlefield of the world in triumph. He is the One—He is the One—who will pass in His royal garments through every palace hall on earth. He will swing His mighty scepter over every crowned head on this planet, while the hosts angelic and the hosts redeemed rend the very skies with their hallelujahs as they say "He is the King of kings and Lord of lords, and He shall reign for ever and ever and ever. Hallelujah!"

COMING EVENTS CAST THEIR SHADOWS BEFORE

REV. P. W. PHILPOTT

Pastor of the Gospel Tabernacle of Hamilton, Ontario, a church which he founded and has rebuilt four times, doubling its capacity with each rebuilding.

When the Convention Committee requested me to address you on "The Signs of the Times," I consented with some little feeling of hesitancy and diffidence, for this phase of the advent testimony is so vast and so important, and moreover, can so easily become controversial, that I would have liked had the task been undertaken by some of my brethren who I feel are much better qualified to present it than myself.

Godly men now fallen asleep and saintly men living and toiling with us have, probably without realizing it, made it very difficult for others to proclaim these glorious and solemn prophetic truths. Moved as they have been with the grandeur and importance of the subject and impressed with the very large place that it occupies in the New Testament, they have allowed themselves to be carried from their Scriptural moorings into forbidden waters, having forgotten, or ignored the fact, that one of the clearest revelations concerning the Second Coming of Christ is that, for the sons of men, God has left "the day and hour" just as uncertain, as the fact itself is certain.

The teachers to whom I refer are those who have figured out a definite date for Christ to appear. How anyone can dare to do this in the face of such declarations as those made by the Master Himself in Matthew 24:26; Acts 1:7, it is hard to understand. The amazing part of this date-figuring business is, that although our friends have failed again and again, they keep right on at it. We have all known of instances where the day was definitely fixed. It came and went, and He did not appear, but undaunted, they coolly and confidently sit down and fix up a new schedule. Now I am sure that this kind of thing has brought nothing but discredit and harm to the glorious truth that they and we so dearly love. I would suggest that when any Bible student is tempted to go into the date-fixing business, that he pray with the Psalmist, "Lord, keep back thy servant from presumptuous sins; let them not have dominion over me: then shall I be upright, and I shall be innocent from the great transgression."

"That day and hour," "the times and the seasons" are among the "secret things" which "belong to the Lord our God," "which the Father hath put in His own power" (Deut. 29:29; Acts 1:7). And yet I think I should say, that the overstudy of prophecy is not nearly so serious as the failure to study it at all. We must remember that the prophetic Scriptures were given for our instruction and that God has encouraged the study of prophecy by a distinct benediction. This is especially true of the Book of Revelation, which is preeminently a book of prophecy (Rev. 1:3).

To me it is deeply significant, if not a sign of the times, that the interest in the prophetic Scriptures is much greater at the present moment than in any other period during the whole history of the church. The Bible is being read and studied as never before and the number of those who believe in the Second Coming of Christ is very rapidly increasing.

I am also very credibly informed that the sons of Jacob are turning to the Old Testament prophets and seeking for light in these dark days in a way they have not done since the times of Ezra and Nehemiah.

The Apostle Peter tells us that the prophetic Scripture has been given that the children of God may have light in just such days as these in which we are living (2 Pet. 2:19). Jesus told His disciples that His coming would fall "as a snare on all that dwell upon the face of the whole earth" (Luke 21:35), but we are also informed that His disciples are not to be surprised and overtaken as a thief, by that event (1 Thess. 5:4). We are to have a light in the darkness and that light is the "sure word of prophecy."

Now, it is not only our privilege but it is our duty to read in the light of prophecy the events that are now transpiring. When here upon earth, Christ upbraided the religious leaders of that day because while they were able to read certain weather signs, they were not able to discern the signs of the times (Matt. 16:1-3) and in these days we read our weather forecasts, the signs of the times as to trade, stocks, markets and national movements, and our reading of them powerfully affects our business life and conduct, and yet we fail to discern the signs of the times.

Let us keep in mind that while we cannot fix the day for His appearing, yet the Scripture gives us approximate signs of the end of this age—I say approximate, mark you—because I believe that they enable us only to approximate, certainly not to calculate—the time of the end.

In Matthew 24:3, we have the disciples asking the Master a twofold question, "What shall be the sign of Thy coming, and of the end of the age?" and all that follows in chapters 24 and 25, was given by Christ in reply to those questions, and those chapters should always be read in the light of the questions asked.

Now in considering the signs of the second advent as given to us in the Scripture, we might classify them as Political, Commercial, Social, Moral, Spiritual, and National or Jewish signs. I shall barely mention some of these in passing and endeavor to emphasize the last, because it is the most significant.

The Political Signs. The Master announced that the end time should be particularly marked by terrific wars of unusual magnitude and horror (Matt. 24:6). Here He tells us that the whole age from that time until He should return would be characterized by "Wars and Rumors of Wars," and we know how very literally that prophecy has been fulfilled. You will observe, however, that in this verse He tells them that "the end is not yet"; but in verse 7 we have just such a cataclysm of strife, suffering and death as we are now witnessing on the blood-soaked fields of Europe. Surely we have come to the time when "nation has risen against nation." And these "are the beginning of sorrows." Let me read from Luke 21:25-26. "And there shall be signs in the sun, and in the moon, and in the stars, and upon the earth distress of nations, with perplexity; the sea and the waves roaring; men's hearts failing them for fear, and for looking after those things which are coming on the earth: for the powers of heaven shall be shaken."

Yes, we have come to this place in the history of the nations; and if these are but the "beginning of sorrows," what will the consummation be? Let every believer note verse 28, "And when these things begin to come to pass, then look up, and lift up your heads; for your redemption draweth nigh."

I believe that to-day there has come into the hearts of God's people everywhere a feeling that we are living in the end times, and not a few of us are waiting for His appearing.

Commercial Signs. In Daniel 12:4, we read that

in the time of the end "many shall run to and fro and knowledge shall be increased." We have reached the age of travel and applied science. Millions are rushing to and fro upon the earth, under the earth, on the sea, under the sea, and through the air like eagles. I was in Southern California last month and they told me there that in that State there was an automobile for every twelve persons, and that by a bit of crowding they could take the whole state for a motor trip on any given day. From the poor attendance at the churches, I imagine that they do go on a trip every Lord's Day. Someone has said that the 19th century advanced human progress more than all the centuries before, and that the first decade of the 20th century surpassed the whole of the 19th. If this is true of the first ten years of this century, what shall we say of these last four years? Surely we have reached the very acme of human genius and invention. I believe that all this is not only a sign of the times, but it is a *foregleam* of that most glorious day which is yet to dawn for this world. The Scriptures call it "The Day of the Lord." It is the day when He shall reign from the rivers to the ends of the earth, and all of these instruments of destruction and death shall be placed in channels of blessing where they will be utilized for the higher purposes of His kingdom.

Social Signs. (James 5:1-8). Here we have a most accurate picture of conditions that characterize these very days. It is an ominous picture.

I do not believe that these conditions prevailed in the days of the Apostle, but a man must be blind who cannot see that we are living in the times of which James wrote. The few own everything and control all, and even in these days of suffering and sorrow, selfishness and greed have raised their ugly heads and are fattening themselves on the blood of the poor. God have mercy on these profiteers who make themselves rich on the common necessities of life while our boys are bleeding to death in the defence of our liberty.

I read a little parody on one of our hymns the other day and it was not without point.

"Let us gather up the sunbeams, lying all around our path,
Let us keep the wheat and roses, give the poor the thorns and chaff,
Let us find our chiefest pleasure, hoarding bounties of to-day,
And the poor will get scant measure, and two prices have to pay.
We might corner e'en the wind god, and confine him to a cage,
And through some patent process, we the atmosphere might gauge.
Then we'll squeeze our little brother, when his lungs he tries to fill,
Put a meter on his wind-pipe and present our little bill."

I read in one of your morning papers to-day of a schoolgirl who receives from her father's estate $12,500 a year, and she complains that it's not nearly enough to meet her ordinary expenses, and appeals to the Surrogate Court in New York to have the allowance increased to $20,000. Among the items of expenses which she files to substantiate her claim, I noticed for manicuring, shampooing and hairdressing the sum of $3,000; for entertainments, dinners, and dances, $2,000; while she asks the modest sum of but $5,000 for the upkeep of her automobile, and $3,000 for other social duties at the school. It is this kind of selfishness and luxurious living that breeds anarchism of the worst kind. It is no wonder that James said "a terrible day of retribution" was coming for such people.

Yes, the spirit of selfishness is everywhere most evident. Yet I think it fair to say that we except from these strictures all those noble men and women who have come into possession of great wealth and are honestly striving to solve the problem of their stewardship, and are using their money for the uplift of their fellow-kind and the spread of the glorious gospel.

Moral Signs. (2 Tim. 3:1-4). "Why are you a premillennialist?" asked a brother the other day, and I replied, "Because Jesus said that at His coming He would find the world in a condition similar to that of the days of Noah and Lot." We all know that those were days of moral midnight. What are the facts to-day? Are we growing better? Are we becoming more Godlike? Now, friends, many of our brethren say that we are improving in spite of all that is transpiring. Where they get the evidence of the improvement is a great puzzle to me. You talk about the gospel saving the world. I have yet to find a city or a town, a village or even a hamlet, that is entirely

Christian. If we go back to the very country where Jesus lived and died and rose again, where the church had its beginning, what do we find? That not only is that country still in darkness and the shadow of death, but there is hardly a trace of Christianity within its borders. No, when we look the world square in the face, there is only one verdict and that is, that the very sins that made the judgment of Sodom a necessity, that corrupted the whole world in the days of Noah, are rampant and working mightily in our midst. I know that it is when we talk like this, the other fellow cries, "Pessimist" but we are not much concerned about that name. The desire of every man who believes his Bible is to be a "truthist," letting the world think and say what it likes. If the ministers of the Gospel do not know, the medical men of our country are aware of the fact that social conditions are most appalling, and I must speak with care here, for we have to-night as our Chairman one of America's most noted surgeons (Dr. Howard Kelly, of Baltimore). I sometimes wonder if my brethren in the ministry who oppose these teachings have taken the trouble to find out what grotesque and mischievous things are being preached in the name of Christ, these days—how that Spiritism is spreading at an alarming rate. This is especially so in England since the war. I fear that many of my brethren do not realize the magnitude and menace of this movement. It is essentially a doctrine of demons (1 Tim. 4:1-3; Rev. 16:14). It is the recrudescence of those frightful forms of evil that made the Flood a necessity (Genesis 6:2-5), and also brought destruction to the Canaanites (Numbers 13:33).

Spiritual Signs. (2 Peter 2:1-2) Dr. Cortland Myers has spoken of these, but I would like to say it seems to me that we are rapidly coming to the place where the man who believes in the fundamental teaching of the Scriptures, such as salvation only through faith in the sacrificial work of Jesus Christ, the Virgin Birth, the Resurrection, Ascension, Second Advent, will be looked upon not only as a back number, but as a fanatic, if not a heretic.

Last evening, Dr. Riley was talking about the evils of Christian Science and other kindred cults, but I can tell you of something that is more dangerous and a thousand times more sad, and that is, when a Methodist, Baptist, or Presbyterian minister stands up in pulpits that were founded by men who sacrificed and suffered for the truths which these men now ridicule and deny. I tell you, brethren, God is not going to wink at this apostasy, and there are many who think with Dr. Myers that German theology has a great deal more to do with the judgment that has now fallen upon Christendom, than some people suppose.

I was simply amazed the other day on reading a statement made by a professor of a prominent university. This learned Doctor is a bitter opponent of all who believe in the premillennial coming of Christ and not being able to answer the argument from the Scriptures, he resorts to the base method of arousing prejudice against the lovers of this truth by accusing them of being traitors to their country. I will read what the professor has said: "Two thousand dollars a week is being spent to spread this doctrine (the doctrine which we are preaching in this Convention). Where this money comes from is unknown, but there is a strong suspicion that it emanates from German sources; in my belief this fund would be a profitable field for government investigation." All this from a man who is supposed to be a scholar and a Christian gentleman. This university pretends to be right up-to-date, in fact a little ahead of the rest of us, but here is a professor of the Divinity School of that institution resorting to the most cowardly method of misrepresentation. worthy only of the dark ages.

If the professor desires to know where the money comes from to spread these truths, I can tell him very frankly. It is given by men and women who "love His appearing." These Second-Coming people are great givers; for instance, this Conference will incur considerable expense; yet not a collection is being taken, because the Committee has underwritten the entire amount. I happen to be the pastor of a church made up almost entirely of working people. That church supports twelve missionaries on the foreign field, in addition to all its home activities, without ever resorting to any questionable methods of raising money—in fact everything is given voluntarily. We not only look after the interests of the church, but I think if you care to investigate, you will find that we keep up our end for patriotic purposes during these days of our country's trial. Besides that, we have over three hundred men from the congregation in France at this very hour. Four of these happen to be my own sons, and I also have the honor of having a daughter a Red Cross nurse. Surely the aforesaid professor must have been very desperate when he made that statement. Personally, I would suggest that the theology of the university he represents might furnish a better field for the government investigation, for a great many thinking men have felt that this second-hand German theology which is being retailed by that institution is very largely responsible for the conditions of to-day.

The Apostle Peter tells us that "there shall be false teachers among you, who privily shall bring in damnable heresies, even denying the Lord that bought them . . . And many shall follow their pernicious ways; by reason of whom the way of truth shall be evil spoken of" (2 Pet. 2:1-2). I believe that we have come to this time. Paul makes it plain that the "last days" will be marked by an apostasy. "The Spirit speaketh expressly, that in the latter times some shall depart from the faith." That is what a great number of our preachers have done, and the result is, to-day we have a form of godliness without any power. Whoever heard of a soul being saved through the preaching of the New Theology? If you want to see men and women turned from sin to righteousness, you must go where they believe and preach the old Book. The gospel is the power of God unto salvation.

The other day, one of these up-to-date men asked what I should do if one of our young college men came to me regarding the first three chapters of Genesis. "Why," I said, "I should ask him if he understood the third chapter of John." "What has that to do with it?" he replied. "Why, everything—if a man has come to an understanding of the third chapter of John's Gospel, to my mind he will not have much trouble with the first three chapters of Genesis." "But now, hold on!" said my friend. "If your child was ill with diphtheria and the physician was about to treat the little one with the Old School method by which thousands of children died of that disease, would you not insist that he treat the child with the up-to-date anti-toxin treatment?" "But," said I, "brother, the analogy will not hold here. Supposing that under the old treatment no one ever heard of a baby dying, while under the new, no one ever heard of a baby being saved, would I not say in that case, if the doctor attempted the new method, 'Hold on, friend! You try that on your own kid?' Just give me the old thing by which babies are always saved."

If one of these New School men desires a revival or anything like a spiritual awakening, he is obliged to call a man who still believes and preaches the great fundamental truths of the Bible.

National or Jewish Signs. There have been times in the past when the political, social, and moral signs were very similar to what they are to-day, but there never has been a time for the last two thousand years when all these signs were manifest at the same time. The Jewish sign has only recently been hung out, and that is why we feel the others are so deeply significant. (Matt. 24.) He spake a parable of a fig-tree. A little time before this, He had cursed the fig-tree because of its barrenness, and that tree withered. Undoubtedly the application is to the Jewish nation. He told that nation that it was to be scattered among all the nations of the earth and that their land was to be desolate until the time of the end, but over and over again we are told that the people are to be gathered back to that land again. Surely no one could possibly doubt this who has listened to Dr. James M. Gray during this Conference. The valley of dry bones in Ezekiel 37 is a type of the nation Israel. The fig tree typifies the same people. The "bones" are coming together before our very eyes and the "fig tree" is surely budding. We must be blind indeed if we cannot see this.

Since I have been in my present pastorate, the first national council of the Jewish nation has been held. Think of it—for 2500 years without a king or leader, and for nearly 2000 years without a country, scattered and peeled, hated of all nations, and yet, they have survived and thrived, they have never been swallowed up by any nation.

If any nation attempted it, it soon followed the example of Jonah's whale. Since the founding of the Zionist Society in 1896 the Jewish nation has made its presence felt in a manner that is nothing short of marvelous. If I had the time, I could show that as legislators, educators, and financiers, they are represented out of all proportion to their numbers. We hear a great deal about patriotism these days, but I do not think that there is any patriotism equal to that of the orthodox Jew. For nineteen centuries they have been out of their land, but ever longing for home. I tell you, friends, it is God that has fostered that love of home in the heart of this nation. We have all heard of sacrifices being made for country since this war began, but I do not think that many have equaled the sacrifice of Dr. W. E. Weizmann, the Russian Jew who having discovered or invented a certain chemical essential to the manufacture of munitions, the lack of which in the crisis of the war was more serious than will ever be known, handed the formula over to the British Government. This chemical was worth millions to that government, and they would have been willing to have paid any sum Dr. Weizmann might have demanded; but he gave it and then gave himself to oversee its manufacture, asking but one thing, viz., that the British Government would favor the re-establishment of his people in the land of Palestine.

The Jew loves money, but here is a proof that he

loves his nation and the city of the Great King more than he loves gold.

I could wish that my brethren in the ministry who oppose this teaching would take up their Bibles again and read those prophecies of the regathering of Israel in the light of what is now transpiring. I am sure you would see that the Lord is turning again to His people Israel and that the Times of the Gentiles are just about full. The fig-tree is budding. God has hung out this Jewish sign and He said, "When ye shall see all these things, know that it (He) is near, even at the door."

I would not have dared to bring to you to-night these moral signs, these political signs, these spiritual signs, were it not that God has already hung out the Jewish sign. There are other times in the period of the history of the world since Jesus went away when moral conditions were bad and these are similar, but is it not a remarkable thing that never since the day that Jesus Christ was here on earth, was there such a combined movement on the part of the Jewish people. The flesh is coming upon the bones, and I believe some of these days they will be back in their land. How else can you account for this movement among the Jewish people? I have a Bible class and we are studying Revelation. We have had all the way from 800 to 1200 every Friday night. We take an offering once a month. Twice we have taken up offerings and given it to our Jewish friends for relief work. One time the class gave them $300.00.

When I took the offering to the rabbi, he said, "Preacher, I think this is the first time on record since the Christian church was founded that there has been an offering taken especially for Jewish relief. There always was some evangelistic string attached to it." I told him that we were just giving him this money to feed his poor and take care of the children. They had a convention and to show a vote of thanks, they honored me by asking me to give an address. I went to the convention. They had rabbis from New York, they had rabbis from other cities, and I didn't know what in the world I was going to say. "I was among the rabbis," and I'm an Irishman, or rather *I am a Canadian.* I was there among these rabbis. I didn't know what in the world I was going to say. They talked in Yiddish and a New York rabbi told how the Jews were going to be back in their land and about the declaration of the British Government. I got my cue and began by saying, "Brethren, you are going to have the land; it is your land; God has decreed it. Your prophets have prophesied that you are going back. It looks to me as if the door is opening and you are soon to be there. The flag of Judah is going to float again over the city of David." They jumped to their feet and they hugged each other, and some of them took off their hats and threw them in the air. I never was so affected in my life. You talk about patriotism. You know some people tell us that we should not be patriots. When the war broke out up there in Canada, some of my church members criticized me, some of them left my church because my boys went to the war. One man wrote me a long letter. He said, "Preacher, why is it you, as a Christian believing in the New Testament, think more of the British nation than of the German nation?" and I read his letter to my people; I thought they ought to know. I said, "He wants to know why I think more of the British nation than I do of the German nation." I said, "He had as well have asked me why I thought more of the Philpotts than I did the Joneses." I said, "The Joneses may wear better clothes than the Philpotts and they may live in better houses, but the Philpotts for me, if you please!"

"Breathes there a man with soul so dead
Who never to himself hath said
This is my own, my native land?"

Jesus loved his own city, but when he beheld His city, He wept over it. Paul was a patriot. He said, "I could wish myself accursed for my brethren, my kindred." You see, beloved friends? And when I saw those Jews, think of it, hugging each other, after their forefathers had been away from that country 2000 years, what in the world ever put that longing in their hearts for their land? God put it there. Their faces are turned back toward the Holy City. Jesus said, "Now learn a parable of the fig-tree; When her branch is yet tender, and putteth forth leaves, ye know that summer is nigh: so ye in like manner, when ye shall see all these things, know that it is near, even at the doors." We are living in the end time. The time seems to be nearly here. May the Lord God help us to go out of this building with solemn hearts! The night when I first got this truth,—when I listened to Rev. Arthur T. Pierson and Rev. A. J. Gordon conduct a convention years ago, I got my view point changed. My whole life changed. I was preaching His truth quite a bit at first and one night as I was going to my bed I heard my daughter Grace moving in her cot and I went into her room and she was awake. I said, "Grace, why are you not asleep?" She said, "Father, I was lying here wondering if Jesus might not come." I thought, "I have terrified this child." She said, "Father, do you think He will come to-night?" and do you know what I found out, that while I couldn't say the hour nor the day when He will come, I could not tell the hour or the day that He wouldn't come. I did not dare say to that child, "No, He will not be here to-night." I said, "Grace, He might be here, what then?" I'll never forget her little face. It was aglow. She clapped her little hands and said, "Oh, Daddy, wouldn't it be lovely?" I say, "Come, Lord Jesus, come quickly." When I think of my boys, all those I love and those who are lying beneath the poppies of France, I say, "Come, Lord Jesus, and take the scepter and reign. Come and cover the face of the earth with righteousness and peace. Come, Lord Jesus."

In opening the Conference sessions for Thursday—Memorial Day and the day set apart by the President for public humiliation, fasting and prayer—Mr. Charles L. Huston, Chairman, said:

In view of news received this morning, and in view of this day which is set apart as Memorial Day; and, further, the call of our President to spend not only to-day but all this week in humiliation and prayer before God; it seems proper to read the President's proclamation as a preliminary to the devotional hour which will be in that direction. When Israel of old, hard beset by their enemies, humbled themselves before God and confessed their sin, turning to Him for help, the full victory came. When, in our revolutionary war in the beginning of this country's history, President Washington bowed the knee before God in prayer, only then did the victory come. When did the tide turn in our fearful civil war? Only when President Lincoln issued a proclamation calling on the nation for a time of humiliation and prayer, and that call was responded to by the country, did the tide turn in that fearful catastrophe. Let us hope that the confession of sin and prayer for victory of this day, set apart by our nation and probably observed throughout all the countries that are joined with us in this fearful clash, may turn the tide of battle. I will now read the proclamation:

By the President of the United States

A PROCLAMATION

Whereas, The Congress of the United States, on the second day of April last, passed the following resolution:

"Resolved by the Senate (the House of Representatives concurring), That it being a duty peculiarly incumbent in a time of war humbly and devoutly to acknowledge our dependence on Almighty God and to implore His aid and protection, the President of the United States be, and is hereby, respectfully requested to recommend a day of public humiliation, prayer, and fasting, to be observed by the people of the United States with religious solemnity and the offering of fervent supplications to Almighty God for the safety and welfare of our cause, His blessings on our arms, and a speedy restoration of an honorable and lasting peace to the nations of the earth";

And whereas, It has always been the reverent habit of the people of the United States to turn in humble appeal to Almighty God for His guidance in the affairs of their common life;

Now, therefore, I, Woodrow Wilson, President of the United States of America, do hereby proclaim Thursday, the thirtieth of May, a day already freighted with sacred and stimulating memories, a day of public humiliation, prayer, and fasting, and do exhort my fellow-citizens of all faiths and creeds to assemble on that day in their several places of worship and there, as well as in their homes, to pray Almighty God that He may forgive our sins and shortcomings as a people and purify our hearts to see and love the truth, to accept and defend all things that are just and right, and to purpose only those righteous acts and judgments which are in conformity with His will; beseeching Him that He will give victory to our armies as they fight for freedom, wisdom to those who take counsel on our behalf in these days of dark struggle and perplexity, and steadfastness to our people to make sacrifice to the utmost in support of what is just and true, bringing us at last the peace in which men's hearts can be at rest because it is founded upon mercy, justice, and good-will.

In witness whereof I have hereunto set my hand and caused the seal of the United States to be affixed.

Done in the District of Columbia this eleventh day of May, in the year of our Lord nineteen hundred and eighteen, and of the independence of the United States the one hundred and forty-second.

WOODROW WILSON.

By the President,
ROBERT LANSING,
Secretary of State.

Rev. W. W. Rugh conducted a devotional service at this time, reading Psalm 24 and Habakkuk

3:17-19, and commenting thereon. The Conference was led in prayer by Rev. R. T. Ketcham.

After the singing of "Break Thou the Bread of Life," Dr. Harris H. Gregg delivered an address on the subject,

WHAT IS TO BECOME OF THE CHURCH?

REV. HARRIS H. GREGG, D.D.

"Behold, I show you a mystery: we shall not all sleep, but we shall all be changed, in a moment, in the twinkling of an eye, at the last trump: for the trumpet shall sound and the dead shall be raised incorruptible, and we shall be changed. For this corruptible must put on incorruption, and this mortal must put on immortality" (1 Cor. 15:51-53).

"But I would not have you to be ignorant, brethren, concerning them which are asleep, that ye sorrow not, even as others which have no hope. For if we believe that Jesus died and rose again, even so them also which sleep in Jesus will God bring with Him. For this we say unto you by the Word of the Lord, that we which are alive and remain unto the coming of the Lord shall not precede them which are asleep. For the Lord Himself shall descend from heaven with a shout, with the voice of the archangel, and with the trump of God: and the dead in Christ shall rise first: then we which are alive and remain shall be caught up together with them in the clouds, to meet the Lord in the air: and so shall we ever be with the Lord. Wherefore comfort one another with these words" (1 Thess. 4:13-18).

The Word of God is the only thing standing to-day. It alone abides when sin has brought in death. In righteousness it curses the unbelief of Cain, and, in grace, blesses the faith of Abel. It buried Babylon, and will yet build Jerusalem again. It was true though Christ was in the manger, when Caesar ruled the world. Therefore the cross of Christ is mightier than the crown of Caesar. Israel impaled itself on the cross of Christ for these centuries of suffering. His Word alone will take them off, and end their sufferings. The world to-day is impaled upon its rejection and crucifixion of God's Word, and, therefore, like Israel, hangs, bleeding and helpless, on the cross of Christ. The Word of God alone will come to their help, who cannot save themselves. The Roman Empire, through Pilate, ordered that Christ's legs be broken on the cross. But for a thousand years the Word of God had said that not a bone of His should be broken. He Himself was dead, but His Word stood; not Pilate's. Seeing that Christ was dead, the soldier decided that it was not necessary to break His legs, and that he would simply pierce His side. The Word of God, which he did not know, controlled the soldier in that decision. Pilate did not order that Christ be pierced. But the Lord had said, in His prophecy, "They shall look upon Me whom they have pierced" (Zech. 12).

The Word of God alone stood that day. Everything else went to pieces. Everyone else but Christ was confounded. So to-day. The Word of God alone enables us to be undeceived by what man is saying, undismayed by what he is doing, and undisturbed by what he is reaping. "For My thoughts are not your thoughts, neither are your ways My ways, saith the Lord. For as the heavens are higher than the earth, so are My ways higher than your ways, and My thoughts than your thoughts. For as the rain cometh down, and the snow, from heaven, and returneth not thither, but watereth the earth, and maketh it bring forth and bud, that it may give seed to the sower, and bread to the eater; so shall My Word be that goeth forth out of My mouth: it shall not return unto Me void; but it shall accomplish that which I please, and it shall prosper in the thing whereto I sent it" (Isa. 55).

CREATION A PREFACE AND PROPHECY OF REVELATION

Creation is God's unwritten Word. The Bible is God's written Word. The Lord Jesus is the living Word. Creation was a preparation for man. In its typical forms it was a prophecy of man's creation and coming. In its symbolism it is a parable of all the great fundamental truths of the Word of God. Its adjustments reveal God's purposes. Its progressive orders and periods unfold God's program. Creation is God's preface to His Word. It is so found in the Scriptures, in the first chapter of Genesis. Creation is a veiled revelation of redemption, and a prophecy of the new creation. It is the tabernacle of the Most High, foretelling that the Word that was God, by whom all things were made, would tabernacle among us, and that, thus, we would "behold His glory, the glory of the only begotten of the Father, full of grace and truth" (John 1).

There are seven days (Gen. 1) mentioned in connection with the creations of God. The earth had become a chaos. "When" and "why" are not essential here. Darkness and the deep cover the earth. God works from darkness to light, and from death to life. The Spirit of God brings in light the first day. But the light fades and the night comes, and one might have thought that light had failed and God had plunged earth back again into perpetual darkness.

But the darkness again is driven back by the dawn of the second day, when God brings in something more than on the first day. And this day does not last, but is turned into night. But in God's order and program He brings in the third day with its resurrection message: the earth comes up out of the water, and vegetation out of its grave. But vegetation does not finish God's program. Another night; and when the fourth day comes God is garnishing the heavens, as if He had left the earth. Following the next night comes the sixth day, and God creates the animals, and then, in counsel, creates man in His own image, to manifest God, and be over the works of His hand. But man's day, too, ends in darkness;

and then comes the seventh day, with no mention of succeeding night, for it is the rest, and day, of God. It was towards this nightless day that God had been working from the first. While God thus worked, and thus revealed His purposes and methods in His calendar of creation, God had in mind a greater work: the finished work of His Son, on which He would build His new creation, and through which He would accomplish His eternal purposes, and abide with His redeemed in an unbroken rest, unto the ages of the ages, in a glory above all His glory displayed in any other creation.

CREATION IS CONSUMMATED IN THE NEW CREATION

Let us take a brief summary of the Bible as the background for the proper setting of our subject, "What is to Become of the Church?"

"In the beginning God created the heaven and the earth," and the last thing that He created was man. God made man a trinity. God said, "Let Us," not "let Me"; "let Us make man in," not "My image," but "Our image." God made him a trinity: spirit, soul and body: three natures in one person: one person in three natures. The Bible is the only book that unveils man to his veiled, sinful heart. The sinner has no capacity to unveil himself, nor to unveil God. God was veiled even by the humanity of Christ. When the veil—that is to say, His flesh—was rent by His death on the cross, His glory was revealed to eyes anointed by the Word of God. When Peter confessed: "Thou art the Christ, the Son of the living God," the Lord Jesus answered: "Flesh and blood hath not revealed it unto thee, by My Father which is in heaven." It is the same to-day. Christ is always exposing sinners to themselves, and where they submit to their unveiling, through His Word, He exhibits the glory of His own Person, and the grace of His salvation. "For the Lord God is a sun and shield." Those who submit to the light of His Word being poured upon their darkness, He shields. To such "the Lord will give grace and glory." If the world would submit to the exposing light of God's Word, there would be no darkness and unbelief in the world. There can be no darkness where the sun is.

Adam became, through sin, what the earth had once been (Gen. 1:2) a chaos, covered with darkness and buried in depths, from which alone the Spirit of God can deliver, by bringing light and producing resurrection life. In righteous discipline God turned Adam's dominion into a chaos, that he might live daily in a parable of his own condition. Because of man's sin, nature is as much out of gear as man. Man cannot throw light upon himself any more than he can upon nature. All light comes from the heavens. Man can no more straighten out himself than he can straighten out nature. He can no more stop wars and rumors of wars than he can stop pestilence, famine and earthquakes, while Satan is loose and man, like him, remains a murderer and a liar. In all recorded history there are less than three hundred years when there is no record of war. Only He who can calm the storm on the sea of Galilee, is able to make "wars to cease unto the end of the earth." Only a confederation that can stop earthquakes can stop wars.

When man became a chaos and turned the earth into a chaos, God's plan did not have to be changed. Before He created the heaven and the earth, God planned that a Man, not an angel, should be over His works. But He planned that His Son should be that man (Eph. 1). God did not immediately send His Son into the world to become Man, when the first man sinned. God waited in order to give man a long chance to show what he became, when he became a sinner. All of human history up to the time of the crucifixion of Christ, "the Second Man," was a display of what man had become as a sinner. In the sight of God man's history ceased when he killed God's Son. God expects nothing further from him. From henceforth man is described as being himself dead in trespasses and sins; while from the third day Christ is announced as risen from the dead and alive for evermore. Therefore all of God's expectations for man are in Christ risen from the dead. As risen from the dead Christ is called "the Last Man." As such He is the final thought of God for man. This last, risen Man is the man God had in mind when He created the first man. We have never seen a man, and never shall, until we see Jesus Christ our Lord and Saviour.

Christ carried the name of "man" entirely to the glory of God during "the days of His flesh." Then He displayed it upon the cross. Then in forty days of resurrection He unfolded its new and eternal glories. Now the throne of God's grace, in the glory, is its home, and the power of its ministry. He is the Pattern of every redeemed one. "We shall be like Him"! Disappointed in ourselves and in things around us, we can at any time look up, through His Word, and see sitting on God's throne God's Pattern and Pledge of what we shall be. Think of that!

THE RISEN CHRIST IS THE BEGINNING OF THE NEW CREATION.

As risen from the dead Christ is not only "the Last Man," but He is the first-begotten from the dead, "the beginning" of the new creation. The work of His new creation is going on, with Himself in heaven and the Holy Spirit here on earth, in His calling to Himself a heavenly people out from among all nations, while Israel, His earthly people, is scattered among all nations. This is His church, His body and His building, every member of which is a "new creature in Christ Jesus." But earth is to be the sphere of His glories, as well as heaven. For He is to have His glories where He had His sufferings. For He is the risen Son and Heir of David as well as the sacrificed, and risen, Heir of Abraham. When He has completed His church and completed its salvation by resurrection, and translated it to heaven, He must needs return to bind Satan and cast him into the pit, to redeem and restore Israel to Himself and their land; to establish God's throne, in the house of His father David, in righteousness and peace in the earth; to redeem nature from its curse and groanings, in this "regeneration"; and to fill the earth with His glory that once filled the most Holy Place of the Tabernacle, and the Holy of Holies of the Temple. His kingdom over the earth will share in the glory of His new creation. But even this is not final. For after it He creates the new heaven and the new earth, and returns the kingdom to His Father, that God, then and there, may be all in all. In the first creation, God begins it with a heaven and earth, and finishes it by creating a man, Adam, in His own likeness. In the new creation, Christ, "the Last Man," risen from the dead, is the beginning of it; and the end of it is a new heaven and a new earth. Satan will not be there; neither sin, nor death, nor pain. "And there shall be no night there"! The Bible begins and ends with God! As it then begins with the creation of heaven and earth, the Bible ends with the creation of the new heaven and earth. God's plan for His church is, therefore, not His plan for Israel, nor is it His whole plan for the earth. His church was the theme of God's counsels and eternal purpose, but it is only a segment in the circumference of His revealed Word.

THE SEVEN DAYS OF THE NEW CREATION

As God had seven days (Gen. 1) in connection with this creation, so, in "the feasts of the Lord," we have revealed to us the seven days of His new creation: God's Calendar of human history. In all of these feasts God has in mind, and is working towards, the day of God, the sabbath that remains for the people of God, in the new heaven and earth. The feasts tell out the methods and stages of its accomplishment. Only God can tell us the day in which we live.

Four of these feasts are in the spring: Passover, Unleavened Bread, First-fruits and Pentecost. Three are in the autumn: Trumpets, Day of Atonement and Tabernacles. Three of them were linked together—Passover, Pentecost and Tabernacles—as being the three days when all the men of Israel must be at Jerusalem.

Passover is the first feast. The death of Christ, "the Lamb of God," is the foundation of redemption and of the new creation. The cry of Christ on the cross rent the veil of the temple, the rocks of the earth, and the graves of the saints. His death was God's judgment upon sin and the creation ruined by it. But His death was also God's immovable foundation for His new creation which can never be ruined. Christ died at Passover.

The Feast of Unleavened Bread was the second

feast, and was inseparably connected with Passover. Leaven represents sin and error. As there was no sin in Christ, He is the Unleavened Bread of God's household. He who is our salvation is also our spiritual food. He feeds us upon Himself in His Word, and always makes His redeemed people holy, like Himself.

The Feast of First-fruits is the third. It was the day following the Passover Sabbath, and was therefore one of the days of the Feast of Unleavened Bread. On it Christ rose from the dead, "the first-fruits of them that slept." Redemption is completed in resurrection, and holiness is the power of a risen life.

Fifty days after the Feast of the First-fruits came Pentecost, another feast of first-fruits and the fourth and last of the spring feasts. On the day of Pentecost the Lord Jesus in heaven baptized His apostles and disciples in Jerusalem with the Holy Spirit sent down from heaven. The Holy Spirit gathered to Christ that day three thousand souls out from many thousands gathered from the ends of the earth in Jerusalem. It was his first-fruits from among the nations. That is all that the Holy Spirit gathers while our Lord is having His Feast of Pentecost. For Pentecost is not God's autumnal harvest. His church is His first-fruits, His out-gathering from Jews and Gentiles. His Pentecost brings Him His church; but not Israel, nor the world.

Summer followed Pentecost. The rains ceased. The streams went dry. The fields were parched.

The shepherds hunted pastures. The wolves fed. At last, late in September, the Feast of Trumpets, the first of the autumn feasts, broke the silence. It is the seventh month: the time for God to complete what He has begun. It was a memorial of the blowing of the trumpets around Jericho, when Israel entered upon her promised inheritance. It was also a prophecy of Christ again calling Israel and, in His new covenant, fulfilling His oath to Abraham and His oath to David. Christ will have His Feast of Trumpets, which will proclaim His victories and manifest His glory.

The followed the Feast of the Day of Atonement. Passover began on the tenth day of the first month and the Day of Atonement was on the tenth day of the seventh month. Thus redemption and atonement are inseparable. Passover was established in the land of Ham, and a door of salvation for a believing Gentile as for the believing Jew. But the Day of Atonement was peculiarly for Israel and was established among them in the wilderness. Alone, and on that day only, and not without blood, God's appointed high priest entered into the Holy of Holies in behalf of Israel, and his coming out again meant God's acceptance of the atonement and His acknowledgment of Israel as His redeemed people. No student of the New Testament needs to be told that Christ has passed into the heavenly sanctuary with His own blood. When He has His Feast of the Day of Atonement, the Jews will be in their "day of Jacob's trouble" (Jer. 30), and Christ shall come out of His heavenly sanctuary to earth for Israel's salvation. He will baptize that nation with the Holy Spirit.

After His Day of Atonement the Lord Jesus will have His last feast—the Feast of Tabernacles: the feast of the whole harvest: the conversion of the world: the baptism of the Gentile nations. The baptism of Israel and the nations are both on the other side of the sounding of the trumpets, and not before.

THE TIME OF THE MYSTERIES

In the New Testament, after Israel's rejection of Christ and the Holy Spirit, one reads of many "mysteries": "the mysteries of the kingdom of heaven," "the mystery of Christ and His church," "the mystery of godliness," "the mystery" of the church's translation, "the mystery" of Israel's present unbelief, "the mystery of iniquity." There is no need at this time to explain them. Gather them up and connect them with Christ's Feast of Pentecost. Group them there. They belong to the Pentecostal age.

THE TRUMPETS OF THE NEW TESTAMENT

There is no need here to explain all the trumpets of the New Testament. Simply group them about Christ's Feast of Trumpets, and thus learn of the important part of God's program for the world to be carried out after all the trumpets have sounded. The nations redeemed then, Christ will govern in righteousness and peace. It is said of all Israel in that day, "they shall all know Me (the Lord Jesus Christ) from the least of them unto the greatest of them" (Jer. 31). And the Lord Jesus shall be King then over all the nations. All nations shall worship Him: "And it shall come to pass, that every one that is left of all the nations which came against Jerusalem, shall even go up from year to year to worship the King, the Lord of hosts, and to keep the Feast of Tabernacles." The church is born before the Feast of Trumpets. Israel and the nations are born again after the Feast of Trumpets. Paul said, "I am born out of due time": that is, ahead of the due time for my people Israel to be born again. It is true of each Gentile member of Christ's church gathered out from all nations. We are all born again ahead of our nations. The "due time" for the conversion of nations is after the Feast of Trumpets. The work of the church is to gather out the church. That is all the Holy Spirit has ever done since Pentecost. He has never converted Israel; and His conversion of all other nations awaits His conversion of Israel (Rom. 11).

PASSOVER, PENTECOST AND TABERNACLES

The theme of the Old Testament is "the sufferings of Christ" in connection with Israel, "and the glories" of Christ, also in connection with

Israel. He had His sufferings in connection with His Passover. He will have His glories, in connection with Israel also, when He has His Feast of Tabernacles. Pentecost is not mentioned by Ezekiel, nor in the Gospel of John, where Passover and Tabernacles are both mentioned, because Christ has His Feast of Pentecost while absent from the earth and while Israel is left to her unbelief. While Pentecost is unknown by name in John's Gospel, our Lord, in miniature, walks through it, as He does through Passover and Tabernacles. His Pentecostal program is: "But ye shall receive power, after the Holy Ghost is come upon you: and ye shall be witnesses unto Me, both in Jerusalem, and in all Judea, and in Samaria, and unto the uttermost part of the earth" (Acts 1:8). In John the Shepherd goes before His sheep. Beginning at Jerusalem, He gathers first-fruits, and goes out into Judea, where John greets Him as Bridegroom of His church; He proceeds through Samaria and passes on into Galilee of the nations (John 3 and 4). While He has His Feast of Pentecost, our Lord is in heaven, His church is on earth, Satan is the god and prince of this age, and Israel is scattered among the nations. In the age to come (Eph. 1; Heb. 2), the Feast of Tabernacles, Christ will be on earth and His church in heaven, Satan will be in the pit (Rev. 20) and Israel in the holy land. Only the Lord Jesus can bring these things to pass. He says that He will.

Passover and Tabernacles being largely the

theme of the Old Testament, we are not surprised to learn that the church is "a mystery": that is, not revealed to Moses and the prophets. It was foretold by Christ (Matt. 16), but fully developed by the Holy Ghost, after the day of Pentecost. Christ chose Paul, and the Holy Spirit used him, for this purpose. Peter knew of the character and glory of the kingdom of heaven when Christ returns. He had been given a vision of it on the Mount of Transfiguration (Matt. 17; 2 Pet. 1). But he did not know of the calling and destiny of the church. From the glory, after Paul's conversion, Christ gave Peter a vision of the heavenly calling and destiny of the church, in the sheet let down and caught up into heaven. There is no one common or unclean in that sheet. All are washed in the blood of the Lamb. When He gathers all His church, the sheet will be caught up into heaven.

If the church is a mystery, so is its destiny. It is so called by Paul (1 Cor. 15:51-58). The church's destiny is, to be caught up from among the dead and living nations, in resurrection bodies, to meet the Lord in the air (1 Thess. 4: 13-18); and, in the "age to come," to reign, from the heavenlies, with Him over the earth (Rev. 5). This is Christ's coming into the air for His church, and not His coming afterwards, with His church, to the earth to redeem Israel and the nations and nature.

BEFORE CHRIST RETURNS TO THE EARTH

The mystery of godliness and the mystery of iniquity must be completed before Christ will stand again upon the Mount of Olives (Zech. 14).

"And, without controversy, great is the mystery of godliness: God was manifest in the flesh, justified in the Spirit, seen of angels, preached unto the Gentiles, believed on in the world, received up into glory" (1 Tim. 3:16). God was manifest in Christ, and now in the church born of the Spirit. Christ was received up into glory before He was received by the Gentiles. The mystery of godliness includes both Christ and His church. "Received up into glory" refers to the destiny of the church. It is conditionless and timeless.

After the mystery of godliness is completed, by the church being caught up into heaven, then the mystery of iniquity (2 Thess. 2) will rapidly develop and head up in Satan's Antichrist, the man who will claim to be God. When Satan brings forth his man-God, the God-man, Christ Jesus our Lord, will return to earth and smite him with the brightness of God's glory.

Lucifer was a brilliant creature before God's throne (Isa. 14; Ezek. 28). He became the devil by attempting to get out of the realm of his creaturehood into the realm of God. He came and put the same prize before Eve in the garden of Eden. She attempted it by believing Satan's lie, and her first child was, like Satan, a murderer and a liar. She had been created in God's likeness.

But the Lord Jesus (Phil. 2) thought it not a prize for Himself to become God, for He is God. But He thought it a prize to stoop beneath angels, and down beneath the power of Satan, and be numbered with transgressors: to enter the sphere of our death and judgment and identify Himself with us, that He might identify us with Himself for ever. When by death He had put away our sins and condemnation, He arose from the dead, taking with Him His redeemed, and, passing by principalities and powers, placing us in a nearness to God created beings will never have: only His redeemed. Israel! His glory shall cover thee on the earth. Church of God! His glory shall shine in you in the heavens. We are daily looking unto Jesus in His grace. We are daily looking for Jesus in His glory! "Even so, come, Lord Jesus!"

WILL THERE BE ANY TEARS IN HEAVEN, AND WHY?

REV. P. W. PHILPOTT

I am to talk to you this morning about the Judgment of Believers' Works. There is a great deal of confusion regarding the judgments spoken of in the Scriptures. Not a few Christian people talk about a "general judgment day" some time in the future; when all kinds of people will stand before a great judgment throne and find out whether they are sheep or goats. Now I am not saying that sarcastically, though I may have given that impression myself some time when I have been speaking on the Judgment that is sure to come. But this morning we want to be clear. There are at least four judgments spoken of in the New Testament. Three are yet future, while one is past; that is, past for all those who have accepted Christ as their Saviour. That was the judgment of sin and Satan that took place on Calvary, when the Son of God met every claim of justice, every demand of the law, and all the penalties of sin, for those who trust in the precious blood of Jesus Christ.

You remember that, in the sixteenth chapter of John, when speaking of the coming of the Holy

Spirit, the Lord told them that He, the Spirit, would convince the world of sin, of righteousness, and of judgment (not judgment to come), rather a judgment past, "of judgment, because the prince of this world is judged."

Thirty-five years ago, one night, I became convicted of sin by the Holy Spirit. A little later I was convicted of righteousness in Jesus Christ. This I accepted, and the very next morning a good layman met me on the way to work. He congratulated me on the stand I had taken and then he turned to the fifth chapter of John's Gospel and the twenty-fourth verse. He asked me to read it, and I saw that morning that judgment for sin, as far as I was concerned, was past for ever. "Shall not come into judgment" is the word of Christ to the man who has received eternal life. In Matthew 25:31-46, we have the judgment of the nations. There will be no resurrection in connection with that judgment, just the living nations. Then in Revelation 20:11-15, you have the judgment of the unsaved dead. All who stand before that great white throne are raised from the dead, and they are judged by the things that are written in the books.

There is another judgment, it is the judgment of believers' works, when "every man's work will be tried, of what sort it is." This will take place just after the Church has been raptured into the presence of her Lord. In Hebrews 11:6, we read that "without faith it is impossible to please Him, for he that cometh to God must believe that He is, and that *He is a rewarder* of them that diligently seek Him." He is a *rewarder.* As Dr. Pierson has said, "With many disciples, the eyes are yet blinded to this mystery of rewards, which is an open mystery of the Word. It must be an imputed righteousness whereby we enter, but having thus entered by faith, our works determine our relative rank, place and reward."

The key-note of this Conference has been, "Behold He cometh!" but He has told us that when He comes, He will reward every disciple according to his work (Rev. 22:12).

This morning, I read a word that was solemnizing and sanctifying in its effect: "And all the churches shall know that I am He which searcheth the hearts, and I will give unto every one of you according to his works" (Rev. 2:23). *"The churches shall know."* In 2 Corinthians 5:10 and Romans 14:10-12 we are shown that "we must all appear before the judgment seat of Christ, that every one may receive the things done in his body, according to that he hath done, whether it be good or bad. So then, every one of us shall give an account of himself to God."

I can imagine there may be some tears at that time, for we not only shall face the good things that we have done, but also the things that have been evil in our lives.

Last night, I was speaking to you about Matthew 24. You remember that when He answered the question of the disciples He finished the address with two striking illustrations, one of the

Ten Virgins and the other of the Talents. I believe that that illustration of the Ten Virgins is a picture of the test that is coming to Christian profession. I do not think this parable has anything to do with those outside of our Church life, making no profession whatever. Those virgins represent persons who are professing at least to be Christians, but half of them are deceived. They have managed to pass all the tests that may be applied by our membership committees and are looked upon as Christians, but when He comes, the discovery will be made that a lamp and garb of a Christian will not be sufficient to take them into the presence of the King. The essential thing in that moment will be a light, and in order to have a light, you must have the oil, which typifies the Holy Spirit. Without the Spirit of Christ we are "none of His" (Rom. 8:9). I fear there are too many to-day that are depending upon church membership and profession, but that day will reveal who are the wise and who are the foolish virgins.

The next parable tells of the test that is coming to Christian Service. As servants, we are called before Him, and must give an account of ourselves to God. Then our works shall be made manifest of what sort they are. It is then that a certain King shall make a reckoning with His servants (Matt. 18:23); and Paul tells us who that certain King is, "the Lord, the righteous Judge" (2 Tim. 4:9). That judgment will include every Christian. "*We all,*" i.e., "them that are sanctified in Christ Jesus, called to be saints, with all that call upon the name of the Lord in every place" (1 Cor. 1:2). It is also to be individual. "Every one of you." I am not responsible for any other man, but God has made me king of my own heart and life. He has also made provision for me to live the life I ought to live, and to do the thing I ought to do; and as an individual, I must answer to Him. Then that judgment is inevitable. "Every one of you *must*"; and it is responsible; "give an account of himself to God." This is surely a very solemn word.

Now if you will turn to 1 Corinthians 3:11, you will find that judgment seat of Christ in operation. You will notice here that it is the superstructure that the builder places upon the foundation that is being tested, not the foundation. That already has passed the test. God has laid the foundation (Isa. 28:16). It is a "sure foundation." We have nothing to do with that, only that we, as wise master-builders, like the Apostle Paul, should lay in our preaching what God has already laid in fact, the sure foundation, which is Christ the Lord.

I was delighted last evening to hear Dr. Riley emphasize so strongly that "there could be no such thing as a church where the deity of Christ was denied." I would go a little further than that, and say that there can be no such thing as a Christian, unless that believer is standing on the deity of Jesus Christ. "He that believeth on

Him is not condemned, but he that believeth not is condemned already," and why? Because he is a drunkard, or a thief, or a liar? No, but "because he hath not believed in the name of the only begotten Son of God" (Jno. 3:18). He may believe whatever else he likes. If he denies the deity of the Lord Jesus, he is not a Christian. I am saying that, friends, because it is the Scripture. That is the foundation upon which we build. If not, we will find that, no matter how grand our superstructure may be, it is doomed to fall, because it is not founded on the Rock.

It is our building that comes under the fire test. The kind of material that we put in the building is the thing that will tell in that day. You know that the selection of the material lies within the choice of the disciple. Every builder has absolute control over the materials with which he builds, and contending motives sway the choice. For instance, the desire for *popularity* has a terrific influence. The desire for *fame,* or for *social standing,* the *love of money, pleasure* or ease. These are great stubble makers. On the other hand, love to Christ, fidelity, a sense of truth, the recognition of the fact that you are an ambassador for Christ—all these have a wonderful effect upon the selection. There are many voices calling us to-day, but there is only one true voice to the wise master-builder, and that is the voice of the Word. Everything else will pass away, but this will abide forever.

A woman came to me the other day with a

complimentary ticket for a celebrated lecture on one of the new religions of our time. Upon my refusal to accept the ticket, she seemed to be greatly amazed and asked for an explanation. "Why," I said, "I would not go there on my life; I am afraid of myself." She could not understand, and remarked that she thought a strong Christian should not be afraid to hear the discussion of any subject. I told her that I was afraid because I would be putting myself upon the devil's territory, and God makes no promise to keep me while I am on that ground. I told her that I did not care to hear this man, because I had heard another Man that fully satisfied me. "My sheep hear my voice, and they know not the voice of strangers." The people that are running after these fads are those who have never heard the true voice. The man who builds the Word of God into his ministry is building gold, silver and precious stones. These alone will stand the fire test. Are there Christian workers here who sometimes are tempted to discouragement? Let me say a word to you. Go forth sowing the precious seed, I mean the seed of the Word, not too many baby stories, not too much sentimental stuff, but faithfully sow the Word. Some may fall on the rocks to die. Some may be caught away by birds of prey. Some will be choked with the thorns, but bless God, *"some will fall on good ground and bring forth fruit."*

We should not wait until the fire falls, let us prove our work to-day (Gal. 6:4).

Now I wanted to speak to you about our reward, but the time is gone and I will hurry. The Apostle Paul tells us that we are seeking an incorruptible crown. I confess to you frankly that I want that reward. I will not be satisfied in heaven without it. I wonder if anybody will be happy; I wonder if there will not be a great many people shedding tears as they stand before Him on that day, having nothing to show for their life and ministry on earth.

> "Not at death I shrink nor falter,
> For the Saviour saves me now,
> But to meet Him empty-handed,
> Thought of that now clouds my brow."

First we have the crown of incorruption (1 Cor. 9:24-25). Here the Apostle urges us to run so that we may attain. We do not get the crown for running, mark you; it is for attaining. Second, we have the crown of rejoicing (1 Thess. 2:19). Paul's joy at the judgment seat of Christ was to be the joy of meeting those whom he had turned from darkness to light through the preaching of the Word. No man can expect this crown who has never won a soul for the Master.

> "Oh, what joy it will be when His face I behold,
> Living gems at His feet to lay down;
> It would sweeten my bliss in that City of gold,
> Should there be any stars in my crown."

Then there is the crown of glory (1 Pet. 4:1-4). This is for taking care of the flock of God, for feeding the sheep. Do you think a shepherd will receive a reward for tending the flock, if he never did it? There is also the crown of righteousness (2 Tim. 4:7, 8). This comes for watchfulness, so you see that our love of premillennial truth is worth while after all. There is a crown for loving his appearing. Can a man receive this if he is not among the watchers? Then, the crown of life (Jas. 1:12). This is given for resisting temptation. I suppose we all have our temptations. Some people would like to have their places changed, that they might be freed from the trial that they daily have to face, but it is well for us to remember that God has a special crown for the woman, for example, who must live with a husband who is a grouch; and may I not say, this crown will also be given to the husband who has a nagging wife but who keeps sweet in the hour of temptation. It is not for succumbing to the temptation, but for resisting it, that we get the crown of life.

I urge you in the words of Jesus: "Hold fast that which thou hast; see that no man take thy crown" (Rev. 3:11). Prebendary Webb-Peploe, one of the Keswick teachers, has said, in speaking of these crowns, "If I can thus be crowned, can I be otherwise than a fool if I am not prepared to sacrifice everything to win them?"

Chairman: Mr. Huston:

As announced this morning, Dr. Chapman is with us just for a little while this afternoon after having conducted and addressed the noonday meeting for business men in the Garrick theatre, and we will ask him to give a brief testimony as to the effect of the message of the Lord's coming in his soul winning work. As you know, Dr. Chapman has been favored of God to girdle the globe with meetings, and has carried this message with him as he has gone, and is able to give the very best kind of testimony.

Dr. J. Wilbur Chapman:

I should like first of all to express my keen appreciation of the honor which was conveyed in the invitation which was extended to me to have a share in this program. I had fully intended to be one of the speakers, and thought it would be one of the greatest privileges of my ministry. Then a divine providence seemed to prevent my coming. And just on the eve of the making of the program I found I could be here for this little time. So I had the privilege of the midday meeting. I make this explanation because I want my name to stand with the names of others who believe in the premillennial hope of the return of our Lord. I also make this explanation because I should like to have the privilege of saying what this belief has meant to me. I suppose I could best express it in the Scripture which I used at the noonday meeting, which was the blessed hope. I did not always accept this interpretation of the Scriptures. I knew there was something lacking in my ministry. The Bible seemed to me to be somewhat confused. I could not, somehow, find out clearly regarding its teachings. But I came under the influence of a very remarkable woman, who was a member of my church, and a member of my household. Some of you will remember her. Mrs. Agnes P. Strain, of sacred memory. It was she who told me that the Lord was coming back, and that He might return soon. Under her skilful direction, I began the study of God's Word with this in mind, and long years ago I came to see this wonderful truth; and I have no hesitation at all in saying to-day that it completely transformed my ministry. If I have had any success in soul winning, if I have had any ability to turn men to righteousness, I think I must lay it all to the influence of this wonderful truth. It has kept me with my eyes upward. It has kept me with my heart longing for His return. And I, as I said at the noonday meeting, have always believed that the church is an elect body, and that some day the body will be completed, and the house builded, if you change the figure; I have always thought that perhaps sometime in my meeting, or in the meeting of another, the last soul might come to Christ and the body be complete. And I have never given an invitation to men and women to accept Christ as their Saviour that I have not had this in mind.

This glorious truth has done more for me than any words of mine could express. I was led to it also because of the fact that Mr. Moody was such a firm believer in the coming of the Lord. Sometimes men say to us—indeed I read it this past week—that belief in the second coming of Jesus Christ is pessimistic. To believe in His coming would be to cut the nerve of special effort, it would simply mean to sit down and wait and do nothing. But when I recall the names of Moody, and Spurgeon, and Muller, and Murray, and John Wesley, and a man like Dr. Munhall, and a man like Dr. Riley, I tell you that these men, so long as they lived and now that they are still living, some of them, have been incessant in their service, toiling by day and night. I think you will agree with me when I say that to believe that the Lord is coming back does not at all mean that you are to fold your hands and do nothing. I think you will also give me the privilege of saying that I have toiled a bit myself, and my only regret is that in these past years I couldn't have done more. My resolve is, that in these days ahead of me I shall do more, that when He comes He may find me busier than ever and filled more than ever with a desire to do His will.

This great gathering in Philadelphia is one of the most significant events in modern church history and I, with all my heart, praise God for it. Of course you must understand that if you accept this truth and look for the Lord's coming, you cannot make your plans so very far ahead; some of them may be suddenly changed. Perhaps you have heard (I should like to say if you have not heard what I am about to relate I can vouch for the truth of it), that before the war a devout Christian was talking to the Kaiser, and talking about spiritual matters, and this subject of the Lord's return was presented, when the Kaiser was seen to drop his head in his hand. Then lifting his face and shaking his head, he said, "I could not accept that. That would disturb all my plans." And I stand here to-day to say, I wish the Lord would come and smash the Kaiser's plans. But while He tarries, no people in this world, and I know I speak for them, will be more faithful in upholding the government, in standing for a righteous peace, in giving of money or giving of life for the winning of this war than the people who are represented in this great gathering in this city of Philadelphia.

Dr. Chapman closed by leading the Conference in prayer.

PRAYER

Blessed God, our Father, in the name of Jesus Christ, we offer up our prayers unto Thee. First of all, we come in confession of sin, sins individual, sins national. Oh, Lord, our God, search us and know us, see if there be any wicked way in us. Lay Thy finger upon the spot of weakness, and make us right. We come to Thee, our Heavenly Father, praying for Thy blessing to rest upon our soldiers and our sailors and our men in the air as they are upon the Western front at this moment. The time seems to be so serious, the crisis in the world's history seems almost to have been reached. O Lord God, keep our faith strong; increase our confidence in Thy Word, increase our loyalty and affection and the thought of Jesus Christ. Make the prayer which goes unto Thee from these thousands of people sweep across the seas and its influence stay the onrush of the enemy, give victory to our armies and before this meeting closes this afternoon, our God, send us news from across the sea that right is prevailing and our boys are safe. We are all willing to make sacrifices, O God, for the cause of righteousness. We have given our best, our time, our money, our children; they have all been placed on the altar, and now, O Lord, just because we believe it would be for the honor and glory of Jesus Christ, for the establishment of righteousness and for the advancement of the kingdom, O Lord our God, we pray Thee stop this awful onrush of the men who would overthrow righteousness if they could. This is our prayer. Amen.

SPECIAL PRAYER IN BEHALF OF BOYS AT FRONT

Blessed God, we lift our precious boys up befor Thee. We do not allow ourselves to think of the blow which would fall upon us if the message should come that they have paid the great price, and so, O Lord our God, this afternoon we ask Thee to hold our boys and all who stand with them fighting for the right; give victory, we beseech Thee—victory, victory—for the honor and glory of Jesus Christ. Amen.

CHAIRMAN: Owing to the fact that Dr. Scofield is physically unable to be present in this conference, according to the message read to us on the opening day, his subject at this hour, "The Coming Glory," will be brought before us by the Rev. W. L. Pettingill.

THE COMING GLORY

By Rev. W. L. Pettingill

Dean of the Philadelphia School of the Bible

It is a pleasure to talk about the coming glory at any time, and in any place, and for anyone, but I count myself particularly happy this afternoon in the opportunity to speak upon this theme, in this place, to this audience, and in the service, under God, of one whom I love as a father. Dr. Scofield has put us all under tremendous debt in these last days, and it is my one regret in connection with this great and wonderful conference that Dr. Scofield himself is deprived of the precious privilege, as I know he esteemed it, to be here in person. I thank my God upon every remembrance of him.

Now, I am to speak to you about the coming glory, and I reckon that the sufferings of this present time—great though they be—are not worthy to be compared with the glory that shall be revealed in the approaching day. It is according to the eternal purpose of God that one day this rebellious province in His universe, which is called the earth, shall be reconciled to Him, and that the earth shall be filled with His glory; and as God has purposed, so shall God perform. We learned this morning afresh, through that powerful message brought to us by Dr. Gregg, that the Word of God cannot be broken.

God proposed to use the people of Israel, in the very morning of their national history, for bringing in the glory. He took them out of Egypt. He brought them through the wilderness, and at Kadesh-barnea He said, "Go in and possess the land." They turned back from Him, and when He threatened to destroy them, and to build up a nation out of Moses' loins, and Moses interceded for them, Jehovah said, in the words recorded in Numbers 14:20, 21, "I have pardoned according to thy word. Nevertheless, as I live, the earth shall be filled with the glory of Jehovah." That decree has not yet been accomplished, but nothing in heaven, or on earth, or under the earth, can possibly hinder our God from doing all that He has said. "God is not a man that He should lie; neither the son of man that He should repent: hath He said, and shall He not do it? or hath He spoken and shall He not make it good?"

Our God is a wonderful God. Our God only doeth wondrous things. How wonderful it is that He has saved us, and that He has already "shined in our hearts, to give the light of the knowledge of the glory of God in the face of Jesus Christ!" No more wonderful thing can He ever do than He did when, by His matchless grace, He gave His Son to die on the cross of Calvary, in order to bring us to Himself. Justification is an old-fashioned doctrine, but there is nothing more beautiful, nothing more wonderful, nothing more glorious, in all the universe, than justification, by grace, through faith in the blood of the Son of God. You and I have the right by that blood to enter into God's presence. As it is written, "Having therefore, brethren, boldness to enter into the holiest by the blood of Jesus, by a new and living way, which He hath consecrated for us, through the veil, that is to say, His flesh; and having an High Priest over the house of God; let us draw near with a true heart in full assurance of faith, having our hearts sprinkled from an evil conscience, and our bodies washed with pure water. Let us hold fast the confession of our faith without wavering (for He is faithful that promised); and let us consider one another to provoke unto love and to good works: not forsaking the assembling of ourselves together as the manner of some is; but exhorting one another: and so much the more, as ye see the day approaching" (Heb. 10:19-25). The newspaper reports to the contrary notwithstanding, the day approacheth, and I call you this day to look toward that day; for ye are not of the night, but of the day. That day ought not to overtake you unawares. It is to the coming day, with its coming glory, that we now address ourselves. And there are four things about the coming glory that I desire to say now. They are: (1) that the coming day will bring glory to the Jews; (2) that the coming day involves glory for the Gentiles; (3) that the coming day involves glory for the church of God; and (4) that, better than all, the coming day involves glory for our Lord and Saviour Jesus Christ.

I. That day will bring glory to the Jews. It is God's purpose, one day, to take up this poor, despised, dispersed, persecuted, punished people, and to make them to be, not the tail, but the head, to lift them out of the dust to become a kingdom of priests unto Him. And no matter how great their guilty separation from Him, no matter how great their degradation in this present time —and I quite agree with you that their guilt is great, that their degradation is great, that their separation from God is great—yet no matter how great all this, all the greater the glory that shall come to them one day, when God has accomplished His purpose with them. The covenants of God are obligations. God has no temptation to repudiate His treaties as "scraps of paper." He remembers His promises. How glad we are to-day that our God is faithful, and that He never appeals to the statute of limitations to relieve Him of doing all that He has promised! I thank God to-day for what He proposes to do for the Jews.

In the 23rd chapter of Jeremiah, verses 5 to 8, it is written: "Behold, the days come, saith the Lord, that I will raise unto David a righteous Branch, and a King shall reign and prosper, and shall execute judgment and justice in the earth."

in the earth! Judgment and justice are already in heaven, but there is going to be a bringing about of judgment and justice in the earth. People will insist upon establishing the throne of the Lord Jesus in heaven, or in the believer's heart, but the Word of God says, in the earth. Now see: "In His days Judah shall be saved, and Israel shall dwell safely, and this is His name whereby He shall be called, THE LORD OUR RIGHTEOUSNESS. Therefore, behold, the days come, saith the Lord, that they shall no more say, The Lord liveth, which brought up the children of Israel out of the land of Egypt; but, The Lord liveth, which brought up and which led the seed of the house of Israel out of the north country, and from all countries whither I had driven them; and they shall dwell in their own land."

If language means anything—and language does mean something when it has proceeded out of the mouth of God—then the time is surely coming when God will bring His people Israel out of all the lands where He has driven them, and they shall dwell in their own land. And, as Amos tells us, when they are thus planted in their own land, they shall never be plucked up any more for ever.

In that day, according to Isaiah 27:6, "Jehovah shall cause them that come of Jacob to take root." Did you ever try to make a Jew take root? The Jew for the present is an air plant. They have tried to plant him everywhere. They tried to plant him in New Jersey. They tried to plant him in Argentina. They tried to plant him in the Soudan. But all their schemes have failed, for you cannot make him take root excepting in the land which God gave to his fathers, and the land in which God has promised to plant him. God is able to do what men cannot do, and He has said that He will cause Israel to take root downward, and bear fruit upward. Israel shall blossom and bud and fill the face of the world with fruit.

II. Then, in the second place—and this has already been touched upon, for it is quite difficult to keep these divisions of my subject from overlapping—in the second place, in the day that is coming, there will be glory for the Gentile. I mean not now, for the out-called Gentiles, the outgathered Gentiles, but for "the residue of men, and all the Gentiles upon whom My name is called, said the Lord, who doeth all these things" (Ac. 15:13-18).

It is always the program of God, as is abundantly shown in His Word, to bring blessing to men through the Jews. I cannot, for the life of me, see how a Christian can do otherwise than love the Jew, when he remembers that everything he has in the world worth while came to him through the Jews. Why, this very meeting is held in the name of a Jew, who sits at the right hand of the Majesty on high, the Son of a Jewish mother, according to the flesh. The Book that we have in our hands is a Jewish production under God. "Salvation is of the Jew." What a tremendous debt we owe to the Jews! It is an outrage and a shame that we have kept the Jewish gospel from the Jewish people. I would to God that we might be reminded here that the very gospel of our salvation is to the Jew first, and then to the Greek.

Just as blessing has come to us through the Jews, so, though in far greater measure and in far wider scope, shall blessing come to the Gentile world as such, when the Jew has come into his own. May I read now from the 60th chapter of Isaiah, a key-passage, selected out of many passages on this wonderful subject: "Arise, shine; for thy light is come." Who is talking here? Isaiah is talking here. And who is Isaiah? Isaiah was a Jewish preacher. And to whom was he talking? He was talking to his own people, the Jewish people. "Arise, shine! for thy light is come, and the glory of the Lord is risen upon thee. For, behold, the darkness shall cover the earth, and gross darkness the people: but the Lord shall arise upon thee, and His glory shall be seen upon thee"—and then what? "And the Gentiles shall come to thy light, and kings to the brightness of thy rising." Thy rising! The words point to national resurrection. Israel is a dead nation, represented by the dry bones of Ezekiel 37. " 'Behold, they say, our bones are dried, and our hope is lost: we are cut off for our parts,' and we are buried among the Gentile nations. Our future is blotted out by our dreadful past. There is no hope for us." Well, out of that so-called "hopeless" condition, there has come salvation unto us. Through their fall, the Gentile world has been made rich. Through their restoration, the blessing that shall come upon the Gentile world is such as is described in Romans 11 as "life from the dead." Their rising, their resurrection, their coming to national life, will bring universal blessing to the world. The Gentiles shall come to their light, and kings to the brightness of their resurrection. O, what will it be like to have the world filled with Jewish evangelists? To have Paul multiplied by a hundred and forty-four thousand. Call that language symbolic, if you like, but it means something—a hundred and forty-four thousand is what it says. It is the remnant that shall turn to the Lord during the Great Tribulation, and they will then preach the gospel of the kingdom in all the world as a testimony unto all nations. They will not have to learn any languages—they already know them all. They will not need to go anywhere—they are already there. And the missionary propaganda of that day will be such as to put our missionary propaganda to shame, if we are not already ashamed of it, which we ought most heartily to be.

I want now to turn to one of the Psalms under this head—the 67th Psalm. We are apt to forget that this is a Jewish Psalm Book, and thus lose many of its richest lessons. Here is a Jewish prayer: "God be merciful unto us, and bless us; and cause His face to shine upon us; Selah."

What for? Why should God do this for Israel?

Listen: "That Thy way may be known upon earth." What is God's way? The Lord Jesus Himself is God's way. He said, "I am the way." "That Thy way may be known upon earth, Thy saving health"—or, as the revision reads, "Thy salvation among all nations. Let the people praise Thee, O God; let all the people praise Thee. O let the nations be glad and sing for joy: for Thou shalt judge the people righteously, and govern the nations upon the earth. Selah. Let the people praise Thee, O God; let all the people praise Thee. Then shall the earth yield her increase, and God, even our own God, shall bless us. God shall bless us; and all the ends of the earth shall fear Him." This is God's program, to bring in universal blessing, first for Israel, and then, through Israel, unto the Gentile world. This part of my subject is most tempting, but I must hurry on.

III. In the third place, the day that is approaching will bring glory to the church of God. I love to think of this. The church of God is glorious even now to those who look upon it with the anointed eye. Of course, you know that when I use the term, "the church of God," I am not using it as it is often used. There are institutions in the world calling themselves churches; but, as Dr. Riley told us the other day, it is quite impossible for some of them to be churches at all. The church of God includes all those individuals in the world who have been born again, and none other. That is the church I am talking about—

"the church which is his body." Now, the church of God is not yet as it shall one day be. For the present, Christians look very much like other folks, except for one thing, and that is their smile. You cannot counterfeit a Christian smile. The world can grin, but it cannot smile. But, beloved, we do not look like we are going to look; we are not finished yet. I meet many dear Christian brethren who try to make me believe they are finished. But, for their sake, I hope it is not so. People talk to me about the full salvation they have already, and when they say it they actually look at me sometimes through spectacles very much like my own. Or they say it through a mouthful of false teeth, and under a bald head, and all that, and they talk about having full salvation. Why, bless your heart, man, full salvation abolishes all that. You do not suppose, do you, that I am going to have four eyes in heaven? No, I am not; neither are you. The time is coming when the church of God will be put on exhibition for the principalities and the powers in heavenly places. God is going to hold a great world's fair —a universal fair. It will be a great affair. Romans 8 tells us that "the earnest expectation of the creation waiteth for the manifestation of the sons of God"—the word for "manifestation" is "apocalypse"; it speaks of the unveiling of the sons of God.

For nineteen hundred years God has been at work preparing His sons for that day; and on that day when everything is ready—and everything will be ready on time with Him—on that day when He gets all ready, He is going to have all the guests present and He is going to show His family, His family, the sons of God. O beloved, won't it be fine when we see them all together! I do not know how many people this hall will seat—there seems to be quite a crowd of us here—yet it is only a little handful out of the family of God; and in that day we shall shine in the kingdom of our Father in the likeness of His Son. It is the day of the manifestation, the unveiling, the revealing, of the sons of God, and the whole creation is waiting for that wonderful day, because the creation itself also shall be delivered from the bondage of corruption into the liberty of the glory of the children of God. Do you know why we get sick? Yes, even the divine healers get sick, and they die, very much like other folks. That is not in their program, but they do. And what is the trouble with them, and with us? It is because they have not got full salvation. It is because our salvation, though nearer than when we first believed, has not yet arrived. We have salvation from the penalty of sin, and from the power of sin we are getting salvation day by day; but one day we must be saved out of the very presence of sin with all that belongs to it; and among the things that belong to it, and out of which we shall be delivered, is what this Word of God calls the bondage of corruption. You and I live in mortal bodies. We live in corrupting bodies. We live in bodies that are going to pieces—these earthly houses of our tabernacle are dissolving; but one day we shall be delivered from all that and we shall have a house, not made with hands, eternal in the heavens. We shall be free from the bondage of corruption. And not only so, but the whole creation also shall be delivered from the bondage of corruption into the liberty of the glory of the children of God. And further—listen! "For we know that the whole creation groaneth and travaileth in pain together until now. And not only they, but ourselves also, which have the first-fruits of the Spirit." How sorry I am for men who have not the first-fruits of the Spirit! How sorry I am for men who do not know God, who have not been born again! What do men do in these awful times of war, who do not have what you have to depend upon? Other men are sending their sons also to Europe, who know nothing about God, and know not how to pray, and have nothing to lean upon. How do they endure at all? Even we ourselves, who are happy in God, who have this salvation, who have the first-fruits of the Spirit, even we ourselves are not yet satisfied. We groan within ourselves. And what are we groaning about? We are groaning within ourselves because we are "waiting for the adoption, to wit, the redemption of our body." A great day of redemption is coming—the day of our exhibition, the day of our revealing, the day of our manifestation, when in body, as well as in spirit and soul, we shall be perfect like Him whose we are and whom we serve, and whom, having not seen, we love. O, glory be to God for that great day that is coming!

IV. I now come to my fourth point, namely, that in that day there shall be glory for Him, even our adorable Lord and Saviour Jesus Christ. O, beloved, I am tired of hearing the name of the Lord Jesus traduced. I am weary of seeing Him stabbed in the house of His friends. I long to have the day pass when men wearing His livery and calling themselves by His name, transformed as His ministers, may drag His name into the dirt and bring reproach and ignominy upon Him. I am thanking God to-day for the eternal decree of the Father that one day, at the name of Jesus every knee shall bow, of things in heaven, things on earth, and things under the earth, and every tongue confess that Jesus Christ is Lord—Lord! Lord!—to the glory of God the Father (Phil. 2:9-11). That will be glory for Him, and glory like that for Him is glory enough for me. O glorious day!

This day is described over and over again in the Bible. In the 19th chapter of the book of The Revelation, there is a wonderful picture of the coming of our Lord Jesus Christ in the clouds of heaven with power and great glory. I will read a bit of it here:

"And I saw heaven opened, and behold a white horse; and He that sat upon him was called Faithful and True, and in righteousness He doth judge and make war." I want to commend that to my pacifist brethren, "He doth judge and make war. His eyes were as a flame of fire, and on His head were many crowns; and He had a name written, that no man knew, but He Himself. And He was clothed with a vesture dipped in blood: and His name was called The Word of God. And the armies which were in heaven followed Him upon white horses, clothed in fine linen, white and clean. And out of his mouth goeth a sharp sword, that with it He should smite the nations; and He shall rule them with a rod of iron: and He treadeth the winepress of the fierceness and wrath of Almighty God. And he hath on His vesture and on His thigh a name written, KING OF KINGS, AND LORD OF LORDS." That is the King who is my Saviour—the Man who died for me. And when he comes forth out of heaven upon his white horse, followed by his armies, I am going to be in those armies. Behold, the Lord cometh with all His saints. I am one of them. By His wondrous grace, I am one of them. I should never dare to think of myself as a saint, or call myself a saint, for I must confess that I do not look like one, neither do I always act like one, sometimes I do not even feel like one, but He says I am one. By the grace of God, and by the blood of Jesus, I am what I am. And when all the saints come, this one is coming. "I am included."

I also like the picture presented of Him in the 14th chapter of Zechariah. That chapter opens with the great siege of Jerusalem by the confederated armies of the world, led by the Beast of that awful time. Poor old Jerusalem! She knows what it is to be besieged. She knows what it is to be slaughtered and trampled upon; and in this 14th chapter of Zechariah there is a picture of that last awful siege before the millennial kingdom shall be set up. It is when everything seems to be lost—the city is broken down and has capitulated, one-half of the people have gone forth already into captivity, and everything seems to be lost—and then it says: "Then shall the Lord go forth, and fight against those nations, as when He fought in the day of battle." Now, if I were not going to come with Him on that day, I would rather be in Jerusalem than anywhere else in the world, just to see Him come. Over on the east there is seen by a few—for there will be a few Simeons, and Annas, and the rest, in Jerusalem, waiting for Him and believing His Word—they will be looking toward the east, and they will see there a cloud about the size of a man's hand; and as they look upon it, they see it growing, growing, and they will call one another's attention to it, and then shall they cry, "Behold, He cometh!" As they watch the cloud, it grows, and grows, and grows, until it finally hovers over the city; "and His feet shall stand in that day upon the mount of Olives, which is before Jerusalem on the east." I am glad to have it geographically, scientifically, mathematically located. The mount of Olives is not in heaven, nor is it "in the believer's heart," but it is "before Jerusalem on the east." When His feet strike that mountain, the spot whence He went away—He is going to take up His work right where he left it, the mount of Olives—and when His feet shall strike that mountain, the mount of Olives shall split in two. Do I really believe that? Surely; why not? But someone says, "That is impossible." Why, listen, man, you would not say "impossible," would you, in the same sentence with the name of Jesus Christ, the King of kings and Lord of lords? Why, He made that mountain. If I could make a mountain, I could make it split up any way I wanted to. And so He is going to split it up and make a valley run through it, to get the thing done that He intends to do, "and the Lord shall be King over the whole earth. In that day there shall be one Lord, and His name one."

Now, I want to take a moment upon one thing in addition. I know that in a company like this there are many minds confused about the order of events, and they are saying, "We wish somebody would tell us what is to come first, so that we may know what to look for." The first prophetic conference I ever attended was at old Shikellimy, and Dr. Chapman was there, as were also Dr. Torrey and Mr. Huston. I remember that I sat there wishing that somebody would be very simple and tell me the order of events.

Well, I am not zealous about the order of events in detail; but I am here to insist, and I believe that this conference stands for the doctrine, that the first thing to transpire now, is not the coming of our Lord to the mount of Olives, but the coming of our Lord into the air.

"The Lord Himself shall descend from heaven with a shout, with the voice of the archangel, and with the trump of God: and the dead in Christ shall rise first: then we which are alive and remain shall be caught up together with them in the clouds, to meet the Lord in the air; and so shall we ever be with the Lord. Wherefore comfort one another with these words" (1 Thess. 4:16-18). Beloved, we have turned to God from idols, to serve the living and true God, and to wait for His Son from heaven. The Great Tribulation will come after that; and the coming in glory will come after that; and the millennial kingdom will come after that; but whatever comes after that, this comes before all; and this is the thing for which we are to be waiting. We are to be waiting for His shout and His coming in the air to catch us up to meet Him there.

I rather think I know what He is going to shout. I think I do. You know he has to say something when He shouts. When He stood at the tomb of His friend at Bethany, He shouted, and said, "Lazarus, come forth!" and he that was dead came forth. Imagine a Christian denying the bodily resurrection, after that! Lazarus had to come, and if the Lord Jesus had not called his name, every dead body in that cemetery would have come forth.

Well, He knows all our names, but it would take him a long time to call the roll. I think we have His shout for us in the words by which, in Rev. 4:1, He called John up to heaven. What He said to John was, "COME UP HITHER!" and when He says that, I am going.

HAS GOD A PROGRAM?

REV. B. B. SUTCLIFFE

Bible Teacher, Extension Department Staff, Moody Bible Institute, Chicago, Ill.

The subject for this hour is, "Has God a Program?" Listening to the addresses of this Conference, one cannot but believe that God has a program, and is moving along step by step to the working out of His purposes. I am to speak of God's program in relation to Israel, in relation to the nations, and in relation to the Kingdom.

1. God's Program in Relation to Israel.

Israel, as we have heard, is to be regathered in an unconverted state into her own land. This is something more than her return from Babylon after the seventy years' captivity, as Ezek. 37:15-28 clearly shows, especially verse 22: "And I will make them one nation in the land . . . and one king shall be king to them all: and they shall be no more two nations, neither shall they be divided into two kingdoms any more at all." Again the Lord says in Amos 9:15, "I will plant them upon their land, and they shall no more be pulled up out of their land which I have given them" (see also Isa. 11:11, 12; Jer. 33:7, 14-16, etc.). When so gathered into her own land Israel will enter into covenant with the sinister being called Antichrist, which covenant he will break at the end of three and one-half years. Then will ensue such a time of distress and persecution that its equal has never yet been seen. It is called in Jer. 30:7, "the time of Jacob's trouble." Dan. 12:1 says it "shall be a time of trouble such as never was since there was a nation even to that same time." Such will be the awfulness of the persecution and distress in those days that it is said in Matt. 24:21, that "except those days should be shortened, there should none be saved: but for the elect's sake those days shall be shortened" (see also Zech. 14:1, 2; Matt. 24:15-28, etc.). The breaking of the covenant, which gives rise to Israel's persecution, is caused by the idolatry of Antichrist who proclaims himself to be God, and the refusal of Israel to recognize him as such. Then Antichrist will attempt to blot out Israel and with her all knowledge of God on earth. This indeed has been Satan's desire since God had this peculiar nation. He attempted it through Pharaoh long ago in Egypt, through Haman in the days of Esther, and he will finally try to do it through this Antichrist. Antichrist will appear, after the rapture of the Church, as the leader of the world. He will be a man of education, a man of refinement and culture, a man of wide experience, a man clever enough to draw to himself the highest and the best the world affords in the way of learning, intellectual power and all that which the world considers great. As the leader of all the forces of the earth, he will set himself up as God to be worshiped.

But the godly remnant among the people of Israel, refusing to give up the worship of the God of their fathers, will break their covenant with him. Hence will follow Israel's time of trouble. Just when it seems as though Israel would be finally exterminated, the Lord from heaven will appear in His second advent to the earth and bring deliverance to His people. So we read in Zech. 14:2, 3: "Then shall the Lord go forth and fight against those nations, as when He fought in the day of battle." "In that day the Lord shall defend the inhabitants of Jerusalem" (Zech. 12:1-8; see also Isa. 26; Isa. 66:15, 16; Matt. 24:29-31, etc.). Rev. 19 describes this time and adds that Antichrist and his prophet will be taken and cast alive into the lake of fire. The deliverance of Israel is followed by her conversion. Zech. 12:9 to 13:1 says the Lord will pour upon His people the Spirit of grace and of supplication, and there will be opened for the house of David a fountain for sin and for uncleanness. They will see Him as their Messiah (Matt. 24) and seeing Him the nation will be converted, or as Isa. 66:5-13 puts it, the nation will be born in a day. Paul's conversion is an example of Israel's. He was converted as Israel will be, not by the preaching of the gospel but by a vision of the risen and glorified Lord (compare Acts 9; 1 Tim. 1:16; 1 Cor. 15:8, margin).

Converted, and all her iniquities subdued, and her sins cast into the depths of the sea (Mic. 7:18-20), Israel will become a praise and fame in every land where they have been put to shame (Zeph. 3:14-20). She will come to the place of religious leadership in the world (Zech. 8:13, 20-23), and finally to the place long ago promised her of national supremacy in the earth. She will be "the head and not the tail" (Deut. 28:13) among the nations, and the kingdom or nation that will not serve Israel shall utterly be destroyed (Isa. 60:10-12).

II. God's Program in Relation to the Nations.

The nations had their beginning in Gen. 10, 11. The race having turned its back upon God and gone into idolatry, as Josh. 24:2 informs us, God divided it into nations. These nations were formed in idolatry and therein continue. Idolatry is not that which is in the dark groping for the light, but that which has had the light and turns to the dark. We are members of a fallen and a falling race. The world is in deeper spiritual darkness to-day than ever before. Civilization is the exaltation of man, Christianity is the exaltation of Christ. Man's exaltation is the world's endeavor, which will end in the rebellion against all that is of God described in the second Psalm. This final rebellion of the nations will be under Antichrist, and will take the form of the attempt to exterminate Israel, by which nation alone God will be sought after. At the appearance of the Lord for the deliverance of His people the nations will be judged as told in Matt. 25:31-46. They will be separated from one another, according to whether they are sheep or goats. Their judgment will be according to their conduct in relation to the Lord's brethren after the flesh, the Jews. Their destiny will be according to their condition, whether righteous or unrighteous. The judgment of the nations is not to determine the question of eternal life or death, but to discover which nations enter into the millennial kingdom. The ones who do come into that millennial kingdom will find Israel, converted and made a praise and fame among them, to be a blessing as she was a curse (Zech. 8:13). They will follow Israel's religious leadership, as Zech. 8:20-23 declares. God has said that all the nations shall know He is the Lord when He is sanctified among Israel (Ezk. 36:22, 23). So the nations wait for blessing until Israel is restored and converted.

III. God's Program in Relation to the Kingdom.

The coming King is He whose name is Jesus. He will be the center of the world's thrones and will sit upon the throne of His glory, as Matt. 25:31 says. Paul speaks in 1 Tim. 6:14, 15 concerning "the appearing of our Lord Jesus Christ which in His times He will show, who is the blessed and only Potentate, the King of kings and Lord of lords." He will also be the center of the world's homage. He has been given a name "which is above every name, that at the name of Jesus every knee should bow, of things in heaven, and things of earth, and things under the earth, and every tongue confess that Jesus Christ is Lord to the glory of God the Father" (Phil. 2:10, 11). He is now on His Father's throne, "from henceforth expecting until His enemies be made His footstool" (Heb. 10:13.) He will also be the center of the world's hopes, and "unto Him shall the gathering of the people be" (Gen. 49:10). "The government shall be upon His shoulder, and of the increase of His government and peace there shall be no end" (Isa. 9:6, 7).

His government will be one of righteousness, justice and equity. Let all rejoice "before the Lord, for He cometh to judge the earth: He shall judge the world with righteousness and the people with His truth" (Psa. 96:13). "O, let the nations be glad and sing for joy: for thou shalt judge the people righteously and govern the nations upon earth" (Psa. 67:4). "Behold the days come, saith the Lord, that I will raise unto David a righteous Branch, and a King shall reign and prosper, and shall execute judgment and justice in the earth" (Jer. 23:5). It means that a reign of righteousness will yet be on this earth. He, the King of kings, will rule with a rod of iron and will enforce peace and justice throughout the whole world. The effects of such a rule are plainly told in Scripture. "He shall judge between the nations and reprove many peoples: and they shall beat their swords into plowshares and their spears into pruning hooks" (Isa. 2:4; see also Mic. 4:1-3).

This world is yet to have an international court of arbitration, from the decisions of which there will be no appeal. There will be just one Arbiter in that court, but He will be the King of kings. There will be no universal peace in the world until the Lord Jesus Christ sets up this court. If the church could bring in universal peace now in our day, it would be proof that the Bible is false. No greater bit of folly has ever been undertaken than the attempt to have world peace before Christ comes the second time. But, because of the enforcement of law and the reign with righteousness, many will yield obedience while they would like to disobey the King. Psa. 66:1-4, as well as Psa. 18:43, 44 and other scriptures, show that His enemies will yield Him a feigned obedience. This will continue until the final test comes at the end of a thousand years. At that time Satan will be loosed from his prison and man will, as in the beginning, be called on to choose whether he will serve God or the devil. Many will choose to follow the devil, only to be destroyed by the Word of the King of kings. At last all evil will be removed and there will come the new heavens and the new earth, wherein dwelleth righteousness (2 Pet. 3:10-13). There will be no need of the rod of iron, for all will know the Lord from the least to the greatest. During the millennium it will be a rule with righteousness, but in the new earth righteousness will dwell.

In brief, God's program is, premillennial when evil is revealed, millennial when evil is restrained, postmillennial when evil is removed.

The evening devotional service was conducted by Rev. W. Dayton Roberts, D.D., Pastor, Temple Presbyterian Church, Philadelphia.

The Chairman then introduced Rev. Herbert Mackenzie.

DOES THIS TRUTH PARALYZE OR ENERGIZE?

PASTOR HERBERT MACKENZIE

Pastor of the Gospel Church, Cleveland, Ohio, and Secretary of the Erieside Bible Conference

About a century ago, Christendom was being bathed in blood by the sword of Napoleon. The world was then passing through its greatest horrors that have been known for ages, and at that time, while Napoleon was creating havoc and hell among the civilized peoples of Europe, God was planning the invasion of heathendom by the undertaking of modern missions. During those days of terrible trial, a number of the modern missionary movements were inaugurated. The London Missionary Society, the Scottish Missionary Society, the Church Missionary Society, the Baptist Missionary Society, the American Board of Foreign Missions were organized about that time. All these missionary organizations were founded and their first missionaries sent forth under the inspiration of the Spirit, during those dark days of the world's history. During the Napoleonic era the work of the British and Foreign Bible Society also was started, and the work of the Sunday schools was inaugurated by Robert Raikes. Carey was then sent by God to India, Morrison was called for China, and Moffatt was led by God to Africa, and one wonders, looking upon such a congregation as this, interested in the truth of our Lord's return, whether in these days—when the Kaiser has heated the fires perhaps seven times hotter—God has a purpose through such a gathering as this of again sending forth His hosts into the darkest corners of the earth, entrusting to them the light that it may radiate far and wide until it reaches the remotest bounds of earth. For He has said even unto us, "Go ye into all the world and preach the Gospel to every creature." We all recognize our duty as citizens to do our best for our country and for the world in a crisis so grave as this through which we are passing. We recognize too that we have a Leader who is leading us on in a spiritual conflict; that we have a commission which must be obeyed and completed in order that he may come again and receive us unto Himself.

Doctrine always decides duty. It matters much what a man believes, and as we study the doctrine of God's Word as we have studied it during the past three days, we are led to inquire from the Word of God just what he expects of us after receiving the added light and blessing. Doctrine in the plan of teaching always precedes the plan of duty. Doctrine is like a locomotive to which a number of coaches are attached. The doctrine is intended to be the inspiration and gives to us impulse and impetus to obey all the behests of our Lord. The doctrine of God is the foundation designed by God, well and truly laid; and duty is a building which God expects us to rear upon the foundation which He has provided.

In the 6th chapter of the Epistle to the Romans, Paul uses the simile of a mold to express the purpose of doctrine. He wrote to those Romans, "God be thanked that ye have obeyed from the heart that form of doctrine which was delivered you." And the word he used was that which we could correctly translate as a die, a mold or a cast capable of reproducing a likeness, a figure, or an image, just as the die produces an image and the superscription on a coin, or as the engraving or the type prints its likeness upon the sheet of paper, so the doctrine of God is intended to imprint a spiritual superscription upon the service of the servant of Christ which authenticates his message, which puts a divine seal upon his ministry as well as a Christlikeness into his life. "Take heed unto thyself and unto the doctrine, for in so doing thou shalt both save thyself and them that hear thee." And when we speak of doctrine, we do not speak of *doctrines,* for God's doctrine is always referred to in the singular in the New Testament. God's doctrine is intended to carry us on, while the doctrines of men, doctrines devised by men in contrast to the doctrine declared by God, only "carry us away" like wind carries away chaff.

It is our business this evening for a few minutes

to look at a few of the scriptures which link up both the doctrine and the duty of the church. For the glory of the doctrine of the glorious appearing of the Lord Jesus Christ has a large place in the New Testament and our service is only accurate and acceptable to God as it is given shapeliness and soundness by our obedience to the *doctrinal die* which has been delivered unto us. With your permission I would like to read two or three brief verses of Scripture which indicate what God has in mind for us, and I want to take three brief messages from the last chapters of Scripture written by the apostle Paul, the apostle Peter and by the apostle John. In 2 Tim. 4:1 we read, "I charge thee therefore before God and the Lord Jesus Christ, who shall judge the living and the dead at his appearing and his kingdom." Here we have a statement of the doctrine. There we are charged before God in the light of the doctrine and the duty is stated in the next verse and perhaps is summed up almost completely in three words: "Preach the Word." No man can know the doctrine of the appearing of the great God and our Saviour Jesus Christ, without having a burning desire and a deep yearning to "preach the Word" which not only will save but build up His saints upon the most holy faith.

The Second Epistle of Peter, the third Chapter the 13th and 14th verses, have a similar sequence. "Nevertheless we, according to His promise, look for new heavens and a new earth, wherein dwelleth righteousness." A statement of the doctrine to which we have been listening during this conference and then once more our outlined duty. "Wherefore, beloved, seeing that ye look for such things, be diligent that ye may be found of Him in peace, without spot and blameless." The busiest people today in the Kingdom of God, or rather among the nations who are preaching the gospel of His grace, are those who believe in the imminent return of the Lord Jesus and the wonderful program which follows His coming.

The 22d chapter of the Book of Revelation contains a three-fold record of words falling from the lips of our Lord which confirm the promise of His coming. In verse 7 He says, "Behold, I come quickly!" The statement of the doctrine once more, and then, "Blessed is He that keepeth the sayings of the prophecy of this book," a statement concerning our duty. I remember a number of years ago a very saintly and a very gifted servant of Christ telling me that with a dimming of the hope, with the fading of the desire for His appearing, there was always failure in his ministry and that he always needed the reviving of the hope in order that he might tighten the bands between himself and his Christ in order that he might be more firmly bound with the cords of loving sacrifice to the horns of the altar of the divine purpose. "Behold, I come quickly." "Blessed is he that keepeth." "Hold fast that thou hast, that no man take thy crown."

The twelfth verse repeats the prophecy of His

return coupled with a promise of recompense, for His servants. "Behold, I come quickly; and My reward is with Me, to give every man according as his work shall be." The work of the servant of Christ is to be undertaken in the light of the coming of Christ. Perhaps we have at times been inclined to be a little bit discontented with the wages we have received, but the Lord Jesus Christ pledges payment of all arrears of wages when He returns.

Finally in the 20th verse the third statement from His lips is found concerning His return. "SURELY I come quickly." The responsive waiting heart answers with a prayer that we should be praying with ever increasing earnestness if we believe He is coming back and if we love His appearing, "Even so, come, Lord Jesus." In this last chapter of Scripture, in the light of the coming we are instructed concerning something that we should keep, something that we should do and something that we should pray. "Even so, come, Lord Jesus." We are assigned the task this evening of answering the question, "Does the prophecy of the Lord's return paralyze or energize in the work of world-wide evangelism?" Experience, as you know, is sometimes misguiding, and if we would learn exactly what this blessed hope is intended to accomplish, we need to turn to God's own Word, and I want first to refer you to the 24th chapter of the Gospel by Matthew. In this passage which we intend to read you will see that God brings before us two servants. In the 24th of Matthew God deals with individuals in twos. You remember He speaks of two men being in the field, and the one shall be taken, and the other left; two women will be grinding at the mill, and the one shall be taken and the other left, but here He gives us the record of two servants. Reading from the 44th verse, "Therefore be ye also ready: for in such an hour as ye think not the Son of Man cometh. Who then is a faithful and wise servant, whom his lord hath made ruler over his household, to give them meat in due season? Blessed is that servant, whom his lord when he cometh shall find so doing." You and I have been *receiving* meat, and when the Lord comes He expects to find us *dispensing* meat. We are never made to be a temple or a pool for the blessings of God. We are intended *always* to be channels. God ever expects us to break the bread which has been broken to us. He gave to the disciples that they might break it unto the multitude, but here is a man engaged in serving meat to his master's household and he is watching for his master's return. When his master does actually appear he is an exceedingly happy man, for that word "blessed" means joyous, and you and I presently are going to be lifted to the height of joy when our Lord returns if He finds us faithful in service and patient in watchfulness. We will be saying, "I will go unto God, unto God, my exceeding joy," for only God Himself is the joy height of man. Only Jesus Himself is the joy height of the believer.

He then speaks to us about another servant. I want you to notice what He says: "But and if that evil servant shall say in his heart, My lord delayeth his coming; and shall begin to smite his fellow servants, and to eat and drink with the drunken; the lord of that servant shall come in a day when he looked not for him, and in an hour that he is not aware of, and shall cut him asunder, and appoint him his portion with the hypocrites: there shall be weeping and gnashing of teeth." What I want you to notice concerning this servant is that he does not deny his lord's return. He does not brush out of his mind altogether the thought that his lord is coming back. The thought which he seeks to dismiss from his mind is that of an early prospect of his lord's return. He says, "My lord *delayeth* his coming," and with that thought taking root in his mind he begins to deal unkindly with his fellow servants and enters into fellowship with the world. There is nothing that will keep us more clearly separated from the world than the momentary expectation of the return of the Lord Jesus Christ. This man said, "My lord *delayeth.*" He only *"delayeth"* his coming. God forbid that we should suggest that all the servants of Christ who teach His *delayed* coming are like this servant whose example is set before us, but we do know that it is a dangerous thing for us to suggest to ourselves that our Lord will tarry ere He return, for with the unwatchfulness of this servant came unreadiness, and with unreadiness came unfaithfulness, and with unfaithfulness came unkindness, and with unkindness came ungodliness, and all this because he had lost the *present* hope. Those who love His appearing, long moment by moment for His return, for it is the normal outcome of Love to long for the appearing of the loved one.

We turn now to the Second Epistle of Peter, the third chapter, the 3d and 4th verses. You remember well what the apostle says. He tells us there that we should know something first; that is, it is one of the earlier things a believer ought to know concerning Satanic opposition to this truth. "Knowing this FIRST, that there shall come in the last days scoffers, walking after their own lusts, and saying, Where is the promise of His coming? for since the fathers fell asleep, all things continue as they were from the beginning." Frequently there is one word which is the keyword to a book, the keyword to a chapter, the keyword to a verse of Scripture, and it seems to me the keyword here is the word *promise*. Where is the *promise* of his coming? A revival of the old Satanic slur and slander aimed at the *Promiser*. Satan knows that he can never overthrow the fulfilment of the Word of God, the promises of God or the purpose of God, but Satan does believe that he can overthrow your confidence and mine in the veracity of the inspired Scriptures. Consequently, "Where is the *promise* of His coming?" is the query of the mocker. Lower down in the 13th verse the apostle says, "Nevertheless,"—in spite of all they say—"nevertheless we"—not they—"according to His promise, look for new heavens and a new earth, wherein dwelleth righteousness." The attack upon the promise is a renewal of the old Satanic deception employed in Eden: "Hath God said? . . . Ye shall *not* surely die!"

Now the Word of prophecy as relates to our Lord's return energizes in the work of world-wide evangelism because it informs us concerning three things. First, concerning God's purpose; second, of His plan for our life; and third, because of the prospect which is set before us. I want to turn now to the 15th chapter of the Book of Acts and read a brief Scripture frequently referred to during this Conference, verse 14. "Simeon hath declared how God at the first did visit the Gentiles, to take out of them a people for His name." Will you notice please that God is simply *visiting* the Gentiles and that we have two suggestions here: first, a *limited period;* and second, a *limited purpose,* a limited time to work and a limited task to perform. He is not dwelling here among the Gentiles as a fixed plan or purpose. He is simply visiting the Gentiles to *take out* of them a people unto or for His name.

The next word is, "And to this agree the words of the prophets; as it is written." This was a new revelation. A new Word in prophecy. The Old Testament prophets had nothing to say about this revelation declared by Peter. But, says James, this prophecy of Peter is not out of harmony with what prophets have said. It is just like a newly written stanza placed in the middle of an old hymn and which is in perfect harmony with the verses which go before and those which follow after it. This testimony regarding the church, this gathering out of the church from the nations of the earth, while it is not revealed to us in Old Testament prophecy, is in perfect harmony with all that the prophets have said concerning the past and future program of the Lord Jesus Christ—there is no contradiction. Then in the next verse we read, "*I will return,*" and the logical result of our belief of this doctrine that God is working among the Gentiles to take out of them a people for His name is, the sooner the desired people are gathered out the sooner He will return, and if that work of gathering them out has been left in your hands and mine, how busy we should be at this business in order to hasten the return of our Lord and Saviour Jesus Christ.

We were referring a few moments ago to the work of modern missions. I believe during the past century that 75 per cent of those whose lives have been spent in producing the century's results upon the mission field have been those men and women who have drawn their inspiration from this fact of a divine purpose among the nations to bring out a selected people who shall comprise the body of the Lord Jesus Christ and upon the completion of which He will immediately return. Those who have bored into the bush of Africa, those who have gone into the jungles of India, those who have encompassed the walled cities of

China during the past one hundred years and have brought to us a century's results and the missionary prospects that we have to-night upon the mission field—75 per cent of them at least have believed in the near approach of the Lord Jesus Christ.

I am wondering if God wants me to say something here which I have never before publicly stated, just by way of suggesting to you the effect this doctrine has had upon my life. Away back in 1897 I was engaged with Mr. Philpott in seeking to establish this testimony to which we have been listening during the past few days, in various centers in Canada, and I remember going into a city to a given work and having around me four or five people. I remember how through that year my heart was groaning to be able to do something for the mission field, and at the end of the first year I calculated the stipend that I had received from all quarters and I found it to be the sum of about $224.00. Just at that time the Lord laid upon me the burden of doing something for the world, the great world, and I immediately began to pray that He might show me just what He wanted me to do. It seemed perfectly clear that we were to take a missionary offering and although the numbers were few and even although the finances were low and the testimony did not seem to make very much headway, we set apart a day for a missionary offering. Gradually we found ourselves praying for God to send us money, not asking people for money, but for God to send us money into the hundreds, and I remember on that missionary Sunday morning before I preached that first missionary sermon in that little hall, I was asking God to send us that day $250.00. But at the end of that day He had not only exceeded in one day my salary for one year, but He had given us not less than $296.00. As our Brother Whittlesey was praying a few minutes ago, the thought came back to me of that first missionary day. That first missionary money within a very few months was used with other sums to send across the seas our first missionary under the board of the China Inland Mission to preach the Gospel to the heathens in China, and I want to say, dear friends, from that day to this, there has never been one year in my life but what God has succeeded in sending us more money in the one day than He has sent for the pastor's salary year by year. To-day in our church in Cleveland I thank God that we are able to say that our missionary income exceeds the entire income of the church for all other purposes. Thus the energizing of the Hope continues in the life of an individual and of a church. Men who are working with God are sure of what they are doing. A man asked me not so long ago what was the greatest thing he could do for God. I said, "The greatest thing that you can do for Him is to do what He is doing." That is what God wants you and me to do; to long for that for which Christ is longing; and Christ is longing to see a completed body, and that completed body must be drawn out from all the peoples and tongues and tribes of the earth.

Those who know the Lord's purpose do not need any personal appeals. I have never asked an individual for a dollar for missions in 20 years. I have never permitted any of my officials to canvass any members of the church for a penny for missions. Men whose hearts are touched by the inspiration of the Lord's return need only to be informed of the need and they are satisfied to give their best to the Lord, for they live in the light of the gleams of the coming glory. I have a mechanic in my church who ten years ago, when I first went there, was very complacently giving from $2.00 to $5.00 a year for missions. He was perfectly satisfied with what he was doing. But after a year or so the light began to break in. A man who was only receiving mechanic's wages and a married man with a family, purchasing in these days Liberty Bonds and giving to all the other humanitarian enterprises connected with the war. After a little while we found that he was giving $50.00 a year and a little later we discovered that he was giving $100.00 a year, and this year he has given over $300.00 to hasten the return of the Lord Jesus Christ.

Second, this Word of God, this Blessed Hope, is instructing us concerning the plan of God for our service. Somebody has said that Judaism and the heathen religions have respect for boundaries and are content to let everybody else alone, but the man who knows the plan of God is not willing to let anybody alone. It does not matter how near He may be or how far away the man may be who needs the Gospel. I have come to the conclusion examining my own heart that we can never be like Christ or Christlike until we love the world. For Christ loved the world and no man can begin to be like Him until in some measure he too can say, "I love the world."

Will you turn with me to the first chapter of the book of Acts. I want to read the last words of the Lord Jesus Christ before His ascension, and I want to read the first words of revelation uttered after He had ascended. Probably a moment or so before He went away He uttered these words: "But ye shall receive power after that the Holy Ghost is come upon you and ye shall be witnesses unto me." And those disciples knew what He meant by witnesses, for that word meant martyr testifiers. Those men knew when He uttered that word that this testimony to which they were called, this witness which was to be their work, was to be of more value to them than their own lives. There are boys, perhaps your boys, your brother, your friend, who will lay down their life, or are willing to lay down their lives for their country, and there is something wrong with you and with me if our lives are of more worth in our sight than the witness which He has left to our trust. The disciples were told in those last words that they should be witnesses unto Him "both in Jerusalem and in all Judea and in Samaria, and unto the uttermost part of the earth. And when He had spoken these things, while they beheld, He was taken up; and a cloud received Him out of their sight. While they looked heavenward two men stood by them in white apparel; which also said, Ye men of Galilee, why stand ye gazing up into heaven? This same Jesus . . . shall so come in like manner as ye have seen Him go into heaven." You notice the accurate sequence in dispensational procedure. Just before Jesus left, He gave His disciples a commission. Just after He had gone, messengers from heaven gave a promise of His return. Between the commission at the one end and the coming at the other, there must be the completion of the work which has been entrusted to us.

Do we know that a thousand million souls are waiting to-night for the light you and I have been receiving in this conference? and that two and a half million a month have been passing away out from the fields of heathenism during our generation out from this life into the next without hearing a word of the Gospel? Two and a half millions a month since the beginning of the war alone gives to us an appalling total exceeding the entire population of the United States. All the munitions employed and all the conflicts in Europe are not able to overtake the awful death and devastation and eternal destruction being wrought because a church is paralyzed through lack of measuring up its duties to the doctrine which it has been taught.

Years ago, I was traveling through Central Soudan. I found there from the west coast up to Lake Chad about 40 tribes waiting for the Gospel. Only one tribe of the 40 had the complete record of the Scriptures. Forty tribes in ignorance, in idolatry, in nakedness, in superstition, steeped in paganism, with a thousand Moslem teachers and traders sent out to convert them from paganism to Mohammedanism; to one Christian missionary being sent out by the entire church of God. I walked an average of 17 miles a day for 7 days without finding a trace of any person who believed on the Lord Jesus Christ. Thousands of villages and scores of towns are *waiting,* WAITING, WAITING, while you and I are enjoying the fulness of His blessing, sitting at His feet and looking into His blessed face. This Conference testimony cannot fail to scatter us to the ends of the earth in obedience to the heavenly vision.

My time has gone. I want, however, to say this, that there is a Prospect. Somebody has spoken here about rewards. Somebody has said in this conference something about taking a crown and laying it at His feet. I know of no surer way of securing a crown to lay at His feet than by gaining it in the work of soul winning; of making known to the world the glories of His cross. Will you remember this to-night? There was a moment in the life of the Lord Jesus when He stood before that earthly judge, when He took the curse from beneath our feet and He permitted His enemies to take those thorns and entwine them into a crown and place it upon His brow, and when you and I look upon His blessed face, we shall see the marks made by the crown of thorns. He loved us enough to take earth's curse from beneath our feet and lift it to His blessed brow. Oh, what a delight, that some day we may be able to take the crown which He has placed upon our head and consider that the highest that He can give to us for our service is only worthy for the feet of Him whose shoe latchet John tells us we are unworthy to unloose.

WHAT MANNER OF PERSONS OUGHT WE TO BE?

ADDRESS BY DR. WM. B. RILEY

Mr. Chairman, Brethren and Sisters: I am keenly sensible of my honor, in being privileged to close this matchless conference by discussing WHAT MANNER OF PERSONS OUGHT WE TO BE?

The subject is found in the third chapter of Peter's Second Epistle.

The apostle's objective, in this chapter, is easily evident. He is forced to the defensive by critics!

The theme of this Conference was Peter's theme. He would stir up "the minds of his brethren by way of remembrance" and that which he would have them recall is the word of holy prophet and apostle, and also of Lord and Saviour, about the Second Coming.

Peter was not only an apostle, but also a prophet —a seer. God, who "is a Revealer of secrets," had brought the future within the apostle's vision. Even the last days were to him like the open pages of a book, and looking into them, he saw "the scoffers" who would come. The words he puts into their mouths: "Where is the promise of his coming?" etc., his arguments against their infidelity, and his positive declaration of divine truth, might, each and all, be considered under three suggestions.

In this discussion, permit us to fellowship with Peter's convictions and express these three points in the possessive case: Our Creed, our conduct, our Christ.

OUR CREED

The time has come when thinking Churchmen recognize the fact that the Second Coming of Christ is creating and completing a definite fellowship. The men who entertain "The blessed hope" are bound together in a peculiar brotherhood: a brotherhood of increasing sweetness and deepening strength. No single denomination of the many that go to make up modern Protestantism, is as definite in its fellowship and as distinct in its doctrinal teaching as is the brotherhood of premillennialism.

In consequence of that fact, permit us to make three remarks, and then elaborate each in turn.

1. The Second Coming is now being specially emphasized.

Whether we have come to the last days or not, no man can dispute the fact that we have come to the days when the number of Biblically instructed men and women who entertain what the apostle Paul called "That Blessed Hope" is enormous and is rapidly increasing.

The most marked religious movement of the

20th century is the revival of Chiliasm. The Bible training school is its educational expression; the Bible Conference, now indefinitely multiplied in numbers, is its expression in assembly; the thousands of pulpits interpreting the Scriptures from this standpoint, and the increasing wealth of literature devoted wholly to the definition and defense of this doctrine, are the effective medium of this propaganda!

While denying the charge that "the movement is heavily financed" and resenting, with the contempt it deserves, the indictment of disloyalty to the interests of human government, we frankly confess our deliberate determination to employ voice, pen, press, in fact every agency at our command to make known the greatest doctrine of all Scripture, namely, the coming of our Lord.

No longer shall this precious truth be left to the erratic and the irresponsible! Through the lips of sane men, and by the pens of the most scholarly the Church of God knows, and by the lives of the most saintly, this Gospel of the Kingdom shall be preached in all the world for a witness unto all nations.

The only apology the advocates of this faith have to present to the public is one of tardiness. It is nothing short of amazing when a woman, in middle life, born and brought up in a Christian house and, for 25 years, living as the wife of a Christian minister of national reputation, asks, in all guilelessness, as one such recently did, "What is this doctrine about the 'Second Coming'? and what is the word employed, 'premillennialism'—or something of that kind?" Before a question like that the advocates of this great hope ought to hang their heads for shame and determine, once and for all, that God shall no longer be compelled to wink at the times of such ignorance.

When the dean of a theological seminary known, by both office and name, in more than one continent, attempts to discuss the subject, "Will Christ Come Again?" and reveals, in multiplied sentences, an utter ignorance of the premillennialist's position, the advocates of this blessed hope should not so much blame him as blame themselves.

Too long have we been silent on the one theme, to which more of sacred Scripture is devoted than to any other subject about which inspired men ever employed tongues or pens!

But the thousands that have waited on this great Conference, the throngs that packed and overflowed the Moody Church, requiring at times three additional assembly rooms to accommodate them, when four years since the Prophetic Conference was held in Chicago, the literal millions that attend upon the multiplied Bible assemblies and Churches to hear the men who know this truth, the sudden rise and unprecedented growth of Bible Training Schools, these all indicate the final awakening of ministers and laymen alike to that most precious and long neglected teaching, the Second Coming of Christ.

To-day it is in the ascendant, and, for the first time since Daniel Whitby diverted men from this truth, it is accredited deserved emphasis.

2. Along with this new emphasis there has risen a passionate opposition; Peter's prophecy is finding a literal fulfilment, and opponents are saying, "Where is the promise of his coming? for since the fathers fell asleep, all things continue as they were from the beginning of the creation."

One opponent of this truth, apparently troubled by the consciousness of his own choleric spirit, introduces his discussion with an apology to the feelings of the good people he intends to hurt. In a single city, recently, on three great public occasions, the chosen speaker of the hour, discussing in each instance a subject altogether aside, turned from his theme long enough to hold the second coming to scorn.

Go to the book stores and ask for volumes on the Millennial Hope and when the salesman shall have stacked up twenty or more before your face, you will find that well-nigh one-half of them are written from the standpoint of opposition, and while in most instances the titles would lead you to expect a sane and spiritual discussion of the subject, quite often the sub-title is a scoff, as, for instance, "THE MILLENNIAL HOPE, A Phase of War-Time Thinking."

The most amazing fact, in this connection, is found in the circumstance that the line of argument against the Lord's reappearance has as perfectly paralleled Peter's prophecy, as though the writers had either never heard of this apostolic prediction, or knowing it, feared not in the least to take the part assigned them.

In illustration, think of a statement like this: "A modern man has various reasons for doubting the validity of present-day reconstructions of millennial hopes. In the first place, mistrust is aroused by the utter failure of all past millennial programs to produce promised results. The apocalyptic visionary was never privileged to see his impending kingdom of heaven established upon earth.

"All early Christians' millennial expectations have similarly miscarried. . . . And yet even to-day some Christians continue to pursue the millennial mirage, vainly looking for a catastrophic end of the world instead of throwing themselves heart and soul into the task of improving the existing order, whose permanence is attested by centuries of disappointed millennial hopes."

Who could longer dispute Peter's inspiration? If Daniel was granted a vision of empires to come, and so described them that now, at the end of more than 2500 years, the greater part of his prophecy has become history, certainly Peter was permitted to see the day, these 2000 years distant, when men should rise saying, "Where is the promise of His coming? for since the fathers fell asleep, all things continue as they were from the beginning of the creation. . . . But, beloved, be not ignorant of this one thing, that one day is with the Lord as a thousand years, and a thousand years as one day." Children must have promises made them speedily fulfilled; mature men can wait and keep the spirit of expectancy.

The extent to which opposition to this truth may yet be carried we little dream. When the suggestion is made that the Government "investigate the teachings of the premillennialists" with a view to lodge, if possible, some indictment of disloyalty, it is not difficult to imagine the day when another portion of Gospel word shall find fulfilment, "And brother shall deliver up brother, and father shall deliver up child," and God's saints shall have another opportunity to suffer with Him who suffered for them.

But all this only gives pith and point to my third remark concerning our creed.

3. The Second Coming of Christ is as sure as the promise of God.

"The Lord is not slack concerning his promise as some men count slackness; but is longsuffering to usward, not willing that any should perish but that all should come to repentance. But the day of the Lord will come as a thief in the night; in the which the heavens shall pass away with a great noise, and the elements shall melt with fervent heat, the earth also and the works that are therein shall be burned up."

Peter's whole appeal rests upon the plain declaration of divine Scriptures. We would base our contention upon nothing else; we would bring our judgment from no other source! It is Peter's convictions we share; the mouth of the Lord hath spoken it; we verily believe it will stand fast.

What if men do scoff? What if passers-by wag their heads and say aha! aha! Noah met all that, and yet went on building the Ark. One hundred and twenty years is a long time to wait and watch for a flood that shall deluge the earth and destroy unbelievers. Scoffing against his prophecy must have seemed the safest of all procedures and the scoff itself came to sound like the only sanity; and yet, unless the tradition of every nation is mistaken and our sacred literature utterly misleading, Noah's prophecy was fulfilled and a drowned world demonstrated the dependableness of the divine Word.

For hundreds of years the prophets continually asserted the first coming of Christ, but history was so slow in running into that mold of inspiration, childish men ceased to regard what the inspired prophets had spoken. When it eventually found fulfilment, one could count on the fingers of a single hand all the expectant of the earth.

Let the past prepare us against the days that are ahead and remind us of a truth often enough illustrated, that "though heaven and earth pass away, one jot or one tittle shall in no wise pass away from the law till all things be accomplished."

Dr. Arthur Pierson reminds us that when in 1884 the Transit of Venus was occurring, some German scientists at Aiken, S. C., had drawn an elliptical circle upon a great stone from which they made their observations. Later they presented a request to that city that this particular stone might remain undisturbed until 120 years had passed and another Transit of Venus had occurred, at which time the then living scientists might make their observations and compare them with the work of 1884.

Dr. Pierson remarked that 120 years is a long time. "Every throne of earth would have been emptied of occupant after occupant," but, said he, "prompt to the year, to the day, to the hour, the minute, the transit of Venus will be on, for such is the accuracy of science."

Read Zechariah's description of the first appearance of Jesus in his triumphal entry into Jerusalem, "riding upon an ass, even upon a colt, the foal of an ass," and remember this, that over 700 years intervened between the declaration and the deed. Generation after generation passed, countless kings came and went; governments perished from the earth to be replaced by other forms; the little sentence, for the most part, was forgotten by Bible students, or if they remembered it at all, the men of their day reminded them that literalism was insanity, and that Scripture should be interpreted spiritually. And yet, in perfect accord with the Word of God, it occurred. He rode into Jerusalem upon an ass, "even a colt, the foal of an ass."

The minor sentence concerning His first appearance was never overlooked of God, forgotten, or fulfilled after some spiritual and unexpected way;

but literally, accurately, exactly. So will it be again! "His feet shall stand upon the mount of Olives" and "His law shall come forth from Jerusalem" and His scepter "shall extend from sea to sea, and from the rivers to the ends of the earth." This is our creed!

But our creed, if it is worth anything to us, or has any value for the world, must eventuate in conduct. What then ought to be

OUR CONDUCT?

"Seeing then that all these things shall be dissolved, what manner of persons ought ye to be in all holy conversation and godliness, looking for and hasting unto the coming of the day of God?" If it were permissible to change the phrasing of Holy Writ, I would like to write this text, "Seeing then that all these things shall be dissolved, what manner of persons ought *WE* to be in all holy conversation and godliness, looking for and hasting unto the coming of the day of God, wherein the heavens being on fire shall be dissolved, and the elements shall melt with fervent heat?" (2 Pet. 3:11-12).

In the judgment of Peter, premillennialism contains in itself a definite, spiritual appeal. If we follow him to the end of the argument in this matter, we will find that he expects this teaching to eventuate in definite and desirable practice. He thinks the hope of the Second Coming should eventuate in sanctity. He argues this hope is to voice itself in sacrificial service, and he maintains that this hope should establish both mind and soul.

The hope of the Second Coming should eventuate in sanctity. "Seeing then that all these things shall be dissolved, what manner of persons ought 'we' to be in all holy conversation and godliness, looking for and hasting unto the coming of the day of God?"

Truth is important to the individual holding it or to the people hearing it, in proportion as it is translated into practice. The times upon which we have fallen exhibit a turning away from "sound doctrine," but even this defection from the faith is not so serious a hindrance to the cause of Christ as is the present day defection in conduct. The worst heresy possible is not one of creed, but rather of character.

That there is an intimate relation between false thinking and false living no man questions, and if we are to impress the world with the value of the "second coming" propaganda, we will only do so by a diviner practice.

Upon this subject the Scriptures leave us in no uncertainty. We are enjoined to "sincerity" in view of the Second Appearance, "that we may be sincere and without offense till the day of Christ."

We are enjoined to sobriety in view of the Second Appearance, since the day of the Lord cometh as a thief in the night, "let us watch and be sober" (1 Thess. 5:6).

We are enjoined to "purity" in view of the

Second Appearance. "And every man that hath this hope in him purifieth himself, even as he is pure" (1 John 3:3).

We are enjoined even to the "mortification of fleshly lusts" in view of the Second Appearance. "When Christ who is our life shall appear, then shall we also appear with him in glory. Mortify therefore your members which are upon the earth" (Col. 3:4, 5).

We are enjoined to holy conversation and godliness, in view of the Second Coming (2 Peter 3:11-13).

In the language of the inspired apostle, "time would fail" me to tell of the victories that are related to this doctrine, as conclusions are related to premise, as result to cause. But I recommend the reading of W. E. Blackstone's book on "Jesus is Coming," where you will find a catalogue of forty practical doctrines that rest with the coming of Christ.

Historically, sanctity has commonly been a consequence of this faith! Ignatius of Antioch was a holy man. He entertained this hope. Polycarp, the disciple of John, was a holy man. He entertained this hope. His friend and companion, Papias, not only taught this truth, but lived as became a man who entertained it. In fact, the Church Fathers, with few exceptions, were men known by two outstanding characteristics, viz., their confident expectation of the return of the Lord and the holy, spiritual character of the lives they led.

That the relationship of doctrine to practice is not destroyed by the progress of time, becomes evident when one recalls the names of John Bunyan, Richard Baxter, John Jewel, John Knox, John Milton, Samuel Rutherford and Thomas Chalmers, Paul Gerhardt and Michael Hahn, and in later time of Horatius Bónar, George Whitfield, while with the modern school of Chiliasts, successors in this faith might be illustrated from the lives of such men as Charles Spurgeon, George Muller, Andrew Murray, J. Hudson Taylor, Arthur T. Pierson and A. J. Gordon.

We are confident that other pastors could bear an exact testimony with Dr. James M. Gray of Chicago, who declares that in his experience as a pastor he had found the members of his church who knew this truth to live spiritual lives and to be devoted to spiritual things. They also made up the most intelligent of his Bible students, manifested special power in prayer, exercised self-denial in giving, were most deeply interested in Home and especially in Foreign Missions, understood the great truths concerning the Holy Spirit and lived altogether the most consistent lives.

We may wisely hold such conferences as this for the propagation of this precious truth, but we should well know that after all, the practice of godliness on the part of those who entertain and teach it, will be the finally effective power in rendering it popular in the Church of God.

Once more then, in the language of Peter, "What manner of persons ought 'we' to be in all holy conversation and godliness, looking for and hasting unto the coming of our Lord."

This hope should voice itself in sacrificial service. "Nevertheless we, according to His promise, look for new heavens and a new earth, wherein dwelleth righteousness. Wherefore, beloved, seeing that ye look for such things, be diligent that ye may be found of Him in peace, without spot, and blameless" (2 Pet. 3:13, 14).

The opponents of this precious truth have tried to make it appear that it paralyzes the individual endeavors of men, converting them into lazy lookers for a catastrophic end of the present social order and an easy introduction of the Utopian dream. But upon this matter, history has a right to be heard, and its pages are replete with results.

I speak not alone for my own denomination, but from a somewhat wide knowledge of the pastors and outstanding churches of other denominations, and I affirm it to be my observation in several countries and upon at least two continents that the most diligent service to the King of kings and the most self-sacrificing spirit in His behalf are found in those pulpits and pews where this precious hope is known.

The denominational annuals would be a positive proof of this fact, and the statement would obtain not alone with reference to the larger gifts to Home and Foreign Missions and the establishment of desirable Christian institutions; but even in the realm of social service—such as giving to the poor, providing for the hungry, clothing the cold, visiting the sick, sympathy with the soldier, with the bereaved, showing brotherhood to the imprisoned and love for the social outcast, the advocates of premillennialism have never been surpassed.

It is an illustration worthy of mention that one man in my church who holds this doctrine most intelligently and advocates it most ardently lives sixty miles distant, and owns a little farm of ten acres worth not more than $5000. He is a keeper of bees and of royally bred chickens. He comes to church about four times a year, namely, at conference or special meeting times, and remains a week at a stretch.

When ten years ago I baptized him he amazed me by sending the treasurer $300.00 to be used for special missionaries on foreign fields, and with each returning season, he increases my amazement. When last February I was ready to enter my pulpit to make the annual appeal for foreign missions, the treasurer stole softly into my study and said: "Pardon me; but I thought this little bit of paper might be an inspiration"; and he handed me a check for $846.00, which, at a later time, was increased to the thousand mark. If this hope "cuts the nerve of missions," would God that every man in my church had his nerve cut in the same manner. For a long time faithful folk have been praying that God would put it into the heart of some millionaire to give millions for foreign missions. Not long ago the prayer was answered and an honored citizen of

Pennsylvania turned over two million dollars to be used for foreign missions. Yes, Peter, "diligence" in the service of our God should be the result of this blessed hope.

But Peter finds a third result which should be always and everywhere manifested. **This hope should establish the mind and the soul.**

He writes: "Ye therefore, beloved, seeing ye know these things before, beware lest ye also, being led away with the error of the wicked, and fall from your own steadfastness" (2 Pet. 3:17).

This statement is to be interpreted in the light of the context, for in the 16th verse Peter speaks of those who stumble from this doctrine because there are some things hard to be understood in it, and being unlearned about it, and unstable, wrest the Scriptures to their own destruction as they do also other Scripture.

Have you ever thought of the point of Paul's reasoning in the 15th of First Corinthians? It is after he has elaborated "the blessed hope," the resurrection of the believer's body and the consequent fellowship of all saints that he says, "Therefore, my beloved brethren, be ye steadfast, unmovable, always abounding in the work of the Lord, forasmuch as ye know that your labor is not in vain in the Lord."

Steadfastness of faith; immutability in creed, the apostle claims as natural consequences of the great second coming truth, and we have reason to-night to thank God that church history is giving proof that advocates of that faith are not even failing in this evil time.

In thirty years in the ministry I have not known a single man who entertained at one and the same time the blessed hope of the Lord's return and yet called into question either the deity of Jesus Christ, the inspiration of the book, or the final and utter authority of either.

Dr. B. H. Carroll, of Texas, the real founder of the public school system of that state, the moving spirit in the establishment of the great Waco or Baylor University, the father and founder of the Southwestern Theological Seminary, the most matchless preacher it has ever been my privilege to hear open his mouth in the name of the Lord, was commonly counted a postmillennialist, and so esteemed himself. The last time it was my privilege to look upon his dear face he held my hand and with trembling voice said, "Riley, we have never seen eye to eye concerning the millennial period, but I want to say to you again as I said to you some years ago, that I hold in unfailing affection, the premillennial brethren, and I declare it my conviction that in loyalty to the Word of God as well as to the deity of Christ, they are not equaled by any company of men the world has known!" Yes, it stabilizes both mind and soul!

But ere I conclude, let me join again with the great Apostle in a brief tribute to

OUR CHRIST

He, after all, is the basis of our creed and He alone is the adequate inspiration of conduct! I regret the necessity of abbreviating when I speak of Him. Peter does not conclude this argument until he pays tribute to Him; but he knows how to unite his praise to Christ with an appeal to Christians! "But grow in grace and in the knowledge of our Lord Jesus Christ. To Him be glory both now and forever. Amen." How rich the suggestions which we may bring from this verse! But it clearly involves the necessity of our spiritual growth.

Of Christ's grace we should have an increased experience. Regeneration is essential to spiritual existence, but is only the beginning. The "grace that is in Christ" is equal to much more than a mere beginning. The mother who brings the babe to birth has in her own being the infant's sustenance, and the Christ who, by the Holy Ghost, begets us into a new life, has in Himself all spiritual sufficiency.

Our ascended Lord has "gifts" for men and a Christian who anticipates His descent should utilize those gifts and mark growth for himself.

This growth is extended by increasing knowledge of Him. In the judgment of the apostle, to the experience of His grace we should add the acquisition of His "knowledge." In fact, Peter aforetime said, "Grace and peace be multiplied unto you through the *knowledge* of God, and of

Jesus our Lord, according as His divine power hath given unto us all things that pertain unto life and godliness, through the knowledge of Him that hath called us to glory and virtue" (2 Pet. 1:2-4).

Finally, **to His name we should bring expressions of never-ending glory.** "To Him be glory both now and for ever. Amen."

It is impossible to dwell upon the riches of His grace and increase in the knowledge of Him, without coming to the point where one is compelled to glorify Him.

Matthew Bridges, reflecting upon what Christ has been, what He is, and what He is to become, calls upon men to break forth into praises and voices himself after this manner. Shall we not conclude this—the greatest premillennial convention yet held on any continent—by joining with him in saying:

"Crown Him with many crowns,
The Lamb upon the throne,
Hark, how the heavenly anthem drowns
All music but its own!
Awake, my soul, and sing
Of Him who died for Thee;
All hail Him as thy matchless King,
Through all eternity.

"Crown Him the Lord of years,
The Potentate of time,
Creator of the rolling spheres
Ineffably sublime.
Crown Him, the Lord of Love;
Behold His hands and side,
Which wounds, yet visible above
In beauty glorified:

"No angel in the sky
Can fully bear that sight,
But downward bends his burning eye
At mysteries so bright.
Glassed in a sea of light
Whose everlasting waves
Reflect His form—the Infinite
Who lives and loves and saves."

THE RETURN, THE RESURRECTION, AND THE RAPTURE

REV. WILLIAM B. RILEY, D.D.

Pastor of the First Baptist Church of Minneapolis;
President of the Northwest Bible School;
Bible teacher and lecturer.

Of all the privileges accorded me in this great Conference, I most highly esteem the opportunity of speaking to you, my fellow preachers.

These three great words, the Return, the Resurrection, and the Rapture, deserve each a separate and extended discussion. The only reasons, therefore, for trying to bring them within the limits of a single discourse exist in two circumstances. First, the other discussions brought to this Conference have involved very many of the features of both the return and the resurrection; and secondly, Paul, by the pen of inspiration, links these all together in both logical and doctrinal order. With that marvelous brevity which is the soul of inspiration, he presents them in five short verses: "But we would not have you ignorant, brethren, concerning them that fall asleep; that ye sorrow not, even as the rest, who have no hope. For if we believe that Jesus died and rose again, even so them also that are fallen asleep in Jesus will God bring with Him. For this we say unto you by the word of the Lord, that we that are alive, that are left unto the coming of the Lord, shall in no wise precede them that are fallen asleep. For the Lord Himself shall descend from heaven, with a shout, with the voice of the archangel, and with the trump of God; and the dead in Christ shall rise first; then we that are alive, that are left, shall together with them be caught up in the clouds, to meet the Lord in the air: and so shall we ever be with the Lord" (I Thess. 4:13-17).

This inspired statement is to the whole subject of the return, the resurrection, and the rapture, what the architect's preliminary sketch is to the finished structure. In each instance it remains for the workers to fill in, and to fill up. A good student will, in a Spirit-led research of the Word, find material at hand for the completion of the great doctrines that Paul here briefly, yet boldly, outlines. As the stones wrought into the temple of God were each ready for its place, requiring not the touch of the hammer, but rather, a perfect knowledge of the plans and careful placing; so the man who works on these great doctrines, with Paul's plan before him, will find no need to change, carve, or unnaturally constrain the sacred sentences of Scripture. When properly put together, they give perfect proof of the divine plan, and provide an unanswerable argument for premillennarianism. Men have sometimes sought to set Peter, or Paul, or John, against Jesus; but on this subject it will be seen that inspired servants and divine Lord speak together.

In the presentation of these great themes to the Thessalonians, Paul speaks of the second coming, the first resurrection, and the supreme rapture.

THE SECOND COMING

IT IS TO BE BOTH LITERAL AND PERSONAL. To speak of the Lord's return as a mere figure of speech that is to know no literal fulfilment, is little less sacrilegious than the total denial of inspiration. To identify that return with the coming of the Holy Spirit, or with the experience of death, is to despise the Master's own differentiations. He was extremely careful to distinguish between the office of the Son and that of the Spirit. The Son was manifested in the flesh—"The Word became flesh and dwelt among us" (John 1:14); the Spirit was contrasted with the flesh—"That which is born of the flesh is flesh; and that which is born of the Spirit is spirit" (John 3:6). The Son's office was that of sacrifice and substitution—"The good Shepherd layeth down his life for the sheep" (John 10:11); the Spirit's office was that of illumination—instruction—"But the Comforter, even the Holy Spirit, whom the Father will send in My name, He shall teach you all things, and bring to your remembrance all that I said unto you" (John 14:26). The Son's personal absence from the earth He declared to be a necessity to the Spirit's appearance in the church—"It is expedient for you that I go away; for if I go not away, the Comforter will not come unto you; but if I go, I will send Him unto you" (John 16:7).

If the plain references to the return of the Lord do not involve a personal coming, language has lost its meaning. For the comfort of His disciples, sorrowing over His approaching departure, He said, "If I go and prepare a place for you, I will come again." In the same discourse He said, "I will not leave you desolate: I will come unto you." The angels that attended Him in the ascension said to the anxious onlookers, "Ye men of Galilee, why stand ye looking into heaven? This Jesus, who was received up from you into heaven, shall so come in like manner as ye beheld Him going into heaven" (Acts 1:11).

It is little wonder, then, that Paul, writing to the Thessalonians, employs the phrase, "The Lord Himself shall descend from heaven, with a shout, with the voice of the archangel, and with the trump of God." There is not a hint in Scripture that the Lord is ever to be identified with death—which the Bible denominates an "enemy" to be eventually "destroyed" (1 Cor. 15:26). This attempt is, as Ottman suggests, a shift, by which some have sought to blunt the keen edge of Scripture. That Christ is representatively present in the world by the Spirit, no man disputes; but that there is another coming "for which we look," a revelation of His presence, which "every eye shall see," is the contention of the Book. Our hymnology—than which no truer theology has ever been written—sets that hope to sweetest harmony; and yet to tear the expectation of a personal return out of your best hymn-book would not leave it in such tatters as would be that more blessed Book—the Bible—when you had torn the same from its sacred pages.

THE TIME IS INDEFINITE; THE EVENT, IMMINENT. "Of that day and hour knoweth no one, not even the angels of heaven, neither the Son, but the Father only." But, "Be ye ready; for in an hour that ye think not the Son of man cometh." It is little wonder that Paul—perfectly familiar with his Lord's speech—should have written to Titus, concerning the grace of God, which had appeared, bringing salvation to all, "instructing us, to the intent that, denying ungodliness and worldly lusts, we should live soberly and righteously and godly in this present world; looking for the blessed hope and appearing of the glory of the great God and our Saviour Jesus Christ" (Tit. 2:12-13).

The wisdom of making this great event imminent, and the date of it indefinite, exists in the fact suggested by Baines, namely, that disciples were to be so living in the hope of it, that they would not be surprised if it occurred, while not so confidently dating it as to suffer disappointment in its delay. The argument that this event could not be "at hand" nearly two thousand years ago, and yet so remote as time has proven it to have been, ignores alike the difference between man's and God's computation of time, and the transcendency of the event. If, with God, "a thousand years are as a watch in the night when it is past," we see no difficulty in the Spirit's expression, "the time is at hand."

Again, the proportions of this event are such as to make that language not only permissible, but accurate. In the far West a carload of passengers were excited by the announcement, "We are coming to Shasta; look!" Windows were pushed up, men and women put out their heads, to behold that snow-capped peak, full before them. And yet, as one put it, "I rode on and on, from a little after break of day until high noon, and still we had not reached its base; and when the Western sun had dipped far toward the horizon, glancing backward, we beheld its bold, beautiful peak, glorious with the vesture of the sun." You could not have said that of a hill. A hill a mile away is not at hand; but one hundred and fifty miles away, and Shasta is "at hand." The second appearance of Jesus, as compared with the most important of human events, is so splendidly transcendent that no wonder those seers, realizing something of its mighty significance, should have lost the sense of distance and time, and exclaimed, "The day of the Lord draweth nigh!" or else, speaking for that Spirit who does not measure time by minutes and hours, but rather as it relates itself to eternity, say, "The Lord is at hand" (Phil. 4:15).

HIS COMING WILL PERFECTLY ACCORD WITH PROPHECY. For some time there has been a discussion in the premillennarian ranks as to whether the "any moment" theory of the second appearance could be retained; one school contending that that is a necessity of the interpretation of Scripture, and another that we can certainly recognize the fulfilment of prophecy, and that some portions of this, not having occurred already, must come to pass before we see in the heavens the "sign of the Son of man." This problem finds its solution in the very fact that the last letter of prophecy, named as preliminary to the Lord's appearance, may have its perfect fulfilment, and yet most professed Christian men fail so to mark the movements of time as to clearly recognize the perfecting of the divine plan. When Jesus appeared the first time, how few there were that saw in the Babe of Bethlehem the completion of prophecy! The visit of the star-led men from the East and the inquiry of the song-surprised shepherds seem to have found an answer in the faith of Simeon and Anna and in the fears of the criminal Herod, but to have left unmoved multitudes of men that were supposed to be the great Scripture students of the day.

Again, the certainty of a lapse of time between the coming of Christ for His people and His coming to the earth with them, cannot be disposed of by dubbing it "a theory created to meet a difficulty of the premillennarian view." There are two comings described in the twenty-fourth of

Matthew that are so absolutely unlike as to demand an explanation. That explanation is found in the fact that Christ comes for His saints (1 Thes. 4:16-17, and 2 Thes. 2:1); an appearance which is apart from "the coming of our Lord Jesus with all His saints" (1 Thes. 3:13), to take His throne and "judge the world in righteousness"; and to this period the Tribulation seems unquestionably assigned. The conversion of the Jew is at its close, and the "wars and rumors of wars, earthquakes, convulsions of nature," etc., both naturally and scripturally belong to the same time!

The full proof of these assertions I have published in "The Evolution of the Kingdom." But for the present, let the Word of the Lord Jesus instruct us, "For verily I say unto you, Till heaven and earth pass away, one jot or one tittle shall in no wise pass away from the law, till all things be accomplished" (Matt. 5:18). Dr. Arthur Pierson tells us that in 1884, when the transit of Venus was occurring, some German scientists, at Aiken, S. C., had drawn an elliptical circle upon a great stone, from which they made their observations. Later, they presented a request to the city that this stone might remain undisturbed until one hundred and twenty years had passed and another transit of Venus had occurred, at which time the then living scientists might make their observations and compare them with the work of 1884. Pierson reminds us that one hundred and twenty years is a long time; every throne will have been emptied of occupant after occupant, and the map of the world will have been made over; for aught we know, the march of the millennium may have begun; but prompt to the day, the hour, the minute, the transit of Venus will be on. Such is the accuracy of science! But again and again the even greater accuracy of prophecy has been put past dispute. Read Zechariah's description of the first appearance of Jesus in His triumphal entry into Jerusalem, "riding upon an ass, even upon a colt the foal of an ass," and remember this, that over seven hundred years intervened between the declaration and the deed. Generation after generation had passed; almost countless kings had been born to the various thrones of the earth; the little sentence, for the most part, was forgotten by even Bible students; and yet, in perfect accord with the Word of God, it came to pass. So it will be again when "His feet shall stand upon the Mount of Olives," and "His law shall come forth from Jerusalem," and His scepter shall extend "from sea to sea and from the river unto the ends of the earth," "for the mouth of the Lord hath spoken it."

THE FIRST RESURRECTION

IT WILL BE CONCURRENT WITH THE SAVIOUR'S APPEARANCE. "The Lord Himself shall descend from heaven with a shout, with the voice of the archangel, and with the trump of

God, and the dead in Christ shall rise first." The word "first" here simply assigns the resurrection of the righteous dead—when the "corruptible puts on incorruption"—to precedence over the marvelous change of the living saints—when "the mortal puts on immortality." The rest of the sentence, however, makes the return of the Lord and the resurrection of the saints concurrent events—the latter the instant resultant of the former. At the last trump that resurrection will occur "in a moment, in the twinkling of an eye" (1 Cor. 15:52). "Then they that are Christ's at His coming" (1 Cor. 15:23). A. J. Gordon truthfully remarks, "Any doctrine of the resurrection dissociated from the Advent, must be false; . . . no atonement apart from the cross; no resurrection apart from the coming." It is "at the coming of our Lord Jesus Christ that there is to be a gathering together unto Him" (2 Thes. 2:1).

IT WILL BE ACCOMPLISHED BY THE SAVIOUR'S VOICE. "The Lord Himself shall descend from heaven with a shout, with the voice of the archangel, and with the trump of God, and the dead in Christ shall rise first." It is doubtful if there be a great event of the future that has not already been enacted upon a small scale—an adumbration of that which is to come; it is equally to be questioned if there be a great truth that has not found its symbols in some circumstances of the past. The resurrection is no exception! The resuscitations of the New Testament are the shadows of the resurrection. They were accomplished, every one, by the Saviour's voice. To the widow's son He said, "Young man, I say unto thee, arise; and he that was dead sat up and began to speak" (Luke 7:14-15). To Jairus' daughter, "I say unto thee, arise. And straightway the damsel rose up and walked" (Mark 5:41-42), while to Lazarus, who had lain "four days in the grave, He cried with a loud voice, Lazarus, come forth; and he that was dead came forth" (John 11:43). It is said that Calhoun was unwilling to die until they should bear him again to the Senate chamber, that he might listen to Clay's voice once more—the voice he regarded as the most eloquent known to the tongue of man. But the voice of Christ will be so much more eloquent that by it the dying shall be revived and the dead quickened into life again. "The dead shall hear the voice of the Son of God; and they that hear shall live."

THE FIRST RESURRECTION WILL CONCERN ONLY THE SLEEPING SAINTS. "The dead in Christ" are all that are mentioned as having any part in this resurrection (1 Thes. 4:16). The explanation is at hand. "The rest of the dead lived not until the thousand years should be finished. This is the first resurrection. Blessed and holy is he that hath part in the first resurrection" (Rev. 20:5-6). It will require a more ingenious man than has yet employed tongue or driven pen to disprove the two resurrections of Scripture. The number of instances in which the first and second resurrections are spoken of, the easy explanation of such passages as Daniel 12:2 and John 5:28, together with the meaningful phrase "the resurrection clearly elective"—form the chain of argument which such men as Baines, Blackstone, Gordon, Brookes, West, and others too numerous to mention, have forged on the anvil of the Word. The translation of Daniel 12:2 by Tregelles, "And many from among the sleepers of the dust of the earth shall awake. These (that awake) shall be unto everlasting life. But those (the rest of the sleepers who awake later) shall be unto shame and everlasting contempt," instead of being "a theory created by a premillennarian to carry his point, and absolutely unknown to commentators," as one writer at least contends, is approved by such eminent rabbis as Saadia Haggion and Eben Ezra and employed by some of the best commentators, while the refusal to let the word "hour," in John 5:28-29, refer to at least as long a period as has already been covered by its use in John 4:23 and 5:25, reveals an indisposition to be convinced. However, the utter absurdity of straining, or spiritualizing Scripture is only reached when one opponent of two resurrections comes to treat Rev. 20:4-6, and contends that the first resurrection, there spoken of, is not that of persons at all, but of "principles," an interpretation which, as one has already suggested, would present the spectacle of "principles" being beheaded "for the witness of Jesus," "principles" refusing to worship the beast, "principles" with foreheads and hands on which they decline to receive a mark, and "principles" over "which the second death hath no power," but which shall be "priests of God and of Christ." Following this to its logical conclusion, "the rest of the dead" must also be "principles," so that we could have no resurrection of persons at all.

It is no argument against two resurrections to remind us that for centuries "reverent students of the Bible" knew nothing of it, any more than it is against the Great Commission, which, for the same length of time, was overlooked, neglected, and, when brought to light, ardently disputed. But to accept this biblical doctrine is to receive an inspiration to holy living such as that which characterized Paul, who, cutting loose from all things that bound him to the world, affirmed his willingness to count them all but loss, "if by any means he might attain unto the OUT-RESURRECTION FROM THE DEAD."

THE SUPREME RAPTURE

Returning to our preliminary sketch again, we find the apostle describing it in these words: "The dead in Christ shall rise first; then we that are alive, that are left, shall together with them be caught up in the clouds, to meet the Lord in the air: and so shall we ever be with the Lord."

Three features of the rapture are here clearly suggested. It will be signalized by the re-wedding of body and spirit; it will be characterized by the change of the mortal and the corruptible, and it will consummate the communion of the saints and the Saviour.

IT WILL BE SIGNALIZED BY THE REWEDDING OF BODY AND SPIRIT. The clear significance of the phrase "even so also them that are fallen asleep in Jesus will God bring with Him," is to the effect that "the spirits of just men made perfect" are now with God. But their bodies lie buried in sea and on land. Our coming Christ will bring the spirits down with Him, and at the sound of His voice the graves shall give up their dead. And when the body and the spirit, divorced by the last enemy, meet in the presence of our Master, He, by His word, will so wed them together that neither man nor devil will ever again divide them asunder. If one could conceive the glory that shall clothe these bodies of ours, when, redeemed from humiliation, they are "conformed to the likeness" of our Lord, and the splendor that shall mark our "spirits"—"made perfect"—he would somewhat realize the meaning of the eternal marriage of the two. This is the hour, and the event, of which the apostle wrote to the Romans—"The earnest expectation of the creation waiteth for the revealing of the sons of God, . . . for we know that the whole creation groaneth and travaileth in pain together until now; and not only so, but ourselves also, who have the firstfruits of the Spirit, even we ourselves groan within ourselves, waiting for our adoption, to wit, the redemption of our bodies." It is little wonder, therefore, that an Old Testament prophet, who was speaking to quicken Israel—"dead in trespasses and in sins"—should have expressed the very thought that will characterize that glad hour when the voice of the Son shall proclaim the approaching rapture; and men shall know the more remote and more blessed meaning of Isaiah's words, "Awake and sing, ye that dwell in the dust, for thy dew is as the dew of herbs, and the earth shall cast out her dead" (26:19). We have read Ingraham's "Prince of the House of David," and have tried to imagine the joy of that marriage occasion when Lazarus, whose recent decease had thrown every participant into pitiful sorrow, now resuscitated, lends, by his living presence, such surpassing happiness as no wedding party had ever before experienced; but we confess frankly that the joy of the hour when all perfected spirits and all glorified bodies shall be joined by the word of the Lord Jesus cannot be compassed by the imagination! RAPTURE is the word.

IT WILL BE CHARACTERIZED BY THE CHANGE OF THE MORTAL AND THE CORRUPTIBLE. "The dead shall be raised incorruptible, and we shall be changed. For this corruptible must put on incorruption, and this mortal must put on immortality. So when this corruptible shall have put on incorruption and this mortal shall have put on immortality, then shall come to pass the saying that is written, Death is swallowed up in victory." What an hour! At that moment those that have come out of their graves, in the full realization of their eternal conquest, will almost tauntingly ask of their defeated foe, "O grave, where is thy victory?" while those that have not slept, but, by the coming of Christ the Master, have put on their immortality, will voice their conscious triumph in the speech, "O death, where is thy sting?" and sing their joy in the sentence, "Thanks be to God, which giveth us the victory through our Lord Jesus Christ." Dr. Gordon's comparison, "The charcoal and the diamond are the same substance; only that one is carbon in its humiliation and the other carbon in its glory; so is this tabernacle in which we now dwell, in comparison with our house which is from heaven," is not only full of beauty, but biblically justified. When, however, one comes to speak of the saints perfected in body, soul and spirit, there are no objects of earth with which to liken them. Jesus said, "They are equal unto the angels and are sons of God, being sons of the resurrection" (Luke 20:36).

IT WILL CONSUMMATE THE COMMUNION OF THE SAINTS AND THE SAVIOUR. The phrase "shall together with them be caught up in the clouds to meet the Lord in the air, and so shall we ever be with the Lord" involves a twofold communion—the communion of one with another, and of all with their Lord. The closeness of that communion, and the sweetness of that fellowship finds no expression sufficient, short of the marriage relation. "They that were ready went in with him to the marriage feast" (Matt. 25:10). It is little wonder that on the consummation of this event there should be heard the voice of a great multitude as the voice of many waters, and as the voice of mighty thunder, saying, "Hallelujah, for the Lord our God, the Almighty reigneth; let us rejoice and be exceeding glad. And let us give the glory unto Him, for the marriage of the Lamb is come and His wife hath made herself ready" (Rev. 10:6-7). We confess frankly that when all of this imagery of prophetic promise passes before one's mind, he begins to understand the spirit and speech of Samuel Rutherford, who, while he languished in prison at Aberdeen, divided his time between singing God's praises on the one side, and pleading for the reappearance of His Son on the other, and we marvel not at his speech: "O fairest among the sons of men; why stayest thou so long away? O heavens, move fast! O time, run, run, and hasten the marriage day! for love is tormented with delays!"

THE GOSPEL FOR WAR TIMES

Rev. W. B. Riley, D.D.

Mr. Moderator and Brethren of the Ministry: I have elected to speak to you to-day on the war-gospel, and I ask your thought to Matt. 24:14: "This gospel of the kingdom shall be preached in all the world for a witness unto all the nations; and then shall the end come."

The question of whether there be a "gospel for war times" is one too important to be despised and too insistent to be dismissed. The minister of the present moment cannot be indifferent to the crisis into which the world has come, and the consequent demands being made upon the church of God. Prof. T. G. Soares says: "There are two immediately possible attitudes for the minister to-day. One is to preach the old gospel, and the other is to curse the Kaiser. One is to go on in the performance of one's pulpit duty as if nothing was happening; and the other is to become a patriot orator. In one case you say that religion is more important than any changing human interest; and you will lead men to a salvation that is unaffected by the tragedy of the hour. In the other case you say that winning the war is the supreme interest to which everything, including religion, must give way." In his judgment, "either of these courses is an abdication of the pulpit"!

If "preaching the old gospel," then, becomes an abdication of the pulpit, some of us would not hesitate to pay the price for that privilege, preferring a dry goods box on a street corner with that gospel to a carpeted pulpit in a sanctuary without it. But, at the same time, we insist that the old gospel is not inadequate to the crisis to which we have come; and that its true exponents and veritable prophets have a definite and needful message for a sinful world, weltering in the blood of its slain.

The declarations of Scripture are never best interpreted by an utter detachment from all context. When Jesus anticipated the very hour to which we have come, of "wars and rumors of wars"; when He saw "nation rising against nation, and kingdom against kingdom"; when, with prophetic vision, He sat in the midst of "famine and pestilence and earthquake," and realized that all of these were but "the beginning of sorrows"; when He remembered the agony to which His own brethren in the flesh—the Jews—and many of His own faithful followers, were to come; when He saw the hatred that would one day be engendered and the destroying one of another that would be accomplished; when He reminded Himself that these things would take place on a day when "false prophets" would be multiplied, and multitudes of plain people would be "deceived" by other gospels, that were not other; when He looked to the beginning of the twentieth century, where iniquity should conquer and "the love of most should grow cold"—having it all fall upon His vision, He then said, "And this gospel of the kingdom shall be preached in all the world for a witness unto all the nations; and then shall the end come."

To three things He definitely refers in that text—The War-Gospel; the Age-Witness; and the Age-Windup. Within the limitations of our time, I may get through with only one of these:

THE WAR GOSPEL

In the judgment of many of us, there is a specific gospel for this special hour. Yesterday, when the world was at peace, the gospel of grace—whether it received it or not—deserved the ascendency; to-day, when the kingdoms of this world are in the clash of battle and the confusion of bloodshed, when their future is as uncertain as their merits are unstable, it is the time to preach "the gospel of the kingdom." The definition of "the gospel of the kingdom" we defer till later; but certain characteristics of the same deserve to be set in order. Certain characteristics of the old gospel are needed now as never before. To three of these we call attention.

It is a gospel that exalts the divine Christ rather than human culture. For something like fifty years the drift of the age has been in the wrong direction; and for twenty-five years past, the influence of Darwinism has been increasingly felt, and the result has been an ever increasing laudation of Adam—the sinful man—and a corresponding depreciation of Christ—the saving Man. In no country in the world have these counter-philosophies marked such progress as in Germany! There Darwinism has found its most ardent followers; "kultur" its most capable exponents and defenders; and there the claims of Christ have been most seriously called into question, and the "faith once for all delivered" most effectually de-vitalized. Dr. Shields, of Toronto, remarks: "It will be generally conceded that no nation in the world has surpassed Germany in her educational zeal. As an illustration of the thoroughness of her system, I may tell you that in 1901, of more than one-quarter million recruits, only 131, or less than one-half of one per cent, were found to be illiterate. No nation has given more attention to higher education than Germany. She has more than twenty universities, and in the winter of 1907-8 there were in these nearly 47,000 students," and that number later increased. For a full century her one objective has been "kultur"! That she has realized that objective is now painfully evident to the entire world. Within recent years certain Americans have been "daffy" over one word—"Efficiency." For its full meaning we may look to the constitution of the German army, and as the culture of the Jewish scribe and the effectiveness of the Roman soldier once combined to nail Christ to the cross, so Modernism—the intellectual boast of the centuries—and Militarism

—the acme of mechanical accomplishment—have alike triumphed in Germany, and have combined to strike Christianity the most deadly blow it has received since the day when Augustine united a sick church with a stinking State.

Prof. Herbert Williams, of Oxford, declares that Friedrich Nietzsche was perhaps "the one European thinker who has carried the evolution principles and ethics to their logical conclusion." And he names him as the most orthodox exponent of Darwinian ideas the world has known. But Prof. Williams reminds us also that Nietzsche saw clearly that, to be successful, evolution ethics must involve "the transvaluation of all values and the demoralization of all ordinary morality," and he says that Nietzsche "accepted frankly the glorification of brute strength, superior cunning, and all the qualities necessary for success in the struggle for existence." Multitudes of men in America, England, and other parts of the civilized world, crazed with the desire to be counted "cultured," have received Nietzsche's philosophy and become its apostles. They do not even now see that Bernhardi, when he contends that, "since Germany is the most civilized nation in the world, she is the only one fitted for leadership and entitled to supremacy," is but taking the logical step of putting that philosophy into practice and bringing into the world again the philosophy that once embruted men, de-virtued women, and destroyed nations; namely, that "Might is right," or "the survival of the fittest."

It is a philosophy that strikes truth to the earth, exiles righteousness from civilization, and, as another has said, "leaves justice weaponless, blind and bleeding on the field over which battle has passed; and honor like Tamar, who, in token of the shame of her violation, with ashes on her head, her garments rent, lays her hand upon her head and passes out of the presence" of men, sobbing as she goes.

If the damnable, dastardly deeds of German "kultur" do not awaken the unthinking world to the realization of the fact that brutal man is unfitted to rule it, then we have a fresh demonstration of the fact that the human mind is too fallen to ever right itself and the human heart too prostitute to be instructed even by unspeakable suffering.

And yet, at the very time when the page of history is such a blot of blood that one cannot even read from it "the signs of the times," a man has the effrontery to stand up in a pulpit and in the name of "Modernism" ask us to sing with Swinburne, "Glory to man in the highest," saying, "For man is the master of all things"; and, in order to give poetical afflatus to his heretical philosophy, measures it off in feet, expressing it in verse:

"Spirit of Man, ascend thy throne!
Men, cities, nations, wait for thee;
Wan captives cry, dull toilers groan—
Hearken! Arise, and set them free.

> Before all pride of rank and race,
> Beyond all pomps that flourish now,
> Beneath all shams, all commonplace,
> Above all empires, Man, are thou!"

It is a doctrine of devils!

Again, the old gospel is a gospel of divine redemption versus human democracy. For full two thousand years the best instructed Bible students the world has known have anticipated the day when kingdoms and autocracies should perish from the face of the earth. They have read Daniel, and, looking into past history, they have seen how the Babylonian empire passed, as he foretold; how the Medo-Persian took its place, as he declared it would; how the Greco-Macedonian came in the very order symbolized by the belly and thighs of brass; and how at last the Roman, that iron monarchy, arose, and then, as the legs of a man, divided and established a capitol at Constantinople in the east and one at Rome in the west, and how out of that empire little kingdoms came, as the toes grow from the feet; and they have known that the vision was not ended. The time is yet to come when "the Stone cut out of the mountain top"—the place of the divine residence—"without hands"—no human power having aught to do with its appearance—will be cast against "the kingdoms of this world" and "grind them to powder," and they will be swept from it as the chaff parts from the threshing-floor before the rising breath of the evening wind.

But now we have a new philosophy to the effect that when the kingdoms pass away

A DEMOCRACY

is to take their place, and we are told that its value is such that we can afford to purchase it with the blood of our boys if it take the last of them from the land. If our great and noble President has breathed a single sentence that is likely to make his name immortal, it is this, namely, "Make the world safe for democracy." With that sentiment we have no controversy; but who will rise, and when will he come, to make *democracy safe for the world?* The world has long had its democracies, and we admit that, on the whole, they have been more satisfactory than autocracies. But if the man has never yet been born who, apart from God, could guide his own steps aright, how can any thinking man imagine that when you multiply him into thousands and millions, power will be imparted by the multiplication; and "the enmity against God," which belongs to the old nature, will be reduced, if not destroyed, by addition?

Unless the democracy that now seeks ascendency in the world comes into the hands of men who are redeemed by "the blood of the Son of God," we shall be no more safe under its supremacy than the Armenians are safe in the hands of the unspeakable Turk, or Belgians are safe in the captivity of the country which has kept the profession of godliness, but whose leaders have crucified afresh and put to an open shame the Christ of the Gospels. For full twenty-five years I have listened to a never-ending refrain in favor of "a social gospel," and have given hours of fleshly weariness and mental disgust to famed orators who repudiated "the shed blood" while they pleaded for the service of man to man—asking for higher salaries, fewer tenement houses, finer education equipments, more adequate appliance of mechanical devices, and, above all, flowers in the front yards and gardens against back walls. I should be a brute not to desire these things for every faithful citizen; but I should count myself a sacred fool to suppose they could ever be made a substitute for the gospel of the shed blood which atones for sin, and while entertaining such thought I could never turn my mind to Germany without an intellectual rebuke. Her people have been well cared for; poverty has not cursed them; education has not been lacking; entertainment has been provided for all classes; they have had their flowers in the front yards and their gardens at the back walls. But their leaders have denied the deity of Christ; they have disputed the authority of the Bible; they have dethroned God and put the spirit of Germany in His seat; and while doing it they have lifted "the lid off hell" and permitted that evil caldron of the universe to pour its fumes of living death and its lava streams of destruction. Since entering the ministry I have ceased not to declare the necessity of redemption;

but this day of war has impressed me with that need as never before, and I feel impelled to plead with my brethren in the ministry not to permit the modern voices to lead them to substitute democracy for the divinely appointed plan of divine REDEMPTION, lest just when we think we are honoring Christ we discover we have enthroned the Antichrist.

And yet once more: This old gospel is an appeal to sacrificial versus selfish living. Its noble Founder came "not to be ministered unto but to minister, and give His life a ransom for many." Thomas Tiplady has written a most readable book entitled, "The Cross at the Front." In that he makes a plea for such a chivalrous religion as our citizen soldiers are certain to require, and he reminds us of the fact that the first and finest expression of Christianity is love. "God is love"! "Love is the fulfilling of the law"! Love is Christ's acme of all virtues! According to Christianity, of "faith, hope and love, these three, the greatest of these is love"! And he tells us that if we love we shall not be self-seeking. And he tells us the truth! And yet ministers rise up and say, "See what a religion we have; and how much of it! Look at the sacrifices men are making now in defense of the weak of the earth, in help of the helpless! See big England and great America stand by their bleeding little sister—Belgium—and defend her with their lives!" God forbid that I should speak aught that would detract from the true glory of genuine heroes, or take from the heroism that is in the defense of helpless nations; but, on the other hand, let us not practice a self-defense and join it so easily to self-applause. England well knew that if she went not to Belgium's defense her own borders would be invaded; and America has come slowly to the conviction that if she joined not the Allies she would fight with Germany alone when once that brute force had finished with her close neighbors; and whatever the magnitude of our heroism, we can hardly claim that it is unselfish. Had it been wholly unselfish, it would not have been so tardy in its expression! I thank God for the work of the Red Cross! I count it an evidence of the salt of Christianity in modern society. I thank God for the ministry of the Y. M. C. A.! It is God's medium of ameliorating human suffering. I thank God for ministers who offer their services to government as soldiers and chaplains, combined. By their presence and their preaching, more of morals will be retained and Christ will be better known at the battle-front. But I cannot forget that we have long had equal occasion of heroism and have neglected it, and equal opportunity of sacrifice and have despised it, because our profession of Christianity has not been sufficiently sincere to make it, like its Lord, sacrificial. Many a Londoner is giving millions now to wage war against Germany, who, five years ago, walked into his palace at night and forgot the thin, pale faces of East End children; forgot the ragged, starving mothers, who slept not because hunger was a mortal agony; and unpaid fathers, who faced a monthly deficit that made it impossible properly to feed and keep the child at school. Thomas Tiplady says, "I had a stray dog in my tent to-night and offered her buttered toast and she declined it; but where in East London is a child that would turn away from buttered toast? When at Christmas time we gave them bread spread with jam, and cheap cake, they stuffed themselves like ravenous wolves and then, by stealth, hid what they could under their clothing." And Thomas Tiplady adds, "The faces of those children haunt me as the horrible sights on the Somme have never done and can never do." Who that has lived in New York or Chicago has lacked opportunity of chivalry and self-sacrifice?

For years our foreign mission boards have pleaded for more money and the Macedonian cry has been a wail coming to us from every country; and yet men have gone on hoarding millions, not much disturbed; and churches have been complacent and content with contributing pennies and nickels and dimes to the unwelcome contribution box that glided past the noses of comfortably seated pew-renters; and now that the time has come when the Government taxes everything we have, and the world-war compels us to put up our thousands and millions, we would much like to congratulate ourselves with the idea that we are a great and generous and unselfish people; but, unfortunately, the facts of yesterday face the effrontery of to-day, and if it were less bigoted it would not boast, but often blush with shame.

Has it ever occurred to us that when the great day of the final judgment comes, Jesus may say, "I was in the trenches and you sent Me no socks; I faced the French winter and ye had knitted Me no sweaters; My ears were bitten with frost and you forgot to provide Me a helmet," but it is settled He will say, "I was an hungered and ye gave Me no meat; thirsty, and ye gave Me no drink. I was a stranger and ye took me not in; naked and ye clothed Me not; sick and in prison and ye visited me not."

Let no auditor *dare* to say that I have spoken aught against adequate and sacrificial provision for the soldiers. My own lads are among them, two from my family and one hundred from my church. I could not endure to have them neglected. One hundred of my young men and women are in the battle-line; I should be ashamed to minister to my church if it for one moment forgot them, and I should not forgive myself if one of them were hungry and cold and I did not share in the sacrifice essential to his comfort; but what I am trying to burn into the hearts of men and blister my own heart with at one and the same time, is this fact, viz., that every church in the world and every Christian man on earth is daily situated in the midst of sacrificial opportunities, and in proportion as we accept the Spirit of Jesus Christ, the selfishness that has been our weakness and that threatens even to work our personal and collective ruin, we will put away, and will wage that greater war against the devil and all his agencies, with all our might, for, however we may hate the German atrocities, we cannot forget that they are but a single feature of the age-long and world-wide war that Satan wages against God and righteousness. Our greatest war is not with the Kaiser and Germany, it is with the devil and hell; and the old gospel—the Book—is our only effective instrument of battle.

I could wish for time to develop the other points mentioned:

THE WORLD-WITNESS

Let me just outline in conclusion. The ministerial mind will see the possibilities. "This gospel of the kingdom (Christ's kingdom) shall be preached."

1. That witness should be in the language of the Word and the power of the Spirit.

2. That witness will only be borne by true and intelligent believers.

3. That witness will, however, be carried to the world's borders.

"Then shall the end come."

THE AGE-WINDUP

1. It will for ever end Satanic sovereignty.
2. It will abolish human government.
3. It will establish Theocracy in the earth.

"The mouth of the Lord hath spoken it."

QUESTIONS AND ANSWERS

Noon Session, Thursday, May 30, 1918. Conducted by

REV. W. B. RILEY, D.D.

WRITTEN QUESTIONS

Brethren, I come to-day, as you understand, I think, not to make any address at all, but to answer some questions that have been submitted in writing. The number is not great, and I think I may be able to take them up in a very brief time.

Ques. 1. "What is the best point of contact to discuss the gospel of the second coming with the higher critics?"

Ans. The point of Bible teaching! It is the only point or basis on which to proceed. I don't think it much worth while to engage in debate if the Bible is ruled out. The whole question is a Biblical question; that is why it is amazing to me for an international man to write upon the subject, "Will Christ Come Again?" and never quote a text. I thought this was a matter of Biblical discussion, and I still believe it.

Ques. 2. "Will you define the difference between the kingdom of God, and the kingdom of heaven?"

Ans. I do not think there is any difference! The phraseology in the New Testament covering these points uses the terms interchangeably. The kingdom of God looks to government, the kingdom of heaven refers to the character of that kingdom, and yet you will find them employed interchangeably.

Ques. 3. "Can the church hasten or delay the coming of the Lord? If so, please explain."

Ans. We have already given proof to the world that we can delay it! I do believe we can hasten it. I think there is a divine program, but human instrumentalities are involved in the question. Dr. MacInnis referred to the fact that Christ is waiting for the church to do the work assigned to it. I am quite confident that what we have done here, these three days, has to do with hastening the return. I am equally confident, too, that one on a foreign mission field or any one doing the work of God in any way has something to do with His return. This gospel of the kingdom shall be preached in all the world for a witness, and then shall the end of this age come, and Christ with it. We call people out; we hasten His coming!

Ques. 4. "Are there prophecies that must be fulfilled before He can come?"

Ans. A study of that Book will show you that some remarkable things will yet come to pass; perhaps the most of them after the church is caught away, and a readjustment of national alliances occurs, such as will not come until that time. History may then move so rapidly as to amaze men in the utter fulfilment of the last word of prophecy.

Ques. 5. "Are not people baptized in the Holy Spirit to-day in the same way as on the day of Pentecost, which was evidenced then by speaking with other tongues?"

Ans. I think I know what this writer is driving at! If I had a copy of my pamphlet here, "Speaking with Tongues," I would give it to him. I believe tongues came at that time as one result of the Spirit. I do not find in my Bible anywhere that tongues are an essential sign of the Spirit, upon which the Spirit's presence or power depends. I do find that the 14th chapter of First Corinthians, the one chapter in the New Testament devoted wholly to tongues, says some things that I have not seen regarded as yet in the so-called tongues movement. Among other things, it says this: that not more than three of those who have received tongues are to speak in any one meeting, and they are not to speak except an interpreter be present, and when they speak they are to speak in order and not two at a time. And I have not seen many cases where those three instances were regarded. I believe in the gift of tongues. I believe it will come again. I find also, that according to the same apostle, instead of being the absolute, essential proof of the Spirit, it is mentioned as one of the least of the gifts of the Spirit—"to be able to speak five words in a known tongue is better than ten thousand in an unknown tongue." I think there have possibly been in the movement some instances of genuine tongues. I have had occasion to scientifically demonstrate that there is spurious work in it.

Ques. 16. "Is the church synonymous with the kingdom?"

Ans. Never! I do not exactly know what you mean by that; but I think you will find it an absolute fact, that your Bible never identifies the church with the kingdom. They are different words and are always so used. One of them, the church, grows up in the world, is growing now, and has been since the days of Pentecost—and even the plans for it, in Israel, for that matter. The other is set up, and it is a different word that is employed with reference to its coming into being. One of them, the church, is of the present. Dr. Lummis, the great Methodist scholar, says that, while there are many instances of references to the kingdom in the future, and some tenses that are indefinite in describing it, there is not in your whole Testament one single instance of its being spoken of in the past tense, as a thing already accomplished. The kingdom is a future thing; that is why the Lord taught us to pray, "Thy kingdom come." But He followed it with a definition which destroys its identity with the church. "Thy will be done on earth as it is in heaven." That is the definition of the kingdom. The kingdom is not made up of flesh and blood. They cannot inherit the kingdom of God. The church is made up of flesh and blood. A rich man cannot enter into the kingdom; he can get into the church with little difficulty. Church and kingdom are never identified in the Word. People confuse them. Make a study of this matter, and differentiate where the Bible does. The church will be more powerful when that discovery is made!

Ques. 7. "In what place of the earth will Jesus be during the millennium?"

Ans. In every place, I suspect. I imagine that His rulership will be from Jerusalem. I am disposed to think, as a rule, the Scriptures say what they mean and mean what they say, and yet I am not disposed to imagine He is kept there in His risen body. He exhibited ubiquitous ability by His risen presence that He did not have in His earthly body.

Ques. 8. "Will all human government cease during the reign of Jesus?"

Ans. Yes, except that which is subsidiary to Him. He will be solitary King. But His saints will reign with Him. That is human government. They will have places and power of authority.

Ques. 9. "Will the world continue to be populated?"

Ans. Yes; I used to think that the world was going to be destroyed. I studied the language on that! Peter tells us that it is going to be destroyed by fire, but he also said that it had been destroyed by water. That did not put it out of existence. Simply wiped the old generation off the earth, and I am confident that the earth itself will be indestructible. Science says nothing can be destroyed. That is exactly why annihilation is not in the Word of God, as it is not in science. You can change its form, but "one generation follows another and the earth abideth for ever."

Ques. 10. "If the Lord came for His saints this moment, what time would elapse before He returned to reign?"

Ans. I think without doubt if you study the Scriptures, you will find it stated clearly enough that our Lord will come first for His saints, and later with them. I will come to that later. In the second appearance of the Lord, after the saints are taken, there is a period of three and a half years in which the Antichrist is doing his devilish work on the face of the earth—1260 days, spoken of as three and a half years; forty and two months, and time, times and half a time. All of them are the same, according to the Jewish calendar. A period of tribulation in which the real character of the Antichrist will be discovered. Back of that time he will be so smooth a citizen that the world will wonder after him and the nations will receive him with acclaim, and the greatest democracy, apparently, that the world ever had, will come to pass, and men will be delighted until his real character is revealed, and that will be revealed, I think, after the church is taken away. By persecutions, bloodshed, death, he will continue until Christ Himself shall reappear with His saints and destroy him.

Ques. 11. "Please state the strongest proof from the Scripture regarding the two stages of the second coming of Christ—the coming for, and the coming with, the saints."

Ans. I am not particularly anxious to debate. The church is not to go through the Tribulation, although I think we may see some dark things on the earth before it is caught away. Scriptures in favor of the escape from the Tribulation seem to me to be Daniel 12:1; Isa. 26:20-21; 1 Cor. 15:51-53; 1 Thess. 4:17; Luke 17:31-37; Rev. 12:6; and Rev. 3:10.

Ques. 12. "In the light of hope of the near return of the Lord, and considering the fact that our citizenship is involved, should ministers have anything to do with politics? Should they vote?"

Ans. I vote with a vengeance, and I fight for sobriety with all the ability that is in me. I have had three debates in my life. One was a liquor fight in my city. We won the fight, defeated the opposition, and knocked out a portion of the saloon section of the town; and I would do it again if I were back there. When I read articles from brethren saying we have another and a higher mission, I confess to you I hardly know who is the right man. We are citizens of this earth, and yet at the same time we have a citizenship in heaven. Paul had a citizenship in heaven. Yet when time to use it, he referred to his Roman citizenship and employed it to the utmost. We have to regard the dual citizenship. Men who live correctly will produce more results than all the voters that go to the polls. I do not think Christ ever voted. It is difficult to prove that He had anything to do with politics of His day. Yet the life of Christ has changed the politics of the centuries.

Ques. 13. "Is there any Bible testimony concerning the so-called ten lost tribes?"

Ans. I don't know!

Ques. 14. "Seeing the Holy Spirit came when the Lord Jesus went away, will He, the Holy Spirit, be withdrawn from the world when the Lord returns?"

Ans. I don't think so. The Spirit was in the world before Jesus went away. A special baptism of the Spirit was promised with reference to His ascension, and it came. Those who listened to Dr. Gregg will not need to ask this. In the last days the first nation to receive a baptism will be the Jewish nation. He will then also pour out His Spirit upon all flesh, and I am inclined to think that is going to be the way in the millennial period. What a time, when the devil is in the pit and the Spirit of God is poured out on all flesh! Every tongue will confess to His glory. As a lad about eighteen years of age, I was in Cincinnati, visiting some cousins. They said, "William, would you like to hear a preacher from Kentucky preach?" I listened to the minister. He was about three inches taller than I am, straight as an Indian, with black hair, and he said, "Brethren, when I get through with my ministry here, I am going to hell to preach to the spirits in prison and lead them to heaven." I was amazed! I never heard anything like it. The longer I think about it, the less it impresses me—favorably. It is hard to win souls in Minneapolis, and it is worse in St. Paul. Excuse me from the endeavor in hell.

Ques. 15. "Will Jesus deliver up the kingdom to the Father when He comes?"

Ans. The kingdom is not, until Jesus comes; it is not the Father's when He comes, but when He has reigned a thousand years. When He has consummated His endeavor on earth! It is at the end, not at the beginning.

Ques. 16. "You said that the words kingdom and church were never synonymous. 'Ye must be born again, or ye cannot see the kingdom of God.' Does not that refer to the church of God?"

Ans. Not at all! Unregenerate men get into the church easily. But they cannot enter the kingdom!

Ques. 17. "What are you going to do with the teaching that is abroad at the present day, that the church has no right to pray the Lord's Prayer in these days—that that is for the Jews?"

Ans. I have never taken that position, so I do not have anything to do with that.

Ques. 18. "Is the Lord to be continually visible during the thousand years?"

Ans. I suspect so; I know of no reason why He should not be.

Ques. 19. "My question is this: Will there be any sin, sorrow, and death during the millennium?"

Ans. Yes. I will give you proof. There can be sin, sorrow, and death during the millennium. First, 1 Corinthians 15 says, He shall reign "until

He has put down all rule and all authority and all power." Rule and authority and power, put down by Christ, must be rule and authority and power that oppose Christ or it would not be put down. He is going to put it down. Second, God's Book contains an absolute program, and you never hear Him say that there will be no sin, no sorrow, no death, in the 20th chapter of the Book of Revelation. The moment you have had that judgment over, heaven breaks—21st chapter—eternity begins, and for the first time it is stated that there shall be no sickness, sorrow, nor pain, nor any more death.

Ques. 20. "In Ezekiel 38 to 39, does Germany figure at all, as was indicated yesterday?"

Ans. Well, this much may be said on that subject. I was profoundly interested yesterday. A while ago, when I had no reason in the world to believe that Russia would break from the Allies, I gave myself one week, when I was on a train most of the week, to constant study of the prophecies along that line, and I said to Mrs. Riley that there is one striking thing about this business. If these prophecies are clear to me, it looks like Germany is there in the "North Country," and Russia is tied up with her.

Ques. 21. "Whom do you think the harlot woman mentioned in the gospel is?"

Ans. I don't know. Some contend that it is Rome. I think some features of Rome, but more than Rome!

Ques. 22. "In the hymn which we sing,

'All hail the power of Jesus' name,
Let angels prostrate fall.
Bring forth the royal diadem
And crown Him Lord of all.'

do you believe Jesus' name is the antecedent of Him? Does it mean that Jesus Himself shall be crowned Lord of all? I thought the Father would be crowned Lord of all.''

Ans. Both. Christ will be crowned Lord of all for one thousand years, until He has subjected all to Himself, then He will turn over all to God the Father, and Himself become subject, so the Word says. See 1 Cor. 15:24.

THE LORD'S RETURN

REV. J. WILBUR CHAPMAN, D.D.

Former Moderator of the General Assembly of the Presbyterian Church in the U. S. A.

A BRIEF NOONDAY ADDRESS DELIVERED AT THE GARRICK THEATER

Of course everybody who believes in the Lord at all believes in His coming back again to earth to reign upon the earth. There are some who say, however, that He is coming after the world is prepared for Him, and that therefore the gospel must be preached and His kingdom set up, and being set up He will come to take His throne.

There are others who believe that the world can only be made better by His personal return, and that when He comes the world will be as God intended it should be. His throne will then be established. He will overthrow unrighteousness and will be crowned King of kings and Lord of lords.

I personally accept the second view; to hold to the first would certainly cause one to be very much discouraged, for with all the preaching that we have done, with all our foreign missionary work, with all the churches established, we find practically the entire world at war and there never has been such sorrow and so many heart-breakings as to-day.

I did not always hold to my present position. I was never taught very much about the Lord's return when I was in preparation for the ministry, and it was not until after I was in the pastorate that I came in touch with a wonderful woman who was a member of my household and of my church as well: Mrs. Agnes P. Strain, and she it was who gave me my first instruction in what has ever since been to me a blessed hope. It has been the inspiration of my ministry and it is a blessed hope to me because it has inspired me in my evangelistic work.

Some people say that to believe in the Lord's near return is to cut the nerve of Christian effort, but this could hardly be true when we realize that this was the belief of John Wesley, of C. H. Spurgeon, of D. L. Moody, of A. J. Gordon, and of a multitude of other men who still live and work. Indeed, I do not know of any men in all the world who are more diligent in season and out of season than the so-called premillennarians. I believe that the church is an elect body, and that some day the body will be completed, or, to change the figure, the house will be completed; and when the last one comes home, then the Lord will come back again. And I have not preached a sermon in years without thinking, as I have been preaching, that perhaps I may have the privilege at this time of leading the last one home, and so I have preached with special zeal.

The true believer in the Lord's return accepts the Bible as the inspired Word of God; believes in the deity of the Lord Jesus Christ; is loyal to the church; and is of course loyal to the Government.

This is a blessed hope also to me because at any moment the Lord may come back again, and should He come, sorrow will cease, wars will be at an end, troubles will be for ever over, loved ones will be united.

I do not know when He is coming; the Bible does not say, and I dare not theorize.

"It may be at morn when the day is awaking,
When sunlight through darkness and shadow is breaking,
That Jesus will come in the fulness of glory,
To receive from the world His own."

We sometimes hear people say that such and such a thing is certain as death. Death is by no means certain. I do not at all know that I shall die. I know that God's Word tells me that "the Lord Himself shall descend from heaven with a shout, with the voice of the archangel, and with the trump of God: and the dead in Christ shall rise first."

Then I am told that "we which are alive . . . shall be caught up . . . to meet the Lord in the air: so shall we ever be with the Lord."

"Oh joy, oh delight, should we go without dying,
No sickness, no sadness, no dread, and no crying!
Caught up through the clouds with our Lord into glory,
When Jesus receives His own."

It is a blessed hope to me because it settles questions for me which otherwise I could not settle at all. I should be confused regarding the judgments did I not believe in the Lord's near return. I never expect to stand in judgment for my sins. Why should I? for He was judged for me. As a matter of fact there are four judgments. One took place when He hung upon the cross in my stead. The other is to take place when His own stand face to face with Him and they are judged, not for their sins, but for the works they have done, whether they be good or evil. Another is to take place when He will gather all the nations before Him; but it is to be noticed that in this judgment there is no mention of anyone that is dead. Another is to take place at the great white throne, when the dead, small and great, stand before Him; but it is to be noticed that here there is no mention of anything that is living.

I should not know what to do with the Jew except for this blessed hope. Believing in my Lord's return and in all the truth that accompanies it, I know that the Jew will go back to Jerusalem in unbelief; indeed, he is going back now; and I also know that finally when the Lord comes and they look upon Him whom they have pierced, then a nation shall be born in a day, the Jew will recognize Him as the Messiah and turn to Him in faith.

I could wish for my friends no greater joy than that which is mine in the thought that He is coming back and may come soon. I do not think it has ever made me fanatical; I do not see how it could.

This is a blessed hope to me because "every man that hath this hope in him purifieth himself even as He is pure." It does not mean every man that hath this hope in himself, but in Jesus as the Son of God, and in His near return. The thought that He is coming back again keeps one pure, for how could we be worldly and indifferent if at any moment He might appear? So I am looking for Him and longing for Him, and as I look and long, I toil the best I know how.

I can think of no one truth that would bring more zeal to the minister, more power to the church, more joy to the children of God, than the thought that the Lord might soon return again to this earth.

So I'm watching and I'm waiting
Each moment of the day,
For it may be morn or evening
When He calleth me away.
And it makes the day go faster
And its trials easier borne,
When I'm saying every moment:
To-day the Lord may come.

I am glad to have my name associated with those who have called this great Conference. I am glad for the thrill of these wonderful meetings. I have felt nothing like it in years, if indeed ever before in my life. I think our Lord is greatly honored by what has been said in the various addresses. I only regret that I have been unavoidably detained from many of the sessions of the Conference. I honestly believe that there has been no more significant gathering of Christians in a generation.

With all my heart I find myself saying, "Lord Jesus, come quickly." I cannot help but think that our Lord is soon to return. There are unmistakable signs of some great crisis not far removed, and I like to think that they are but the signs of His coming.

The angels said to the wondering disciples gazing heavenward: "In like manner as ye have seen Him go into heaven," He shall return. He said Himself that He was coming back.

St. Paul, St. Peter, St. John and hosts of others in Biblical times believe it. Why should not I have this blessed hope?

Some day, I know not when, our Lord shall come;
And when He comes I know He'll take us home.
So keep us trusting, Lord, whate'er befall,
And make us ready when we hear the call.

It may be He will tarry through the night,
Or it may be He'll come with morning light;
But whether it be day or night, He'll come,
And when He comes I know He'll take us home.

But if His coming is not very near,
And if He wills that we should tarry here,
Of this one thing I'm sure—I know it well—
It will be heaven just to do His will.

Dear Lord, we long to see Thy blessed face;
Our feet are often weary in the race.
We wait Thy coming, when each day is done.
Lord, tarry not, oh, tarry not, but *come.*

J. W. C.

ONE OF THE CONVENTION PRAYERS

"He did it; I couldn't have done it."

Rev. Dr. D. M. Stearns, pastor of the Church of the Atonement at Germantown, was speaking. One of the managers of the Conference was congratulating him upon his appearance on the platform, as it had been feared that the infirmities of age and his recent illness would prevent his attendance. The old veteran soldier of the Cross gave God all the glory in his reply, and that the Holy Ghost was upon him in remarkable power was evident from his prayer. Every heart was thrilled with the conviction that God was giving him the words he should speak as he offered this petition:

"Our Heavenly Father, God and Father of our Lord Jesus Christ. Oh, we do thank Thee for Thy Word, which is 'forever settled in heaven,' written by the Holy Spirit, and we thank Thee, O God, for telling us in Thy Word of Thine eternal purpose, of Thy plan to fill the earth with Thy glory. We thank Thee for telling us there is just one thing to do if we are redeemed, and that is, to live to make Thee known as quickly as possible, and to make known this great salvation, so that Thy church, Thy body, shall be completed and the marriage of the Lamb come. We cannot help thinking, although we do not know really, but we cannot help thinking that the redeemed in glory have just one great topic. It does seem so to us. If we are wrong, forgive us, but it seems that there must be just one topic to the redeemed in heaven—the approaching marriage of the Lamb. May it be our great privilege to live wholly for Him who loved us and gave Himself for us, and to make known this great salvation everywhere, so that in all the world, all the 'whosoevers' may come, who shall form Thy bride! We thank Thee for the redeemed in glory, some of whom we have known, who have lived to tell these things, and have passed over and are waiting there while we are waiting here. We thank Thee for the redeemed on earth. We thank Thee that we have the forgiveness of sin, that our names are written in heaven, that we are joint heirs with Jesus Christ, that He is longing to show us the glory which the Father gave Him. Blessed Lord, we thank Thee for those words in His prayer on the last night on earth: 'The glory which Thou gavest Me I have given them,' and 'Father, I will that they also, whom Thou hast given Me, be with Me where I am,' to behold Thy glory. Oh, we thank Thee for the love of Thy heart, revealed to us on that last night ere Thou wast crucified. We know Thou canst not fail; we know Thou art not discouraged; we know the church will be builded: Thou hast said it, every member of Thy body shall be gathered in and Thou wilt come in Thy glory with Thy redeemed to set up Thy kingdom, to bind the devil, to shut him up for a thousand years, to convert Israel, to make Israel a righteous nation, the first on earth, and through them Thou wilt fill the earth with Thy glory. We thank Thee for telling us; we never could have thought it out. Thou hast made it so plain. And we thank Thee with all our hearts for this time, when so many people are hearing these truths right here, and in other Conferences that shall be held in our land. We thank Thee for the testimonies of yesterday. May there be a special anointing upon all that shall speak today! May they lose sight of every one but Thee! We thank Thee for a special anointing upon all who speak today and upon all who have had any hand in bringing about this Conference. We pray Thee, grant unto each one of us, that we may go out as missionary Christians, seeing nothing worth while but to know Thee better, and to live to have others know Thee, and thus hasten the completion of Thy church. We pray Thy blessing upon the millions of Gospels and Testaments being scattered among our soldiers. O Lord, make bare Thy holy arm in the eyes of the nations, that the ends of the earth may see Thy salvation. Thou hast told us, 'See that ye be not troubled.' May we not be troubled, but be strong in the Lord!—every moment, every hour, every day, in Thy hand for Thy pleasure. May the Spirit have full control in these services and Thy will be accomplished! We ask it in the name of our Lord Jesus Christ. Amen."

CHRIST and GLORY

Addresses delivered at the

NEW YORK PROPHETIC CONFERENCE

CARNEGIE HALL,

November 25-28, 1918

Edited by

ARNO C. GAEBELEIN

PUBLICATION OFFICE "OUR HOPE,"

456 FOURTH AVENUE

NEW YORK CITY

TABLE OF CONTENTS

Introduction

THE Prophetic Conference which met in Carnegie Hall, New York City, during the last week of November, 1918, was the greatest of its kind ever held in this country. Divine Providence guided in its arrangement and Divine power was blessedly manifested throughout the meetings.

It was in the fall of 1913 when it was laid upon the heart of the writer to suggest to the Dean of the Moody Bible Institute, Mr. James M. Gray, that a Prophetic Conference should be he held in the Moody Church in the early part of 1914. The conference was at once planned, largely attended, and was felt in its blessing all over our land. When that conference was planned no man knew that a few months later the great world-war would break out. But the Lord knew all about it and He knew the need of a strong prophetic testimony for His Church. The Chicago Conference supplied that need. The printed report was used much in the revival of the study of Prophecy during the war.

Since that conference different brethren, including ourselves, desired that a similar testimony be given in the great Metropolis of our country. We made several attempts to call such a conference, but without success. During the summer of 1918 we received the strong conviction that the time had come for a large prophetic testimony in New York City. The same conviction was shared by a number of brethren, especially by our friend and brother, Mr. Alwyn Ball, Jr. After an exchange of thought it was decided to call a number of brethren to form an executive committee, for the planning of a New York Prophetic Conference. The committee consisted of the following brethren: Alwyn Ball, Jr.; George S. Dowkontt; Chas. Gremmels; W. M. Strong; Delevan Pierson; George Carter; J. Richards; Oscar Rixson; H. Raud; Charles Young; Hugh R. Monro and A. C. Gaebelein. After much prayer and consultation it was decided that the Conference should be held in Carnegie Hall, the most prominent hall in New York, during the Thanksgiving week. A call was then sent out signed by almost one hundred prominent New York preachers, professional men and business men. But no one knew that when the appointed time for the Conference came the world-war would be over. The Lord knew that it would be so and that another prophetic testimony was needed to call attention to the real character of the age and the divine forecast of the future. We believe the Lord graciously met this need through these addresses given.

Some had expressed doubt if Carnegie Hall could be filled. That doubt was settled by the very first meeting. When the meeting had started at 7.30 p. m., every available seat was taken and several hundred were unable to get into the Hall, so that an overflow meeting had to be held in the Church of the Strangers, as well as on on other evenings. The Hall was filled to overflowing every night, Tuesday and Wednesday nights several hundred were standing throughout the lengthy service. The morning sessions on Tuesday and Wednesday filled the spacious Marble Collegiate church building, on Fifth Avenue and 29th Street. The morning session on Thanksgiving Day was held in Carnegie Hall and over 2,000 attended. The afternoon sessions also filled the Hall except the uppermost gallery.

The power of God was manifestly present in each service.

INTRODUCTION

Many of God's people said that they had never attended a series of meetings in which the presence of the Lord was so evident as during this conference. Thousands received great help and inspiration. Many Christians had their eyes and hearts opened to the second, pre-millennial coming of the Lord. The power of God in salvation was likewise present. As a result of the first meeting held, several accepted Christ and since then we have heard from a good many that they were saved as a result of the testimony given.

The singing was under the able leadership of Charles M. Alexander, who, with the magnificent choir of over two hundred voices, contributed largely to the success of the Conference. Such singing! Everybody said, we have never heard such wonderful singing before. The hymn mostly sung, besides "The Glory Song," was the one with the inspiring chorus:

> "Living, He loved me;
> Dying, He saved me;
> Buried, He carried my sins far away;
> Rising, He justified freely forever:
> One day He's coming—
> O, glorious Day!"

And who would have thought that the beloved brother who wrote this hymn, J. Wilbur Chapman, who gave such a clear testimony during this Conference, should so soon be called home to be with the Lord.

And now we send forth this volume, giving most of the addresses delivered at this remarkable Conference. "Christ and Glory" we have called this report, for the testimony given exalts our ever blessed Lord Jesus Christ, His glory and our coming glory. We know this printed testimony will be largely used. It should have a nation-wide, yea, more than that, a world-wide circulation. It should be placed into the hands of every preacher in the United States and Canada.

To accomplish this a large sum is needed, and we are confident that the Lord whom we desire to honor and glorify in this work, will put this upon the hearts of His people, and that through them a world-wide circulation of this volume will become possible.

ARNO CLEMENS GAEBELEIN.

456 Fourth Avenue,
New York City.

The Pre-eminence of the Lord Jesus Christ and His Coming Glory

By Arno C. Gaebelein, Editor of "Our Hope."

"Who is the image of the invisible God, the Firstborn of all creation; for by Him were all things created, that are in Heaven, and that are in Earth, visible and invisible, whether they be thrones, or dominions, or principalities, or powers, all things were created by Him and for Him. And He is before all things, and by Him all things consist. And He is the head of the body, the church, who is the beginning, the Firstborn from the dead, that in all things He might have the preeminence."—Colossians i:15:18.

We meet in this Prophetic Conference to exalt and glorify one Person and one Name, the Name which is above every other Name. And He whom we desire and delight to honor is in our midst, for He has said "Where two or three are gathered together in my Name there am I in the midst" and again "Lo, I am with you always even unto the end of the age." May we remember in each service that the unseen One, our Saviour-Lord is with us.

There was a brief moment in the earthly life of our Lord, when suddenly His garb of humiliation was changed into glory. It took place upon that mountain where He had taken His three disciples. All at once the glory of the Father covered Him. His blessed face shone like the sun and His raiment was white as light. That transfiguration glory was the foregleam of His coming glory. Such is His glory now at the right hand of God; with such glory He is, some day, coming back to earth again.

Yet it was then that human lips uttered words which marred that glory. Peter said "Lord it is good to be here." He suggested to make this glory permanent. He spoke as if there could be glory without suffering, a crown without a cross. Greater still was his mistake when he added "If thou wilt let us make here three tabernacles; one for thee; one for Moses; and one for Elias." What was his error? He put the Lord of glory into the company of mortal, sinful men, such as Moses and Elias were. He lowered His dignity and glory. It was therefore while He was yet speaking that the voice of another was heard. It was a voice which spoke from above. It was the voice of God the Father vindicating the honor and glory of His own Son, the Lord Jesus. Listen! "This is my beloved Son in whom I am well pleased; Hear Him". Not a man like other men; not a saint like other saints; not a lawgiver like Moses; not a prophet or reformer like Elias, but my beloved Son.

What was suggested on that mountain by Peter, to place the Lord on the same level with other men, is the common thing today throughout Christendom. They call Him the carpenter, the man of Galilee, a good man, a great man, the best of man. They place Him alongside of Buddha, Confucius and Socrates. In doing this His fullest glory is denied and the Lord of all is dishonored.

The portion of the Scriptures read at this time tells us that pre-eminence belongs to our Lord Jesus Christ. In all things He has the pre-eminence. Let us then see the sevenfold pre-eminence of our Lord we find revealed in the Bible.

PRE-EMINENCE OF THE LORD JESUS

1. *His is first of all the pre-eminence in creation.* Creation itself is for man an unsolvable mystery. How did the things we see, this earth, the universe the fathomless heavens with their millions of stars come into existence? When and how did it all originate? Is matter eternal or had it a beginning? What is the future of this universe? These are but a few of the many questions which man has asked. Sages and philosophers of all races and ages have been occupied with such questions concerning the origin of creation. It would greatly amuse us if we were to state some of the utterly ridiculous theories which great thinkers of different nations in the past invented to explain how things seen came into existence. Not less foolish is the theory which is so widely taught throughout our country, in our schools and colleges—the so-called evolution theory. It is nothing less than an attempt to find some other cause for the existence of nature than nature's God as revealed in His infallible Word. Without answering the claims of evolution let me give you two reasons why a Christian must reject it.

In the first place the evolution theory makes God the author of evil. He must be held responsible for all the misery, sorrow, suffering and death which are in the world today, for He Himself imparted it when He started the supposed protoplasm evolving. If that were true then God would indeed be the author of all the horrors in the world and man would be without any responsibility at all. And furthermore evolution knows no remedy for the evil which is in creation. It denies and rejects the great redemption as made known in the Gospel of God.

If the creature is to know anything about creation, since searching cannot find it out, it must be made known by revelation. And such a revelation we have in the Bible.

PRE-EMINENCE OF THE LORD JESUS

"In the Beginning God created the heavens and the earth." Creation is the work of God. When we examine the New Testament Scriptures we discover that creation is ascribed to the Son of God. What a great statement we have here in the Epistle to the Colossians, who like so many professing Christians today, had listened to false teachers and were being misled by evil doctrines. Listen again. "For by Him (the Son of God) were all things created, that are in heaven and that are in earth, visible and invisible . . . all things were created by Him and for Him". Was this the opinion of the Apostle Paul? How could he ever have made such a great statement unless God revealed it unto him by His Spirit! Nor is he the only writer of the New Testament who makes this known. John in the beginning of his gospel gives the same testimony. "All things were made by Him and without Him was not anything made that is made." And again, "The world was made by Him." (John i:3, 9.) From these inspired statements we learn that the pre-eminence in creation belongs to Him whom we worship as our Saviour-Lord. Therefore all who believe the Bible believe on Him as the omnipotent Lord, the creator of all things.

Nor must we forget how wonderfully He manifested the Creator's power and the attribues of the Godhead when He walked among men in deepest humiliation in the form of a servant. That humble Nazarene, as they called Him, displayed omnipotence. Look at Him as majestically He spoke to the waves and the wind with His command "Peace! Be still!" The wind was hushed; the waves became a calm. Who else but the Creator, who made the sea, could do this. And so it took the power of an omnipotent One to change the water into wine. And look again and see sickness and pain banished by the loving touch of His hand; and more than that He raised the dead. How great too was His omniscience! He knew the secret thoughts of His disciples and the plottings of His enemies so that His own confessed "Lord Thou knowest all things." Away then with the miserable and lying inventions of the enemy, so prominent in the twentieth century, by which it is claimed that Christ was only divine in the sense as every other human being possesses divinity and other inventions which deny His Godhead and rob Him of His highest glory.

II. *He also has the pre-eminence as the Upholder and Sustainer of all Things.* The Bible tells us that "by Him all things consist" and that He "upholds all things by the Word of His power". It means that He sustains this universe, that without Him all would collapse. He occupies a throne and in His hands rests all power. Well may we remember this in days when thrones crumble into dust, when everything is shaken, and testing times are upon man and man's government as never before, that there is a throne which cannot be shaken, nor can it be affected by what is going on down here. His throne is an everlasting throne of righteousness, and ultimately righteousness will be victorious. The Son of God our Lord has the pre-eminence in government, upholding and sustaining His creation. And think of it child of God, that He is your Lord. The hands which uphold all things uphold His people down here in conflict, in sorrow and in every trial.

III. *But furthermore He has the pre-eminence in the Bible,* the revelation of God. And well it is that we speak of this blessed Book as the infallible, the inerrant Word of God. How tersely it was put some two years ago by our good President Mr. Woodrow Wilson when he penned the inscription for the soldiers New Testaments, beginning with this statement "The Bible is the Word of life" and closing with the testimony "The Bible is the Word of God." Well said—the Bible, the Word of Life and the Word of God. Many voices throughout Christendom ridicule and deny these statements, which embody the faith of our fathers. They tell us that perhaps the Bible contains here and there some kind of a revelation, but they claim it takes scholarship to ascertain what is really truth and what is merely human opinion, myth or legend. And blessed little scholarship some of these critics possess. The solid truth the Bible *is* the Word of God, as God's people always believed, has been changed to a statement of camouflage—the Bible *contains* the Word of God. How prominently the horrors of the past four years are connected with the rejection of this Book divine as God's Word and God's revelation must be clear to every thinking Christian. Destructive Criticism and the new Theology robbed Germany of the faith in the Word of God and the Gospel of Christ; and then they were, under Satanic delusion, plunged into that which outraged the laws of God and man. Let a nation stand by the Bible as the Word of God; honor the Bible, read the Bible, believe the Bible and its message of God's love in His Son and that nation will always prosper. And here permit me to say that we have a message to give from the President. We wrote Mr. Wilson asking him for a message to this Bible Conference. His Secretary replied that on account of the pressure of his official life he could not do so, but sent instead the copy of an address he delivered several years ago, with the permission to use anything of it. Let me then read to you this sentence and let us consider it as his message. "I have a very simple thing to ask of you. I ask every man and woman in this audience that from this night on they will realize that part of the destiny of America lies in their daily perusal of this great book of revelation—the Holy Scriptures."

Our good Vice-President Mr. Thomas R. Marshall sent from Washington to the speaker a direct message. He writes "Out of the Babel of tongues now in the world proclaiming—Lo here is salvation, lo there is salvation—all history proves that the only sure salvation for the individual or the nation is the knowledge of and obedience to the revealed Word of God. Read it. Strive to obey it."

In this wonderful Book the Son of God, our Lord Jesus Christ has the place of pre-eminence. Years ago a certain father brought home to his children a children's game by which he intended to teach them the geography of our land. It consisted of a paste board map of the United States, cut up in small pieces of different shape. They were to fit piece to piece till the map was reconstructed. It took them five minutes to complete the task. And when the father inquired how they succeeded so soon, they turned the map over. On the other side was the figure of George Washington. All they did was to put the man together, the arms and legs, hands and feet; and thus the difficulty of the map on the other side was completely solved. In this Book of all books there is revealed a Person, the Lord Jesus Christ, the Son of God. He is the key to the Scriptures. Not "Science and Health" as it is claimed is the key to the Scriptures, nor the mad ravenings of Russellism, or any other ism, but the Lord Jesus Christ is the key to the whole revelation of God, the key which unlocks the treasure house of God to the human soul. Wherever we turn in this Book, which has outlived every attack, the anvil upon which infidelity has broken its hammers, we behold this majestic Person and all His glory.

From the Book of Genesis, the book of the beginnings of all things, to the great capstone, the Book of Revelation with its unveiling of the future, He stands out in solitary majesty. Moses speaks of Him; every prophet tells out His matchless person, His work and His glory. We see Him and His work in the offerings and sacrifices, in Israel's earthly worship, in historical events—His face may be seen on every page in this Book. And then the names He bears! Hundreds of names which tell out His worth, His love, His grace as well as His glory.

Christian! Whenever you read your Bible, and daily you must read it prayerfully if your Christianity is to be a reality, look always first for Himself. Remember the written Word makes known to your soul the living Word, the Son of God. He Himself said concerning the Scriptures "They testify of Me." Approach then this Book with the simple prayer "Father by Thy Spirit show me Christ and His glory, show me Him who is altogether lovely." Pray this and you will never pray in vain.

IV. *But let us see next His pre-eminence in Redemption.* Man is the lost creature of God. Man is a sinner and alienated from God, destitute of righteousness; he is in the place of death and therefore on the road to an eternity of darkness and separation from God. Man therefore needs redemption. He cannot redeem himself. Well did Job cry out, uttering the old, old question "How can a man be just with God"? And afterward he confessed the hopelessness of his own efforts when he said "if I wash myself with snow water and make my hands never so clean, yet shalt thou plunge me in the ditch and mine own clothes shall abhor me" (Job ix:30-31) Nor can an angel or any other created being redeem and save man from the horrible place into which sin has brought him. If man is to be redeemed God must do it Himself. The One who alone is able to redeem and to save man is the Son of God, the Lord of Creation. To accomplish the great work of redemption He left the bosom of God. He left the glory behind and came down to this earth of sin and death. He who was rich became poor. Born of the Virgin He became man and as the God-man He lived that perfect life, that holy life, that blessed life, that life of trust and obedience and in it all He made God, the invisible God known to man. He brought God to man but to bring man back to God something else besides incarnation and a holy life was needed. Redemption could only be procured for a guilty race by the Cross. On that cross, He who knew no sin was made sin for us. There He met and owned God's Holiness and righteousness—there He took the sinners place in judgment. On that cross He was forsaken of a holy God and all the waves and billows of divine judgment passed over His head. On that cross He paid the price of redemption and shed His precious blood, by which the believing sinner is cleansed from all sin and put beyond condemnation. Oh that wonderful Cross with its wonderful work!

A few months ago I looked once more upon that great, majestic mountain on the pacific coast, Mount Rainier. Twilight came on. And then the great giant, towering almost fifteen thousand feet above sea level, with its summit capped in eternal ice and snow, was suddenly glorified by the rays of the setting sun. The summit seemed partly bathed in blood red and over yonder the red merged into a tinge of yellow like shining gold. And as I looked upon it the Cross came back to my mind, the cross on which the Lord of Glory died. Calvary is such a peak reaching from earth to heaven. The blood was given there and the glory secured. In that cross His glory as the redeemer is made known, the Lamb of God who meets perfectly God's righteousness and reveals His great love. What a glory then is His through the work of the Cross! He has, by His work, procured the power to bring sinners from eternal night to eternal light, from eternal shame to eternal glory, from the dunghill of sin and death to the throne of life and glory. And that cross can never lose its glory. It can never be dimmed; its glory will never diminish; it can never be forgotten in all eternity, even as it was known from before the foundation of the world.

And therefore He has the pre-eminence in redemption. There is no salvation in any other "for there is none other name under heaven given among men whereby we must be saved." (Acts iv:12.) There is but one way to glory and that is the way of the cross, to believe on the Son of God who died for our sins. All who will be in the Father's house were brought there through the blood of the Lord Jesus Christ. Every other gospel, so called, salvation by character or the new thought gospel, or anything else is a miserable counterfeit. And that includes the foolish invention, which for a time became so popular in Great Britain, that the soldier who dies on the battlefield goes straight to glory because he gave his life in a good cause. No! a thousand times No! Christ alone can save. His then is the pre-eminence in redemption.

V. *There is another pre-eminence, His pre-eminence as the risen Man in glory.* We speak of the created heavens. But there is also an uncreated Heaven. God is a Person. He has no beginning. For Him there must have been a dwelling place before all time and all creation. That place is the third heaven, the uncreated heaven. When the Son of God had finished the work and God raised Him from the dead, He passed through the heavens and entered into the heaven of heavens. There He received as the risen Man, in His glorifid body the highest place which God could give to Him. He seated Him at His own right hand in the heavenly places, far above all principality, and power, and might and dominion, and every name that is named, not only in this world but also in that which is to come. He put all things under His feet. And now as the glorified Man He fills the throne, angels and authorities and powers being made subject unto Him. There too He receives the homage of the heavenly hosts. All heaven glorifies and adores Him. In such glory John in the isle of Patmos beheld Him when He saw Him in the midst of the golden candlesticks. Wonderful sight to see the One whom Isaiah announced as the Wonderful, the Counsellor, the Mighty God, the Everlasting Father, the Prince of Peace, to see Him, who was once made a little lower than the angels for the suffering of death crowned with glory and honor, to see Him as the Priest in yonder Holiest ever living and interceding for His own blood bought people.

VI. *There is also His pre-eminence in the new Creation.* The old creation has upon it the stamp of sin and death, the new creation is life and glory. The only way which leads into this new creation is the new birth. To belong to the new creation one has to be in Christ. "Therefore if any man be in Christ Jesus he is a new creation, old things are passed away; behold all things are become new." (2 Cor. v:17). He is both, the author of this new creation, and the Head of it. All sinners saved by grace form the body of Christ, which is the church and He is the head of that body. He sustains and keeps and ministers to this spiritual body as He sustains His physical creation. And some coming day this new creation will be complete. The redeemed body will be joined to the glorified head, the Lord Jesus Christ. All the redeemed will share His glory.

When that blessed consummation comes then His pre-eminence in that new Creation will be acclaimed in that never ending glory song "Thou art worthy . . . for Thou wast slain and hast redeemed us to God by thy blood out of every kindred, and tongue, and people, and nation; and hast made us unto God kings and priests and we shall reign over the earth." (Rev. v:9.) And hear how this hymn of worship and praise increases, rises higher and higher in the coming day of glory. "And I beheld, and I heard the voice of many angels round about the throne and the living creatures and the elders, and the number of them was ten thousand times ten thousand, and thousands of thousands; saying with a loud voice, Worthy is the Lamb that was slain to receive power and riches, and wisdom, and strength, and honour and glory and blessing." Such is His glory which He will receive as the pre-eminent One in the new creation, the head of the body. And this is the glory which awaits all who are in Christ. Oh, the blessed thought that some day we shall see Him as He is! Oh, how it thrills the heart to think that we shall look into that face of glory, that we all shall have a face to face meeting with the Lord of glory, the pre-eminent Christ! And what a destiny it is to be ultimately like Him, to share the vast inheritance of glory with Him and to live on, and on, and on in the glory fellowship with the Lord.

VII. *Finally He will receive the pre-eminence as King of kings and Lord of lords over this earth.* This is His coming, future glory. What will the future bring for this earth and the human race? This has been and is still the important question all thinking people ask. Throughout the past four years of the world war with its unspeakable horrors and suffering, uncountable thousands have asked "what shall be the end of these things?" And now that victory has come, autocracy is dethroned and democracy is enthroned, we still have our questions concerning the future. Will the coming league of nations maintain peace on earth? Will the sword never again be unsheathed? Listen to wise words of another, I believe spoken from the platform of this great hall. Col. Roosevelt said: "Let us never forget that any promise that such a league of nations or any other piece of machinery, will definitely do away with war, is either sheer nonsense or rank hypocrisy." Very true Mr. Roosevelt! What about the dark shadow of lawlessness, the beast of the pit which despises all government and would sweep away every law and order? Indeed never before in the history of this age has the human race faced such problems and perplexities as we face today. It is as our Lord told us. "Upon the earth distress of nations with perplexity, the sea and the waves roaring. Men's hearts failing them for fear, and looking after those things which are coming upon the earth" (Luke xxi:25-26). What then is the future to bring for this earth and the people upon it? No Christian needs to speculate about it, for we have a sure word of prophecy in which the Lord, who knows the end from the beginning, has revealed the future. Oh! the pity that the church of Jesus Christ has neglected this magnificent portion of God's holy Word, so full of light, of hope and comfort.

This Word tells us all about the things to come. It tells us that the time will come when Monarchies and democracies will give way to another form of government. God Himself will set up on this earth a Kingdom, the Kingdom of heaven, the Kingdom of the Son of His Love, the Kingdom of righteousness and peace. A Kingdom will ultimately come into which all the nations of the earth will be gathered, a Kingdom which extends from sea to sea, in which nations learn war no more; a Kingdom in which God's will is done as it is done in heaven. And God's word is equally clear how that Kingdom comes. Not by the efforts of man; not by the progress of civilization; not by reformation or education. Not even by the work of the church. That Kingdom comes when the Lord Jesus Christ comes back to earth again. Some day these heavens will be covered with His glory and He who lived once upon this earth, who died the sinners death, was raised from the dead and ascended upon high, He who is now at the right hand of God, yea this same Jesus, will come again. Then He receives that Kingdom and the glory time for this poor world will come. But above all it will be His glory-time, for He who was once crowned with thorns will then be crowned the Lord of all. These great, forgotten and neglected truths will be more fully unfolded in this conference. Before our brother Dr. Torrey speaks to us on "that blessed Hope" let me ask you this question. In all things the Lord Jesus has the pre-eminence, have you given Him the pre-eminence, the first place in your life? He is your creator, your sustainer, your Savior, the Lord who loves you. Why then is He not the pre-eminent One in your life? No real happiness, no real peace and joy can you know till you give Him the pre-eminence, as your Saviour and your Lord. All our troubles and difficulties in our

Christian lives have but one source—we have never crowned Him Lord of all in our lives. This very first meeting give Him the pre-eminent place in your heart and life.

"That Blessed Hope"

By DEAN R. A. TORREY, Los Angeles, Cal.

I have not a doubt that it is providential that this prophetic Conference is held at just this time. Of course when these brethren arranged for this Conference and selected the date, they had no idea that an armistice was to be signed and an end brought to the immediate hostilities before this Conference could ever assemble. But God knew it. And now that the armistice has come, the minds of people on both sides of the water are filled with all kinds of fantastic hopes and anticipations that are doomed to disappointments. We are entertaining all kinds of hopes nowadays, but there is only one hope and that is the blessed hope of our Lord's return. And that is not only a blessed hope, but it is a sure hope built upon that Book, which is beyond a peradventure, as Dr. Gaebelein said it was, and as the President said it was, and as the Vice-President said it was and is, the Word of God. In other words, it is God, who cannot lie, who has promised the return of our Lord and Saviour Jesus Christ.

We are hearing a great deal in these days of how men are dreaming, and planning, and speaking of a league of nations and the permanent peace that is to follow. Such hopes are delusive; they will end in disappointment and dismay. There may be a league of nations, but no peace will come from such a league except a temporary peace, and then the most awful universal war that this old world has ever seen will follow. We have had holy alliances before. What came of them? Disappointment and calamity. We have had the triple alliance of the Central Powers, and the triple entente of France, England and Russia. And what came of them? The present war. And if a league of nations comes, what will come of it? As I have said, first peace, and then the most awful war that this world has ever seen, culminating in political chaos, out of which shall emerge another and a greater Napoleon.

Then is there no hope? Yes, there is hope, a hope both sure and steadfast, a hope that is absolutely certain, a hope that is built upon the inerrant and infallible Word of Him that cannot lie. It is about that hope in its relation to the believer in Jesus Christ that I have been asked to speak to-night. I have been asked to speak on that hope as it is set forth by our Lord and as it is interpreted in another passage by an inspired commentator, the Apostle Paul.

Will you turn in your Bibles please to the 14th chapter of John, the first three verses. You all know them, but I want you to look at them again. For a great many years every Saturday at our family worship my family has repeated this chapter of John together, so that after years of repetition it is fairly burned into our hearts.

"Let not your heart be troubled: believe in God, believe also in me. In my Father's house are many mansions; if it were not so, I would have told you; for I go to prepare a place for you. And if I go and prepare a place for you,

I come again, and will receive you unto myself; that where I am, there ye may be also."

The whole keynote of the chapter is found in the opening words, "Let not your heart be troubled: believe in God, believe also in me." The 27th verse closes just the same way: "Let not your heart be troubled," and with this addition, "neither let it be (Revised Version) fearful." And between the first verse and the 27th verse of this chapter are thoughts for the comfort of Christ's disciples during His absence. And the one great all inclusive thought is that the way to escape heart trouble is "believe in God, believe also in me." That is God's great cure for heart trouble; that is God's great cure for despondency under any and all circumstances. That is God's cure for pessimism, chronic or acute,—faith in God, and especially faith in God as He is revealed in Christ.

But along with this keynote, and following this keynote, our Lord Jesus, in anticipation of the overwhelming event of the next day, when all their hopes seemed about to be laid in the dust, gave them several specific thoughts for their comfort, and the first one and the great one is the second and third verses: "In my Father's house are many mansions. If it were not so, I would have told you; for I go to prepare a place for you, and if I go and prepare a place for you, I come again and will receive you unto myself; that where I am, there ye may be also."

Now there are a great many interpretations of this coming again of our Lord Jesus. Even so good and reliable a commentator as Godet, in his great two volume commentary on the Gospel of John, says that the coming here refers to the coming of our Lord to the individual believer at his death. Was he right in this instance? We are not left to speculate about that, for God in His wondrous grace has given us an inspired commentary on these three verses of John xiv.

That inspired commentary is found in First Thessalonians. iv: 13-18.

"But we would not have you ignorant, brethren, concerning them that fall asleep; that ye sorrow not, even as the rest, who have no hope. For if we believe that Jesus died and rose again, even so them also that are fallen asleep in Jesus will God bring with him. For this we say unto you by the word of the Lord," —that is, by express commandment of the Lord Jesus Christ— "that we who are alive, that are left unto the coming of the Lord, shall in no wise precede" or anticipate "them that are fallen asleep. For the Lord himself shall descend from heaven, with a shout, with the voice of the archangel, and with the trump of God: and the dead in Christ shall rise first; then we that are alive, that are left, shall together with them be caught up in the clouds, to meet the Lord in the air: and so shall we ever be with the Lord. Wherefore comfort one another with these words."

I say that is an inspired commentary on John xiv: 1-3. What warrant have I for saying it? Because there are just four points in each passage, and those four points exactly cover one another. The Lord's word, "I come again"; the apostle Paul's comment, "the Lord Himself shall descend from heaven." The Lord's word, "I will receive you unto myself"; The Apostle Paul "We shall be caught up to meet the Lord in the air." The Lord's own language, "that where I am there ye may be"; the Apostle Paul, "and so shall we ever be with the Lord." The Lord's word, "Let not your heart be troubled"; "comfort one another with these words." There cannot be a possibility of doubt about it that 1 Thessalonians iv, 16 to 18 is an inspired commentary on our Lord's promise that He is coming again. So we are going to take this as the interpretation of His own Word.

"THAT BLESSED HOPE"

The first thing here is the blessed hope of the coming of the Lord for believers, when believers are caught up to meet Him in the air. We are told first of all that it will be a coming in person, "For the Lord *himself* shall descend." It will not be the coming of some great social reform, it will not be the coming of some great religious revival. You know we have a way nowadays of speaking of a revival of religion as the coming of Jesus Christ; and so it is in a certain sense, but it is not the coming that is spoken of in this verse. It is a personal coming, "The Lord himself shall descend from heaven." "I come again." Social reformations have their place, we need them badly enough. They do not last very long though when they come, do they? Thank God for religious awakenings if they are real and in the power of the Holy Spirit and not mere human enthusiasm.

But, O friends, what we who really know the Lord, and love the Lord long for, is not a reformation, or religious revival; it is the Lord Jesus Christ Himself. We thank God for the messengers of His grace, we thank God for the daily gifts of His grace; but what the Christian is longing for is a person, not a message, not a gift, but the Lord Himself.

Many years ago, when I was a pastor in the city of Minneapolis, a godly old man, who really loved the Lord, wrote an article in one of the denominational papers in which he told us we should not look for a personal coming of the Lord Jesus, that that was not what the Word of God meant, but that we must learn to see Him and be satisfied with Him as coming more and more in all the wonders and glories of this century. Now I believe that man really loved the Lord. He had made great sacrifices to be a missionary among the Indians, endured great hardships. He had given practical proof that he loved the Lord; and yet I never could see how a man who really loved the Lord could ever have written those words. I want the Lord Jesus Christ. Oh, I delight in His Word as I find it in this inspired Book; I delight in those wonderful experiences of His grace that He gives me by the power of His Holy Spirit; but I want the Lord Himself; "And the Lord Himself shall descend."

Suppose when I left my wife out in Los Angeles, I had said to her, "Clara, I am coming back soon; I do not know just how soon. I am coming back soon; I do not know just when. I want you to be waiting for me." Now, every day since I left her I have written her a letter. And suppose, too, I had sent her some beautiful and perhaps costly gifts since I have been away. And then all the time she was looking not for letters, but she was looking for me. And then suppose somebody should go and say to her, "Mrs. Torrey, what are you looking forward to?" "To my husband's coming home." Then suppose they should say, "But you do not expect him to come personally, do you?" "Why, certainly." "Why?" "Why, because he said he was coming." "Oh, yes, but he did not mean he was coming personally. Hasn't he written you a letter every day?" "Yes, every day." "And hasn't he sent you some gifts?" "Yes, he sent me some gifts, tokens of his love." "Now then, what he meant was not that he was coming back personally, but he wanted you to see him and be satisfied with him as coming in these letters he was writing and these gifts that he was sending."

She would say, "I don't want his letters, I don't want his gifts; I want *him*." And while I thank God for the wonderful gifts of Christ that He bestows upon me, and I thank my risen Lord for sending His Holy Spirit to be the indwelling guest in my heart, I want *Him!* The Lord Himself shall descend."

Dr. Brooks of St. Louis, used to tell about a young lady in his congregation that married an army officer in the regular army; and not long after their marriage he received word to go to another post, and the post was of such a character that he could not take his wife with him, and separating from her he said, "I may not be gone very long. These transfers oftentimes are for a very short time, and I may come back perhaps in a few days, perhaps longer, but probably soon." And after he went he sent her letters and beautiful gifts. One day she was sitting in the parlor with an open letter in her hand that she had just received from him, and a great box of the gifts that he had sent. While she was looking at the letter and going over the beautiful gifts, there was a little noise at the front door and there was a footstep. She looked up and there her husband stood in the doorway. She dropped the letter; in her haste she stumbled over the box and scattered the gifts, and next she was clasped to his heart. She did no longer want his letters, nor his gifts. She had him! We shall have Him, the Lord Himself.

We are told then in this passage that this coming of our Lord, when He comes in the air to receive His Saints, and when He comes with His Saints, is to be a bodily coming "The Lord *Himself* shall descend from heaven. It is the picture of the coming down of a Person. Then we shall be caught up to meet Him. Who caught up? Raised ones, and we that are still living will be transformed, meeting with those who are raised. What is raised? Spirits are not raised; they never die. They do not have to be raised. But the body falls, the body crumbles into dust; and this crumbled body, this dissolved body, will be raised. If we are living, it will be transformed, then all the Saints will meet and meet Him in the air. Oh, no such coming as Pastor Russell told his dupes, that it occurred way back in October, 1874, that nobody saw. One day I was preaching on the subject of the second coming in the Moody Church in Chicago, and at the end an apostle of Pastor Russell, one of his ablest teachers, who had sat through it all—came to me at the close and said: "Now, Mr. Torrey, you do not really mean to say that we will see Christ with these physical eyes? You do not believe that, do you? I said, "It does not make a particle of difference what I believe; the question is what the Word of God says, and the Word of God says in Revelation I:7, "Every eye shall see him, and they that pierced him." Of course that has to do with the time when He comes with His Saints, but even when He comes for the Church it will be a coming of our Lord Jesus Christ Himself. Some years ago I was on a council for the installation of a minister. In those days they used to put questions to men who were candidates for installation, and to this minister, who was thoroughly orthodox on the great fundamentals of the faith, I put the question: "Do you believe in the personal, visible return of our Lord to this earth?" He said, "No, I don't." "Well," I said, "what do you do with Acts i:11? You know what the heavenly messengers said, as the disciples stood gazing after Him and looking up in the heaven where he had gone. "Why stand ye gazing into heaven! This same Jesus which was taken up from you to heaven shall so come in like manner as ye *saw him going.*" I said, "What do you do with 'shall come in like manner'?" "Oh," he says, "His coming is just as certain as His going, but it does not mean a bodily coming and a visible coming."

Now it is absolutely impossible to put that construction on the Greek words. The Greek words mean "in the manner which." It cannot by any possibility of Greek construction mean anything but "manner," a bodily, visible coming.

Then the next thing is that this blessed hope of our Lord's coming in the air for His own is a future coming. It has not taken place yet. All the things that are described here, did they ever take place? "The Lord Himself shall descend from heaven with a shout, with the voice of the archangel and the trump of God. And the dead in Christ shall rise first, and we which are left shall be caught up together with them to meet the Lord in the air, and so shall we ever be with the Lord." Did that ever occur? A good many people say it has; at least they say He has already come. Pastor Russell, as already stated, said He came in October, 1874. How anybody could ever identify Russellism with pre-miliennialism is more than I could understand. Russellism is very closely akin to the most common form of post-millennialism, such as is taught by Shailer Mathews and others. It is practically the same thing. Some say that the coming refers to His coming at death to the believer, and that therefore it is fulfilled in the experience of each individual believer as he dies. Some say that He came at Pentecost, or when the Holy Spirit comes in the individual experience of the believer. Some say that the coming refers to the destruction of Jerusalem long ago. Just stop for a moment and look. Take first of all the death of the believer. You have no doubt been present at the triumphant deathbed of a believer. But is it His coming? Did those things occur when you stood there by the bedside? Did the Lord descend with a shout, with the voice of the archangel? Did you hear any trump of God? Were you, as his spirit left his body, raised then, and were you that stood at the bedside caught up together with him to meet the Lord in the air? I simply have to ask the question.

Take the coming at Pentecost. Did any of these things occur at Pentecost? Take the coming of the Holy Spirit. That is in a sense a coming of the Lord Jesus. Further on in this same chapter, the Lord Jesus after having promised the coming of the Holy Spirit, says in the 15th and following verses: "If ye love me, keep my commandments," or, as the Revised Version puts it, "ye will keep my commandments. And I will pray the Father, and he shall give you another Comforter, that he may be with you forever, even the Spirit of truth: whom the world cannot receive; for it beholdeth him not, neither knoweth him: ye know him; for he abideth with you and shall be in you. I will not leave you desolate: I come unto you." But did these things occur when the Holy Spirit came? Did the Lord descend with a shout, with the voice of the archangel, and the trump of God?

Take the destruction of Jerusalem. Now, the destruction of Jerusalem was beyond a question in a certain sense a type and precursor and prophecy of the day of the Lord that is coming in connection with our Lord's return to this earth, and that is spoken of in the New Testament in the 24th chapter of Matthew and the 15th of Mark. But did any of these things occur at the destruction of Jerusalem? Were believing saints raised? Were living saints transformed and caught up to be forever with the Lord? If that is the true interpretation, it is pretty hard on the Russellites, for they are all left behind and they are all here yet. And it is pretty hard on the rest of us too.

No! not in the death of the individual believer, not in

Pentecost, not in the gift of the Holy Spirit, not in the destruction of Jerusalem, not in any event or series of events that have already occurred, have those inspired Words of God been fulfilled. It is still in the future, and as we hope, —though in the face of Acts i-7 we would not dare predict, the very near future.

When He comes with His Saints to this earth, He comes with great publicity, as we are told in Matthew xxiv, the 26th and 27th verses, "When they shall say unto you, Behold he is in the desolate place, go not forth: Behold, he is in the inner chambers, believe it not. For as the lightning shineth out of the east and shineth even unto the west; so shall the coming of the Son of Man be."

Every little while somebody arises and proclaims themselves as the second coming of Christ in some desolate place or some obscure corner. Now it is Dora Beekman in Minnesota; then it is Prince Michael in Detroit, Michigan, until he was sent to the penitentiary at Jackson for unmentionable vices; then it is some other one in Chicago, and then it is Mary Baker Eddy at Concord. Oh, all these inner chamber and secret corner comings of Christ are long since predicted and exploded delusions.

My sister, now with the Lord, once in the city of New York was asked to attend a Christian Science service. She refused to go for awhile, but finally went. And when they were coming from that service, the lady who had asked her to go, and who was a very ardent Christian Scientist, said to her, "Well, Edith, how did you like it?" She said, "I didn't like it at all." She said, "Why not?" She said, "There wasn't any sermon." She said, "What do you mean by a sermon?" She said, "I mean an exposition of God's Word." "Why," this Christian Scientist said, "we never have anything of that kind. That is human." "But," said my sister, "the Reader stood up there and read for half an hour out of Mrs. Eddy's 'Science and Health.'" "Oh," she said, "that isn't human. That is the second coming of Christ." It isn't the second coming of Christ that is predicted here. If the revelation of Christian Science to Mrs. Eddy was in 1876, as is claimed to be; if it was a revelation—it wasn't a revelation by God but simply a downright theft of Dr. Quimby's child up in Maine, which Mrs. Eddy re-baptised and redressed as her own child.

One more thing I wish to say. It will be a triumphant coming. "The Lord Himself shall descend from heaven with a shout." It is the shout of command, the shout of a victor, the shout of a leader of hosts. Ah, He is coming with a shout of command, the Great triumphant One. We are talking about Foch the victor and Petain and Haig and Pershing. But there is a greater victor coming. Oh, He is the victor! His is the shout. The victory here that is set before us is the victory over death, referring back to what our Lord Jesus says in John v:28-29: "The hour is coming in which they that are in their graves shall hear His voice"—and what? When He descends with a shout of command, the blessed dead shall arise, the wicked dead a thousand years later. Victor over death; and, as we see elsewhere, victor over all the forces of Satan; victor over evil in all its forms. That is the great solution of this world's problem. Oh, all the dreams of social philosophers, all the dreams of poets and lovers of humanity will be more than realized in that day. To sum it all up, it means a redeemed and glorified spirit in a perfectly redeemed and glorified body in a redeemed and glorified society in a redeemed and glorified universe,—a new heaven and a new earth. Is it any wonder that every intelligent heart today, as we take up the newspapers has but one cry, "Even so come, Lord Jesus." As I walked at the noon hour today I never was so glad that the Lord Jesus was coming again as I was then. As I looked at the headings in the newspapers, how the conservative socialists had been put down, and the red anarchists evidently triumphed; and I saw these little groups of men—yes, big groups of men, the sidewalk packed with them, whispering and talking together I was glad I believed the Book. War over? Trouble just begun. Autocracy is a dangerous thing; anarchy is a far more dangerous thing. But as I hear the low rumblings of the thunder of the coming storm, as I go over to the East Side in New York, as I go across the river in Chicago, as I walk the streets of Milwaukee, as I go down the Los Angeles streets and see the soap box orators of the I.W.W., my heart is not heavy, not a bit. When men's hearts are quaking for fear, says our Lord Jesus, look up, for your redemption draweth nigh. The Lord is coming.

Oh, how those words ought to thrill our hearts. He is coming! Perhaps within a year, perhaps in a month, perhaps in a day, perhaps tonight. Would you be glad if right here now before another song is sung, or anything is done, there should burst suddenly upon this audience the voice of the archangel, the trump of God, the shout of command?

But it is not a blessed hope for every member of the professing Church. Many of them are not saved. It isn't really a hopeful blessing for many who profess to believe in the Lord Jesus Christ's return, and talk a lot about it. It is one thing to talk about it and go to conferences about it and applaud when things are said about it, and it is something quite different to live in the power of it.

Some of you business men who have a great deal to say about the personal premillennial return of our Lord, how are you conducting your business? On Christian principles? No! Ah, but for you who are out of Christ, unbelievers—not unbelievers in the sense of being infidels, but unbelievers in the New Testament sense that you have never accepted Jesus Christ as your personal Saviour, surrendered to Him as your Lord and Master, openly confessed Him before the world, it is not a blessed hope for you. When the Lord comes it means you are to be left behind, left behind when God takes away the restraining power that holds back the manifestation of the anti-Christ. Do you want to live in this world when the salt of the earth is gone? Why, look at Petrograd and Moscow when even human power was removed. See what came. But think of it when the church is gone, when the Holy Spirit as a dispensational agent is gone—do you want to be here? I don't. And then darker and darker and darker and darker until it is the midnight of eternal despair. The common argument today for immediate repentance and acceptance of Jesus Christ is that you may die at any moment. That is not the Bible argument. The Bible argument is, "Be ye ready, for in such an hour as you think not the Son of Man cometh." Are you ready?

The Crowns of the Lord Jesus Christ

By Lewis S. Chafer, Bible Teacher and Author.

"And the soldiers platted a crown of thorns and put it on his head." (John xiv:2.)

"But we see Jesus, who was made a little lower than the angels for the suffering of death, crowned with glory and honor." Heb. ii:9.)

"His eyes were as a flame of fire, and on his head were many crowns." (Rev. xix:12.)

I. Crowned With Thorns.

The crown of thorns symbolized Israel's rejection of her King. The nation was not rejecting a God-given sacrifice for their sins, though He became a Saviour for all men through their rejection of Him. Because of much prophecy the nation was expecting their Messiah-King. The Old Testament, by itself, would be a disappointing book. It discloses the final earthly blessings of Israel and the nations, but these blessings were not realized. The book closes with the predictions concerning the coming of "The Sun of Righteousness," the Messiah, with His forerunner, but they had not been seen. The New Testament opens with the birth, presence and ministry of the King and His forerunner. It also records the offer of the kingdom to Israel with all its promised blessings. One of the greatest highways of prophecy is that of the "Son of David," the Messiah-King. Because of these predictions, every devout Jew was awaiting the appearing of the One Who was to be the "consolation of Israel." A few received Him and rejoiced in His presence; but with the multitude this Scripture was fulfilled:

> "As a root out of dry ground: he had no form or comeliness; and when we shall see him, there is no beauty that we should desire him. He was despised and rejected of men; a man of sorrows, and acquainted with grief: and we hid as it were our faces from him; he was despised, and we esteemed him not."

But in spite of all this, He was the Son of the Father's love in Whom the Father was well pleased. He was, and is, the King of Israel. Since the Jews expected that the Messiah was to come, their test of faith was to believe that Jesus of Nazareth was that promised One. They knew about the man Jesus and of His mighty works; but very few would own Him to be the Christ of God, the King of Israel. Saul of Tarsus knew Jesus of Nazareth and hated His name; but when Saul was saved, he began immediately to reason with the Jews in their synagogues that Jesus is the *Christ*. This was the issue with the Jews. Was Jesus of Nazareth the King of the Jews? An individual might believe Him to be that King; but the kingly claim was made to the nation, and the nation made answer. In spite of the fact that He was a King by birth in the Davidic line, and that He fulfilled every prophecy and expectation, they answered the question by the assassination of their King. Before His death He offered Himself as the King of a *nation:* since His death He is offering Himself as Saviour to *individuals* of every nation and kindred and tribe. There is need of special emphasis here, for there are those who are unable to distinguish the fact that the Lord Jesus was first a "minister to the circumcision," or Israel, to "confirm the promises made unto the Fathers," and that through their rejection of Him, and through His death, He became Saviour to all men so that Gentiles may now glorify God for His mercy and grace. Such offers of His saving grace as were announced before His death were made in direct relation to His death. We read: "For God so loved the world, that he gave his only begotten Son, that whosoever believeth on him might not perish, but have everlasting life." Every promise to Israel, though once rejected, will yet be fulfilled by the King when He comes again. This is not a theory; it is the teaching of the Word of God. Some claim to find difficulty in believing that God would offer the kingdom to Israel when he *knew* that they would reject the King and His kingdom. But God created man when He *knew* he would fall. He provided a redemption for the whole world when He *knew* that it would be rejected by the vast majority in the world. He commissions us to preach the Gospel to men whom He *knows* will not receive it. He took Israel into Egypt when He *knew* they would suffer and forget Him. He took Israel out of Egypt when He *knew* the long record of their sin and final apostacy. He took them to Kadesh-barnea and offered them a glorious entrance into the land when He *knew* they would rebel. Certainly we create no *new* problem when we discover that God offered His King to the people to whom He was promised, when He *knew* that they would reject their King. Such a revelation is in harmony with the records of *all* the dealings of God with the children of men.

Prophecy anticipated the birth of the King: "Behold, a virgin shall conceive, and bear a son, and shall call his name Immanuel." So, in the Second Psalm, it is prophesied of the Son that He would rule with a "rod of iron." Prophecy likewise anticipates the nation's rejection of the King. "He was despised and rejected of men." They "esteemed him not." Again, according to prophecy, His very rejection was to open His saving grace to all men:

"But he was wounded for our transgressions, he was bruised for our iniquities: the chastisement of our peace was upon him; and with his stripes we are healed. All we like sheep have gone astray; we have turned every one to his own way; and the LORD hath laid on him the iniquity of us all."

So, also, prophecy anticipated the return of the King when He will not be rejected, but shall reign over regathered Israel and the Gentiles in the earth. A prophecy by Moses, written thirty-five centuries ago, states that Israel will be regathered from their great dispersion when the Divine Presence *returns* to the earth.

"That then the LORD thy God will turn thy captivity, and have compassion upon thee, and will return and gather thee from all the nations, whither the LORD thy God hath scattered thee. If any of thine be driven out unto the outmost parts of heaven, from thence will the LORD thy God gather thee, and from thence will he fetch thee" (Deut. xxx:3, 4).

Like many others, a prophecy found in Amos ix:11, 12, has never been fulfilled; but the Spirit of God quotes this prophecy from Amos in The Acts xv:13-18, and there indicates the conditions under which it will be fulfilled. This Scripture states:

"Simeon hath declared how God at the first did visit the Gentiles, to take out of them a people for his name. And to this agree the words of the prophets; as it is written, after this I will return, and will build again the tabernacle (house) of David, which is fallen down; and I will build again the ruins thereof, and I will set it up: that the residue of men might seek after the Lord, and all the Gentiles, upon whom my name is called, saith the Lord, who doeth all these things. Known unto God are all his works from the beginning of the world."

Two divine purposes for the Gentiles are mentioned in this passage. God, at the present time, is taking out from among the Gentiles a people. Later there is to be a blessing for *all* Gentiles; but Israel's kingdom and its blessings over all the earth are here again said to be realized when He *returns*. When it is taught that Christ was born Israel's King and that they rejected the King and His kingdom; that through His rejection and death a redemption for all man-kind has been secured; and that the rejected King and His kingdom will be received by Israel when the King returns to the earth, it is no clever scheme of interpretation held by some "school" of students of prophecy. The Spirit has witnessed to this exact arrangement throughout all the prophecies of the Old Testament and we rejoice to discover every word of it to be fulfilled according to the New Testament.

All of this prophecy is now accomplished excepting His return. He has come as Israel's King. He has been rejected. The blood redemption has been accomplished for all men. God is calling out a heavenly people from among the Gentiles. He will as certainly *return* and build again the Davidic order, which is Israel's kingdom, and all Gentiles will come to His light and kings to the brightness of His rising. The Son of God came first to the nation Israel as their promised King. At that time He did not minister to Gentiles. Few Gentiles saw Him or spoke to Him. He said, "I am sent but to the lost sheep of the house of Israel."

During those days He sent His disciples out as heralds of the King and His kingdom and commanded them, "Go not into the way of the Gentiles, and into any city of the Samaritans enter ye not: but go rather to the lost sheep of the house of Israel."

It was when He was rejected and crucified that He became God's Lamb "that taketh away the sin of the world." Not one of the rulers said: "I will not believe on the Lord Jesus Christ and be saved;" but they did say: We will not have this man to reign over *us*. To thrust the present issues of salvation into this and similar Jewish situation, is to confuse two distinct dispensations. It obliterates the great lines of prophecy, and robs the Gospel of its distinctiveness and power. We are not now saved because we acclaim Jesus to be King, or because we bow to His authority. We are saved now by *believing* on a Saviour. It is one thing to face the kingly authority of the Lord Jesus as did the Jews; it is quite another thing to face the particular claims which His sacrificial death have made on every soul. Peter said, "Thou art the Christ, the Son of the living God," meaning the expected Messiah-King of Israel; but immediately after this Peter rebuked his Lord when the Lord Jesus had spoken of His death. Christ cannot save by His crown, by His authority, or by His glory. He can save only by His precious blood. Even His power cannot save us apart from the atoning sacrifice which He has made.

The Lord Jesus Christ was scourged, mocked, spit upon, set at naught and crowned with thorns in the common hall. And this in derision of His kingly claim. The Scripture states:

"Then Pilate therefore took Jesus, and scourged him. And the soldiers platted a crown of thorns, and put it on his head, and they put on him a purple robe, and said, Hail, King of the Jews! and they smote him with their hands." Pilate said unto them: "Behold your king!" But they cried out, "Away with him, away with him, crucify him." Pilate saith unto them, "Shall I crucify your King?" The chief priests answered, "We have no king but Caesar." "Then delivered he him therefore unto them to be crucified."

Pilate said to the Jews, "behold your King!" God says to us, "Behold the Lamb!" In crucifixion the Son of God "was lifted up" as Moses lifted up the serpent in the wilderness. There is life in a look at the Crucified One. It is hardly possible to have looked to the Saviour as being the solution of all the problems of our lost estate and not be, to some degree, aware that we have looked to Him. To be saved is a personal consciousness, not of emotions, but of dependence on Christ: "I know whom I have believed." If we have not this consciousness, we do well to reconsider the grounds of our hope. The rejection and crucifixion of Christ was "according to the determinate counsel and foreknowledge of God." God permitted His Son to be crowned with thorns, rejected and crucified. But God was accomplishing His own great purpose in all this. He was reconciling the world unto Himself.

II. Crowned With Glory and Honour.

The Lord Jesus Christ arose from the dead and ascended up on high where He now is seated at His Father's right hand. There, too, He has been crowned with glory and honour. His present position and work is especially revealed in the letter to the Hebrews. One passage speaks of His present coronation.

"For unto the angels hath he not put in subjection the world to come, whereof we speak. But one in a certain place testified, saying, What is man, that thou art mindful of him? or the son of man, that thou visitest him? Thou madest him a little lower than the angels; thou crownedst him with glory and

honour and didst set him over the works of thy hands: Thou hast put all things in subjection under his feet. For in that he put all in subjection under him, he left nothing that is not put under him. But now we see not yet all things under him. But we see Jesus, who was made a little lower than the angels for the suffering of death, crowned with glory and honour: that he by the grace of God should taste death for every man."

This passage is taken from the Eighth Psalm. There reference is made to the first man, Adam, in his original position over the earth; but the first man lost all this position through the fall and we are immediately introduced to the position and authority of the Second Man, the Last Adam, the Lord Jesus Christ, Who, after the fall, fills all the Father's vision. The Last Adam was made a little lower than the angels for the suffering of death. He died and rose again; for it was not possible that He, the Prince of Life, should be holden of death. The Word of God gives us the exact facts concerning His present position, and faith may now see Him in the highest heaven, "crowned with glory and honour."

As very God, He was always the embodiment of the highest glory and honour; but a new glory and honour had been made possible by His work of redemption. Returning from earth into the full blaze of His eternal glory He carried into heaven those new glories and honours which had been acquired through His ministrations on earth. In heaven, the return of the Son of God from earth was an event of greatest moment. How great was His victory as seen by the Father and the holy angels! What honour and glory was His in the eyes of those who fully comprehended the eternal value of His redemption for a crushed and fallen race! Far too little consideration is given to the importance of the home-going and present ministry of the Son of God; yet there is no lack of emphasis in the Word of God. Fourteen passages describe the ascension of Christ and His present position in glory. Three may be noted:

"While they beheld, he was taken up; and a cloud received him out of their sight."

"The Lord said unto my Lord, Sit thou at my right hand, until I make thine enemies thy footstool."

"When he had by himself purged our sins, sat down on the right hand of the Majesty on high."

He ascended into heaven as (1) the perfect Man, (2) the perfect Saviour and (3) the perfect God.

(1) *The Perfect Man.*

While here upon earth He was both the perfect human and the perfect God. He functioned His life within one or the other of these spheres; but never did He co-mingle them. He could say "Whom do men say that I the son of man am?" as though He did not know. This was perfectly human. Yet John tells us that "He needed not that any should testify of man: for he knew what was in man." This was perfectly divine. As perfectly human He could say: "My God, my God, why hast thou forsaken me?" Yet in that cross it was God that was in Christ reconciling the world unto Himself. As Son of Man He was hungry: as Son of God He could turn stones into bread; but He did not minister to His human need by His divine power.

There are aspects of His presence and position in heaven which are to be classified as either human or divine. He now appears in heaven with His glorified human body in which the scars of crucifixion are forever to be seen. It will not do to speak of the days of His earth-life as the days of His incarnation. He has not ceased to be incarnate, nor will He ever cease to be. He carried His perfect humanity into heaven itself. He required no mediator, or priestly sacrifice for sin. As the Son of Man He was received into the highest glory on the grounds of His own perfection in the sight of His holy Father. Thus John saw in heaven, a man, in a glorified body, and he heard Him say: "I am he that liveth, and was dead: and, behold, I am alive for evermore." Through His death and resurrection the highest positions were given unto Him. He is the "Firstborn from the dead," as to actual victory over death, and, being raised from the dead, He is seated at the right hand of God "far above all principality, and power, and might, and dominion, and every name that is named, not only in this world, but also in that which is to come." All things are put under His feet and it is given unto Him to be Head over all things to the church, which is His body, the fulness of Him that filleth all in all. So, also, the highest title is given unto Him. Because of the cross it is said: "Wherefore God also hath highly exalted him, and given him a name which is above every name."

(2) *The Perfect Saviour.*

He is a perfect Saviour as to what He has accomplished on earth, and He is a perfect Saviour as to what He is now doing in heaven. He finished a work; yet He continues to work. Thus He is still a Saviour, even in heaven. He was a perfect Saviour as to what He did here on earth; for He faced "the wolf"—SIN; He conquered death; He vanquished Satan; and He "led captivity captive." Every aspect of this mighty victory over our foes is now guaranteed for us by His presence in glory in a human body that bears the scars of crucifixion. His work was accepted in heaven when He was received into heaven. By our union with Him, He is our present Saviour even though in heaven. We are "crucified *with* Him," "dead *with* Him," buried *with* Him," "raised *with* Him," and "seated *in* Him." We have life *from* Him, we are righteous, justified and accepted *in* Him. By being our "Advocate with the Father," He is our present Saviour even though in heaven. In this great ministry He does not make excuses for our sins: He does not plead for mercy in our behalf: He presents His own scars as evidence that He has borne the last condemnation for every sin. "There is therefore now no condemnation to them which are in Christ Jesus." By interceding for us, He is our present Saviour even though in heaven. This means that He both prays for us and shepherds our souls. He saves us from a thousand pitfalls and snares of Satan. "I have prayed for thee." "The Lord is my shepherd; I shall not want." "Wherefore he is able also to save them to the uttermost that come unto God by him, seeing he ever liveth to make intercession for them."

Crowns are promised to the believer; but the Lord Jesus Christ has won them all on the highest plane. He must have the superlative "crown of glory" for He is the Chief Shepherd over the flock of God.

As our Lord in the glory and as Head over all things to the church, He is directing all service here below, and will direct,

> "Till we all come in the unity of the faith, and of the knowledge of the Son of God, unto a perfect man, unto the measure of the stature of the fulness of Christ."

(3) *A Perfect God.* On returning to heaven He took again the robes of glory which had been so freely laid aside in order that He might suffer in our stead. The Twenty-

fourth Psalm records the song of heaven which was sung when He returned to His place in glory.

> "Who shall ascend unto the hill of the LORD? or who shall stand in his holy place? He that hath clean hands and a pure heart; who hath not lifted up his soul unto vanity, nor sworn deceitfully."

Only One such has ever gone up into heaven from this sin-cursed earth. He was pure; He was holy; He was undefiled.

> "Lift up your heads, O ye gates; even lift them up, ye everlasting doors; and the King of glory shall come in. Who is this King of Glory? The LORD of hosts, he is the King of glory."

As He now appears in heaven, the glory of God is on the face of Jesus Christ.

> "For in him dwelleth all the fulness of the Godhead bodily."
> "Crowned with glory and honour,"
> "Whom the heavens must receive until the restitution of all things."

He will then come forth as very God and very Man to take His own throne, the throne of David, and reign in righteousness and peace on the earth. He shall reign Whose right it is to reign, and He will then be

(III.) *Crowned With Many Crowns.* The last pages of of the Bible describe the consummation of the ages. The Scriptures trace the purposes and mighty working of God from the beginning of those purposes, even before the foundation of the world, to their end. It is fitting that the closing pages of God's Book should record the final triumph and victory over all rebellion against God, and picture the eternal glories of the restored order that is to be. The second coming of Christ is the consummating event for which creation has so long waited and upon which the fulfillment of the purposes and promises of God are made to depend. This consummating event has been described a number of times in both the Old Testament and the New; but the last description is complete and language fails adequately to portray the power and glory of His return. It is then that He is to be "crowned with many crowns." In many references to His second coming it is stated that He is to come in "power and great glory."

1. *He comes with power.* The Lord of glory proceeds forth from His wedding, out from heaven, followed by His spotless bride. Behold Him as lightning shining from the one part of heaven unto the other! He has a "rod of iron" in His hand with which to dash the nations "in pieces like a potter's vessel." "His eyes are as a flame of fire" and "out of his mouth goeth a sharp sword, that with it he should smite the nations." That wicked one shall He consume with the spirit of His mouth and destroy with the brightness of His coming.

"The Lord Jesus shall be revealed from heaven with his holy angels, in flaming fire, to take vengeance on them that know not God, and that obey not the gospel of our Lord Jesus Christ."

"Behold the nations are as a drop of a bucket, and are counted as the small dust of the balance; behold, he taketh up the isles as a very small thing. And Lebanon is not sufficient to burn, nor the beasts thereof sufficient for a burnt-offering. All nations are before him as nothing; and they are counted to him as less than nothing, and vanity. *** And he shall blow upon them, and they shall wither, and the whirlwind shall take them away as stubble."

"God cometh from Teman, and the Holy One from Mount

Paran. His glory covereth the heavens, and the earth is full of his praise. And his brightness is like the sun: rays stream from his hand; and this is the hiding of his power. Before him goeth the plague and burning pestilence follows his feet. He stands and measures the earth: He looks and makes nations tremble; the everlasting mountains are broken in pieces, the eternal hills sink down: His ways are everlasting."

"Our God shall come, and shall not keep silence; a fire shall devour before him and it shall be very tempestuous round about him."

"Who is this that cometh from Edom, with deep red garments from Bozrah? This that is glorious in his apparel, travelling in the greatness of his strength? I that speak in righteousness, mighty to save. Wherefore is redness in thine apparel, and thy garment like him that treadeth the winefat? I have trodden the winepress alone, and of the people not a man was with me: and I have trodden them in mine anger, and trampled them in my fury; and their blood is sprinkled upon my garments, and I have stained all my apparel. For the day of vengeance was in my heart, and the year of the redeemed was come."

Here is the Messenger of the covenant, a refiner's fire, a purifier of the sons of Levi.

"He shall set up an ensign for the nations and shall assemble the outcasts of Judah from the four corners of the earth."

"And he shall send his angels with the great sound of a trumpet, and they shall gather together his elect from the four winds, from one end of heaven to the other."

"For he cometh, for he cometh to judge the earth."

"They that dwell in the wilderness shall bow before him; and his enemies shall lick the dust. The kings of Tarshish and of the isles shall bring presents: the kings of Sheba and Seba shall offer gifts. Yea, all kings shall fall down before him; all nations shall serve him. Lift up your heads, O ye gates; and be ye lift up, ye everlasting doors; and the King of glory shall come in. Who is the King of glory? The LORD strong and mighty, the LORD mighty in battle."

In these Scriptures we have an unfolding of the sufficiency of God in His power to transform the earth and to change the shadow of darkness and sin to the ineffable light of His glory. What He hath promised He will fulfil. All the lines of hope from the first promise of final victory given in Eden, to the present hour are focused upon the return of the King in His power, majesty and strength, and He will compass every issue of the ages and vindicate every purpose of God. We should not marvel that He is to come in renovating judgments to the earth; the marvel must ever be that He, the King of Glory, should have bowed the heavens and come down to this earth to die as an unresisting Lamb. The great conquerors of the earth have depended upon power and allegiance of their armies to execute their will. The King of Glory will conquer *alone*. His power by which He created all things is sufficient to bind the forces of darkness, transform the universe, and to consummate the hopes of all the ages.

2. *He comes with great glory.*

His return in glory is recorded in Rev. xix:11-16. His glory is fourfold and is indicated by the four titles which He bears In the New Testament the Holy Spirit has given four portraits of the Lord Jesus Christ. They are the four Gospels. In Matthew He is the Lion-King; in Mark He is the faithful Servant-Ox; in Luke He is the Man Christ Jesus; and in John He is the Eternal Word of God, symbolized by the eagle, the bird of the highest altitudes. He will possess His eternal glory as the "Word of God" which He had as very God before all creation. He will have a particular glory as the "Faithful and True" Servant; He has acquired a glory through the sacrifice of His human body and because of that sacrifice God hath highly exalted

Him and given Him a name which is above every name. It is His human name of Saviourhood, the glory and extent of which no man can ever know. He will also have the Kingly glory of David's throne in a thousand, thousand times more splendor than that of Solomon. He will then be "King of kings and Lord of lords."

The passage reads:

"And I saw heaven opened, and behold a white horse; and he that sat upon him was called Faithful and True, and in righteousness doth he judge and make war. His eyes were as a flame of fire, and on his head were many crowns; and he had a name written, that no man knew, but he himself. And he was clothed in a vesture dipped in blood: and his name is called The Word of God. And the armies which were in heaven followed him upon white horses, clothed in fine linen, white and clean. And out of his mouth goeth a sharp sword, that with it he should smite the nations: and he shall rule them with a rod of iron: and he treadeth the winepress of the fierceness and wrath of Almighty God. And he hath on his vesture and on his thigh a name written, KING OF KINGS, AND LORD OF LORDS."

As a crown is the fitting symbol of authority, pre-eminence and distinction, the Lord Jesus Christ, once crowned with thorns and now crowned with glory and honor will then hold every crown of authority by right and title. He will have won every crown of pre-eminence and distinction that can ever be in heaven above or earth beneath. It will be our unspeakable joy to cast our crowns at His feet and to join with the angelic host in the coronation hymn:

"Bring forth the royal diadem and crown Him Lord of all."

Advent Hope From Primal Expectation to Final Manifestation

W. Leon Tucker, *Bible Teacher.*

Simply and sublimely the Word of God opens with a sentence containing seven words. This wonderful sentence, "In the beginning God created the heavens and the earth," speaks of the original creation. The second verse of Genesis I is not a continuation of verse 1; there has been an arrest. Verse 2 does not continue the record of creation; verse 2 shows the original creation brought into chaos and confusion. The reason for this we are not now to discuss save that God did not create the heavens and the earth originally in chaos. He created them with the perfection which marks everything which comes from His hand. In Genesis 1:3 we have a reconstructive era, the beginning of reconstruction. The original heavens and earth in their creation in Genesis 1:1 are not a matter of chronology. There is no date, there is no information, there is no calendar, there is no chronology for the original creation. How long the original creation remained in a state of chaos no one knows, but Genesis 1:3 is the beginning of a recreation in which the original heavens and earth are now restored by the mighty hand of the One who in the beginning created all things; for not only is He Creator, but He is also re-Creator.

Genesis 1:3 begins the recreation of the earth. It occurred in six days of time, twenty-four hours for each day, and during those days the progressive unfolding and development of the Divine purpose can be seen. In Genesis at the close of chapter one we find a finished creation and a Sabbathic day.

In Genesis ii we behold man, the first man and the first woman, in their dominion over the earth. We find this marvelous union of Adam and his bride-to-be associated in the Book of Ephesians with the mystery concerning Christ and the Church; for said the Apostle Paul, "I speak of a great mystery concerning Christ and the Church." In Genesis iii there comes into the new creation the intruder. One who brought sin first into the universe and upon the first creation, now brings it into the second. The original sinner in the universe of God is not Adam; there was an aboriginal. The original sinner in the universe of God was Satan. I John iii:8 declares, "He that sinneth is of the devil; for the devil sinneth from the beginning." In Genesis iii sin enters the world. The way sin enters the world according to Romans v:12, "Wherefore, as by one man sin entered into the world, and death by sin; and so death passed upon all men, for that all have sinned." And it is found that the source of human life was so corrupted that from that day until this day there has been no flesh that could stand before God. God never has taken over human flesh; God has no way of salvage for human flesh. God nails flesh in the place of death and deals with it in no other way, for its issue is death and corruption, desolation, sin, sorrow and suffering. And the first child produced from the loins of corrupt man was a murderer. And whatever may be the sympathy which the rationalists try to create concerning

Cain, we are through with human reason, and rest upon Divine revelation; for this Book says that Cain was of that evil one, and this Book declares that his brother whom he slew was of a line which was known as the line of faith. The first man that was born was a murderer, and the second one was murdered; the first one an anti-Christ, and the second one a figure of the Christ which was to come. In Genesis iv we find the results of sin in the world,—death and murder; and man by nature has been a murderer from that day unto the hour in which I am now speaking unto you. And in Genesis v, which has been called aptly and marvelously in my judgment the epitah chapter of the Word of God, death is reigning. Adam begat sons in his own likeness and they died. He could produce them only in his likeness, and he himself was dead in sin; and you can get nothing out of the flesh but a reaping of corruption. Genesis v shows everyone dying until we have reached the seventh from Adam, and he saw not death; for he escaped death by the one and solitary and single means of escape from death, and that was by translation. God has only one way that any may ever escape death, and that is by the way of translation. So God took the seventh from Adam out of the way by translation because a judgment was due the earth and God had made no provision for Enoch during the judgment which was to be on the earth; for in the Sixth chapter the corruption and the violence which was filling the earth made necessity in Chapter vii for the preparation of a place of security and shelter for God's own purpose, and Enoch would have had no place in that ark. Indeed he would have been a strange and pitiful figure; for God had planned that ark for the three sons of Noah, that He might preserve the nations of the earth alive and take them through the judgment of the flood. He had no provision for Enoch's transportation, so He gave him a translation; and God has no provision for the transportation of the Church of God through the coming tribulation; He is going to give the body of Christ a translation; for He never confuses His purpose. The Jew and the Gentile and the Church of God are never one in the Book of God. So we find in the Sixth chapter the corruption of the earth; more than corruption, eruption. In the Seventh chapter the beginning of the flood, in the Eighth chapter the flood at its full, and in the Ninth chapter the flood at its finish.

At the close of Chapter ix is one little prophecy which outlines national life from the time that prophecy was made until the time I am now speaking, and beyond the time I am now speaking and throughout all history. There you have the destiny of those three sons; for into that ark Peter says, eight souls were taken. There was Noah, his wife, his three sons and their wives, Ham and Shem and Japheth; and in that ark God was preserving alive the nations of the earth. And will you believe me that then and there all the nations on the face of the earth dwelt in pacification perhaps for the first time since nations have been known to exist. There they dwelt together peacefully.

Chapter x outlines all the nations on the face of the earth. And who were the passengers in that ark? The nations of the earth. The nations are divided into three: the Hamitic peoples, the Shemitic and the Japhetic peoples, God saving the nations for His purpose in that ark. And not only did we have all the nations in that ark, but we had this Book in that ark, because the Shemitic people gave us every word of this Book from the beginning of Genesis to the end of Revelation. And not only that, but Jesus Christ was in that ark Himself, for He was in the loins of Shem; and so God gave the living Word and the written Word security in that ark as well as the nations. And when they come out upon the new earth a prophecy is outlined; Hamitic peoples to be the servants; Japhetic people to be the civilizers, the enlargers of the earth, to take possession of its great boundary lines; but the Shemitic people to be the people in whom God would dwell; for in the tents of Shem God dwells, and never has God been down to this earth that He has not been down in the tents of Shem. When the tabernacle was built He dwelt between the cherubim; He was dwelling in the tents of Shem. When the temple was reared, and the Shekinah vision, He was dwelling in the midst of Shem. When God came down in Christ in the incarnation, He came to His own, He was dwelling in the tents of Shem. And when again He comes and His feet touch Mount Olivet, He will once again dwell in the midst of the Shemitic people. So the tenth chapter of the Book of Genesis is a record of all the nations on the face of the earth. National life is there written in advance. The Word of God is the information which the old world needs today concerning great national problems, because this Book is a universal and a national Book. From this wonderful tenth chapter of Genesis, where the Hamitic, Shemitic and Japhetic nations are outlined, we pass along to the eleventh chapter, where, according to Deuteronomy xxxii:8, the Most High was the One who began segregation for civilization; for by the confusing of tongues He separated them, and by the separation into their tongues they took their habitable place on the face of the earth.

And so in the twelfth chapter of Genesis, after the babel is over, we see now Abraham with the choice, God taking to Himself a nation for His own purpose. And the reason God took this nation Israel was a two-fold reason, that He might give revelation two-fold: first in the written Word, and secondly in the living Word. So we get from the Jew not only the written Word, but also when Christ came He was of the Shemitic race, He was of the seed of David according to the flesh.

In the rest of the Book of Genesis we find Abraham bore a son whose name was Isaac. Twice Abraham got Isaac from the grave: First, from the dead womb of his mother with the Messianic promise and hope. They were all depending upon Isaac. Then Isaac having been delivered from the dead womb of Sarah was delivered from the altar on which he was placed, from which he came out as a figure of the resurrection of a greater Son of Abraham. Isaac then bears a son whose name is Jacob, and Jacob bears twelve sons, and one of the twelve one day appears with a garment upon him which is not what sometimes we would attempt to make our children believe in the Sunday School; but the coat of many colors was a garment which signified that the father had conferred upon him the honor of the first born, and all the children must look to him. Joseph was the object of their envy and their enmity, and when they saw him they said, "The father has honored him. He is made the heir. Come, let us kill him." And in the life of Joseph we have Jesus set forth in type.

For many years I attempted to discover why Joseph was a type of the Lord Jesus, until in the 89th Psalm I read and found. "He hath ordained a type, or a testimony, in Joseph." Joseph was loved by his father, hated by his brethren, sold out of envy, raised exalted to a throne. A Saviour for the Gentiles and finally of his own brethren.

So we find the Book of Genesis ends with Joseph leading his nation down into Egypt, Jacob rising in his bed, lifting up his head, and in the forty-ninth chapter outlining Jewish history down to the end of time.

Then what? The Book of Genesis closing in Egypt and the Book of Exodus opening in Egypt with a great and mighty international menace, for Israel had so increased that the Hamitic peoples now see in them a problem and therefore—a suggestion which was satanic—they attempted the obliteration of the race through generations, and the first born was preserved and kept from the wrath of the king.

In Exodus v-ix we see the judgments upon Egypt and upon Pharoh. In chapters xi-xiii we have the Passover; and in chapter xiv the passing out, and in chapter xv the miracle of the Red Sea. In the rest of the Book of Exodus the murmuring begins and the tabernacle law is given, the instruction for the building of the tabernacle; and when you reach the close of Exodus Jehovah is dwelling in the tabernacle. And what He said in the tabernacle is the record of the Book of Leviticus. When you reach the Book of Numbers there is forty years of wandering, because in Hebrews xi, when there is put on record the things which have been done by faith, there is nothing done by faith from the time that Moses takes the children of Israel out of Egypt by faith in the Passover blood until the time of Joshua and the walls of Jericho fall down. Within that time there is not a thing that is of faith. It is 40 years of wandering through the wilderness.

Then having entered the land, having driven out next to extermination the Canaanites, we find them placed under judges because of the hardness of their hearts. Then came kings, three of them, for they cried for a king. God gave them a Saul for 40 years. He gave them a David for 40 years. He gave them a Solomon for 40 years; and in Solomon the glory of national Israel reached its highest height until the present time, but not the height to which it is yet to come. And after the death of Solomon, Rehoboam and Jeroboam, and the disruption of the nation. There were ten tribes moved to Shechem and then into Samaria and the ten were called Israel. And there is only one instance, for there is no theological etymology could ever make Israel in this Book mean anything but the natural descendants of Jacob. And here we find that when the ten were called Israel and moved down to Samaria, the seat of their government was there. And in about 1775 years before Christ what? The dispersion of the ten tribes, but Judah continued in Jerusalem, two tribes.

Then follow a number of dynasties of which I shall not now speak; and 606 years before Christ approximately Nebuchadnezzar, a Chaldean king, was battering away at the north walls of Jerusalem. Jeremiah sat down after the siege and wrote lamentations and cried out and said, "Oh, how has a mighty city become tributary!" For Judah is now dispersed, and beginning with Nebuchadnezzar there is what is known in the Bible as the "times of the Gentiles," a time during which Gentile nations shall subject the land of Palestine and the people of Israel; and, as our brother showed this morning in his address. It was a marvelous thing how, when Christ was born, a tax had been levied upon the whole world. The fourth part in the image seen by Nebuchadnezzar, the fourth world empire exercised universal rule over Israel and now levied a tax upon the whole world, and the whole world was paying tribute to him in the days of Augustus Caesar. And since the day the Roman Empire began as the fourth world empire it has never ceased to be on the map of Europe. What is "Kaiser" but a contraction of "Caesar?" What is the Czar of Russia but another Caesar?

So in the days of the fourth world empire He was born; but Matthew's Gospel does not open the New Testament; the New Testament is not opened by Matthew's Gospel. No; we are still on the ground of the old covenant when the blood of bulls and goats maintained. You have no New Testament until He dies, for it is a covenant in His blood. And you cannot therefore bring the Sermon on the Mount into gospel preaching as a means of salvation, because salvation is not in His life; it is in His death. I know that He did what He did because He was what He was; and I know if He had not been what He was, He could not have done what He did. But what He did had value because He was what He was; He was and is Christ the Son of God.

So we find that when the Gospels close He has died, has been raised again, and has been exalted to the right hand of God. And then we find on the day of Pentecost the birthday of that Church which was spoken of in the sixteenth chapter of Matthew, and the Jew Peter arising and crying out, "You men of Israel, you have crucified your Lord, but God has raised Him from the dead." This was the sure mercies of God. Death and hades could not hold Him. He is out and gone and has the keys of them on his girdle. Therefore Peter says, "You men of Israel, you slew Him." They said, "What must we do?" And he said "Go back to John's baptism; repent and be baptised for remission of your sins. What John and Jesus told you, I tell you." Because there is no remission of sin in these days by the act of baptism; only by faith in Him is there salvation. So we find in the remaining chapters of Acts the Jews have turned away from the risen Messiah. And then Paul went out and preached to the Gentile world. And Christ is in the heavens, a rejected King, but nevertheless the King. He is the rightful heir and the only royal seed of the throne of God. God send Him back soon! That is the purpose of this mighty convention; mighty because of the presence of the Holy Ghost; not mighty because men are here, but because He is here to speak through them.

Then the Book of Romans is next to be seen, which is the greatest international Book of all, moving out from the Jewish world to the Gentile world. And when the Book of Romans is finished we come to the Epistles, which are a record of the occupation of Christ at the right hand of God. Oh, I wish I could get the Church of God to turn her eyes to the place where her Lord is. That will be the cure for her worldliness, occupation with Christ in heaven. I have forgotten the occupations of the earth apart from my service, which I trust is a sacrificial service. I am occupied with the One who is at God's right hand; and though I am a sinner ruined by sin, ransomed by blood, regenerated by the Holy Ghost, raised in power,—though I am that, I want to tell you it is because Christ is in heaven that I am there with Him. I would be yet in my sins if He had not died for me and took them to the grave, arose for me and took me up with Him when He went, and that is where I am with God, and that is where every believer is; and if we could only get the believer occupied with Christ at the right hand of God, and less with our condition down here on earth, there would be a new victory in the Church today. It is Christ at the right hand of God; and it is the agency—if I dare use that word—of the Holy Spirit to keep the believers's eyes wherever Christ is. Call me a dreamer if you desire, a star gazer if you want to, but I have my eyes only upon the wonderful Man yonder in the heavens, Christ Himself. And He can never appear before God again apart from me, and I can never appear before God apart from Him, we two are so joined. That is the view of the Epistles. The four gospels contain the good news of the Son concerning His Father, but the Epistles contain the good news of the Father concerning the Son; and that should be the subject of our service.

And then the most remarkable thing that is recorded in those Epistles and one of the most wonderful things took place, that never could be any other way than this way. For in the Epistles we have the revelation of a pacification that is above everything that has ever been known. Do you think the Jew and the Gentile will ever dwell together in peace? I know of a place where the Jew and the Gentile dwell together in peace; and I know Who made the peace. There was a time when there was a middle wall of partition between the Jew and the Gentile, and God intends that to maintain in the age to come, that His people shall still be a separate people and a sacrificial people; but I know a place now where all are one. I know a place where the greatest pacification has been wrought in the history of all the universe. I know a place where there is not to be found anywhere a Jew or a Gentile, a bond nor a free, a male nor a female; where racial distinctions are gone, where all social distinctions are erased, and where all sexual distinctions are gone. There is neither a Jew nor a Gentile, a bondman nor a free, male or a female in Christ Jesus. And that is the position which we now occupy in Christ Jesus. Ephesians tells us how it is. He hath by the blood of his cross made of the two one new man, breaking down the middle wall of partition which was between us, raising us up to heaven, where we are all sitting together. The only place in which a Jew and a Gentile are together is in Christ.

That is the only place God wants them to be. The heavens still receive Him, and the world still rejects Him, because we cannot be united with Him without rejection of the world which rejected Him.

The heavens still receive Him, and if the Church of God were left here to pass through the coming judgments, then God's purpose would be confused, because those judgments, says the Book of Romans, represent the nations in tribulation, "upon the soul of every man, to the Jew first, and also to the Gentile." But we are neither Jews nor Gentiles, for if any man be in Christ he is a new creature. You cannot change Hamitic, Shemitic and Japhetic over into the blood of Christ. That does not mean that God is through with the Shemitic race, or the Hamitic peoples, or the Japhetic peoples; but He must get the Church of God out of the way, for they are not an earthly folk to hinder His earthly plan; and inasmuch as no judgment is due, for judgment has all been settled for the Church of God once upon Him, there is nothing to do but for God to let loose His vials of wrath. And the only difference between the book of Daniel and the book of Revelation in subject matter is this: "Daniel, seal up your book; it is for the time of the end." Revelation: "John, take the seals off your book, for the end time has come." And just as soon as the Church of God has gone, the Book of Revelation begins in its judgments, its seals having been broken, which cover the entire figure in my judgment,—the sounding of the trumpets, the pouring of the vials of the wrath of God upon Jew and Gentile. And then, thank God, the return of the Lord in the clouds of heaven, to deliver His people Israel in the hour of their peril, to establish the Shemitic race in the land, to give them the reorganization of the tribes, the rehabilitation of the Jews, the incarceration of the devil and the establishment of His Kingdom.

I want to tell you in closing that there is upon the earth today a throne on which there is no king, and it has fallen down. There is in heaven today a King who has no throne. He is at His Father's right hand. For He said, Son, they have rejected Thee; sit on my right hand, until one of these days,—until one of these days the kingless throne will receive the throneless King. May God hasten the day.

A Pastor's Testimony

By OTHO F. BARTHOLOW,

Pastor of First M. E. Church, Mt. Vernon, N. Y.

I have been for years as a minister of the Gospel, a prisoner of hope. I have longed for that day to come when in some sane, rational, beautiful way, to me the foremost doctrine of the Holy Scriptures and the one with more dynamic, more solution of all human and national ills in it than any other doctrine within the sacred pages revealed, should be presented in this great metropolis. That hour has come, and our hope is realized. The most precious truth has been associated in the past for so many years with error, with people that had more earnestness than perhaps intelligence at times, and has always been coupled with some particular fad, that it has been a delight to my heart to know that under the leadership of these scholars and these followers of Christ such a meeting as this could be held. And I wish here this afternoon for a moment to express a conviction and an experience.

In the first place, the conviction. Let us understand clearly that we are using a great many shibboleths just now. "The world safe for democracy"; nobody seems to know just what it means, but perhaps we do. "The league of nations." As I read history, the past is full of dead democracies, and the world was no safer with the democracies of the past than with aristocracies; and yet we believe in a kind of a government of the people that will in the end be a blessing to the earth. But, beloved, I am convinced more and more the only rule we may look for in this world that will consummate the union of nations and of hearts is the coming of our Lord Jesus Christ as King of kings and Lord of lords. And my prayer is that the King now in the heavens may inspire the statesmen of the world to understand a little more about this, and that you and I may not be carried away with this shibboleth, "Everything is going to be new now." New how? And the inference is by evolution. Evolution has failed, if you please. We have had that illustrated to us as never before in the history of nations, and our hope now is for the glorious appearing of the great God our Saviour and the coming of His kingdom. We have been so lost in the kingdom, concerned and absorbed in the kingdom, that we have lost the King. Thank God, we are coming back to the emphasis of that which is central, Jesus Christ incarnate, the human, glorified Lord coming as King of kings and Lord of lords. My conviction.

Now my experience. I was educated in a Methodist Theological Seminary, educated in the post-millennial theory. I tried to preach it. I thought I was called at times to fight the pre-millennial theory. I tried to do that and had a hard time. I took my Bible by commentaries and by the professors' authority. I made up my mind a few years ago I would take it for myself, as God intended I should, study it anew; and as I read it from Genesis all through to Revelation a light came to me. "Young man, you have been mistaken. You have been preaching an error. The truth is the pre-millennial theory, the coming of Jesus Christ for His own and to fulfil His promise in Israel,—King and Ruler, And the saints to be caught up to meet Him in the air."

Then the great truth came to me; "and I began to preach it." I was just enough of a theorist to say, "The proof of a thing is what it does. I am going to see what it does." I preached to my people. A new spirit came into the church. A few months ago I got into a conference where there were eight men who were post-millennarians arguing against one pre-millennarian; eight to one. Well. it takes eight of them to overcome one of us; then they cannot do it. But this philosopher said: "The only trouble with the pre-millennial idea is, it cuts the nerve of action. It causes a man to cease his efforts in this world to bring men to Christ. It paralyzes activity, makes us visionaries and impracticable; therefore, it cannot be true." My experience was this: It put power in the church; it gave energy for every field of activity.

I want by the power of the Holy Ghost to prepare the bride for the coming of the Bridegroom, to prepare the bride to be caught up with Him. New life came. I began to teach it to men ten years ago; began with ten men in a Bible class to teach this great fundamental doctrine. To-day I have fourteen hundred men in the largest Bible class in this country. I began to teach it to women. We started with twenty. We now have seven hundred women studying the Scripture of God, this great blessed truth that holds with all that is in the Scripture that we hold true, and the hope of the nations and the very longing of our hearts this afternoon. Talk as you please, Jesus as the pre-eminent Lord, Jesus as the eternal incarnate, perfect Man, and very God, shall come and reign; and then after the millennium He will bring the consummation.

Signs of the Times

DAVID JAMES BURRELL,

Pastor of Marble Collegiate Church, Fifth Ave. and 29th St., N. Y. City.

I know why I am here, but some of my friends do not. One of them said to me a little while ago, "I should think among all those pre-millennarians you would feel like a cat in a strange garret." I said, "Why?" He said, "I didn't know you were a pre-millennarian."

Well I will tell you this: A man is known by the company he keeps. I am going up to Carnegie Hall to find some good society, and I can depend upon the people who are looking for the coming of Jesus Christ to believe in Him, and to believe in His blessed Word. And that is why I am here; and you can call me a pre-millennarian if you want to. I never call myself anything else; but I am not going to stand for any names, you understand. I am here because *I love His appearing,* and *He is coming.* Put that down! My Lord is coming one of these days, coming out of heaven, and with these eyes I shall see Him. It may be looking over the ramparts of heaven, or it may be down here working tomorrow morning with some of you, that He will come; but when He comes I am going to be on the watch and with these eyes I shall see Him. I am not at all sure that I can interpret prophecy as well or as much in detail or particular as some of my friends. I don't know so much about prophecy as some of them do. Now I am not criticising them—God bless them all—but I simply say that prophecy to my mind is a revealing and it involves also an adumbration; otherwise it would be a mere statement of fact. All real prophecy is very much like a Japanese picture, which has no very visible perspective; but there is one thing about a Japanese picture you can always see; you can always see Fujiyama, the great mountain, in the background, snow capped, white crowned, glorious. That is the way with the Scripture prophecy; we cannot always catch the perspective. I cannot as well as some of you men, like Mr. Gaebelein, and others, I cannot always get what is intervening, but I can always see that cloud capped hill: our Lord is coming again.

It was a great day, oh, it was a wonderful day upon Mount Olivet, when the disciples were met, wondering when they were going to see Him again. He had an appointment with them, as He has with us; and while they stood there all at once He stood among them. He stood there among them and told them some wonderful things as to the business of their lives; and when He was through there was a rift in the clouds and the heavens opened to receive Him. He rose with His hands stretched out in benediction; and the disciples stood gazing up, and they may have heard a rustle of wings and they may have seen great gates, great crimson gates, roll back, and they heard voices afar in the distance: "Lift up your heads, O ye gates; and be ye lifted up, ye everlasting doors; and let the King of Glory enter in." And if I had been there I would have stood gazing up into heaven, too. I would have been gazing up until today for the very wonder of it. But then the shining ones stood by and said, "Why stand ye gazing up into heaven?" Well, where would they gaze? "Why stand ye gazing up into heaven? He shall so come as ye have seen Him go." Now that is enough for me. "He shall so come," on clouds of glory seated; oh, wonderful shekinah! And there will be the rustle of wings, and there will be the rolling back of the golden gates, and there will be men looking up, and Christ coming down to reveal Himself again.

And I don't know so much about the signs as some of my brethren do. I am to talk about the signs of the times,—the roll of heavy artillery, the march and countermarch of armies; our great army marching one way, and another great army, thank God, going the other way.

The first of the signs is war. "And there shall be wars and rumors of wars." At the end of the tenth century, at the completion, that is to say, of a round cycle of a thousand years, it was generally supposed that Christ was coming. The hands had swept around the dial and the clock had struck, and people put on their ascension robes and got ready for the appearing of the Lord.

And the Emperor of Germany—the Emperor of Germany now is a horse of another color—but the then Emperor of Germany put on his ascension robes, and he went out everywhere among the hamlets, and villages, preaching the coming of Christ; and on that last night of the thousandth year of the Christian era he also waited for the great coming. And the night wore on, and the midnight bell struck, and the day dawned, and the world woke as if from a paralysis and went back to its accustomed tasks. There had been wars. There had been famines and pestilences insomuch that men called it Armageddon, and that is why they looked for the immediate coming of Christ.

Well now, after the completion of almost another cycle of a thousand years we have been talking about Armageddon. The foundations of the great deep have been broken up, and the skies have been lurid above us, and the world never saw such a commotion as we have seen in these last days. But what said the Master? "Now," He said, "do not be too sure. Ye shall see wars and rumors of wars, but do not be troubled the end is not yet."

Now there is another sign. A second sign is that of the harrow. "There shall be great tribulation in those days." There is coming a future great tribulation. The word "tribulation" is from "tribulum," meaning a great harrowing; and the early Christians supposed the persecutions to which they were subjected were to be followed immediately or quite so by the coming of Christ. The men who were distressed and harrowed by Nero in his successive persecutions betook themselves to the catacombs, and there under the dripping of the night dew and in the solitude and in their fearful hours they greeted each other in the dawn not by saying good morning, but by saying "Maran-atha," "The Lord cometh." And when the night came there in the deep darkness, they did not say goodnight, they said, "Maran-atha,"—the Lord cometh. And the years have passed and He has not come yet. But He is not slack as some men count slackness. The years are nothing to Him. No pendulum swings with God. No hands sweep around His great dial. You and I live and must needs talk in terms of space and time. To Him the past is as the future. He has travelled through it; and His coming will be sure and it will be a quick coming in the chronology of the Infinite God.

I am not putting it off, mind you. It may come tomorrow morning. I am on the watch; only I say that I am a little careful; I want to be a little careful about any absolute statement as to time. The persecutions of the past have gone by. We are not subject, thank God, to persecution in these days. But the opposition to the Gospel so far from ceasing with the end of persecution is more vigorous, more strenuous and bitter today than it ever has been in the history of the world. And that is the meaning of this war. It is the opposition of the world against the Christ of God. "The kings of the earth have set themselves"—the great powers—"the kings of the earth have set themselves, and the rulers have taken counsel together against our Lord and against His Christ, saying, "Let us break their bands asunder, and cast away their cords from us." Listen. "He that sitteth in the heavens shall laugh; the Lord shall have them in derision." He shall declare His decree. What is it? "Thou art my Son; this day have I begotten thee. "Ask and I will give thee the heathen for thine inheritance, and the uttermost parts of the earth for thy possession." O men and women, was there ever such a prayer as that which Christ offered when He stretched up His pierced hands upon the cross and pleaded with God, like a great Atlas with the world resting on His breaking heart, "O my Father, as the fruit of the travail of my soul give me the heathen for mine inheritance and the uttermost parts of the earth for my possession." That is the answer of God to the harrowing of the world. And yet I am not prepared to say even in the interpretation of the sign of the harrow that the end will be today.

Then there is a third sign, that of the apostacy. There is a future abomination of desolation. In our own day the abomination of desolation is the Trojan horse which has been wheeled within the gates of the Church of God. You don't know an atheist today or an out and out infidel. We used to have Ingersoll and Bradlaw, the last of the old guard, who stood like Goliath, shaking their spears like weavers' beams, and crying out against God Almighty. And there is something frightful in the thought of old time infidelity. But, gentlemen, it has gone out of vogue, and the only atheism and infidelity in the world today which has any fight left in it is within the professing Church. It is in the pulpit, it is in the pews, where Christ is denied and travestied and reduced to the meanest dimensions of a diminutive man; and where the Bible is derided so that it is no longer even the best of books, far from it, not true, only true in occasional spots. The Word of God! All that inside of the Church. I am not given to throwing these harsh criticisms at the bride of Christ, but, brethren, I am speaking God's truth. The only belligerent, aggressive, effective, destructive infidelity in the world today is from the belly of the Trojan horse that has been wheeled within our gates.

Now if the apostasy was ever a sign, it is a terrific sign of the coming of Christ in these days, and yet in view of all the patience of the Lord in the centuries gone by, I am not ready to say even yet that He will come before another morning. But there is a fourth sign. That is the sign of the wakening of the bride. Do you know that all the Gospel is in two little words? One is "Come," and of course the other is "Go." The Church long ago decided to come. Oh, all you people and everybody else that professes to love Jesus Christ, have come. "Come unto me, all ye that labor and are heavy laden, and I will give you rest." And the Lord pity us, the most we do get when we come is rest; and here we sit. The best hymn that we can sing is:

"When I can read my title clear to mansions in the skies,
I'll bid farwell to every fear and wipe my weeping eyes."

And it does not make any difference how many weeping eyes there are in Belgium or over in Armenia, or anywhere else. We are just as busy as we can be wiping our own eyes. There is another hymn which strikes me as a thousand times better. It is, "Throw out the life line; someone is sinking today." The Church has not learned it yet. As old Dr Duff said, "We are only playing at missions; we have not begun yet." We have come; we have not learned how to go. That was the word of the Master when He stood on Olivet. Do you think He came back and remained with His disciples forty days for nothing, just to show Himself, and to have them glad for a few meetings and then sorry for a long while? Have you thought He came back and stayed with them forty days for that? He came back because He had something to say, and all that He had to say was in the great commission, "Go." Get up and go. Go out into the highways and hedges; go out into the remote frontier; go out into the regions beyond. Go; evangelize. That is the thing the Church has not learned yet. The Church is asleep today. We can raise more money for the campaign in northern France in twenty-four hours in America than all the Christian people in America will give for a ten years' campaign for the advancement of the gospel of Christ.

The Lord said the Gospel must be preached throughout

the whole world; then shall the end be. He did not say the world was to be converted. Now here is what He said: "Go preach the Word; preach the Word; take the Book, the Gospel, and give it to the whole world, and I will do the rest." It is the Word that has saving power. The Secretary of the American Bible Society told me two or three days ago that ten million khaki testaments had been circulated among the armies of the world within the last four years. Thank God for that! It is the Book that does the business, not you nor I, except as God is pleased to use us. The great dynamic is His Spirit ,and the instrument which He uses in His Word, and the great promise is this: "As the rain and the snow cometh down from heaven, and returneth not thither, but watereth the earth, and maketh it to bring forth and bud, and give seed to the sower and bread to the eater; so shall"—your word? Oh, no—"so shall my word be that goeth forth out of my mouth. It shall not return unto me void; but it shall accomplish that which I please, and prosper in the thing whereto I sent it."

Well, I don't know now at the end. Am I a pre-millenarian? Am I good enough for such folk? Well, I declare I feel at home among you. I love the Lord's appearing. He is coming; coming to reign in glory. I do not see Him yet, but I shall see Him with these eyes.

In the meantime what are we going to do about it? I see the Lord coming this way. He is wiping the perspiration from His face. He has had a busy day of it. "My Father worketh hitherto, and I work." He has two sickles with Him. He is coming this way. If you and I stand here idle in the market place, called His name, He will say: "My friend, I have been out reaping Here is my sickle; here is a cycle for thee. Come thou with Me. Say not it is yet four months, and then cometh the harvest? Lift up your eyes and see. The fields are white unto the harvest. Come with Me." Oh, that is the glory of manhood! It is great to be saved, but it is stupendous to be called with our high calling to be laborers together with Him. Now find what He wants us to do.

One of these days some of us will be walking along the street—you and I, Doctor, may be walking along the street—and talking politics, or talking about the weather, or about business conditions, or something of that sort, and something will happen. There will be a bright light; there will be a rift in the clouds. I will drop your arm. "Doctor, look, look, look! Maran-atha! The Lord is coming!" And afterward the mountains and the hills shall break forth into singing, and all the trees of the field shall clap their hands for joy; and the tabernacle of God will come down among men, and He will dwell with them, and they shall be His people, and God Himself shall be their God. Amen. Even so come, Lord Jesus.

"Roll swift around, ye wheels of time
And bring the welcome day."

The Manifestation of the King in the Gospel of Matthew

By FORD C. OTTMAN, Author and Bible Teacher.

Let us look at this time for a little while into these Gospel pages and see how our Lord was presented to the nation to which He came. You have but to open the pages of the New Testament, and at once His identity is made known: first, by His legal royal descent, and secondly by His supernatural birth. As the King of Israel He needed the one, as the King of the Kingdom of Heaven He needed the other; and He had both. John the Baptist, His forerunner, declared that every mountain and hill should be made low and that every valley should be exalted; so that on this dead level, this plain, all mankind was to stand before God; and on this level meeting humanity, John the Baptist, foreordained of God to run before the King, introduced His Kingdom as at hand.

You will notice that one of the first things so far as the Gospel of Matthew is concerned is that we have no chronological record here of the life of our Lord. You will notice in this Gospel of Matthew, which by common consent of us all is the Gospel of His kingdom, that when He was introduced to that nation and when He had been tested in His humanity as to His ability to accomplish that for which He had been sent by the Father into the world, that immediately going up into a mountain, He announced those principles according to which His kingdom was to be constituted, instituted and governed. And immediately after He had announced the constitutional principles according to which His kingdom was to be established and governed, we find that this Divinely guided man Matthew, nothing but a man who had been seated at the receipt of custom hitherto, but now filled and governed by the Holy Spirit, proceeds at once to identify for his own people the King who had thus announced the principles of the Kingdom that He had come into the world to establish.

In the eighth and the ninth chapters of Matthew—perhaps all chapters of the Bible are equally remarkable—but there is something extraordinarily remarkable to me in these two chapters that follow the so-called Sermon on the Mount, and which precede the sending forth of the disciples to proclaim throughout the length and breadth of Israel the Kingdom that our Lord had come to establish. In these two brief chapters there are given to us the identification marks of the King. There are twelve great signs that manifest in a most marvelous way the King of Israel; twelve great signs that are grouped together not in chronological order, but in a Divine order, as Matthew was guided by the Spirit to give it. And these are in three groups of four signs each. In the first group there are four miracles of healing; in the second group there are four miracles of power; and in the last group there are four miracles of healing. Our Lord came down from the mountain, and there came to Him a man full of leprosy. He did not come chronologically at that time, but Matthew puts him there and for a purpose. This man that was full of leprosy came and fell at Jesus' feet and said, "Lord, if Thou wilt Thou canst make me clean"; and immediately He cleansed him and sent him away to the priests to offer the gifts required by the law of Moses for a testimony unto them. A testimony as to what? Leprosy in the very nature of it was the symbol and type of sin. With leprosy nobody could deal but God; and yet here is a man filled with leprosy, and by a word he is cleansed. "Go to the priests and offer the gifts for a testimony that now indeed God, who alone can deal with leprosy, is working in Israel." Isn't it a sign? I think so. Demonstrating first of all that He is the Son of God, His supreme title, and always foremost with Him; and denying that, all else must fall into ruin. He is the Son of God. He has proved Himself to be the Son of God by this cleansing of the leper. Then comes the centurion. "Lord, I am not worthy that Thou shouldst come under my roof. Speak the word only, and my servant shall be healed." He marveled and said, "I have not found so great faith, no not in Israel." He is finding faith greater among the Gentiles than in Israel. "I have not found so great faith, no not in Israel." And He spoke the word and the servant was healed. Demonstrating, if they could have seen it, that He was the son of Abraham, because as Abraham's seed in Him should all the nations of the earth be blessed. I think some of us might see also in the third of these miracles, where Peter's wife's mother is restored from her fever, the Lord acting as the son of David, pointing forward to the day now so near when, thank God, the great fever of unrest shall be over and the Jewish people brought back into Divine favor.

And then the fourth and last of that first group: Demon possessed and all kinds of sick people brought to Him at eventide, and the demons are cast out and all the sick are healed, and this in answer to one of the prophecies of Isaiah which declared the blessings that were to come into the world with the advent of the Messiah and the establishing of His kingdom. And He was demonstrated in that miracle as the Son of man, by which title of course He takes the kingdom and brings in the glory.

In the second group of four miracles—they are not exactly all miracles of the same kind, but the first would be miracle enough to many of us—a man says to Jesus, "I will follow Thee whithersoever Thou goest." And the Lord says, "The foxes have holes, the birds of the air have nests, but the Son of man hath not where to lay His head." And I say that here is a sign of sovereignty, a peculiar sign of Divine sovereignty, the Son of man in the place of creature necessity not subject to His circumstances, but absolutely sovereign over them, and saying to a disciple that would follow Him, "The birds of the air have their nests, and the foxes have holes in the ground, but the Son of man hath not where to lay His head." And isn't it fine for us to think today that Jesus when He was here in humanity was never once governed by His circumstances, but always compelled His circumstances to minister to Him and to bear witness to His glory.

We have an expression that has become so common that none of us seem to be able to escape from its use: "How are you feeling this morning?" "Very well, thank you, under the circumstances." I never heard anybody say, "Very well, thank you, supremely and serenely above all circumstances." They are always under them. And the very word itself, "circumstances"; circum, around, a thing that is standing around. Why, these circumstances are a thing that has been put around you. It is the very hedge around you, the very thing to protect you; and how was it possible that you ever got under? That is where your trouble lies. You are under the circumstances. Jesus in all the glory of His human life was never once subject to His circumstances. Jesus compelled His circumstances to minister to Him. "The Son of man hath not where to lay His head." I say that this is a sign of sovereignty, of sovereignty over any and all circumstances, which we may rejoice in as we think of the Lord this afternoon.

The second sign in this second group is a mark of sovereignty. It is the storm on the sea, and Jesus, wearied in His humanity, is asleep and the boat is filling. The disciples have got all the evidence on their side, for the boat is sinking; and they go over to Him and waken Him and say, "Lord, carest Thou not that we perish?" And notice that before our Lord pays any attenion to the storm or to the filling of the boat, He says to the disciples, "Oh ye of little faith, wherefore didst thou doubt?" And then with a word He stills the tempest. And they all marveled and said, "What manner of man is this, that the winds and the waves obey Him?" Sovereign over nature! And when anybody comes to talk to me about the sovereignty of physical law and the reign of law, I think that you and I can rely that the great Framer of these laws did not tie His own hands when He framed them, and He could set them aside when He wished and when He willed, and without one single jar in the movement of the spheres. He is sovereign over nature.

I used to say something in my earlier ministry that young people hiding their heads under a blanket during a thunderstorm were far safer, if they only realized it, with the Lord, this same Lord who holds the winds and the waves in

His hands. It was He that set the boundary to the ocean and said, "Here shalt thou come and no further, and here shalt thy proud waves be stayed." He is absolutely sovereign over all the forces of nature.

When He gets across the sea to the other side, in the land of the Gergesenes, there come out two demons to meet Him. Notice that nobody ever passed that way before unchallenged. Two demon beset men. Mark says that they bound them with chains and they could not hold them. Nobody ever touched that territory; you wouldn't. But here comes One that neither fears nor flees; and these demon possessed men run and kneel at His feet, and they say to Him, "Thou Son of the Most High God." Notice it, these demons speaking in these possessed men are proclaiming His deity. "Thou Son of God." I have sometimes thought that men in the folly of their wisdom might deny the supreme glory of the person of Jesus Christ, but demons never; they know better. And the Lord with a word expels the demons; and I say that that is a mark of sovereignty, that the demons are still within the limit of His controi. It may be indeed that the devil may walk to and fro in the earth. It may be that there is license, but for all this the Book declares that the Lord Jesus is sovereign over all the forces of evil.

The fourth in the group is where they open the roof of the house and let down the man with the palsy. How precious as we come to these marks of sovereignty. He said to him, "Arise, take up thy bed and walk"; a fine thing to say to a man that has palsy. And he does not arise and he does not get up until there has been time for people to say to themselves, "This is blasphemy. Nobody can forgive sins but God"; which He had said before He said the other imperial thing. He said to them, "Whether is it easier to say this: Arise, take up thy bed and walk, or to say, Son, thy sins be forgiven thee? I will tell you what is the easier. It is very much easier for somebody to say, "Thy sins be forgiven thee," for nobody knows whether they are or not. That is easy; anybody can do that. But if you can bring into my presence a man that is a paralytic, that is incapable of motion or even of sensibility, and if I can say to that man, "Arise and walk," that is ocular demonstration, isn't it? So the Lord said—how wonderful the proof—"That ye may know that the Son of man hath power on earth to forgive sin, (He said unto the man with the palsy,) Arise, take up thy bed, and walk"; and immediately the man arose and took up that whereon he lay, and went unto his own house; and Jesus had demonstrated that He was *sovereign over sin.* The last group is so very wonderful, to me at least, and I feel so utterly incapable of closing with it that do the best I may it will but be a suggestion of what is therein contained. After these eight signs manifesting His royal glory there is a great and wonderful dispensational picture, a dispensational picture which is outlined for us by four miracles of healing, the last of the group. But before our Lord gives us this marvelous picture He has the feast with sinners; a marvelous thing to see Him with the sinners round about Him, and it was a feast for Him. And then making the declaration that the time had come when at last the old legal garment of righteousness was wearing out, and that you could not patch the old garment now with the new cloth, nor could you put the new and expensive wine into the old bottles, because if you did, the old bottles would burst, they could not hold it, and you would spill the wine itself; no, we must have a new garment, and we must have a new place wherein to put the wine. And having said that, the ruler comes and says, "Lord, my little daughter is lying at the point of death." And He said, "I will come and heal her." Then somebody says, "Trouble not the Master, for thy daughter is dead." She is dead. Now can we get it by the grace of God as we close the afternoon. He is on His way to raise to life one that has been pronounced dead. A marvelous thing, isn't it? He is on His way to raise one to life that has been pronounced dead, and as He makes His way with that object in mind in the great throngs which are round about Him, there is a woman whose life is slowly ebbing away; and she says, "I believe if I could get somewhere in the crowd and touch the hem of His garment I should be healed." And somehow she makes her way and reaches out her hand and touches Him, and immediately there goes through her the thrill of a new life. And as He goes on after having healed the woman He comes to the house, and there is the solemn music, the dirge of the dead. And when Jesus had put them all out He said to the young maid, "Arise"; and she came out of death into life. And He went out of the house, and two blind men—notice how Matthew groups it—two blind men cry out unto Him and say, "Thou Son of David, have mercy upon us." And He said, "Believe ye that I am able to do this?" And they said, "Yea, Lord, we believe." And He opened their eyes and they saw. And then they brought to Him a man that was dumb, possessed with a dumb demon, and Jesus cast out the demon from that dumb man, and the dumb man spoke. And this is the great dispensational picture given to us by Matthew through the Spirit of God. I wonder now if we could quite see it. You do not need to accept it as the teaching of these verses, but you must needs accept it as the general teaching of Holy Scripture.

The Lord Jesus Christ divested Himself of His glory. He came into the world for a purpose. It was to raise to life a nation that was spiritually dead; that was His purpose. He came into the world, of course, to seek and to save that which was lost, but His primal ministry, as He himself declares, was to Israel, to bring them up out of their graves, their spiritual death, and constitute them a kingdom, and through them bless the whole world. That was the initial intention. And now while He is on the way to that—it isn't accomplished yet—through all these centuries gone by His purpose and plan concerning Israel is not yet accomplished; but He is moving on steadily toward that great purpose. And if we fail to see it, we fail to see the great objective of Scripture, that kingdom that is yet to be established upon the earth and to fill the world with God's glory. Christ Jesus is on the way for the purpose of bringing Israel out of her grave and constituting her a kingdom. And while He is on His way in this majestic and wondrous sweep through the centuries—well, take myself; I am like the woman with the issue of blood, and with my life forces draining myself away; and somehow and somewhere there has dawned within me the consciousness that if I could but touch the robe of His glorious garments I should be healed; and I touch Him and I am saved; and so the Church has been formed as He marches down through the centuries to the fulfilment of that great purpose that is in His heart.

Possibly we might learn a parable of the fig tree. "When its branch is yet tender and putteth forth leaves, ye know that summer is nigh." And when we see the great homeward trend of the old Jewish people back to renationalization, the flag of David floating, in their unbelief perhaps, some of us might say—yet the fig tree seems indeed to be putting forth leaves now. And Jesus says, "When ye see that, the summer is nigh"; and in a little while—how soon we do not know—but in a little while the Church shall be complete. Through the ministry of the Spirit of God there shall be added that which makes up the full complement of the bride, and we shall be lifted with the departed dead in Christ, transformed, transfigured into the likeness of His glory to meet Him. And then the eyes of the blind shall be opened in response to their appeal to Him again as the Son of David. "Thou Son of David, have mercy upon us." And He will open their eyes, and they shall look upon Him whom they have pierced; and then the demons shall depart, and they shall speak, and Israel shall bud and blossom and fill the whole world with fruit, and the whole world shall be filled with His glory.

The Present Age, Its Characteristic and its Predicted End

JAMES M. GRAY, Dean of the Moody Bible Institute of Chicago.

I.

For a true perspective of this subject one needs to take his stand in the Garden of Eden after the fall, when God pronounced judgment upon the serpent, who represented Satan, saying, "I will put enmity between thee and the woman, and between thy seed and her seed; it shall bruise thy head, and thou shalt bruise his heel" (Gen. iii:15). In these words God announced His gracious purpose to redeem the human race through a personal Redeemer, our Lord Jesus Christ. But some two thousand years after this announcement, and when the race has demonstrated by its iniquity the need of such Divine intervention for its salvation, God is pleased to reveal a secondary instrument, or servant, by which it shall be brought about, viz: the nation of Israel, the seed of Abraham, coming out of his loins. The king chosen of God for this nation and who is the beginning of a line of kings, is David, the son of Jesse, and the centre of his government is Jerusalem. To David, God gives the promise that his son shall sit upon his throne, and that his kingdom shall be established forever. Later scriptures leave no doubt that this son is the seed of the woman promised in Eden, the seed of Abraham as well, the personal Redeemer, the Son of God, our Lord Jesus Christ. Centuries elapse before this Son is born, centuries of sin and the penalty for sin, in the history of the Theocratic Kingdom, and when at length the Son *is* born, it is only to be rejected of His people, to be betrayed, and crucified, to die and be buried in the tomb. Nevertheless, He was declared "to be the Son of God with power, according to the Spirit of holiness, by the resurrection from the dead" (Rom. 1:4); and one day thereafter while speaking to His disciples "of the things pertaining to the Kingdom of God," they asked Him, saying, "Lord, wilt Thou at this time restore again the Kingdom to Israel?" By which I understand them to mean the Kingdom promised to David and over which He, Jesus, the Messiah, is to reign.

Very significantly He replied, not that the Kingdom had been abrogated and never would be restored; but only, that it was not given to them to know the times or the seasons of its restoration, which the Father had put in His own power. Moreover, He went on to say that power would be given them when the Holy Ghost would come upon them, to be witnesses unto Him both in Jerusalem, and in all Judea, and in Samaria and unto the uttermost part of the earth.

"And when He had spoken these things, while they beheld, He was taken up, and a cloud received Him out of their sight.

"And while they looked steadfastly toward heaven as He went up, behold, two men stood by them in white aparel, who also said, Ye men of Galilee, why stand ye gazing up into heaven? This same Jesus which is taken up from you into heaven, shall so come in like manner as ye have seen Him go into heaven." (Acts I 3:11).

II

We now return to a critical point in the days of His ministry, prior to His death and resurrection, when, speaking after the manner of men, He had come most deeply to realize that He had come unto His own, but His own received Him not. It was that day at Caesarea—Philippi, when he asked His disciples, "Who do men say that I, the Son of men, am?" They were obliged to reply that the most men said of Him was that He was John the Baptist or one of the prophets. He then asked them, "But who say ye that I am?" And Simon Peter answered, "Thou art the Christ, the Son of the Living God" (Matt. xvi:13-16).

We call this a critical point ,because it was then that Christ revealed to them, and to us that mystery which Paul told the Romans had been kept secret since the world began (Rom. xvi:25), viz: that the Gentiles should be fellow-heirs and fellow-members of the body, and fellow-partakers of the promise in Christ Jesus through the Gospel (Eph. ii:5-6). It was then that He said to them through the disciple who had thus confessed Him, "Thou art Peter (meaning a piece of a rock), and upon this rock (not Peter necessarily, but Christ Himself in the confession of His name), *I will build my church* and the gates of hell shall not prevail against it. In other words, the church is this secret which was not made known to men. Nothing is said of the church in the Old Testament. It did not come into being until after the death, resurrection and ascension of our Lord Its birthday was Pentecost, ten days after the return of the disciples from Mount Olivet. "Who founded the Christian church?" asks Dr. Philip Schaff in his well-known catechism. To which he replies: "Our exalted Saviour on the fiftieth day after His resurrection (ten days after His ascension) by the outpouring of the Holy Spirit upon His disciples at Jerusalem. (Ref. Matt. xvi:18; Acts ii:1-11; 1 Cor. xii; Eph. ii:20)."

III

Let us here pause a moment to add some confirmatory evidence that the church and the Kingdom are not the same. Note the terms used representative of each, the church is "built," the Kingdom is "set up." Note the relationship sustained by men toward each, the church has its "elders," "messengers," "servants"; the Kingdom has its "heirs." We "see," we "receive," we "enter" the Kingdom, but we "join" or are "added to" or become "members of" the church. The Kingdom is "advanced" and "extended," the church "cleansed" and "edified." The church will reign with Christ, but the Kingdom will be reigned over by Christ and His church. The church is an election, but the Kingdom will be universal. The church is now in the world, but one day it will be taken out of the world; the Kingdom is still in abeyance, but one day it will be manifested. The church is temporary so far as its earthly establishment is concerned, but the Kingdom is an everlasting Kingdom.

Years ago there lived and ministered in Boston an earnest, zealous, but somewhat eccentric brother, known as Father Taylor of the Seamen's Bethel. He was lacking in the cultivation of the schools, and one day, in preaching, his sentences became inextricably confused. In despair at his inability to find a way out, he at length cut the Gordian knot by exclaiming, "Brethren, I seem to have lost the track of my nominative case; but one thing I know, I'm bound for the Kingdom."

He was right. Though he had been in the church a good many years, he realized that the Kingdom was still future. In which he was wiser than a university president whom I knew, and who, by-the-way, was also a Christian minister, and who is quoted as saying: "The Christian church is the Kingdom of God on earth, viewed in its objective or institutional form, God's Kingdom among men is as old as human history!" We thus see that one may be a successful university president, and even pass as a Christian minister, and yet not be very well acquainted with the Bible!

IV

Let us now return again to the historical thread of our subject. The disciples have returned from Christ, the day of Pentecost has come and gone, the Holy Spirit has fallen upon them, they are baptized into the body of which Christ is the Head, they have been formed into the church, and they have taken up the work of witnessing to Him as they were commanded. At first they preach the Gospel to the Jew only, and limit their ministry to Jerusalem. But a great persecution arises about Stephen, and they are all scattered abroad, except the apostles, and they go everywhere preaching the Gospel. Into Samaria and into Syria they go, and the Gentiles hear the word, and believe it, and are baptized. By special revelation, Peter, contrary to his deepest convictions, is persuaded to preach the Gospel to Cornelius and his household, the Roman centurion, of Caesarea, and a Gentile. And behold! the Holy Spirit fell on them as on the Jews at the beginning, as at Pentecost. These innovatory and revolutionary acts stir the leaders of the church at Jerusalem to the very depths. They resent the introduction of the

Gentile to the privileges of the Gospel on the same footing as the Jew. It seems inharmonious with the teaching of the prophets. It can not be the mind of God.

Therefore a council is summoned at Jerusalem to consider it, which record is found in Acts xv. James the brother of our Lord presides over the council, thus clearly demonstrating that Peter was not the primate at this time as some would have us believe. Peter is called upon however, to give his testimony about Cornelius; and then Paul and Barnabas declare, "what miracles and wonders God had wrought among the Gentiles by them." When suddenly, James calls for silence. The Holy Spirit is about to speak through him and to reveal the solution of the problem.

> "Men, brethren," said he, "hearken unto me; Simeon (i. e., Peter) hath declared how God at the first did visit the Gentiles, to take out of them a people for His Name.
>
> "And to this agree the words of the prophets, as it is written:
>
> "After this I will return, and will build again the tabernacle of David that is fallen down: and I will build again the ruins thereof, and I will set it up.
>
> "That the residue of men might seek after the Lord, and all the Gentiles upon whom My Name is called, saith the Lord who doeth all these things." (Acts xv:13-18.)

Here then is the Divine program, the divinely inspired revelation of the characteristic of this age. It is different from any age preceding it, or to follow it. It is not the age of the Kingdom, but the age of the church. It is not the age of an ingathering, but the age of an outgathering. God is now visiting the Gentiles and taking out of them a people for His Name. Here one, and there another individual from among all peoples, and nations and tongues are hearing the Gospel of redemption and are being moved by the Holy Spirit to embrace its promises, to lay hold of Christ by faith, and so to become baptized into that body of which He is the Head.

In other words Christ is now building up His church. It is not a question of the visible church . That is a multitudinous collection not a gracious election. It is a question of a spiritually regenerated organism, for "he that is joined to the Lord is one Spirit" (I Cor, vi:17). And wonderful is the process by which Christ builds up His church. Paul reveals it to us in his letter to the Ephesians when he says: "Unto everyone of us is given grace according to the measure of the gift of Christ. And He gave some apostles, and some prophets, and some evangelists, and some pastors, and teachers." For what purpose have these gifts been bestowed upon the body by its head? The answer is, "for the perfecting of the saints." For what purpose are the saints perfected? The answer is, "for the work of the ministry," or unto ministering, "unto the edifying (building up) of the body of Christ" (iv:7-12).

The saints are the builders of the church. They are those through whom God is now visiting "the Gentiles to take out of them a people for His Name." What a motive for missions this is, and for evangelism at home and abroad! But the saints need perfecting for this work, and they receive it through heaven-sent and heaven-equipped apostles, prophets, evangelists, pastors and teachers. Would to God that their number might be mutiplied as one result of this Bible Conference.

What a sad story it is of how men frequently get into office and dignity in the Christian church! But let us not be discouraged as though Christ were neglecting His body.

He still continues to give all the ministers, and just the kind of ministers the church needs. And what is more, the true church recognizes these ministers and stands behind them, even when human hands have not been laid upon their heads or the hall--mark of ecclesiasticism added to their names. "Pray ye therefore the Lord of the harvest, that He send forth laborers into His harvest" (Matt. ix:38).

V.

But here is another wonder. This calling out and building of the church is after all, only a means to an end. The process, glorious as it is, has a finish. The church had an earthly beginning and it will have an earthly end. This work of ministering is only to be pursued, Paul tells us, "until we all come in (or attain unto) the unity of the faith and of the knowledge of the Son of God, unto a perfect man (full grown) man, unto the measure of the stature of the fulness of Christ" (Ephes. iv: 13).

Which means "not that each believer should become in himself a perfect copy of the original Christ, in all His fullness, but that the entire body, richly and variedly gifted, and wonderfully fashioned, should as a whole, attain unto the measure of the stature of the fullness of Christ." The perfect, full grown man, which Paul has in mind in other words, is not you nor I as an individual, but that mystical man of whom he has been speaking throughout, and which is constituted of Christ as the Head and the whole blessed company of believers as the body. There is a day coming when that man will be perfected, when the body of Christ will have been completed, when all the elect shall have been called out from among the Gentiles, and what then? Ah! then,

"The Lord Himself shall descend from heaven, with a shout; with the voice of the Archangel and with the trump of God.

"And the dead in Christ shall rise first.

"Then we which are alive and remain shall be caught up together with them in the clouds to meet the Lord in the air.

"And so shall we ever be with the Lord.

"Wherefore comfort one another with these words." (1 Thess. iv:16-18.)

VI

We now approach that part of our subject in which is to be treated not the characteristic of this age which, as we have seen, is the outgathering of the church, but its predicted end. Once more we lay hold of the historical thread of things and return to the council at Jerusalem. James is revealing by the Spirit that "God at the first did visit the Gentiles to take out of them a people for His Name. And to this agree the words of the prophets," he goes on to say, "as it is written:

"After this I will return and I will build again the tabernacle of David which is fallen; and I will build again the ruins thereof and I will set it up."

This is the impending hour in the world's history seized upon by an old English hymn writer whose words were popularized by Charles Wesley, when he sang:

Lo, He comes, with clouds descending,
Once for favored sinners slain;
Thousand, thousand saints attending,
Swell the triumph of His train:
Hallelujah!
God appears on earth to reign!

Every eye shall now behold Him,
Robed in dreadful majesty;
Those who set at naught and sold Him,
Pierced, and nailed Him to the tree,
Deeply wailing,
Shall the true Messiah see.

In other words, according to the inspired teaching of James, after the rapture or translation of the church, the next great event scheduled in the prophetic plan is the return of Christ to set up His Kingdom. It is then that He is revealed from heaven, as indicated by Paul in his second epistle to the Thessalonians, "with His mighty angels, in flaming fire, taking vengeance on them that know not God, and that obey not the Gospel of our Lord Jesus Christ" (I:7-8). Because James cites the Old Testament, and says, "To this agree the words of the prophets," etc.; some have argued that the Gentile outgathering and the setting up of the fallen tabernacle of David are one and the same thing. That the rearing of the tabernacle of David and the building of the Christian church are identical. But such is not the case. To say nothing of its contradiction by the whole trend of prophetic teaching both in the Old and New Testaments, in the present instance the citation is from the closing chapter of Amos, which is clearly a prediction of Israel's literal restoration to her own land in a national capacity. In the second place, the citation adds the words, not found in Amos, *"After this I will return* and will build again the tabernacle of David." This clearly shows that the latter will take place following the outgathering of the church, and connects it directly with the second coming of Christ. In the third place, James does not say, "in this are *fulfilled* the words of the prophet," but with this *agree* the words of the prophets. "Symphonize" is the Greek words used here. "With this symphonize the words of the prophets." As A. J. Gordon beautifully expressed it, "It is but saying that the parts of the great oratorio of redemption perfectly accord, though centuries lie between its differer measures. To show how they accord, the Holy Spirit as in this instance, sounds all the octaves with a single sweep, and lets us listen to their grand unison."

VII

And now, what is that unison?

1. God is now, in this age, visiting the Gentiles to take out of them a people for His Name. He is choosing His people *out of* the world. No universal redemption in His purpose now. That may follow but not in this church age. The vast proportion of the world "lieth in the wicked one," and in comparison therewith, the church is but "a little flock." And yet because the church is an election, it is necessarily not an end in itself but a means to an end. To borrow the figure of another, "it is Christ's great army, gathered out by a Divine conscription from every kindred and people, that it may attend Him as He goes forth to His final conquest of the world" (Rev. xix:11-16).

2. After this He will return and build again the tabernacle, or set up the Kingdom promised to David. By His personal coming in glory after the translation of the church, the purification and restoration of Israel as a nation shall be brought about. "And so all Israel shall be saved, as it is written, there shall come out of Zion the Deliverer, and shall turn away ungodliness from Jacob" (Rom. xi:26). Here is an illustration of Simeon's prophecy of Christ as "a light to lighten the Gentiles and the glory of Thy people Israel." The sun lightens the earth and draws up from it the water drops which form the clouds. But he is the glory of the heavens as their central and most illustrious orb. So Christ as a revelation to the nations exhibits Himself as the brightness of His Father's glory and the express image of His Person, in order, as Dr. Gordon puts it, to win from the

nations a chosen heritage. But he will be the supreme glory of His people Israel, when He at last shall be owned as their Messiah, and reign in the midst of them as their King.

3. All this is to the end "that the residue of men might seek after the Lord, and all the Gentiles on whom My Name is called, saith the Lord, who doeth all these things." Thank God, the day is coming when His glory shall fill the earth. The knoweledge of Him shall cover the earth as the waters cover the sea. But everything in its own time and its own order. To the Jew first and also to the Gentile. When Israel is judged, and purified and restored to God in Christ, then the day of the world's blessing is at hand. It is thus the Psalmist sings: "God be merciful unto *us*, and bless *us*, and cause His face to shine upon *us*. That Thy ways may be known upon earth, Thy saving health among all nations" (Ps. lxvii). Or to express it in the words of Paul, "If the fall of them, the Jews, be the riches of the world, and the diminishing of them the riches of the Gentiles, how much more their fullness? If the casting away of them be the reconciling of the world, what shall the receiving of them be, but life from the dead?" (Rom. xi, 12-15).

To quote Auberlen here: "A new life in the higher charismatic fullness of the Spirit shall extend from God's people (the Jews) to the other nations of the world, compared with which the previous life of the nations must be considered dead."

Oh, how I pity our post-millennial brethren who are denied this outlook. To them the end of the age appears identical with the end of the world. It closes up the only chance of the race. It terminates redemption for the world. The last judgment follows it, in their view, and the fixed eternal state. No wonder they have no love of His appearing, and seldom speak of it. If they could only see it as the opening of the triumphs of the age to come! If they could only see it as Peter did, a 'season of refreshing from the presence of the Lord, and the time of the restoration of all things spoken by the prophets since the world began' (Acts iii: 19-21).

"Come, blessed Lord! Let every shore,
  And answering island, sing
The praises of Thy royal Name,
  And own Thee as their king.

"Hope of our hearts, O Lord, appear,
  Thou glorious Star of day;
Shine forth, and chase the dreary night,
  With all our tears, away.

"No resting place we seek on earth,
  No loveliness we see;
Our eye is on the royal crown,
  Prepared for us—and Thee!"

—Sir Edward Denny.

Saved When the Lord Appears

By J. Wilbur Chapman, Evangelist.

Texts: Acts i; 11—"Ye men of Galilee, why stand ye gazing up into heaven? This same Jesus, which is taken up from you into heaven, shall so come in like manner as ye have seen him go into heaven."

I Thessalonians iv; 16, 17, 18—"For the Lord himself shall descend from heaven with a shout, with the voice of the archangel, and with the trump of God: and the dead in Christ shall rise first: Then we which are alive and remain shall be caught up together with them in the clouds, to meet the Lord in the air: and so shall we ever be with the Lord. Wherefore comfort one another with these words."

These two texts of Scripture are plainly presented and there can be no question as to their interpretation; they mean just what they say, namely, that the Lord Jesus Christ is coming back again to this earth, and just as He ascended from the midst of His disciples, clothed with his physical body, and a cloud received Him out of their sight, so He will come again.

He left a wondering company of disciples when He was on the slopes of Olivet, and from their midst began to ascend up towards heaven, and strange to say He will come back again to a company of disciples, for notwithstanding the plain statements of Scripture with reference to His coming, many in the Church are apparently unacquainted with the fact of His glorious appearing or else are indifferent to it.

This may be because those of us who are in the pulpit have not been faithful in teaching the Word of God, or it may be that the rank and file of Christians have studied the Scriptures indifferently, if indeed they have studied them at all.

All evangelical Christians believe that Jesus Christ is coming again sometime. We have said it over and over in our repetition of the Apostles Creed, and there can be no question about the fact at all. The only question is as to when He is coming; some say before the millennium, and they are called pre-millennarians; others expect Him after the millennium, and they are spoken of as post-millennarians. But if He comes after the millennium He will come to a world made ready for His appearing by human effort, righteousness will be asserting its power, and have in its control all things. If this position is accepted, then His coming is far removed from the present time, for just when men thought the world was rapidly growing better, the world-war was upon us and today the world is scarred and marred by its effects. If He comes before the millennium, then He will come to set the world right; He will set up His Throne and establish His Kingdom. He himself will work mightily in all ways and it will be a world worth while living in when it is all under the sway of His Almighty Power. As for myself, I prefer the millennium which He makes ready rather than the one which might be set up or prepared by man himself, therefore I am a pre-millennarian.

Just what will it mean to be saved when the Lord appears?

To be saved at all is the wonder of heaven and earth. We are saved *from sin's penalty* by His death on the Cross and our personal acceptance of Him. We are saved *from sin's practice* by the indwelling of His Spirit strengthening our wills. This is what the Apostle Paul meant when he said

"I live, yet not I, but Christ liveth in me." We are saved *from sin's presence* by His coming again, for when he comes the last enemy shall be overthrown, temptation will be a thing of the past, and our deliverance shall last forever.

Let us put it in this way:

We have been saved by His death on the Cross and our identification with Him, this has to do with the past. *We are being saved* by His Spirit who makes Christ real to us and makes the Word of God powerful in the changing of our lives, this has to do with the present. *We shall be saved* when He appears and the body of this humiliation is made like unto His own glorious body, this has to do with the future. In order to prevent confusion, we must keep in mind the fact that there are to be two appearings of our Lord:

First—*He comes for His Saints.* This is what the Apostle Paul meant when in I Thessalonians iv:16-18, he said, "For the Lord himself shall descend from heaven with a shout, with the voice of the archangel, and with the trump of God; and the dead in Christ shall rise first. Then we which are alive and remain shall be caught up together with them in the clouds, to meet the Lord in the air: and so shall we ever be with the Lord. Wherefore comfort one another with these words."

Second—*He comes with His Saints.* When the time is up and Scripture has had its fulfillment, he will set up His Kindgom on the earth; His sway will be almighty and His power irresistible.

This truth has always been of the greatest possible inspiration to me. I learned it when I was a young minister, and it changed my whole conception of Christ and my interpretation of the Scripture, and filled me with a zeal to attempt at least to do His Will. It has never made me fanatical, and I am sure that it has not made me listless, and from the first day I received the truth until this present time, it has been to me "the blessed hope." In common with other Christians, I believe the Church to be the body of Christ and that as individuals we go to make up that body and as men are won to Christ and they surrender to Him, they are parts of that body. So of necessity, one day the body will be completed—the last member will be added to it— and I have always thought that perhaps the one who comes under the influence of my preaching, might be the last, and the skies would brighten and the Lord return, and I have hardly preached an evangelistic sermon for years without this in mind. It is to me a glorious hope. I have frequently been asked "Would you not be startled, indeed, would you not be afraid, if suddenly the skies should brighten and the Lord appear?" And my answer is "I might be, except for the statement made in my first text of Scripture, 'Ye men of Galilee, why stand gazing up into Heaven? This same Jesus, which is taken up from you into heaven, shall so come in like manner as ye have seen Him go into heaven,'" it is "this same Jesus" who is coming back; He who was cradled in the manger and wrapped in swaddling clothes, He who lived in Nazareth as a boy, a youth, and a young man, He who preached in Galilee as never man had spoken before Him, He who suffered in Gethsemane until the blood drops rolled down His face, He who died upon the Cross as my substitute, He who rose from the dead when the time was up and the stone was rolled away from the door, He who ascended up into heaven—He is coming back again. How could I be startled when He appears? So human that He grew weary as He toiled, so human that He fell asleep when He was in the little boat with His disciples, so human that He toiled in the carpenter shop, making this implement and that, and making them well.

> "If I could hold within my hand
> The hammer Jesus swung,
> Not all the gold in all the land,
> Nor jewels countless as the sand
> All in the balance flung,
> Could weigh the value of that thing
> 'Round which His fingers once did cling."

So divine that the water blushed into wine when He looked at it; so divine that devils feared Him and went rushing into a herd of swine and drove them into the sea; so divine that disease was staid by His presence and His touch; so divine that death was overpowered by Him, and Lazarus, at the sound of His voice, came forth from the tomb bound in his grave clothes.

He is coming back again and we shall see Him.

> "Just to see Jesus once scarred as Redeemer,
> Jesus, my Lord, from all suffering free,
> Just to see Jesus transfigured forever,
> That will be glory, be glory, for me.
>
> Just to see Jesus when saved ones are gathering,
> Jesus who died upon Calvary's tree,
> Just to see Jesus with all heaven ringing,
> That will be glory, be glory, for me."

He is surely coming back again and it is well worth while to ask the question as to what this coming will mean to certain classes of people.

1. What will it mean to the saved?

SAVED WHEN THE LORD APPEARS

1 Corinthians xv:51, 52.—"Behold, I shew you a mystery; we shall not all sleep, but we shall all be changed, in a moment, in the twinkling of an eye, at the last trump: for the trumpet shall sound, and the dead shall be raised incorruptible, and we shall be changed."

So many times we hear people use the expression, speaking of certain events, "This is as certain as death," but death is by no means certain, it is not at all sure that we shall all die. St. Paul himself tells us we shall not all sleep, and he is speaking of death; some will be alive when the Lord comes back, and perhaps we who are to-day in health and strength, shall be of the company.

(a) Some day the skies will brighten and He will appear, and just as Saul of Tarsus saw what others did not see, so some eyes will be opened to behold Him, while others will be blinded to His coming, and when those who have their trust in Him are taken away, others will remain behind in wonder and in amazement.

(b) Families will be separated. In this household a mother was a humble follower of Jesus Christ and all the others were indifferent to Him. She will be taken; the others left.

In another household the father was a Saint of God. The Bible was his constant delight and Jesus Christ, the man of His counsel, but it was impossible for him to lead his children to Christ, and with the mother he will be taken and the others left; perhaps a wife with an indifferent husband left behind.

A business man who has been careful in all his business dealings, and consistent in his following of Jesus Christ, taken, and those withh whom he is associated, left behind; perhaps the children of a household whose parents were worldly and cared not for Christ and His Church are taken.

(c) It should be remembered, however, that before these are taken, the dead in Christ shall rise first; their spirits safe with Him from the moment of their death, their bodies have been resting in the tomb, and when He appears, the tombs of the Christian dead shall be opened, and spirit and body united. They shall go up to be with Him.

There are some places I should like to be at that wonderful time. I think I should like to be standing here speaking of Him, or I should like to be pleading with an audience to turn to Him, or I should like to be sitting beside some one who is helpless and hopeless and urging them to accept of Him, or I should like to be at the grave of D. L. Moody, and behold his tomb open and see him ascend to meet the Lord whom he so faithfully preached; or I should like to be at my mother's tomb where years ago we placed her and said "goodbye" to her with tears blinding our eyes. To sum it all up, however, I think I should like to be just anywhere, seeking to please Him and trying to find out concerning His Will, that I might do it.

I stood one day in Wales before the grave of the famous Welsh preacher, Christmas Evans, and was told that he was buried in the same grave with a friend, a brother minister, whom he loved dearly, and this was all because they wanted to be together when the Lord came and they be caught up. They had agreed that hand in hand they would ascend to greet Him.

(d) In the Scriptures we read that we who are alive shall be caught up together with them in the clouds, that is, with our beloved who have gone on before. No more separation, no more fear of the cable's message, no more funerals, no more visits to the cemetery, no more going back to the home that has been made empty because the loved one has departed.

"We shall not all sleep, what ineffable bliss,
Some living at present may taste even of this,
His coming, the rapture, the joyful surprise,
One moment a mortal, the next in the skies.

Our Saviour will come in the air, He'll descend,
The living, the sleeping, to Him shall ascend,
Some wait there in heaven, some wait here below,
Then raptured in triumph to Him we all go.

We shall not all sleep, but changed we shall be,
Yes, changed in a moment when Jesus we see,
In the blaze of His glory, the flash of an eye,
All caught up together to meet in the sky."

(e) When St. Paul was nearing the end of his remarkable career, he writes, "That I may know Him, and the power of His resurrection, and the fellowship of His sufferings, being made comfortable unto His death; if by any means I might attain unto the resurrection of the dead."

The expression "if by any means I might attain unto the resurrection of the dead" is literally "the out-resurrection from among the dead"! that is, St. Paul knew that the Lord was coming back, that the Christian dead would rise to greet Him, and he wanted to be of the company, and thus expresses his hope and desire.

I was very much touched recently when Colonel and Mrs. Roosevelt said that they did not wish to take advantage of the offer of the Government to have the body of their son, Lieut. Quentin Roosevelt, returned to this country for burial; they wished to leave him there in France until the resurrection morning, and I feel just as Colonel Roosevelt has felt, for if my son had been obliged to make the supreme sacrifice and die "over there" I would want his body left in France in order that when the Lord appeared, he and all the other Christian dead who had come to know Jesus Christ as a Saviour, might rise up in a company to greet Him in whose name they had fought.

2. What will it mean to the unsaved for Christ to appear?

(a) If they are dead then it will mean that at His appearing their tombs will not be unsealed, they shall wait longer for another great event which is so startling that one shudders even as he reads of it, that is Judgment.

(b) If they are living they will be left behind when others ascend to greet Him with their loved ones in the skies.

(c) And when the time comes those who have rejected Jesus Christ will face the Judgment. In Revelation xx: 11-13, I read, "And I saw the great white throne, and Him that sat on it, from whose face the earth and the heaven fled way; and there was found no place for them. And I saw the dead, small and great, stand before God; and the book was opened, which is the book of life; and the dead were judged out of those things which were written in the books, according to their works. And the sea gave up the dead which were in it; and death and hell delivered up the dead which were in them ;and they were judged every man according to their works." It is a white throne, to me, at least, it is significant that when the saved greet Him there will be "a rainbow round about the throne in sight like unto an emerald." The emerald is green and green rests the eye.

In contrast the full blaze of the white of the throne of God's judgment will be torture indeed.

He will be upon the throne; the One whom men have rejected and despised in spite of his mercy and love. "The dead small and great shall stand before God." There can be no favoritism there. The books shall be opened and on the basis of one's record, men will be judged. Those who have accepted Christ need have no fear of the judgment of the Great White Throne. "There is therefore now no judgment to them that are in Christ Jesus," but if he has been rejected, and finally rejected, we know what the end must be, for the word of the Lord hath spoken it.

Recently the Honorable Elihu Root, in one of his addresses used this expression:

THE TIMETABLE OF THE ALMIGHTY.

What a striking sentence, how suggestive, how true it is to these days, how it fits in to my subject.

(a) The hour has come. Jesus said that as he was nearing the end of his earthly ministry, and when the price of our redemption was to be paid in full.

(b) "Behold, now is the accepted time; behold, now is the day of salvation."

(c) The door of mercy is open; it may close at any moment. "Seek ye the Lord while He may be found; call ye upon Him while He is near."

The Church in the Book of Revelation

By Ford C. Ottman.

The Book of the Revelation is a prophecy. It is the only book of the New Testament that is distinctively a prophecy. It has the two main features: It is a prophecy of the things that are, and of the things that shall be after these things that are. It is a prophecy of the things from the time of John in Patmos until the Lord comes in power and glory.

The prophecy of the things that are is contained in the seven letters of the seven churches. The prophecy of the things that shall be after these things is from the fourth chapter to the ninteenth, covering a period of seven years, the final period of the earth's judgment, covered by the seals and by the trumpets and vials.

This is followed by the revelation of the coming of Christ in glory (in the nineteenth chapter), attended by the armies of heaven. The beast and the false prophet shall be cast alive into the lake of fire, which is then open for the first time. Satan is to be bound and put into the "pit of the abyss." It is God's dungeon, where Satan is to be confined. There is then the sessional judgment of the living nations. The Lord Jesus is received and crowned as King. The whole world is filled with God's glory. And after the kingdom age is past Satan is brought up out of the pit of the abyss for a less mysterious purpose than some of us suppose, and only for a brief season, after which the whole framework of things is destroyed, and there comes before our vision the new heaven and the new earth wherein dwelleth righteousness. These are the momentous themes that are brought to our attention in this great prophecy of the Revelation.

Only briefly will it be possible to speak this morning of the first part of this book and to suggest one or two things that may show how these addresses to the churches that are in Asia have their application not merely to the Church as a whole, but, what is of more importance to us, a direct and personal responsibility. Of course we do not believe for a moment that the application of the truth contained in these letters to the churches was exhausted in any local application. We believe that just as the letter to the Thessalonians is given for all time, and as the letters of Paul to Corinth are given for all time, so are these letters to the churches given for all the time while the Church is upon the earth.

These letters are addressed especially to the messengers, or angels of the churches, and I conceive that herein lies an important statement which indicates the personal application of these letters aside from anything else that they reveal concerning the condition of the Church at large. These letters are addressed to the angel of the church, whoever the angel may be. We are hardly prepared to say to the pastor or the bishop or some other functionary in the church, but they are nevertheless addressed to somebody who is called the angel of the church. But the apostle says when he gives us a description of Him that stands in the midst of the golden lampstands, and is giving us an estimate of their spiritual condition, that He held in His right hand seven stars; and a little later he says that the seven angels are the seven stars. The letters are addressed to the angels, and the angels are the seven stars, and the seven stars are held in His right hand. That is the superscription of these letters.

Who are these stars? Stars shine through the night, and the darker the night the brighter they shine. You remember doubtless that in the long distant past, when God appeared to Abraham and called him out, that He promised him a double seed. God said to Abraham, "Count the stars." You try it. And then He said, "So shall thy seed be." On another occasion He said. "Count the sand by the seashore" Try that. And He said to Abraham, "So shall thy seed be." Why did God tell Abraham to count the stars and promise him a seed like that? Then why was it when God renewed the promise to Isaac, Abraham's son, he said, "Count the stars, so shall thy seed be," but he was not to count the sand. And why was it when he came to the third patriarch, Jacob, He said to him, "Count the sand by the seaside; so shall thy seed be"; never "Count the stars?" And when the whole thing is summed up in Hebrews why does the apostle say, speaking of Abraham, "Therefore sprang there of one, and him as good as dead, so many as the stars of the sky, in multitude, and as the sand which is by the seashore innumerable." Why, certainly you will all admit that from Abraham there sprang two seeds. There was an earthly seed, given us here under the figure of the sand of the seashore; and there was a heavenly seed, represented by the stars of the sky in multitude. If I were a Jew unsaved, if I did not know Christ, if I were a Jew without being a Christian, nationally, racially, in every respect I would still be the answer of God to that promise and be one of the sands of the seashore. And if I am today a believer in the Lord Jesus, I am the child of Abraham by faith in Christ Jesus. I am not of the earthly seed. I am a Gentile, but I claim Abraham for my father. I am the star seed and not the earthly; and so are you if you believe in Christ

Now it is significant to me that if the angel addressed—in every case, whether to Ephesus or to Smyrna or to Pergamos, or any of the last four, the letter comes to the angel—and if the angel is the star, and if the star is held in His right hand, I think I know now to whom these letters are really addressed, don't you? Of course you do if you have followed me and if you believe in this. Take the believer in the Lord Jesus. Is he safe? Is he secure? Do we have in an audience like this to talk about the doctrine of eternal security when Jesus said, "My Father which gave them me is greater than all; and no"—not "man"—the Greek isn't "no man," but "no one," man nor devil, "shall be able to pluck them out of my hand." Seven stars held in the right hand of Him that is inspecting the moral condition represented by the lampstands, addressed to these seven stars, for they are the messengers of the churches. They are the angels of the churches, and these letters are therefore sent primarily to them that they may be instructed as to the Lord's estimate of what the lamp-stands represent.

Now I have been led to say all that because there has been some misapprehension as to just whom these letters were sent to, and if we are to-day believers in the Lord Jesus and hold the doctrine of eternal security because we are in His right hand held safe, then ought we not to be that individual to whom he appeals in every case? "He that hath an ear, let him hear what the Spirit saith unto the churches," the whole corporate body, the Church taken as one, listen to what He says who stands in the midst of the golden lamp stands to estimate their moral and spiritual condition. It is of very small importance to me what the Church historian may have to say concerning the foundation and historic progress of the Church of Christ. It is of course an humilitation to these distinguished professors of Church history to say to them that everything that is of vital importance in the whole history of the Christian Church is all summed up in seven letters to seven churches. That is what we have here. It is a prophecy of the things that are. Why, of course the things were there in that day in the local assemblies, and they are here to-day, and so far as Thyatira and Sardis and Philadelphia and Laodicea are concerned they are to go on until He comes. A blessed thing for us to know that the whole channel and flow of things was foreknown and foretold and He holdeth the stars through the long night in His own right hand.

Now I am speaking this morning about the Church in what the Scripture describes as the patience and kingdom of Jesus. I apprehend that the brother who follows me is going to talk about the Church in what the Scripture calls the kingdom and glory of Jesus. The kingdom and patience of Jesus; the kingdom and glory of Jesus. Let me suggest what the drift has been so far as these letters can briefly put it before us.

In Ephesus it is the loss of first love. That is where the apostasy began in your life and mine, when as the years went by somehow the Lord Jesus was not so precious to us as He was when we first knew Him. That is the root of all the fruit of apostasy, when there is loss of first love. May God in His infinite mercy in these days of prophetic unfolding of His glory win us back. If we have drifted, may He win us back.

One might almost think that Luke was giving us a parable of all this when He tells us about the voyage of the apostle Paul, which was ever toward Rome until it reached Rome. They seemed to be comfortable at first in a place called the fair havens. I like that, the place that is called the fair havens. I sang it long ago when I was a boy and first converted.

"I've anchored my soul in the haven of rest,
I'll sail the wild seas no more;
The tempests may sweep o'er the wild stormy deep,
In Jesus I'm safe evermore."

The place that is called the fair havens. Oh, how glad we were when at last we anchored there. But Luke tells us it was not commodious to winter in. Somehow or other when we got to our anchorage in Christ we felt as if we were rather limited in our harbor facilities, not quite commodious enough, and so there is an anxiety to get out of the fair havens. "And when the south wind blew softly"—that is the character of the south wind, to blow softly—"when the south wind blew softly, supposing they had obtained their purpose, loosing, they sailed close by Crete. But not long after there rose up against it a tempestuous wind called Euroclydon," and that ship went on its tempestuous way until it took Paul and the Pauline doctrine incarnate in him and landed the whole thing in Rome.

And just so sure as you start with Ephesus and the loss of your first love for the Lord Jesus you will begin to drift, and you will drift from Ephesus into Smyrna, and you will find, as they found in Smyrna, persecution. Persecution; but that was not the thing in Smyrna, the devil soon found out. He never learns by experience. He repeats himself all the time. The only advantage is he has got a new lot of dupes every time; but it is the same old trick, the same old limitation, a circumscribed place in which he labored. Long ago he discovered about the people in Egypt that the more they were persecuted, the more they grew; but he does not know what else to do, so in Smyrna he keeps it up. And when he finds that the blood of the martyrs is becoming the seed of the Church, then he changes his tactics and he leaves it. The same old thing. Nothing new under the sun, not a thing.

Mr. F. W. Grant says—and I am perfectly willing to acknowledge where I got a good part of what I am giving you; and it was Mr. Grant who said, that it was the roar of the lion—Listen! "It is the roar of the lion that will drive people into the snare." That is what is heard in Smyrna, the lion's roar of persecution, and into the hidden snare they went, and we get a relapse into Judaism. That was the terrible thing, saved by grace, and then to go back into legalism, with bondage.

"Free from the law, oh happy condition,
Jesus hath bled and there is remission;
Cursed by the law, and bruised by the fall,
Christ hath redeemed me once and for all."

Now say what you will about me—and I know there are a good many things to criticize about me, I know it better than you. I look in the glass every morning and wonder is it possible that I shall ever be like Him; and if you knew all that I know about myself, you would see more things than you have. If I knew all about you that you know about yourself, I would be the same kind of critic that you are of me. But it is that spirit of legalism that has come into the Christian Church. No matter what you are, if you believe in the supreme glory of the Son of God and are a sinner saved by grace, say it to the confusion of the devil and everybody else, and be free, and be not again entangled with the yoke of bondage. Do not get back into Judaism. That is where you get when you drift from your love, because—well, you are away from Him and so you have to kind of—help yourself; see? That is Judaism.

What is the next? Pergamos. Pergamos, where Satan's throne is. Why do they say "seat," where Satan's seat is instead of throne? These translators said, "Well, that is the limit. We cannot give him a throne. Whatever we do with him, we will just keep him short of that." But let us put it back and face the music The church gets where Satan's throne is. And you have not begun to estimate the moral values of this world if you do not realize that this world is under the shadow of the Cross of Jesus, that this is the time of the Lord's rejection, that this is the time when the devil is the god of this age and he has his throne here now. Pergamos, the place of Constantine's conversion, and he was never a Christian. When he made the profession of Christianity respectable and Church membership desirable, of course he gave them pieces of gold, and white robes. He gave them to people to join the Church. and we have so far drifted from that state of things, why, we get them today with a ham sandwich and a cup of coffee. It cost gold and white robes in the days of Constantine when the alliance was first formed, the alliance of the Church and the world, that has never been broken to this day.

And then of course you get Thyatira; and before you get to Thyatira you have the doctrine of Balaam developed; certainly the doctrine of Balaam. Just have the alliance of the Church and the world, and of course you get your pews filled with people who say, "We furnish the cash, and we propose to have the kind of preaching we pay for." That is Balaam. Balaam had a hard time, I can tell you. So do some of these modern preachers. And it is not only the doctrine of Balaam that is developed there, but it is the doctrine of the Nicolaitanes. The Church historians nearly lost their eyesight trying to find those fellows, and there are no such people. And when you are telling there are no such people, or if you invent that kind of people years afterward to fit in here, it does not work. It is the conquering of the people, the conquering of the laity. Certainly that is what you get, the doctrine where the priest is the whole thing, the clergy, and the laity take their place. Whoever heard of clergy and laity in the language of the church? Whoever heard it? It isn't there. It isn't in the vocabulary of the true church. He constituted us all a holy priesthood. Well that is what you get when the alliance is complete between the Church and the world; and you cannot distinguish them. Pergamos where Satan's throne is.

Then follows Thyatira and here it is Romanism complete, Jezebel, suffering her to teach; and you have the woman of the parable putting leaven into the meal offering, which if it represents anything, represents Christ as the food, and the leaven is put in by the "Church" and administered to the "Church's children." You have got your great camp following that came out of bondage. They fell to lusting out there in the wilderness, and they said, "Who shall give us flesh to eat?" We remember the flesh which we did eat in Egypt very well, and the leeks and the onions and the garlic and a lot of other vegetable diet. And now our soul is dried up, for there is nothing but this manna before our eyes. That is what the preacher gets now. "Give us some cucumbers and leeks and a little flesh to eat. We don't want manna any more." That is Thyatira, mixing leaven into the meal offering to make it more digestible, easier to eat; put on a picture show Sunday night; have an ungodly quartet sing a heathen piece in an unknown tongue; anything, anything but pure manna. That is Thyatira; and it goes on to the judgment until the Lord Jesus comes. It goes on beyond His coming to take us, the stars, up to Himself, to withdraw their shining. It goes on until that same schism that dishonored Him shall ride the scarlet beast of world empire, which shall tear and rend her. Of course Sardis is a revolt from all that, as we had in the Reformation; and I believe that it is that returning of heart of the person to the Word of God. Oh, how simple after all. "He that hath an ear let him hear what the spirit saith to the churches." Let us come back, brethren, dropping every difference and every criticism, and in these darkened closing days of the dispensation let us say this shall be our one purpose, we will stand together, we will stand for His Person, and we will stand for His Word, whatever happens. That is Philadelphia.

Then the loud assertion of the people's rights, that is what Laodicea means. We are hearing murmuring on every side, and the whole professing thing ready to be spewed out before the seals are broken and earth's judgment-salvation begins. Let us hear the voice of Him that is standing now outside of the whole thing, who cannot go on with it any longer as if inside of it, but standing in lowly grace. How wonderful, isn't it, when we think of the vision that shall be brought before us of His coming glory and all the holy angels with Him, all heaven filled with His grace, the centre and object of adoration of the universe, when I think of

Him saying to Laodicea, "I am standing at the door and knock. If any man hear me"—the last meal of the day—"I will come in and sup with him, and he with me." And sometimes I think, well, what have I to entertain with? Nothing. As my friend John Robertson said when we were going over this long ago, "Perhaps He will bring His own entertainment with Him." Let us open the door and say, "Lord, come in"—it may be but a barren place—"and sup with me with what I have." And then we shall sup with Him, and the morning shall break and the shadows flee, and we shall be with Him forever.

The Church and the Kingdom. How the Church Will Be With Christ When He Receives the Promised Kingdom.

WILLIAM L. PETTINGILL, Editor "Serving and Waiting."

Will you notice please the relation between Mr. Ottman's theme, who has just preceded me, and Mr. Torrey's theme, who is to speak this afternoon in Carnegie Hall on the glorious return of Christ to establish the kingdom, the difference between these two themes on the one hand, and our theme on the other. We have been hearing about the Church in the present age; we are to hear about the kingdom this afternoon. Now we are to think for a little while of the Church and the kingdom, and how the Church is to be with Christ when He receives the promised kingdom.

There is then a Church and there is also a kingdom. We learned last night through Dean Gray that these two things are far from identical.

The Church is not the kingdom; the kingdom is not the Church. They have many things in common, and preeminently among them they have the same Head. The Lord Jesus Christ is Head over all things to the Church, which is His body; and the Lord Jesus Christ is Head over all things to the kingdom, which is His realm. He reigns over the kingdom, but along with Him the Church will reign over the kingdom as His queen, the wife of the Lamb.

There is, however, even at present a kingdom of God in

the world. Whenever a man is born again he enters into the kingdom of God. He is delivered from the power of darkness and translated into the kingdom of the Son of His love, and he acknowledges the rule and reign of God and of His Son Jesus Christ in His own life. There is such a thing as the kingdom of God in its mystery form, as I have just mentioned; and there is such a thing as the kingdom of heaven, that great mass of profession, in its mystery form. But when we are thinking to-day of the kingdom, we are thinking of its future manifestation, when the Lord Jesus Christ shall come in the clouds of heaven with power and with great glory, and take His great power unto Himself and reign as King of kings and Lord of lords. I will ask you to please turn to the 17th chapter of Luke, where these two things, the present and the future form of the kingdom come before us. Luke xvii:20: "And when he was demanded of the Pharisees when the Kingdom of God should come, he answered them and said: "The kingdom of God cometh not with observation." It cometh not with outward show. It is not a thing to be seen by the outward eyes. "Neither shall they say, Lo here! or, lo there! for, behold, the kingdom of God is in the midst of you." He was not saying, "The kingdom of God is *within you.*" He was talking to a lot of Pharisees, who had nothing to do with the kingdom of God really, but then the kingdom of God was amongst them; the King was there ready to set up the kingdom, and wherever there was one acknowledging His rule, there was the kingdom of heaven in the midst of them. But see, He goes on and says to His disciples—not to the Pharisees now, but to His disciples, for He is teaching spiritual things, which none but His own people could understand:

> "The days will come when ye shall desire to see one of the days of the Son of man, and ye shall not see it. And they shall say to you, See here; or, see there: go not after them, nor follow them. For as the lightening, that lighteneth out of the one part under heaven, shineth unto the other part under heaven; so shall also the Son of man be in his day." You and I are desiring to see it manifested. We do not yet see it, but one day it shall be manifested. It shall come with outward show; and just as the lightening fills the heavens, shining from the east unto the west, so shall the coming of the Son of man be in His day."

But the 25th verse: "But first must He suffer many things, and be rejected of this generation."

Look now at the 19th chapter of Luke, the 11th verse: "And as they heard these things, he added and spake a parable, because He was nigh to Jerusalem, and because they thought that the kingdom of God should immediately appear. He said, therefore, "A certain nobleman went into a far country, to receive for himself a kingdom, and to return, leaving word with his servants, Occupy till I come." That certain nobleman has gone into a far country to receive a kingdom and to return. The kingdom of God was not to immediately appear when our Lord uttered these words: He has gone into a far country, and He is going to return, and He told His disciples to occupy until that time.

Then in the first chapter of the Acts of the Apostles, at the sixth verse. His disciples asked of Him, saying,

> "Lord, wilt thou at this time restore again the kingdom to Israel? And He said unto them, It is not for you to know the times or the seasons, which the Father hath put in his own authority. But ye shall receive power, after that the Holy Ghost is come upon you; and ye shall be witnesses unto me,

both in Jerusalem, and in all Judea, and in Samaria, and unto the uttermost part of the earth. And when he had spoken these things, while they beheld, he was taken up; and a cloud received him out of their sight."

I can well imagine that they were greatly perplexed as they saw him disappear just while He was talking about such interesting things, and they just hoped He would tell them about that kingdom. They had been waiting for it, and they thought, now that everything was done, as they supposed, the kingdom should immediately be set up; and they had just asked Him about it, "Now is this the time when the kingdom is to be restored to Israel? There is the seventh chapter of ii Samuel, and there are all the signs of the Old Testament to be fulfilled. Is this the time when you are going to fulfil them?" And He had just begun to tell them about it, it was not for them to know the times and the seasons, this was reserved for the Father, but power was coming upon them, and they were to witness to Him all over the world; and just while He was saying it, He disappeared. I hope to God when we disappear we will be telling somebody something about God. I can imagine their turning to each other and saying, "Now, there He has gone. My, our hearts failed us when He was crucified; then we were begotten into a lively hope by His resurrection from the dead, and we have been very happy about it for 40 days and 40 nights, and we thought now the time was ripe and the kingdom would be established; and He was just telling us about it, and He has gone. What do you suppose it means?" While they were looking steadfastly into heaven, two men stood by them in white apparel, who said, "Ye men of Galilee, why stand ye gazing up into heaven? This same Jesus, which is taken up from you into heaven, shall so come in like manner as ye have seen him go into heaven." Well, that settled everything; that adjusted everything. That was the keystone of the arch; that was the missing link in the chain; that fixed it all up. And they hurried back to Jerusalem to tell the other disciples about it, that Jesus was coming again. It was just like a new thing to them, because though He had told them about it over and over again, no one believed a thing He said about it. People tell us that the disciples invented the whole business; they tell us that the disciples invented the doctrine of the resurrection. Why, they were the last people on earth to believe anything about the resurrection. When the women said there had been a resurrection, they said the women had hysterics. And why did not they believe in the resurrection? Because they did not believe in the crucifixion. You get a man wrong on the atonement and he is wrong on everything. They were wrong on the atonement. They were not orthodox a bit about Christ. He kept telling them that He was going to be killed; and they would not believe it. They rebuked Him once, and that was enough; He stopped that. They rebuked Him openly. But though they did not rebuke Him openly any more, none of them believed a word He said about it. There wasn't a single disciple in the whole crowd that believed what He said except Mary of Bethany. She believed it; and when she anointed His body for the burial they rebuked her, and He stopped that. He said, "I want this told everywhere when my gospel is preached, what this woman has done." She believed Him. Oh, how refreshing to Him it was to have somebody believe what He said! Now then, when the cross was actually set up and He was nailed to it, they were dumbfounded. They had not believed His testimony about the cross, and so they were not prepared to believe His testimony about the resurrection; and when the resurrection came, they could not believe it until finally the proofs were piled up, and they could not help but believe it. And now for 40 days they had been rejoicing in it, and then He had gone away. And then wasn't it gracious of Him to send those two men down with that testimony, "He is coming back again."

And how is He coming back? Is He coming back in the gradual diffusion of Christianity, or is He coming back at the death of the believer? It took a modern commentator to invent a thing like that. Why, no; they said He is coming back just as He went away. He went away bodily; He is coming back bodily. He went away visibly; He is coming back visibly. He went away in the clouds; He is coming back in the clouds. He went away from the Mount of Olives, and He is coming back to the Mount of Olives. Just as He went away He is coming back, and exactly to the same spot; and when He comes back to that spot, there will be something doing on Mount Olivet.

Now you know that the second chapter of Daniel is the great chapter on the coming of this kingdom. It is a long story, and you are familiar with it.

Nebuchadnezzar was the first Gentile monarch to rule over Jerusalem after Israel became a nation, and with him began that great epoch called the times of the Gentiles, which has been going on now for twenty-five hundred years, in which God is proving out the Gentiles to show that they are not able to rule or reign. Well, they have made an awful mess of it, and now they are about to sit around the peace table to make peace. The Gentiles cannot rule this world; and one day God is going to put His own man, who is a Jew, the man Christ Jesus, upon the throne of this world and establish here, not a universal democracy, but a universal monarchy, such a government as the world has never seen. Now it is all told there in the second chapter of Daniel.

You know how that Nebuchadnezzar dreamed a dream, and wanted to know what he dreamed. The only thing he remembered was that he had dreamed a mighty interesting dream, and he just had to know what he had dreamed. He forgot the whole thing except he had dreamed a dream, and he wanted to know what it meant. He was surrounded by experts on that sort of thing. He had people around him that told him they could tell all about the future, they could tell all about dreams, and he never before had had a chance to put them to the test. So he called them to him and said, "Here is your chance to make good. You have been telling what you could do. Now do it. I have dreamed a dream, and I have to know what I dreamed, and then I have to know what the dream meant. They said, "You tell us what it was, what is your dream; then we will tell you what it meant." "Oh, no," he said, "that is the trouble. You are trying to gain time. Off go your heads unless you tell me what I dreamed, and not only you, but your house shall be a dunghill." That is what comes of despotism when you have the wrong kind of a despot. And so while I am not a democrat, I am not just yet a monarchist, until the Monarch appears, you know. I hope that democracy will sort of hold together until the Autocrat comes whose right it is to rule. Well, you know how the edict went out that everybody's head was to be cut off; there was to be an awful slaughter. And Daniel and his fellows, who had not been consulted, found suddenly it was on the program for their heads to be cut off.

Of course they grew keenly interested in that matter right off. And Daniel sent in word, "Now wait, I will tell the king what he dreamed and the interpretation thereof." And he went to God and got the interpretation, and went in and told the king what he had dreamed.

I think I see that king sitting on his throne high and lifted up. You may let your imagination run riot, for the luxury of the Babylon court was beyond anything you can imagine. You need not think of the king and Daniel having a little interview by themselves, not for a minute. That king was not left alone for a minute. All the courtiers were there; the retinue of servants were all there; and there was pomp and grandeur and glitter and display on every hand; and he sat there on a high throne, and here was this little despised Jew. The others had said, "There isn't a man on earth that can tell the king's matter." And that is where so many ministers make a mistake. They say, "I don't know anything about it. I wasn't taught anything about it in the theological seminary. Nobody knows anything about it; so what is the use?" "There isn't a man on earth that can tell the king's matter." But here was Daniel and he could tell all about it.

I think I see that man sitting upon that throne and looking down on Daniel and saying, "Why, sure enough, that is what I dreamed; that is it. How in the world did he know?" And he asked him how he knew. And Daniel said, "There is a God in heaven who put you on that throne up there. He gave you that throne. You thought you had got it by your own power; not so; He put us down and sat it up. The God of heaven, whom I worship, is also the God of earth and He it is who gave you this dream, and He it is who has given me the interpretation. It is not from anything in me; He did it all."

"Now," he said, "this means that God has given to you the political history of this world for a long time to come. You and Babylon, which you represent, are the head of gold. After you is coming another kingdom inferior to you, of silver; and another third kingdom, of brass, that shall rule over the whole world; and a fourth kingdom, strong like iron; and then finally this fourth kingdom will be divided into parts, and these parts are represented by the toes, and thus the feet and toes are made part of iron and part of brittle clay." He said, "You saw until a stone came down out of heaven, which smote the image upon its feet and toes, and destroyed the whole image, and took its place and filled the whole earth. That means that God one day will set up a kingdom of His own in the world, which will take the place of all these kingdoms, and it shall endure forever. This is what God has said."

Well now, dear friends, I suspect that when Daniel got through the dream and began the interpretation, Nebuchadnezzar was ready to hear what that little Jew had to say; and if that be true, I think that you and I, who live 2500 years afterward, and have seen with our eyes the fulfilment of the greater part of the dream, I think that it is time that you and I gave Daniel a hearing, and let him say his say and believe what he says. Why, everybody who has studied history a little bit knows what has happened. You don't have to study history, if you will just study what the Bible tells you. You know what has happened because whatever the Bible says is bound to happen. In the eighth chapter of Daniel, the second and third of these world powers are actually mentioned by name, Medio-Persia and

Greece, in the 20th and 21st verses. And then if you want to know the name of the fourth kingdom, you have to go to Luke, where you find the whole world being possessed by the emperor of Rome, Augustus, and when you hear the Jews saying, "The Romans will come and take our city." The names of all these kingdoms are in the Bible itself, and history of course has shown that the Bible all the time knew what it was talking about and was all true. I was about to say that history has confirmed the Bible, but history cannot confirm the Bible. Somebody came to old Dr. Weston one time and said, "Doctor, they have just dug up some things over there in the East with their spades that confirm large portions of the Scriptures." And the Doctor wasn't interested at all. He said, "That doesn't amount to anything. Now if you will find some place where the Bible confirms the excavations, that will help some." It is all there. Babylon was succeeded by Medio-Persia, symbolized by the arms and breast of silver. Greece was symbolized by the belly and thighs of brass. Rome, which was divided into two parts—every well developed man has two legs—and when you come to the legs, here you find Rome actually divided into eastern and western Rome, with the city of Rome as the capital of western Rome, and the city of Constantinople, named after that hybrid professing Christian, Constantine, as the capital of eastern Rome. So you have the division into the two parts; and then eastern and western Rome have been divided long ago into sub-divisions. But what about those metals? Gold is more valuable than silver, and silver is more valuable than brass or bronze, or copper, and brass is more valuable than iron, and iron is more valuable than clay. Yes, and God says that means that each of these succeeding metals will be inferior to the one that went before; which is to say that constitutional monarchy, limited monarchy, representative republicanism, democracy, socialism, and all the rest are inferior from God's viewpoint to absolute monarchy as a rule of government.

That isn't a popular thing to say here, I know, but I cannot help it; I did not write this chapter; I am only reading it to you.

Then here is another thing. While it is true that gold is more valuable than silver, and silver more valuable than brass, and brass more valuable than iron, and iron more valuable than clay, it is also true that silver is stronger than gold, and brass stronger than silver, and iron is stronger than brass, but clay is not stronger than iron. What does that mean? It means that as the principle of absolute monarchy, the rule by one man, was set aside in these various empires, and there was mingled with it the seed of men, as the chapter itself says, "They shall mingle themselves with the seed of men,"—as rule by the people became joined to rule by the monarch, there had to be brought in the element of force in order to govern; and so the armies had to be larger and larger, until by and by, when you come down to the toes, the feet and the toes, you find that the armies discover how much strength they have, and so the clay, which speaks of representation of the people, which speaks of rule by the people, which speaks of Bolshevism, which speaks of socialism, which speaks of red flagism,—all those come in in the toes, and displace the strength of the iron!

Don't you see that this whole thing, this whole colossal image of human government is standing upon a very insecure foundation today. Don't you see the foundation is growing very insecure? Why, it was only a few years ago they had such things as czars and kaisers and kings and emperors and such things as that. They are all gone. The iron is disappearing and the clay is coming in like a flood. And you know what is coming, don't you? It is the stone which destroys the whole thing; the Lord Jesus Christ to take up His great power and reign as King of kings and Lord of lords; and that thing is bound to happen, and it is bound to happen soon.

Now then, I will ask you to note that when the Lord Jesus receives the kingdom unto Himself, the Church will be with Him. We are told, you know, in these days by some very sweet Christian brethren who are postmillennialists that there has to come something between us and the coming of our Lord to take us unto Himself. Now I love them, but I do not trust them. I do not thank anybody for putting anything even so thick as a piece of tissue paper between me and my blessed hope. The Word of God, the epistle to the churches, if they teach anything, teach that we are to be serving the living and the true God and waiting for His Son from heaven. If they teach anything, they teach that you and I have been delivered from the wrath to come, that we are not appointed unto wrath, but we are to obtain salvation; that whether we wake or sleep we should live together with Him.

I have just one argument to advance against post tribulation. It is this: The Church is the body of Christ. The Church is Christ. First Corinthians xii:12 says so. "For as the body is one and hath many members, and all the members of that one body, being many are one body; so also is Christ." Speaking about His body of course, but isn't it perfectly legitimate to speak of a person's body as of himself? The Church is Christ, is His body. To say that the

Church must pass through the awful scenes of the great tribulation and have visited upon her the wrath of God in that awful time is to say that Christ Himself must again go through the awful billows of the wrath of God; and I say to you that that thing has no more claim upon Him, that He paid the awful penalty once and for all, and that He and we are not appointed to wrath, but to obtain salvation; that whether we wake or sleep, we shall live together with Him. Oh then, beloved, the kingdom is about to come, but something has to come before the kingdom comes, and that thing that is to come before the kingdom comes is the thing for which you and I should be waiting in these days. Oh, I am sorry for the man who isn't looking for the Lord Jesus. "Do you think He will come to-day?" somebody says.

"I think not." "To-morrow?" "Oh, I think not. Not for a thousand years." That is the way they talk. "In such an hour as ye think not, He will come." Amen. Even so come, Lord Jesus.

The Visible and Glorious Return of Christ God's Final Answer to Infidelity and All Present Form of Error

By DEAN REUBEN A. TORREY.

I have been asked to present this afternoon the subject of the Visible and Glorious Return of Christ, as God's Final Answer to Infidelity in all its forms, and to all Present Day Error.

I. THE SECOND COMING OF CHRIST, GOD'S FINAL ANSWER TO INFIDELITY

First of all, the return of our Lord Jesus in glory will be God's final answer to infidelity. The promises regarding that return that are found in the Bible, both the Old Testament and the New, are very plain and they are also, humanly speaking, very improbable and apparently impossible of fulfillment; and, when they are fulfilled, they will constitute an unanswerable proof of the Divine origin of that book that contains these promises and prophecies. The promises and prophecies regarding the first coming of Jesus Christ, His virgin birth, the place of His birth, the time of His manifestation to His people, the manner of His reception by His people, His death and burial, and the detailed circumstances connected with it, His resurrection from the dead, and His victory subsequent to His resurrection, seemed most improbable when made, but these predictions have been fulfilled to the very letter, and by their fulfillment in Jesus of Nazareth we have conclusive proof of two things: first, that Jesus is the predicted Messiah of the Jews, and second, that the Old Testament is the Word of God. But the Old Testament contains far more detailed and explicit predictions regarding the second coming of Christ than it contains concerning His first coming, and in addition to these Old Testament predictions we have in the gospels and in the epistles and the book of Revelation in the New Testament still more detailed predictions regarding the same event. And when these numerous predictions are fulfilled to the letter, the prediction for example regarding His descent from heaven with a shout, with the voice of the archangel and the trump of God, the rapture and all the events predicted as to follow the rapture, the manifestation of the Antichrist, the time of Jacob's trouble and the coming of the glorified Christ visibly and bodily to the deliverance of His people, and His blessed and glorious reign, then every infidel mouth will be stopped and every knee shall be forced to bow and every tongue has to confess that Jesus Christ is Lord; to the glory of God the Father (Phil. ii:10, 11). There will be no possibility in that day of denying the Divine origin of these predictions and the supernatural inspiration of the book which contains them. The Apostle Peter foretold in 2 Pet. iii:3, 4 that in the last days "mockers" would "come," just as they have come in the person of Shailer Mathews and other theological professors, and that the especial object of their mockery would be, as it is, the second coming of Christ. To use Peter's exact words, "In the last days mockers shall come with mockery, walking after their own lust, and saying, Where is the promise of His coming? for, from the day that the fathers fell asleep, all things continue as they were from the beginning of the creation." But when He actually does come, as He surely will, then every mocking mouth shall be silenced and all infidels and atheists be overwhelmed with fear and dismay, and every mouth, instead of being filled with boastings of a crass evolutionary philosophy, will be filled with cries "to the mountains and to the rocks, Fall on us, and hide us from the face of Him that sitteth on the throne, and from the wrath of the Lamb; for the great day of their wrath is come; and who is able to stand?" (Rev. iv:15-17). The second comingof Christ will be God's own final answer to infidelity and atheism and agnosticism in all their forms.

II. THE SECOND COMING OF CHRIST, GOD'S FINAL ANSWER TO THE DESTRUCTIVE CRITICISM

The second coming of Christ, the visible and glorious return of Christ, will be God's final answer to the destructive criticism. One of the fundamental postulates of the destructive criticism, and of pretty much all that in our day is called "Higher Criticism" (whatever the original and proper significance of the term "Higher Criticism" may be) is that there can be no such thing as minute and detailed and supernaturally inspired, predictive prophecy. So, whenever any minute and detailed prophecy is found in Isaiah, Jeremiah, Ezekiel or Daniel, or any other Old Testament prophet, the destructive critics take that at once as conclusive proof that these passages could not have been written by the person whose name it has borne for so many centuries, but that it must belong to a later period. This fundamental postulate of the destructive criticism has already been proven untrue time and time again by the many minute and exact literal fulfillments of prophecy that have already taken place, for example, by the prediction in Micah v:2, regarding the place of the birth of the Messiah; the prediction in Daniel ix:25-27 regarding the time of the Messiah and His cutting off, i.e., His death; the many predictions concerning the manner of His reception by His people, the manner and details of His death, burial, and resurrection contained in Isa. 53, for we may bring these predictions down to the latest date that the most daring destructive critic ever thought of assigning them to, and still they will be centuries before their minute, detailed and literal fulfillment in Jesus of Nazareth. Furthermore the fact that there are many minute, detailed and specific predictions regarding the Jews in the scriptures of the Old Testament and the New which are being fulfilled before our very eyes to-day. But when the Lord Jesus comes again and the many and detailed predictions connected with His second coming are fulfilled to the letter before the very eyes of men in a way that cannot be misunderstood or mistaken, then the utter folly of the fundamental postulate of the destructive criticism will be seen by all. So the second coming of Christ, His visible return in glory, with all the events connected with it will be God's final and crushing answer to the destructive criticism in all its forms. Destructive critics, listen to what I say and repent of your folly now, and give up a type of criticism that beyond a peradventure was not only made in Germany, the land not only of systematized and *university-bred* and fostered violence, lust, outrage and general deviltry, but the land of systematized and *university-bred* and fostered falsehood, but which is also demonstrably false in its fundamental postulates and in all its details. If you do not repent now the time is coming when all these predictions regarding the visible and glorious return of our Lord will be fulfilled before your eyes and you will have to repent then when repentance is too late to bring salvation.

GOD'S ANSWER TO INFIDELITY

III. THE SECOND COMING OF CHRIST, GOD'S FINAL ANSWER TO UNITARIANISM

In the third place the second coming of Christ will be God's final answer to Unitarianism in all its forms. Unitarianism has already been fully and satisfactorily answered by the resurrection of Jesus Christ from the dead. The resurrection of Jesus Christ from the dead can be proven to be the best established fact of history, but the resurrection of Jesus Christ from the dead is conclusive answer to Unitarianism in all its form. Some one will ask, "How is the resurrection of Christ from the dead an answer to Unitarianism?" Because Jesus Christ when He was here upon earth claimed to be the Son of God, claimed to be Divine, claimed to be the Son of God and claimed to be Divine not in the sense in which many to-day are saying, "Oh yes, I believe Jesus is the Son of God, we are all sons of God. Oh, I believe Jesus Christ is Divine, we are all divine," but claimed to be the Son of God and to be Divine in a sense in which no other is Divine. For example, in Mark xi:6 our Lord taught that while all the prophets of the old dispensation, even the greatest, were servants of God, that He was a Son and the only Son of God. In John v:23 He taught that *all men should honor Him*, the Son, *even as they honor God the Father*. In John x:30 He said, "I and my Father are one," and in John xiv:9 He says, "He that hath seen me hath seen the Father." Beyond a question Jesus claimed to be God manifest in the flesh. Men put Him to death as a blasphemer for making that claim, and if He was not God manifest in the flesh, then the Jews, according to their own divinely given law, were right in putting Him to death, only they should have put Him to death by stoning and not by crucifixion. Whoever denies the Deity of Christ justifies His execution. But before they put Him to death our Lord Jesus said in substance, "You will put me to death for making this claim, but three days after you have put me to death God will set the stamp of His endorsement upon the claim by raising me from the dead." Put Him to death they did; lay Him in Joseph's sepulcher they did; roll the stone to the door of the sepulcher they did; seal it with the Roman seal, which to break was death, they did; but when the hour that Jesus had foretold was come, the power of God raised Him from the dead, and God proclaimed more loudly and more clearly and unmistakably than ever if you should hear His voice speaking from the opened heavens above New York to-day. This man is what He claimed to be. He is my Son. He is God manifest in the flesh. All men should honor Him even as they honor the Father. All men should worship Him and adore Him even as they honor the Father. All men should worship Him and adore Him even as they do me. Ever since that glorious first day of the week when He rose triumphant over the grave and death, Unitarianism has had no logical standing ground. In His resurrection is a complete answer to Unitarianism in all its forms. But His second coming, His Visible and Glorious Return will be God's final answer to Unitarianism. Jesus Christ said under oath to the high priest that He was the Christ, the Son of God, and then added: "Nevertheless I say unto you, Henceforth ye shall see the Son of man sitting at the right hand of power, and coming in the clouds of heaven." "Coming in the clouds," what does that mean? Take your Concordance and look up the word "cloud," and who alone comes in the clouds, and you will see that Jehovah of hosts and Jehovah alone comes in the clouds; that He and He alone "maketh the clouds His chariot." So evidently the thought is that when Jesus comes again He is coming openly manifested as Jehovah and "every eye will see" that He is Jehovah, and the Unitarians and every one who has denied His proper Deity will be overwhelmed with shame. Unitarians, every Unitarian here, acknowledge now what His resurrection has proven, acknowledge Him as God; worship Him. God says in unmistakable terms, "Let all the angels of God worship Him." (Heb. 1:6). You too worship Him. God commands it, reason demands it, the proven facts in the case demand it, that all men should honor the Lord Jesus as they honor the Father. But if you will not do it now you shall have to do it in that day when He comes and when, as God tells us in His own Word, "Every knee shall bow, of things in heaven and things on earth and things under the earth, and every tongue confess that Jesus Christ is Lord, to the glory of God the Father" (Phil. ii:10, 11). It will do you no good to confess it then, if you have not done it before.

IV. THE SECOND COMING OF CHRIST, GOD'S FINAL ANSWER TO RUSSELLISM

In the fourth place, the second coming of Christ, the Visible and Glorious Return of our Lord, will be God's final answer to Russellism. This foul system propagated with such an outlay of money, has ruined the spiritual life and paralyzed the service of thousands. This system is a strange combination and conglomeration of pretty much all the errors that the living church has spued out of its mouth during the eighteen centuries of its history. It contradicts the plainest teachings of the Word of God at points too numerous to mention. It has been satisfactorily answered time and time again, but the final answer to this whole vile system, to all its lies and blasphemies, will be at the second coming of Christ. "Pastor" Russell taught that Jesus has already come, that He came in October, 1874; but when He really comes, *in the way the Bible says He will come,* in a way entirely different from any imaginary coming that has already taken place, Russellism will be seen to be the hollow fraud and lie that it really is. Russell taught that the body of Jesus was not raised, but either removed and preserved somewhere, or else dissolved into gasses, but when the very Jesus who was crucified and then was raised and transformed and ascended, comes again *as "the Son of man,"* as He said He would (Matt. xxvi:64) Russellism will be seen for the hollow lie it really is. Russell taught again that the Judgment is to be another probation and "another chance," but when the Lord Jesus comes, as He said He would, and "sits upon the throne of His glory," and before Him are gathered all nations then living on the earth, and says to those on His right hand, "Come ye blessed of my Father, inherit the kingdom prepared for you from the foundation of the world," and to those on His left hand, "Depart from me ye cursed, *into eternal fire* which is prepared for the devil and his angels" (Matt. 25:31-41). Then Russellism will be seen for the hollow lie and baseless, delusive, deceiving and destroying false hope that it really is.

V. THE SECOND COMING OF CHRIST, GOD'S FINAL ANSWER TO MARY BAKER EDDYISM, CHRISTIAN "SCIENCE FALSELY SO CALLED"

In the fifth place the second coming of Christ, the Visible and Glorious Return of Christ will be God's final answer to Mary Baker Eddyism, Christian "Science falsely so called."

"Christian Science" has been exposed and its every claim exploded times without number, and no one can in this day remain an honest Christian Scientist except through gross and unpardonable ignorance of what Mary Baker Glover Patterson Eddy taught or what the Bible teaches, or else because since they would not receive the love of the truth they have been given over to strong delusion to believe a lie (2 Thes. ii:8-11). But the second coming of Christ, His Visible and Glorious Return will be God's final answer. Mrs. Eddy taught that there was no such thing as the body. that the body is only "illusion," "mortal thought," but when Jesus comes again in the same manner in which He went (Acts 1:11), bodily, and visibly, an actually and forever *incarnate* Jesus, Christian Science will be seen for the empty and ridiculous lie that it is. Mary Eddy taught that the actual *historic Jesus* was not the Christ she belived in, but that the Christ she belived in was the ideal Christ; but when Jesus Himself comes again in the clouds of heaven and all the holy angels with Him, she will know and her deluded disciples will know that the actual historic Jesus who was born of the Virgin Mary, *who suffered and actually died,* who actually and literally rose from the dead, is the true and only Christ and that, as John puts it, "Whosoever denieth the Son, the same hath not the Father" (1 John ii:23), and "he that denieth that *Jesus* is the Christ, this is the antichrist" (1John ii:22). "Christian Scientists" teach that the revelation of Christian Science to Mrs. Mary Baker Eddy in 1876 was the second coming of Christ. But when Jesus Christ comes again, publicly, bodily, visibly, and in great glory, Mary Baker Eddy's claim will be seen unclothed from its gaudy dress of high sounding but empty words in all its naked hideousness. Mary Baker Eddy taught that there was no such thing as death, that death was an illusion and that therefore there could be no proper resurrection of the dead, but when her mentally and financially duped followers hear the voice of command of our descending Lord, and see the graves opening and the dead coming out of them and ascending to meet the Lord in the air, and they themselves left behind to pass through all the horrors of the Great Tribulation, and to feel the stern hand, not of "the Beast of Berlin," but "the Beast" of Revelation, they will see what a mockery was their imagined "Science" and what utter fools they have been.

VI. THE SECOND COMING OF CHRIST, GOD'S FINAL ANSWER TO UNIVERSALISM IN ALL ITS FORMS

In the sixth place, the second coming of Christ, the Visible and Glorious Return of our Lord, will be God's final answer to Universalism in all its forms. Time fails me to dwell upon that. Simply let me point you to one passage in the Word of God, 2 Thess. 1:7-10, "The Lord Jesus shall be revealed from heaven, with the angels of His power in flaming fire, rendering vengeance to them that know not God, and to them that obey not the gospel of our Lord Jesus; who shall suffer punishment, even *eternal destruction* from the face of the Lord and from the glory of His might, when He shall come to be glorified in His saints, and to be marvelled at in all them that believed. . . . in that day." Men are unwilling to believe that any man shall be finally and forever lost, I do not wonder that men are loath to believe it. They try to make out that in some way, in some place, in this world or some other world, at some time, all men shall be brought to repentance and thus saved. Alas: it is a baseless hope, woven of our delusive wishes and not from the teaching of the Word of God. The premises and conclusions of Universalism have been answered time and time again, but the final answer will be God's own answer when the Lord Jesus returns, when, as the passage just quoted declares, "those who know not God" and those who "obey not the gospel" will be punished with "eternal destruction." Oh, impenitent sinners, persistent rejectors of our Lord Jesus Christ, hugging to your bosoms the delusive phantom of a baseless hope that you will have another chance in some after world, throw that delusive and destroying hope to the winds and accept Jesus now while it is time. Surrender to Him as your Lord, confess Him as such before the world, and go forth to live and to please Him in everything day by day. And you false prophets, who are encouraging silly men and women in such a hope, and while posing as their merciful friends are proving yourself their cruelest enemies, cease your well meaning but really destroying work today.

VII. THE SECOND COMING OF CHRIST, GOD'S FINAL ANSWER TO ALL WOULD BE WORLD CONQUERORS AND WORLD RULERS

In the seventh place, the second coming of Christ will be God's final answer to all would be world conquerors and world rulers. God gave Napoleon His answer to his wicked ambitions in 1815, God has given the cruel ambitions of Kaiser Wilhelm II His answer in the past few weeks, but when Jesus comes again God will give all the proud sons of Satan who aspire to rule the nations of the earth their final and crushing answer. His coming will be the solution of all the world's problems and the cure for all the ills of human society. He alone can bring peace and He will. If I did not know that Christ were coming again I would necessarily be plunged into the depths of a hopeless pessimism and despair. If the Lord Jesus were not coming, there would be and could be nothing for this sad world to do but to build its merciless dreadnaughts and submarines and zeppelins and airplanes, and devise more and more destructive gases and more powerful and more frightful explosives and go on fighting one another until this world became transformed into one universal charnal house of maimed, tortured, dying and dead. War will continue, more frightful wars even than this, until He comes, but His coming, the Prince of Peace, will end it all. Boastful man tells us how he will bring all evil to an end by his evolutionary progress and the growth of knowledge. Only a few weeks ago we were saying that when Jenner discovered vaccination for smallpox he put an end to smallpox, and when antitoxin was discovered for diphtheria that put an end to diphtheria; that when the typhoid serum and typhus serum were discovered that would eliminate typhoid and typhus, that there would never be another great pestilence among civilized nations. But what answer came to our foolish boastings? Influenza, and eleven thousand dead in Philadelphia in a single month; forty thousand dead in the State of Pennsylvania; twenty-two thousand dead in the State of Illinois; more dead throughout the world than this appalling war has claimed as victims. O, man, with all thy boastings what a puny creature of the dust thou art. We need God, we need Jesus. When He comes all plagues and pestilences will spread their foul and murky wings and take their flight. When He comes war will end, except for that brief space at the end of the Millennium when Satan shall be loosed for a little season that he may meet his overwhelming and final defeat. Then war ends, tyranny will end, unbelief will end, every evil will end, and "The earth shall be full of the knowledge of the LORD, as the waters cover the sea" (Isa. 11:19). Then, *and not till* then. Even so come Lord Jesus, come quickly.

The Capture of Jerusalem and the Great Future of that City

By Arno C. Gaebelein, Editor "Our Hope"

"For Zion's sake will I not hold my peace, and for Jerusalem's sake I will not rest, until the righteousness thereof go forth as brightness, and the salvation thereof as a lamp that burneth. And the Gentiles shall see thy righteousness, and all kings thy glory; and thou shalt be called by a new name, which the mouth of the Lord shall name. Thou shalt also be a crown of glory in the hand of the Lord, and a royal diadem in the hand of thy God . . . . I have set watchmen upon thy walls, O Jerusalem which shall never hold their peace day nor night; ye that make mention of the Lord keep not silence, and give Him no rest till He estabish, and till He make Jerusalem a praise in the earth." (Isaiah LXII:1-3, 6, 7.)

"Thus saith the Lord of Hosts, Behold I will save my people from the east country and from the west country, and I will bring them, and they shall dwell in the midst of Jerusalem, and they shall be my people, and I will be their God, in truth and in righteousness" (Zech. viii:7-8.)

Jerusalem! Jews and Gentiles love this word. The Hebrew race, God's ancient covenant people and their remarkable history of blessing and suffering is closely linked with that city. Centuries before civilization ever touched Europe, when its nations were still wild Barbarians, Jerusalem was already in existence. It was a city of importance even in the days of Abraham, when the Lord called him as the father of the Jewish nation. From the Tel-el-Amarna tablets we learn that its name was then "Uru-salem" which means the city of peace and there can be no doubt that the King-Priest Melchizedek that King of Righteousness and King of Peace, as well as the Priest of the Most High had that city for his dwelling place. Under David, the never to be forgotten Shepherd-King, Jerusalem became the great center of Israel. He took possession of Zion and made it his residence. His Son Solomon built in it that magnificent temple which Jehovah filled with His glory. And therefore the Jews always loved Jerusalem. When they were at the rivers of Babylon and hanged their harps upon the willows with no song, but only tears they cried out "If I forget thee, O Jerusalem let my right hand forget her cunning. If I do not remember thee, let my tongue cleave to the roof of my mouth if I prefer not Jerusalem above my chief joy" (Psalm cxxxvii). This spirit of love for Jerusalem has never died, nor can it ever die, among the Jewish people. And we Christians love Jerusalem for the same reason the true Jew loves it and more so, because of Him who is our Saviour and Lord, who walked once through its streets, was acclaimed by the multitudes as Israel's King, who displayed His power there and finally was cast out of the city to die. We love Jerusalem because of Christ our Lord.

And what a stir among Jews and Christians when about a year ago the glad news flashed over the wires that Jerusalem had been captured by General Allenby. What rejoicing when it became known that the unspeakably, wicked Turk, with his equally wicked German master had been defeated, that the crescent was downed and the flag of the British Lion wafted over David's City! And then the question, What does it mean this capture of Jerusalem? Rejoicing Jewry and Christian Bible Students looked upon it, as it is in reality, as one of the greatest events of the great world war. And now let us examine this event and the future of this remarkable City.

1. *What is the Future of Jerusalem?* The future glory of the city is revealed by the Prophets of God. Anyone who believes the Bible must believe in the glorious future of Jerusalem. And here let me expose that fatal error into which so many Bible believing Christians have fallen, an error which is responsible for a great deal of the confusion existing in Christendom. So many Christians think when they read of Jerusalem, or Zion, its blessing and its glory, it means no longer the literal, the earthly Jerusalem, but that it means now the heavenly Jerusalem. Others again make of Zion and her glory the Christian church, while many a denomination speaks of the glory of her own particular Zion. All this is wrong. The Church is not Zion nor is the Zion of the Bible the church. It is true there is a new Jerusalem, a heavenly Jerusalem into which the redeemed will be gathered to be forever with the Lord. But this heavenly Jerusalem, the new Jerusalem is nowhere revealed by the Prophets of the Old Testament Scriptures. Whenever the prophets speak of Jerusalem, or Zion, they always mean the literal Jerusalem over yonder in Palestine and not a spiritual thing and much less the church. Begin to read your Old Testament in the right way and remember whenever God's Spirit reveals the glory of Zion and the glory of Jerusalem He reveals a literal glory of a literal City on earth.

And what is that promised future of glory for Jerusalem? We might turn now the pages of our Bibles for an hour and read many Scripture passages which make that glory known and learn from these the answer to our question. We shall read a very few and then give, upon these infallible promises of a covenant keeping God, our own description of the coming glory of Jerusalem.

"And the ransomed of the Lord shall return, and come to Zion with songs and everlasting joy upon their heads; they shall obtain joy and gladness, and sorrow and sighing shall flee away" (Isaiah xxxv:10). "Comfort ye, Comfort ye my people, saith your God. Speak ye to the heart of Jerusalem and cry unto her that her warfare is accomplished, that her iniquity is pardoned for she hath received of the Lord's hand double (in blessing) for all her sins" (Isa. xl:1-2). "Break forth into joy, sing together, ye waste places of Jerusalem for the Lord hath comforted His people, He hath redeemed Jerusalem. The Lord has made bare His holy arm in the eyes of all the nations, and all the ends of the earth shall see the salvation of our God" (Isaiah lii:9-10). "O thou afflicted, tossed with tempest, and not comforted, behold I will lay thy stones with fair colours, and lay thy foundations with sapphires. And I will make thy windows of agates, and thy gates of carbuncles, and all thy borders of pleasant stones. And all thy children shall be taught of the Lord, and great shall be the peace of thy children. In righteousness shalt thou be established thou shalt be far from oppression, for thou shalt not fear; and from terror, for it shall not come near thee" (Isaiah liv:11-14).

"Arise, shine, for thy light is come and the glory of the Lord is risen upon thee. For behold darkness shall cover the earth, and gross darkness the people, but the Lord shall rise upon thee, and His glory shall be seen upon thee" (Isaiah lx:1-2). "Hear the word of the Lord, O ye nations, and declare it in the isles afar off, and say, He that scattered Israel will gather him, and keep him as a shepherd doth his flock. For the Lord hath redeemed Jacob and ransomed him from the hand of him that was stronger than he" (Jerm. xxxi:10-11). "In those days and at that time will I cause the branch of righteousness to grow up unto David and he shall execute judgment and righteousness in the land. In those days shall Judah be saved and Jerusalem shall dwell safely, and this is the name wherewith she shall be called 'The Lord our righteousness'" (Jerm. xxxiii: 15-16). "And the name of that city from that day shall be Jehovah Shammah—the Lord is there" (Ez. xlviii:35). "The Lord also shall roar out of Zion and utter His voice from Jerusalem; and the heavens and the earth shall shake, but the Lord will be the hope of His people and the strength of the children of Israel." "So shall ye know that I am the Lord of your God dwelling in Zion, my holy mountain, then shall Jerusalem be holy, and there shall no strangers pass through her any more" (Joel iii:16). "In that day will I raise up the tabernacle of David that is fallen, and close up the breaches thereof; and I will raise up its ruins, and I will build it as in the days of old" (Amos ix:ii). "But in the last days it shall come to pass that the mountain of the Lord's house shall be established in the top of the mountains and it shall be exalted above the hills and people shall flow unto it. And many nations shall say, Come, and let us go up to the mountain of the Lord and to the house of the God of Jacob; and He will teach us of His ways and we will walk in His paths, for the law shall go forth of Zion and the word of the Lord from Jerusalem. And He shall judge among many people and rebuke strong nations afar off; and they shall beat their swords into plowshares and their spears into pruninghooks; nation shall not lift up sword against nation, neither shall they learn war any more" (Micha iv:1-3). "Sing, and rejoice, O daughter of Zion, for lo I come and will dwell in the midst of thee, saith the Lord. And many nations shall be joined to the Lord in that day and shall be my people—and the Lord shall inherit Judah his position in the holy land and shall choose Jerusalem again" (Zech. ii:10). What promises these are! And how many others we might add! And they all mean what they say. It is not the church, nor is it a kind of spiritual idealism some Jews believe, but a literal glory. What blessings and glories are therefore in store for the City and for Jewish people! They will be regathered from all countries where they are now in dispersion and restored to their God given land. The waste places will be rebuilt; the land will be once more a land flowing with milk and honey. God's mercy, grace and loving-kindness will overshadow the nation and their sins will be remembered no more. Orthodox Jews go on their New Year's day to some running water and practise what they call "Tashlik." They cast some things, like pieces of paper, into the water and recite the three last verses of Micah. "Who is a God like unto thee who pardoneth inquity, and passeth by the transgression of the remnant of His heritage? He retaineth not His anger forever, because He delighteth in mercy. He will turn again, He will have compassion upon us; He will subdue our iniquities; and Thou wilt cast all their sins into the depths of the sea. Thou wilt perform the truth to Jacob and the mercy to Abraham which Thou hast sworn unto our Fathers from the days of old." This beautiful Scripture will be fulfilled when Israel and Jerusalem is restored; their sins will be cast into the depths of the sea. Jerusalem will then become the metropolis of the whole world. A King will reign, the King Messiah and a new government will be set up in that city, the government of heaven, of righteousness and peace. The whole world, all the nations will then turn to Jehovah and worship the Lord of hosts; every instrument of war will be turned into an implement of agriculture. Visible glory will cover the city and rest upon it. Such is the future of Jerusalem, when that city will be like a royal diadem in the hand of the Lord and she shall no longer be called "Forsaken" or "Desolate," but "Hephzi-bah" (my delight is in her) and "Beulah" (married). But that glory has never been in the past nor is it today.

II. A Retrospect: Jerusalem's past history. Let us see next what has been the past history of the city which has such a bright future of glory. For a brief period it had prospered and became a far famed city. That was when the Son of David, Solomon reigned in Jerusalem. No wars were then in progress, and Solomon was the King of peace. He built the house of the Lord which was filled with His glory. The fame of the City and this wise and great King spread everywhere. The Queen of Sheba came from afar and confessed that not the half had been told. What happened when Solomon became old is known to every reader of the Bible. The wise man, the great King became a great fool and departed from the Lord. As a result the Kingdom was divided and with it began that history of strife, sin and shame, which the inspired historical books so faithfully describe. Lower and lower sank the City of David. The temple was often profaned. Idolatries with all its immoral practices held sway. Some of the sons of David, the Kings of Judah, worship Moloch and cast the children into the fiery arms of that idol. While it is true that great reforms took place and several kings did what was right in the sight of the Lord, the tendency was ever downward till the point was reached when God's patient mercy ended. Thus it is written, "They mocked the messengers of God, and despised His words, and misused His prophets, until the wrath of the Lord arose against His people till there was no remedy" (2 Chron. xxxvi:16). Yet when Jerusalem apostatized and turned away from Jehovah, He spoke the loudest through His prophets concerning Jerusalem's destiny and coming glory. When it was the darkest, the lamp of prophecy shone the brightest. Then God used the King of Babylon, Nebuchadnezzar, as an instrument of judgment. The Lord gave Jerusalem into his hands. He took the city, burned the temple, took the golden vessels and carried the house of Judah into captivity. Then began the dominion of the Gentiles over Jerusalem and ever since Jerusalem has had her wars and woes. The glory had departed. After Babylonia came the Persian Empire, then the Alexandrian and finally the Roman.

But without tracing the events in history let me show you that beautiful sight in Babylon, when the seventy years of captivity were about ended. Look at this white haired old man! Seventy years before he had been brought to Babylon as a captive. True to God and true to His Law, God had honored the boy Daniel and made him His mouthpiece, revealing through him the future of the nations of the earth. And now after his long life of vision and service, trust in God and victory, the old Daniel still has his windows open towards Jerusalem. In spite of all the honors heaped upon him, his heart is in his beloved

Jerusalem. One day he sat at that window looking towards Jerusalem, reading the prophet Jeremiah. And then He fell on His knees and prayed. What a prayer that was! You find the words of it in the ninth chapter of the Book of Daniel. He confessed the nation's sins, his own sins, he pleaded with God and humbled himself. He never ended that prayer. As soon as he began the Lord called Gabriel and gave him the message for the prophet. Before he finished his petitions the heavenly messenger interrupted him. The message he brought was concerning the beloved city. One of the great messages of the Word of God it is, and yet how few Christians and how very few Jews have ever examined it. The message gave information as to the definite time when the wall of Jerusalem which had been broken down should be rebuilt. But what makes this message so very interesting are the other events made known which should transpire before the glorious future of Jerusalem comes, before the morning of light and blessing should break.

Gabriel told Daniel that a certain number of years would pass and Messiah the Prince should be cut off in Jerusalem and have nothing. After this event a certain nation was to come and destroy the city and the sanctuary and trouble should be the lot of the city and the nation in the future till finally the day of blessing and glory should come. (Dan. ix:24-37). Wonderful it is that when the number of years mentioned in this prophecy had expired something happened in Jerusalem. For three years a wonderful person moved among the Jewish people. He had healed their sick, raised the dead and drove out demons. He spoke as no other man ever spoke. Many believed on Him as the promised Messiah, the Son of David. On the very day when the

483 years mentioned by Gabriel had expired the Lord Jesus Christ entered Jerusalem riding upon an ass, as predicted by Zechariah. Then He was acclaimed by the multitudes who went before and who followed after as the King of Israel and the glad shouts of Hosannah to the Son of David were heard in the streets of Jerusalem. A few days later and the cry is changed. "Crucify Him—Crucify Him! Away with Him! His blood be upon us and upon our children!" That week they delivered Him into the hands of the Gentiles to be crucified. Messiah, the Christ, was thus cut off and did not receive that Kingdom which is promised to Him as the Son of David according to the flesh. And after that the predicted fate came for the city and for the nation. The Lord Jesus Christ, our Saviour and Israel's King had wept over the city; He saw the armies casting up a trench; He predicted that they should fall by the edge of the sword and should be led away captive among the nations, Jerusalem to be trodden down by the Gentiles till the times of the Gentiles would end. And all came to pass. The very nation announced by Daniel,* the Romans, came and took the city, and burned the sanctuary. For the second time the Temple of the Lord was destroyed. Jewish tradition has it that it was on the same date on which Nebuchadnezzar destroyed the Temple, that is the ninth day of the Jewish month of Ab. And ever since the Jewish nation has been homeless and Jerusalem the prey of Gentile greed and corruption, dragged into the dust of shame and deepest degradation. That it will never be thus forever is vouched for by the promises of God and by the lips of our Lord Jesus Christ.

* For a complete exposition of this great prophecy see "Exposition of Daniel," by A. C. Gaebelein. 230 pages. Price, 75 cents.

III. The End of the Times of the Gentiles; the Significance of the Capture of Jerusalem. The times of the Gentiles will end some day and that end will mean Jerusalem's glory. Is then the end of the times of the Gentiles, during which Jerusalem is trodden down, in sight? Is this age soon going to end? No Bible believing Christian who knows these things can be in doubt on these questions. The signs of the times tell every thinking Christian that a great crisis has been reached in the history of this age. Without speaking of all the great signs of our times, for that is not the object of my lecture, I shall point you to the most significant one, and that is Jerusalem.

For over 25 years the Jewish people have had a great national revival. Zionism, the Jewish State, the return to the old homeland has been strongly advocated. Well do I remember a visit to a small synagogue in the mountains of Romania, some 22 or 23 years ago, and speaking as a Gentile, as I am, to the few old Jews about the revived hope and Herzl's plan, how the tears filled their eyes and rolled down their cheeks.

And Zionism has grown. But when this awful war began, the hope of Zionism seemed to die. And note the striking coincidence, the great world conflict began on the ninth day of the Jewish month Ab, the day when Jews all over the world fasted and wept in memory of the fate which overtook Jerusalem twice on that day. Yes, in the beginning of the war the hope of Zionism was almost dead; and throughout the war the Jews suffered as perhaps no other nation has ever suffered. Who then could have imagined that when the war ended Jerusalem would be free and the whole land delivered from the bloody grasp of the hellish Turk.

The conquest of Palestine by the heroic expeditionary

forces was an almost miraculous achievement and one wonders if not the unseen hosts of heaven were there to fight on the side of righteousness. And here is another remarkable coincidence. General Allenby with his staff entered the city and then bowed the knee thanking God for the great victory and asking God's blessing upon the future of the city. On the day when this happened the Jews celebrated the feast of "Chanukah," commemorating the cleansing of the temple after the profanation and defilement by Antiochus Epiphanes. And here is still another remarkable fact. When this war was about ended, when Turkey was stripped of her power, and the armistice about to be signed which would seal the doom of Germany, the British-Jewish delegation landed in Palestine to undertake the reconstruction of the land. And a few months ago the cornerstones for the great Jewish Universities was laid on the Mount of Olives. We say cornerstones, for they laid 12 stones instead of one; one for each of the tribes of Israel. That is prophetic, too!

Whatever the decisions at the Peace table may be, one thing is sure, Palestine and Jerusalem will pass back into the hands of their original owners they will get it without money, and without price, even as Jehovah declared in the Law of Moses. "The land shall not be bought and not be sold." England, France and our own country have pledged their word to this program. Even the Pope in Rome has expressed himself in favor of the Jewish restoration. It seems then clear that divine providence has used this horrible war to take away Palestine from the Turk and make it possible for the Jewish people to return. This is what our Lord indicated concerning the end of the age, that the figtree should put forth new leaves. The figtree is the emblem of Israel. For this entire age Israel was nationally dead and now the signs of national life appear once more. No wonder that Jewry is rejoicing. Such is the significance of the capture of Jerusalem. To the Jews it means that their hopes are about to be realized. To us true Christian believers it is the sign that the times of the Gentiles are rapidly nearing their close.

IV. What must yet come to pass before Jerusalem's Glory and blessing comes. We have seen the Capture of Jerusalem is indeed a great and significant event, that it opens the way for the realization of the Zionistic hopes, but one thing is certain this event in itself cannot produce or bring about the glory promised in God's Word to Jerusalem. Before the Jewish people can get the blessings which a covenant keeping God has so graciously promised to them, before they can be regathered and possess the land in its promised dimensions, from the Nile to Euphrates, before Jerusalem can become the metropolis of the earth, before the nations will worship the Lord of hosts, something else must take place. The divinely predicted history of the Jewish people, recorded in this infallible book, contains an unfulfilled chapter. If some people now think that perfect peace is in store for Jerusalem, and the restoration of the land will settle forever the future of the land and the people, they are very much mistaken. This war is not the last war which the holy land has seen. This Book predicts a final invasion of Israel's land by an enemy who will at that time be broken to pieces. The Word of prophecy speaks of a time of great tribulation in store for the restored people in that land, even the time of Jacob's trouble. By and by when the Jewish hope is all realized, when they have Jerusalem, when the Jewish university is finished, when another temple stands there once more, then this final drama will be enacted. Gentile nations once more invade the land and a final siege of Jerusalem will come. Let me point you to the Scripture where we find this record.

In Zechariah Chapter xiv we read of what has never been in the past history of Jerusalem. Here is something which reveals the real deliverance of Jerusalem. Listen to what the prophecy saith. "Behold the day of the Lord cometh, and thy spoil shall be divided in the midst of thee. For I will gather all nations against Jerusalem to battle; and the city shall be taken and the houses rifled, and the women ravished and half of the city shall go forth into captivity and the residue of the people shall not be cut off from the city." But some one might say, has not this been one of the sieges of Jerusalem in the past? Let us see what it saith in the next verse—"Then shall the Lord go forth, and fight against those nations, as when He fought in the day of battle." Has this ever been? It cannot mean the taking of the city by General Allenby. No such thing happened then nor at any other time. But let us read some more. "And His feet shall stand in that day upon the Mount of Olives which is before Jerusalem on the east . . . and the Lord my God shall come and all the saints with thee." Surely this has never been in connection with any past siege of Jerusalem. We ask then, Whose feet will stand in that day of Jerusalem's final calamity upon the Mount of Olives? Who is He that comes to deliver His suffering people Israel? Every Christian believer knows the answer. It is the Lord, the same Lord who walked once with weary feet through Jerusalem, the same Lord who entered the city upon an ass, the same Lord who was crucified outside the city wall, the same Lord who was laid in Joseph's tomb, who rose from the dead on the third day and who stood upon the Mount of Olives from whence He ascended upon high. The angels said then "This same Jesus shall come again in like manner as ye have seen Him go into heaven." And here is the prophecy, "His feet shall stand in that day upon the Mount of Olives." That day is the day of His glorious, personal and visible return to the earth.

These are the coming events for Jerusalem. At present we witness the soon coming restoration of the Jews in unbelief. All Zionism stands for, and more, will be realized. Then comes the time of Jacob's trouble when a false Christ, the Anti-christ will rule them, the final invasion of the enemies of Israel and the climax of all, the Return of Israel's King, the once rejected Lord Jesus Christ, the Son of David after the flesh. He comes to deliver His people. They will know Him by the prints of the nails in His hands and the pierced side. Then will they look upon Him whom they pierced and worship at His feet. After that he will give the Glory to Jerusalem and as this final vision of Zechariah declares "The Lord will be King over all the earth."

That is how the Glory will come to Jerusalem, through Him whom the nation Israel once rejected, and just as Joseph in Egypt became the Saviour not only of the Gentiles, but also of his own brethren, so the Lord Jesus Christ will in His coming again be the Saviour of His people Israel. In that coming day His Kingdom of righteousness and peace will be established and Jerusalem will be the capital of that kingdom. From there the nations will be governed. It will become the glory spot of the earth, the place where once more the Shekinah rests and the angels of God ascend and descend upon the Son of Man. How God-like this is! The city of suffering and tears, the city through which He walked once in humiliation, through whose streets He was dragged as the Lamb of God, the city which witnessed His suffering and His shame, the city out of which He was cast as a criminal and nailed to the ignominious Cross, that same city He will choose as His glorious rest and fill it with indescribable glory.

The name of the city will then be "Jehovah Shammah" the Lord is there. In its midst tears and sorrow will be unknown. His redeemed people will sing His praises and shout their Hallelujahs. The nations of the earth will join with their Hallelujahs and from above, the New Jerusalem where the redeemed, the Saints of God are gathered in His glorious presence will answer with a mighty Hallelujah. It is the coming Hallelujah Chorus of redemption. Oh! let us praise and worship Him now, the Lord of Glory our Saviour and Israel's coming King.

The Last Days; the Last War and the Last King

By W. B. RILEY, Pastor First Baptist Church, Minneapolis, Minn.

Micah iv:1-7 has come to the time of its inning. The man to whom, in the light of present events, it does not appeal in a new and magnificent meaning, is a poor student of Scripture. For four years, two themes have occupied and dominated the thought of the entire world, and the two are War and Peace. Magazines, books, newspapers, have centralized upon these subjects, they could do no other. They have become the all-absorbing theme of all thought, and the controlling motive of individual, social and national conduct. Micah, the Prophet of God, dwelt in troublous times, and sickening of the smoke and cloud and fog, and its resultant depression and fear, he climbed the mount and stood in the upper air beyond it all, and looked out over the ages to see whether the future would be better than the present, whether the last days would improve upon his own day; and the vision he caught was both disconcerting and comforting. It showed no improvement in man, but it did reveal the marvelous and blessed plan of God; and, when Micah came down from the mount, he told the people what he had seen, and with his quill he set it down, that all centuries might understand that we are living to-day in the midst of what Micah saw, and to-morrow we will come into a realization of more of it.

THE LAST DAYS

To three things, set forth by the Prophet, let me call your attention: The Last Days: The Last War: and The Last King.

THE LAST DAYS

"In the last days it shall come to pass" (Micah iv:1). Who can tell what the last days are? Who can determine when they began and when they will end!* Beyond all doubt, God has divided time at one point. The first days were the days before Christ came, and the last days are the days sweeping in between His appearance in humility and His re-appearance in glory. It is difficult to dispute the time of their beginning: it is more difficult to determine the time of their end. Peter fixed the time of their beginning, quoting from the Prophet Joel—"It shall come to pass in the last days, saith God, I will pour out my spirit upon all flesh: and your sons and your daughters shall prophesy, your old men shall dream dreams, your young men shall see visions, and also upon the servants and upon the handmaids in those days will I pour out my spirit, and they shall prophesy." Peter said of the pentecost, "This is that which was spoken by the prophet Joel." It is evident, however, in the last days, saith God, I will pour out my spirit upon all flesh, that the last days are to have their last days; that the very latter time, the closing of this dispensation, is fairly and fully set forth in Scripture, and Micah seems to have had that brief concluding period in mind—the last of the last days.

* The meaning of the Hebrew "B'achrith Hayomim" is rather "in the end of days"; the days of Messiah are meant, when Christ has come back to earth and is revealed in His glory. Then and not before can the glorious blessings of Micah iv and Isaiah ii be realized.—Editor.

If we understand him clearly, there are certain characteristics of the last days that will mark them: there are certain conversions of the last days that are assured, and there is a certain kind of education that will be accomplished in the last days.

The characteristics of the last days. One method of Bible study indulged by Mr. Moody, and often advised by him, was the topical method. Any man would be profited who followed it, and "the last days" would be an interesting theme. If you take your Concordance and run it through you will find "mockers" would come in the last days (Jude 18), men who make light of the faith, and who especially laugh to scorn the second coming of Christ (2 Pet. iii:3); you also find that the last days will be characterized by "perilous times" (2 Tim. iii:1). That the last days will be marked by "false prophets," "wars," "rumors of wars, famines, pestilence, earth-quakes." (Matt. xxiv:1-14); the last days are also characterized by disobedience to parents, unthankfulness, unholiness, 2 Tim. iii:2. It must be conceded that the world has seldom seen more scriptural signs of "the last days" than now characterize it. There is, in some quarters, a disposition to feel that the present world-war is an anacronism; that it just happened to occur because one man was thoughtless enough to shoot another, and one country ungracious enough to make unreasonable demand upon the country to whom that homicide belonged! But not at all so! The nations of the earth have planned to war; they expected to war, they have compelled history to run into "the mould of prophecy," that "the last days" might be exactly as God said they would be. Great standing armies have characterized the European peoples;

have had considerable place also in Asia and in the Americas. The one thing that Germany will never be able to explain, no matter how studied her words nor how deceiving her phrases, is the historical fact that in the face of all the efforts of pacifist diplomats, peace conferences of international import and the decisions of the Hague, etc., Germany went on maintaining and increasing the greatest standing army the world had ever seen, until she had it far bigger and more ready for war than she was in her last conflict with France; and, at the same time, by inventions, she believed herself ready by her submarines to whip the British navy from the seas. Famed writers among her, long before war was declared, attracted attention by advocating preparation for war, and saying that when it came it must be "relentless war" until "Germany's power" was "increased" and "her dominion extended." Christ, then, was no false prophet—"In the last days there shall be wars and rumors of war," and if these be not the very last, then greater wars yet remain to deluge the world with blood, and the day will break when two hundred million of men will bear arms in the fulfillment of prophecy (Rev. ix:16).

But Micah, being a true prophet of God, is not the special exponent of pessimism. We have already said that he saw things that were disconcerting; but he saw equally things that were encouraging and inspiring.

The conversions of the last days! He saw "the mountain of the house of the Lord established in the top of the mountains; and exalted above the hills, and the people flowing into it. He saw the nations coming, and saying, Let us go up to the mountain of the Lord, and to the house of the God of Jacob; and he will teach us of his ways and we will walk in his paths."

The notable premillennial brethren of England, in the Manifesto which they put forth sometime since, expressed their absolute confidence, that, "in the last days there would be an out-pouring of the Spirit upon all flesh."* There are people who think we are just now on the eve of that revival; and there are some who contend that this war itself will produce it. Perhaps the most popular pulpit men at the present moment, in all political and war circles, are the very men who are saying that this world-war will produce a world-wide revival of religion and eventuate in wholesale redemption, such as the earth has not yet seen. We are told that millions of men, looking death in the face, are turning from the sight of his horrid features to God, and are bending the knee in prayer. We are told that chaplains, Y. M. C. A. secretaries and camp pastors are undertaking more for men than has ever been undertaken, since man had a beginning on the earth; we are told that the fruit of this combined endeavor, associated as it is with the marvelous work of the Red Cross, and all the ameliorating influences inspired by the scenes of suffering and death, are spiritual in nature and character, and will tend to lead men to God.

Far be it from me to speak one disparaging word against

* But this promised outpouring of the spirit of God upon all flesh does not come now, while the church is on earth. The Holy spirit came on the day of Pentecost to baptize believers into the body of Christ, the church. This is constantly going on during this age. No second baptism of the Spirit is promised to the church. The second chapter of Joel where it is written, "And it shall come to pass afterward, that I will pour out my Spirit upon all flesh" shows the time when this outpouring takes place. It will be after Israel has passed through the time of Jacob's trouble and when their restoration has taken place.—Editor.

the magnificent endeavor that is being made for the men; God will honor it and the work of the true secretary, and the true camp pastor, and of the true chaplain and nurse, but one of the sanest articles that I have seen from the pen of any man calls attention to certain great facts that are too often overlooked by the impassioned orator who loves the hand-clap and knows how to secure the same. He says, "So far as facts can be ascertained from those, both in official and unofficial position as Christian workers with the armies, there is nothing strikingly religious in the life of our soldiers. It goes without saying that they are magnificently courageous, careless of all danger, inspired with splendid passion, and governed by a high sense of honor. But these things are not necessarily an expression of Christian faith and purpose. To the great majority the spiritual nature of the conflict in which they are engaged is simply unrecognized. They are face to face with death, and with the duty of dealing death to the foe. They are living amid circumstances of unprecedented discomfort, and are often herded together in a manner which makes anything like open confession of the christian faith and cultivation of the devotional life well-nigh impossible. Many have found themselves unable to stand the normal strain of it all, and have lost what religion they had. Others, staggered at the apparent overthrow of their early conceptions of God by the mere fact of the War, have renounced such faith as they formerly professed. And as for the rest, familiarity with death has by no means produced anything like a general sense of the need of Divine protection. The mission of amusement has been considerably overdrawn. . . . Is there not something wrong in that conception of the serious realities of life, at such a time as this, which expresses itself in an unwearied round of entertainments? And is not positive harm done to men who are thus familiarized with a type of so-called Christian work in which anything like definite religion is almost apologized for?" It is a vain imagination, therefore, for us to expect that when our boys come back to us they will all come back clean, upright, christian, men. It is very doubtful indeed if we can expect, in view of the trials which they must endure, the loss of the sacred influences from which they have been removed, that they will come back as clean in character as they went forth; and as christian in conduct as they were before they faced this holocaust of iniquity. If there was ever a time when the Church of God should emphasize evangelism it is the very moment when that practice of a social gospel, which is a poor substitute for the shed blood, is in the ascendent; and that is now. No! this revival will come in the last days but it will not be the consequence of war. Micah does not so state; nor did he so believe. It will have an altogether different source; an altogether different inspiration will characterize the period of final peace! but it will come; as sure as there is a God in Heaven it will come! And nations shall come and say, "Let us come up to the mount of God and to the house of Jacob, and he will teach us of his ways and we will walk in his paths." It is a blessed promise; it is a bright prospect; it is as sure as the speech of the eternal God himself: it is His speech; and it will come to pass!

The education of the last days! With it, then, will come a new kind of education for "the law shall go forth of Zion, and the word of the Lord from Jerusalem." The one reason why we are in the throes of war, the one reason why man has lost respect for his brother, disregard the virtue of his sister, the one reason why the human hyena has triumphed over humanity itself, is the doctrine of evolution, leading us to suppose we could make great men and build up great nations by the way of physical and mental development. We have supposed that magnificent muscle and trained minds would produce the Darwinian dream of a super-man, and it has all been as false as the philosophy of the Satan who suggested it; and the Germans who have been its ablest exponents; and the world could never have gotten a better illustration of the utter lie contained in that conception than Germany has produced. Her men were men of perfect muscle; their stockily built forms were the fear of their opponents, and their well-nigh universal education the despair of competing nations. And yet their neglect of the law, and their discrediting of the Word of the Lord left the brute in the ascendent, trampled the very breath from the body of Christianity, and left the Fatherland the form thereof without its power—a stale religion still wearing the name of Christ, from which the Son of God, grieved to death, long since departed. The most rotten theology that has characterized and cursed man in twenty centuries has been making in Germany for the last fifty years, and imported to every part of the earth. No, we do not educate a man properly when we begin and end with his muscle: we do not educate man properly when we add his mind to his muscle: we do not educate him acceptably to God when we set the key note of his learning to anything else than the experimental and the spiritual, and when the last days come, and God bares his arm to give to the world an illustration of what He can do, you will see a new system of learning introduced, and the Bible will not be banished from the public schools, refused a hearing in the State Universities, discredited and scoffed in the denominational schools, neglected and forgotten by individuals and families, but, breaking forth with a new beauty and new power, "the law shall go forth of Zion, and the word of the Lord from Jerusalem." And as Germany has boasted her culture—referring to the head of man—the world will then boast a new education, but the reference will be to the heart and to a knowledge of the living God, which alone can make wise unto salvation. Thank God that that education shall characterize the last days, "For the law shall go forth from Zion and the word of the Lord from Jerusalem."

There are some features of this prophecy that the church of this period needs to dwell upon. I call your attention to the fact that it is not the Czar of Russia that will judge among the people: that it is not the Kaiser of Germany that will judge among the people: that it is not King George of England that will judge among the people, that it is not even President Wilson of the United States, that will judge among them. I saw a learned article lately to the effect that America would end war, and teach the world how to live. No man loves his country better than I, or his flag more devotedly; but such teaching is not according to my Book. America has had very much to do with the ending of this war; a most important part in bringing it to a conclusion. In spite of the tremendous advantages that were with Germany, almost insurmountable—the advantages of conquered territory, the advantages of a long disciplined army, the advantages of trench warfare on French and Belgian and Servian and Russian soil, the advantages of short distances for shipping, the advantages of a homogeneous people and the advantages of the mechanical invention in which she surpasses. She weakened and America's strong arm dealt her such a stunning blow, that, crawling upon her knees, sick and dizzied, she consented to the peace terms already pronounced by our noble President; but that is not the end of world-wars, and Micah makes some things so plain that to dispute them would take the meaning from human speech!

Let me call your attention to three of them.

1. *The Lord shall bring peace to this world. He* shall judge the nations; *He* shall rebuke strong nations afar off; and they shall beat their spears into pruning hooks; nation shall not lift up a sword against nation, neither shall they learn war any more." There was a meeting in Minneapolis a while ago, held in the name of Christ, with great men sitting in it, representatives of a great denomination, and they drafted a Resolution and sent it to our great President, asking him if possible to restore to the world a lasting peace. Alas! Alas! men have not yet looked to the real power for peace; they are still depending upon their poor fellows instead of depending upon the mighty God. It is a vain dependence! President Wilson of America, and the power back of him, has compelled a temporary world-truce, but as for *lasting* peace, that remains with the Lord, and with Him alone; and it is profound pity when men who are supposed to be preachers of the Word point their fellows to any other source for lasting peace, or let them look to any other person than that of our coming King. Joseph Parker, that remarkable London minister, once said, "The thing to be remembered is this, you can never have peace until you have righteousness." And then he illustrates—"Only one thing can carry the earth and that is gravitation. Gravitation will pick it up; but your hands cannot; your institutions cannot; your politics cannot; only one thing

keeps the universe right, and sends it whirling through its musical revolutions, and that is gravitation. Gravitation can pick up a thousand universes, and hold them all."

But what is gravitation? God's right arm, and He who can hold the universes in His own right hand, can with his lips, speak to the storm-swept world as He spake to the little lake of Galilee, "Peace be still," and instantly its winds and its waves obey Him. The *Lord* shall bring peace to the world!

The Lord shall bring prosperity to the world. It is when He judges among the people and rebukes strong nations and compels swords to be converted into plowshares, and spears into pruning hooks, and pronounces a permanent peace, that they "sit every man under his vine and under his fig tree;" and none shall make them afraid. That is another lesson we need now to learn. Already we are crying reconstruction! We are going to need education the world over; and we are going to need new methods. We are going to be under the necessity of rebuilding shattered men, and we are going to be under the necessity of revamping commerce; and some of our great financiers have already prophecied the most remarkable period of prosperity the world has ever seen. They expect the new national alliances, the new forms of education, the new means of transportation, to compass it all; and the greedy are getting ready now to get rich now that the war is over, and men in America expect our country to forge to the front in all relations, and become the dominating commercial power of the world. In all probability she may; and if so, and if the Lord delay His coming, that prosperity will not be extended by anything akin to this text, will not produce that new social order in which each man shall be a land-holder, it will not even effect that peace in which man is content to "sit every man under his own vine and fig tree," where none shall make afraid. It will have in it all the old elements of trial and sweat and oppression and contention and hatred and hell. I am not enamored of the prospect of what can be accomplished in the world that makes its god a god of gold; I am not at all charmed by the promise of commercial advantages such as the world has never seen, when the description of them makes no mention of my Christ and gives little or no consideration to His cause; and if any greater calamity could befall our country than to have this war followed by another period of unprecedented prosperity in which prayers should continue to wane, and Bible study continue to be neglected, and spiritual exercises continue to decline, and spiritual experiences grow increasingly seldom, and in which "every man walks in the name of his god," and makes his god Venus, Bacchus, or Gambrinus, according to the pulsing appeals of his own passions! I want to see peace come to the world, and it will come! for "the mouth of the Lord hath spoken it." I want to see prosperity the portion of every man—and it will be so, for that He also hath said that; but I want the realization of the Prophet's further vision!

The Lord shall have praise from the whole world. "And we will walk in the name of the Lord our God forever." Prosperity will never be the portion of all men while kings and czars and potentates sit on man-made thrones and administer man-made laws and despise alike God and His Word. This war seems at an end, but the peace that follows it will not be a lasting peace if the Lord be forgotten. I am in sympathy with the aims of "the League for the Enforcement of World Peace," and I think no greater folly was ever indulged than that which slaughters men by the millions, and which, in the end, will enrich no country nor give higher supremacy to any potentate; but I know my Book too well to expect that either peace or prosperity will be the universal portion until men have turned from their false gods and are ready to pay tribute to Him who alone sitteth upon the circle of the heavens; and His administration is the lone administration of this world, and that day will come when the Lord comes. In other words, the reappearance of the Lord Jesus Christ will speedily produce the end of the last war.

Let us hope then, that we approach the further fulfillment of Micah's portion of the vision and the

THE LAST KING.

"In that day, saith the Lord, will I assemble her that halteth, and I will gather her that is driven out, and her that I have afflicted; and I will make her that halted a remnant, and her that was cast far off a strong nation: and the Lord shall reign over them in mount Zion from henceforth, even for ever."

Three things in conclusion:

The Lord shall be the last King. The men that now sit upon the thrones of the earth are concerned about their successors. They want their sons to sit where they have sat, and their sons' sons to come in order. They want to keep the throne in the family circle, and they would like to know who would be their successor even in the unborn centuries. I can tell them—"the Lord shall reign," and either themselves, or their sons, or their grandsons, shall finally abdicate in His behalf, and turn over the governments of the world to Him.

Dr. Joseph Parker, in his "People's Bible" interprets this language of the Prophet as meaning that the Church is to be the uppermost institution, the sanctuary of God is to be at the top of things, and out of it is to come law; out of it also is to come the spirit of righteousness, and out of it, day by day, is to come the spirit of peace, the spirit of benediction. The Prophet was not thinking of the church at all; he was not thinking of administration of the church in this age; he was speaking of the King and of His personal reign in the earth; and in anticipation of that glad day, he struck the very harps of Heaven to music. The theme of their paeon was—"The Lord shall reign!"

> "Kingdom of Peace, whose music clear
>   Swept through Judea's starlight skies,
> Still the harsh sounds of human strife
>   Break on thy heavenly harmonies.
> Yet shall thy song of triumph ring
>   In full accord, from land to land,
> And men with angels learn to sing:
>   'Behold, the Kingdom is at hand.' "

Another thing that the Prophet made clear is this:

Under the last King Israël shall have a central place. "I will assemble her that halteth, and I will gather her that is driven out, and her that I have afflicted; and I will make her that halted a remnant, and her that was cast far off a strong nation." The Germans began this war expecting to make themselves a strong nation: England continues to hope to make herself the strong nation. America has taken a hand in it, and the average American confidently believes that in the final windup of all things, this will be the great and glorious country, and that the American people will be the people under the favor of God. These sentiments are natural and are so patriotic that one hates to disturb them; but my Book does not so read. Germany shall not have dominion; England shall not control, America shall not rule; but a nation that is now weak, that is now scattered to the ends of the earth, without a land in which to dwell, a city to become her capital, or even a flag floating for her protection, that nation will be the people of God. Jerusalem now attracts the attention of the world; the land of Palestine is now promised by all belligerents to the Jew. History runs into the mould of prophecy and the day may be nigh at hand.

"O then that I
Might live, and see the olive bear
Her proper branches, which now lie
. Scattered each where,
And without root and sap decay,
Cast by the husband-man away,
And sure it is not far!
For surely He
Who loved the world so as to give
His only Son to make us free,
Whose Spirit, too, doth mourn and grieve
To see man lost, will, for old love,
From your dark hearts this veil remove."

Finally, *His kingdom will be the last and the lasting kingdom.* When Daniel had his vision of the ages he saw four great empires destined to fall in turn—The Babylonian Empire, represented by the golden head of the great image; the Medo-Persian empire, represented by the breast and arms of silver; the Grecian empire, represented by the belly and thighs of brass; and the great Roman empire by the iron legs. After that his vision revealed the toes, or the little nations that were to grow out from the Roman empire as the toes come from the feet. And the next world-empire visioned by the Prophet, and promised to the ages, was the empire in which "the Lord himself should reign in Mount Zion, from henceforth even forever!" And that is the Empire of the future; that is the kingdom to come, and in that kingdom the Utopian dreams of the centuries will find their fulfillment, and the lasting peace for which we pray, its perfect consummation.

The Two Resurrections

By Joseph W. Kemp, Pastor Metropolitan Tabernacle, New York City.

The two resurrections! The title is arresting, for it runs counter to popular opinions and traditional beliefs. It is closely related to the central subject under study at this conference, for any consideration of it apart from the Second Coming of the Lord is inadequate and disjointed. The importance of this theme may be judged from the place it occupies in and the prominence given to it by the Scriptures. Bible is a wonderful book. The Book is occupied with the mightiest themes which can engage the mind of man, and among these, and as occupying the foremost place, is that of the resurrection of the dead, a doctrine, supposed by many, to be more a matter of pious speculation, than of any practical importance in the life of the Child of God. That which is so prominent in the Scriptures ought surely to find a large place in the ministry of our time. But alas it is not so. One fears that the Christianity of today is weakened, and the church's life well nigh paralyzed because of the weak, effeminate and inefficient handling of these great doctrines by those who ought to move amongst them with ease and familiarity. We are missing in these days the great notes which our fathers struck, causing some of us to wonder, if the call for the spicy and the light, for the feathery and the flippant, has not made us lose the vision of our high calling. My own conviction is unshaken on this matter, that when the pulpit of today returns to the preaching of the great words and subjects of the Bible, we shall have brought considerably nearer that glorious day of revival for which many have been praying for years.

The doctrine of the resurrection was among the foremost subjects of apostolic preaching. We are told in the ivth of the Acts that the Apostles preached through Jesus, the resurrection from the dead, and that preaching transformed the ancient world. The apostolic announcement of the coming resurrection, assured by the resurrection of Christ, was the burden of that which they had to proclaim. We shall get the apostolic results when we choose the apostolic method of preaching. God marvellously blessed this primitive evangelism. Within the subject of the resurrection of the dead are wrapped all our hopes as believers. In it is contained the fulfilment of all the Divine promises. By it we shall be freed from the destroying power of sin. It brings to us assurance of eternal glory, and it is the one joy note in the hour of human bereavement. Not death, but resurrection is our hope. Martha only uttered the confession of the Church when she said "I know that he shall rise again."

It is no new thing that this doctrine should be held in dispute for it was so in the days of the apostles. It was denied by the Sadducees, "For the Sadducees say that there is no resurrection, neither angel, nor spirit; but the Pharisees confess both." (Acts xxiii:8). Paul was scoffed at for preaching the resurrection of the dead for "certain philosophers of the Epicureans, and of the Stoicks, encountered him. And some said, What will this babbler say? other some, He seemeth to be a setter forth of strange gods: because he preached unto them Jesus and the resurrection." (Acts xvii:18, 19). It was denied by Agrippa and Festus, for Paul in his defense made the inquiry—"Why should it be thought a thing incredible with you that God should raise the dead?" (Acts xxvi:8). It was doubted by the Corinthians. "How say some among you that there is no resurrection of the dead?" (1 Cor. xv:12); and it was explained away by Hymenaeus and Philetus, who concerning the faith have erred, saying that the resurrection is past already and overthrow the faith of some." Similarly today we have those who deny and doubt and scoff, and explain away, and in certain quarters the resurrection of the dead is as little believed in as in the days of the Sadducees, for the carnal man but dimly after all, grasps the reality of spiritual things, and persists in perverting the plainest statements of the Book. It is difficult to conceive how one who denies the resurrection of the body has a right to be called a Christian at all, for such a one has made shipwreck of the truth and has overthrown the faith of some. Their word is noxious and destructive. Let it never be forgotten that a truth neglected is a truth speedily disregarded and rejected.

What is the teaching of the Book on the subject of the resurrection? We hear of it by Job who says—"I know that my Redeemer liveth, and that He shall stand at the latter day upon the earth, and though after my skin worms destroy this body, yet in my flesh shall I see God." (Job xix: 25-27). We hear of it by Isaiah—"Thy dead men shall live, together with my dead body shall they arise." (Isaiah xxvi: 19). We hear of it by Daniel who says—"And many of them that sleep in the dust of the earth shall awake, some to everlasting life and some to shame and everlasting contempt" (Daniel xii:2). We hear of it by Hosea, who says speaking for his Lord—"I will ransom them from the power of the grave: I will redeem them from death: O death, I will be thy plagues: O grave, I will be thy destruction." (Hosea xiii:14). We hear of it by Paul in his great discourse on the resurrection, 1 Cor. xv and finally, we hear of it by our Lord Jesus Christ himself in the words of the text, which introduce our subject today. Now putting all these passages together, what do they teach? They teach that there will be a resurrection embracing all men—not a simultaneous resurrection, but a universal one, in which all that are in the graves shall come forth" for there will be a resurrection "both of the just and of the unjust" (Acts xxiv:15). They also teach, together with others, that there will be two resurrections. The commonly accepted belief is that there will be but one general resurrection, when all, irrespective of their predeceased moral condition, will rise and come forth to a general judgment. I must confess that I have been utterly unable to discover any scriptural warrant for such a belief. The Scriptures teach no such thing, but most emphatically declare there will be two resurrections. We read in Revelation xx:5, 6—"but the rest of the dead lived not again until the one thousand years were finished. This is the first resurrection. Blessed and holy is he that hath part in the first resurrection; on such the second death hath no power." This is a passage which is a constant difficulty with Post-Millennarians, and they seek to evade the subject by speaking of the first resurrection as the quickening at conversion. Such an attitude is untenable, for these holy dead were quickened before they were beheaded for the testimony of Jesus. One cannot do better in this connection than quote from Dean Alford, who in his "Critical English" Commentary says,—

"It will have been long ago anticipated by the readers of this Commentary, that I cannot consent to distort its words from their plain sense and chronological place in the prophecy, on account of any consideration of difficulty, or any risk of abuses which the doctrine of the Millennium may bring with it. Those who lived next the Apostles and the whole Church for three hundred years, understood them in the plain literal sense; and it is a strange sight in these days to see expositors who are among the first in reverence of antiquity, complacently casting aside the most cogent instance of unanimity which primitive antiquity presents. As regards the text itself, no legitimate treatment of it will extort what is known as the spiritual interpretation now in fashion. If, in a passage where two resurrections are mentioned, where certain souls lived at the first, and the rest of the dead lived only at the end of a specified period after that first, if in such a passage, the first resurrection may be understood to mean spiritual rising with Christ, while the second means literal rising from the grave; then there is an end of all significance in language, and Scripture is wiped out as a definite testimony to anything. If the first resurrection is spiritual, then so is the second, which I suppose no one will be hardy enough to maintain. But if the second is literal, then so is the rest, which, in common with the whole primitive Church and many of the best modern expositors, I do maintain and receive as an article of faith and hope."

Further, let me read what the late C. H. Spurgeon said concerning this passage. It cannot be said that Spurgeon specialized in Prophecy, but he has left us in no doubt as to his attitude toward pre-millennarian teaching, for he said on one occasion, "far rather do I expect to see this world sink into a pandemonium than rise into a Millennium without the King." But that by the way. Here in his statement regarding the text, "There is a passage which apparently teaches us that between the resurrection of the righteous and the resurrection of the wicked, there will be an interval of one thousand years. Many think that the passage intends a spiritual resurrection, but I am not inclined to think so: assuredly the words must have a literal meaning. Hear them, and adjudge for yourselves." And then he repeats the text which I have just quoted. Here then we have the somewhat startling announcement of disembodied souls being re-embodied. The word "lived," as A. J. Gorden shows in his "Ecce Venit" is never in the New Testament used except of man in his complete condition of body and spirit united.

A further objection is that this is the only passage dealing with the two resurrections with a space between and distinct in character, and that since the passage is found in a book which teaches by symbolism, it has not the same weight as if found in the gospels or epistles. Now, as to the first part of this objection, it is hardly accurate, for there are other passages bearing on the two resurrections. But supposing there was no other reference and that we were shut up to this solitary text, it would be enough, for repetition does not increase authority. With regard to the second part of the objection that the passage loses authority because it is found in the book of symbolism: it is well to remember the book is recognized as canonical and authoritative by the Church of God, and, moreover, there is a pronouncement of blessing on those who read and keep the sayings of this book.

Let us review one or two other passages suggesting two

resurrections. In Luke xx, verses 34-36, we have our Lord's allusion to those who "shall be counted worthy to obtain that age and the resurrection out from the dead." In Philippians iii:10, 11, we have a striking and significant passage, where Paul says, "I count all things but loss . . . if by any means I might attain unto the resurrection from the dead," or, as profound Bible scholars tell us, the word is "the resurrection out from among the dead." It is difficult to conceive how the words can refer to anything else than a separation and a quickening to life out from among the dead. In I Thes. iv:16, we read—"The dead in Christ shall rise first." There is no hint of the rising of the dead who are not in Christ. In John v:28; the word is clear. "The hour is coming, in which all that are in the graves shall hear His voice and come forth: they that have done good unto the resurrection of life; and they that have done evil unto the resurrection of damnation." In Daniel xii, it is said "that some shall rise to everlasting life and some to shame and everlasting contempt."

Now, there is nothing modern in this idea, for Toplady said long ago, "I am one of those old-fashioned people who believe the doctrine of the millennium, and that there will be two distinct resurrections of the dead; first of the just, a second of the unjust; the last resurrection of the reprobate will not commence till one thousand years after the resurrection of the elect." Jeremy Taylor, said—"The resurrection shall be universal—good and bad shall rise: yet not altogether, but "first Christ, then they that are Christ's: and then there is another resurrection."

Now, let us pass on to note who will take part in the first resurrection. There will be no mixed multitude. The saints, and saints alone, take part in that first resurrection.

They were separate from the wicked in life and they retained their pilgrim character to the end. They will be separate and distinct in the resurrection. Oneness with Christ now secures for us the glory of that day. Moreover, it is said they will be "blessed and holy." Peculiar blessedness will be theirs at that day, and our Lord alone knows how much that word implies. They are, moreover, preserved from the "second death." The *name* is peculiar, the *thing* is common. Behind the grim figure of the first, which is the cloaked and shrouded shadow feared by man, waiting for all at the turn of the road, there rises the still grimmer form—something at the back of physical death, which can lay its cold grip upon the soul that is separated from the body. What can it mean? The pure vagueness of it seems to shake the heart. The second death! The separation of the soul from Him who is the fountain of life. But, upon the saints this second death has no power. The heart ever hungers for the resurrection exempt from death. There have been those who came from the grave: such as the saints who arose after our Lord's death. Individual cases like Lazarus; the widow's son at Nain; Jairus' daughter; the young man whom Paul brought to life again. But these all lived to die again. Even the analogy of nature mocks us for the bud bursting forth into blushing blossom returns to death. "The morning gilds the sky" but to return to the doom of night. Springtime lifts its head but to go back again to the grave of winter. And so alas! all do but mock. . . .,*Christ's conquest is final*: Death hath no more dominion over Him, and in Christ, the second death has no power. This is life, glorious, full and unhindered. It is that for which we wait.

When will this be? Not until the second coming of our Lord Jesus Christ. In 1 Thes. iv:16 we read—that the Lord

Himself shall descend and "the dead in Christ shall rise first." Without appearing to be controversial, it remains to be said that our own conviction is that the resurrection of the saints will take place before the Millennium—that period of one thousand years of earth's blessedness. Out from the graves the saints will come and be with Christ during his millennial reign.

Now, what shall we say regarding the second resurrection? This will be at the close of the one thousand years: "But the rest of the dead lived not again until the thousand years were finished," and in Revelation xx:12-15, it is said—"and I saw the dead, small and great stand before God, and the books were opened, and another book was opened which is the book of life; and the dead were judged out of those things which were written in the books, according to their works. And the sea gave up the dead which were in it, and death and hades delivered up the dead which were in them, and they were judged, every man, according to their works, and death and hell were cast into the lake of fire. This is the second death." It is a resurrection unto damnation, shame and everlasting contempt. What can it mean? What unrest! what peeling off of capacities, what crushing of ambitions; what destroying of delights! I say it reverently, that God Himself cannot avert the calamity that shall come for the soul that has part in the second resurrection.

It may now be asked what kind of a body is that which will be given to us in the resurrection? Such a question opens up an immeasurable field of research. The body which the believer shall have in the resurrection will be glorious—like unto Christ's; "for we shall be like Him," 1 John iii:2. It will be independent of previous conditions and freed from crippling limitations. It will be capable of service that we cannot now dream of, and of enjoyment, the like of which we have never experienced. In I Cor. xv, we have a description given us of the resurrection body of the believer. The late Dr. A. T. Pierson, following Brown, says there are several features of the resurrection body. First, corruption gives way to incorruption; that is, there will be no liability to decay in the resurrection body. Dishonor is displaced by glory. The body is meant to be the temple of the Holy Ghost, but too often it has been disgraced by evil lusts. Dishonor implies sin, but in the resurrection the body will be a body of glory. Weakness gives place to power. No more infirmity or fatigue. The natural gives place to the spiritual. Then, to the utmost our spiritual powers shall be developed. The earthly gives place to the heavenly. We shall cease to be subject to ordinary laws. Again the mortal shall put on immortality. Death will never be able to reach the glorified body. Not flesh and blood. There will be nothing tainted or decaying? My brethren, this is a practical truth. It is in this connection that we are told to comfort one another. I Thes. iv:18. It is intended to cheer our hearts in prospect of departure, should the Lord tarry. Let the truth teach us to respect our bodies that shall one day be fashioned like unto His own glorious body.

I cannot do better than close with the words of A. J. Gordon who has been repeatedly quoted in this conference, "Let who will," says Gordon, "fasten their hope upon the down calling of mortality 'return unto the dust ye children of men,' we will listen patiently and joyfully for the upcalling of immortality."

"Awake and sing, ye that dwell in dust, for thy dew is as the dew of herbs, and *the earth shall cast out her dead.*" Is. xxvi:19.

The Influence of the Study of Prophecy Upon the Life and Service of a Christian

By W. H. GRIFFITH THOMAS, Professor Wiclife College, Toronto, Canada.

What food is to the body, the Word of God is to the soul. It is milk for babies, it is strong meat for adults; and, as Dr. Pierson used to say, it is also honey for dessert. But it is important that our food for the body should be proportioned and balanced, and so we are told nowadays in various ways, in restaurants and other places, how much of this or that nutriment is in this or that article of food; and we are to eat so much of this, and so much of that, and so much of the other, and not to overdo it with one kind of food, lest we should put on too much tissue, when we ought to put on bone and muscle instead. If this is true of the body, it is equally true of the soul; that every part of the food of God's Word should be our spiritual and intellectual and moral nutriment. There are many people who feed unduly, it may be, upon one part of it, and the result is that their spiritual life becomes lopsided and unbalanced and disproportionate. But the true Christian will see that every part of God's Word has its place in his spiritual life and food, in order that he may grow thereby and grow up into Him, Christ, in all things.

Now there is one part of the food of God's Word which is very often neglected, and that is that part which we designate as prophecy. It has been computed that the Lord's coming is mentioned over three hundred times in the New Testament. And yet this is the part of God's Word which is so often neglected. But surely, anything that is so prominent as this must have real meaning and importance. When you think of the comparative infrequent reference to such subjects as the Church, the ministry, and the ordinances, and then realize the amount of consideration that has been given to these things, we see at once how very serious it is if we neglect that portion of God's Word which has to do with the coming of the Lord.

But some people say it is not practical; it is only speculative, it has no real bearing on our life. And yet here is one text which you find on the program, 1 John, iii:3, "And every man that hath this hope in Him purifieth himself, even as He is pure." Another passage also in the program; 2d Peter, chapter iii, and in verse 11 we are told: "Seeing that these things are thus, what manner of persons ought ye to be?" And in verse 14, "Seeing that ye look for these things, give diligence that ye may be found in peace, without spot and blameless——" The fact is when we realize it as God intends it, there is nothing more practical, more definite, more direct in its bearing on ordinary every day life than this subject of prophecy and the coming of the Lord. I quote from Dean Alford: "There is nothing that so much takes a man out of himself, nothing that so much raises and widens his thoughts and sympathies, nothing that so much purifies and elevates his hopes, as this preparation for the coming of the Lord." That is my theme this morning, the influence of prophecy, and I am wanting to limit myself almost entirely to the thought of the influence of the Lord's coming on the life and service of the Christian, and I think I shall serve my purpose and perhaps your purpose the better if I limit myself to one portion of God's Word; and I hope you will not mind if I give you a Bible reading on that subject from that portion of God's Word. I refer to the earliest epistles of the Apostle Paul, the Epistles to the Thessalonians.

You know there are seven epistles to churches, and these epistles are found in four groups. There are epistles which have to do with the doctrinal foundation, as Romans and Galatians; there are epistles that have to do with Church life, like I and II Corinthians; there are epistles which have to do with Christian doctrines and experiences, like Ephesians, Philippians, Colossians; and there is this fourth group, which has to do with the coming of the Lord, I and II Thessalonians. There are only eight chapters in the two epistles, but the Lord's coming is found in every chapter but one, and even there, there is a definite though indirect reference to the attitude of the Christian in relation to it. So this morning I want to put together as briefly and as quickly as possible these aspects of prophetic truth regarding our Lord's coming and think of their bearing on our life and service.

Now I want you to notice as we go along that this subject of the Lord's coming is at once the inspiration of our life and service because of its application to our life and service. The first of these points is the Lord's coming in relation to hope. You will find that in chapter 1 of the first epistle, verses 3 and 10: "Remembering without ceasing your work of faith, and labor of live, and patience of hope—" There you find the three Christian graces mentioned, faith, love and hope; and all three are emphasized together, as they are in other passages, as essential and integral parts of the Christian life. Faith, we hear a great deal about that; love, we hear a great deal about that; but hope, we do not so often hear about that; and yet here the three of them are found exactly on a level. Faith, why, that looks up and back; love looks around; hope looks on. Faith is concerned with the past and present, love always with the present, and hope always with the future. Faith accepts; hope expects. Faith appropriates, hope anticipates. Faith receives, love reproduces, and hope realizes. Faith is concerned with the Lord Himself as He is now, and as He has been in His redemptive person and work. Hope has to do with the Lord as coming, and never with anything else. You know there are some people that think we cannot look forward without a sort of shrinking. Well, I suppose those people are thinking of looking forward to death. I admit that you cannot look forward to death without shrinking. It is easy of course to idealize death, as sometimes you find it idealized in the poets. It is easy, for instance, for Longfellow to say, "There is no death! What seems so is transition"; and then make that rhyme with "elysian." But that is poetry. That is not the New Testament. The New Testament idea of death is always this: the last enemy. There is nothing elysian in regard to the New Testament teaching about death. Some years ago, a medical man wrote an article in an English paper pointing out that from the purely physical standpoint it was impossible for anybody to look forward to death without shrinking; and if that is true physically, I believe it is equally true morally and spiritually. Whenever you hear of people wanting to die you may be perfectly certain they need a doctor. There is something abnormal and mawkish and unreal in anyone longing to die. Why, some years ago, when I was in pastoral work in Oxford, I said to two or three friends who were near me, "Now if you would like any particular hymns chosen for next Sunday, I will be glad to include them, so that the choir can practice them." And one young lady, bright and beautiful and strong and vigorous—asked me for this hymn: "I am kneeling at the threshold, weary, faint and sore." She was not—she was to be married in a few weeks—but she wanted that mawkish hymn that is only appropriate, and very beautifully appropriate, to an old saint of 80 who has more friends with the Lord than down here. But you see there was the unreality of it. But if you look forward to the Lord's coming there is nothing of that. Death is always, I repeat, the enemy; but the Lord's coming is that which is called the blessed hope; and it is this that ought to figure very largely in connection with faith and love as a part of our Christian character and life. The same thing is true from another standpoint, in verse 10; and may I ask the kind attention of my brother ministers to this. You notice in verse 9 what the Apostle says: "They themselves shew of us what manner of entering in we had unto you"—now this is what the Apostle preached—"how ye turn to God from idols"—that is the work of faith—"to serve the living and true God"—that is the toil of love—"and to wait for His Son from heaven"—that is the patience of hope. And I think as I look at these words that is the kind of preaching that you and I ought to exercise. We ought never to allow the Lord's coming to be far away from our evangelistic preaching. For this was a message to those who were not then Christians. The Lord proclaimed not only as the One who died and who lives, but as the One who is coming again. And so you see the definite bearing of this on hope, whether we think of the Christian, as in verse 3, or the preacher, as in verse 10.

Now will you notice the Lord's coming in relation to *work*. Chapter ii, verse 19: "What is our hope, or joy, or crown of rejoicing? Are not even ye, in the presence of our Lord Jesus Christ at His coming?" The Apostle Paul was a keen soul winner and he loved the souls of those with whom he was associated. A dear old friend of mine in Oxford was fond of telling that he had a letter once from a clergyman who wanted an assistant in his parish to work with him; and telling my friend of the kind of man he wanted he said, "I want a man whose heart is aglow with the love of souls." And so it was with the Apostle; and as he thought of the converts that God had given him in Thessalonica, he looked forward to the culmination of that when they would be associated together; they would be his crown of rejoicing, his unspeakable joy, in the presence of the Lord Jesus Christ at the Parousia, at the time when the Lord Himself should come. That is the culmination of our work as soul winners. We are winning people for Christ here and now, and we rejoice in everything that they show of Christ and His experience in the present life. But we look forward to the time when they shall with us be associated, and that will be indeed the time of joy, that will be glory for every Christian worker when he is able to say, "Behold I and the children whom Thou has given me." There is nothing like the thought of the Lord's coming and our association with our converts at that day to inspire us to holy service for God today in winning souls to Himself.

Then will you notice we have the Lord's coming in relation to *holiness*, in chapter iii. At the end of chapter iii the Apostle prays that they may increase in love for the purpose, "to the end that He may establish your hearts unblamable in holiness at the coming of our Lord Jesus Christ with all His saints." The Lord's coming in relation to *holiness.* He prays that the hearts may be established. Now what is the heart? The heart in Scripture is always the centre of the moral nature. The heart always includes the mind and the emotions and the will. Wherever you find the word "heart" in the Old Testament or in the New you are always sure to find the inclusion of all those three, though, of course, one or other of these points may be especially emphasized in this or that passage. The heart means first of all the mind. You know we are accustomed to distinguish and sometimes contrast the mind and the heart. There was a man once in England who was preaching in the open air, and he was trying to emphasize the necessity for a real work of God, and he said: "It is not what you believe in your head, but what you believe 18 inches lower down." That of course is a very legitimate distinction, but that distinction is not found in the word "heart" in Scripture. The mind, our thought, is part of the heart; our emotions are part of the heart, and our will is part of the heart. And it is this mind and these feelings and this will that he prays may be established, confirmed, settled, unblamable, or rather unblemished in holiness.

Now holiness first of all means consecration. Purification only arises out of it as a secondary result. The first and primary idea is separation, consecration; and the Apostle prays that in that great day when the Lord shall meet them and they meet their Lord, that their moral being,—minds and hearts and feelings and will,—shall be established without blemish in consecration and purification before God and the Father. And do you not see, therefore, how true it is, the

Apostle Peter says, "What manner of persons ought we to be in all holy conduct and Godliness?" If the Lord's coming does not enable us to realize what holiness means, then nothing will, nothing can, because this is intended to be the inspiration of our life here and now. We are to live unblamable now; we shall be without blemish hereafter.

If you will turn now to a well known passage, you will find the Lord's coming in relation to *comfort*, in chapter iv, 13 to 18. You notice that there was a great problem before those Christians of Thessalonica. Between the time that they had sent the message to the Apostle and the first preaching in Thessalonica a number of their beloved friends had died, and having heard about the coming of the Lord, they wondered how those dead ones would fare. Would they be permitted, would they be allowed to join; would it be possible for them to be associated? And the Apostle says when he calls their attention to this problem, "I would not have you ignorant. I do not want you to be without hope, as the majority of people are, because your belief in Jesus Christ as dying and raised again carries with it a belief that those who sleep in Jesus will God bring with Him." How beautiful are the words as the Apostle Paul puts it, "those who have been put to sleep by Jesus." That is true of all the believers who are now with the Lord. They were put to sleep by Jesus; and the belief that God raised Him from the dead involves the absolute belief that Jesus Christ will bring with Him those who are now asleep in Him.

And then comes this revelation, verses 15 and 17. After the problem in verse 13 and the solution in verse 14, there comes the new revelation. "For this we say unto you by the word of the Lord"; and then, as you know, he goes on to say: "So far from these beloved ones who have passed away being inferior, they will be superior in the sense that they will be caught up first, and we who are alive will follow them, so that they will not be behind us; we shall be really behind them." That is how he revealed the new truth to them. And then comes the word of consolation, "Wherefore comfort one another with these words." Many of us during the last four years have, as we know, been in great need of comfort. When we have seen those long lists of casualties in the various papers, we could not help thinking of the many hearts and the many homes that have been desolated. And we cannot help thinking in our joy this morning of the homes on Thanksgiving Day where there will be vacancies and vacant chairs. As we stood in Toronto last Monday two weeks and realized what had happened, as we saw in the great procession of the soldiers the original Canadians of four years ago, the men who were wounded more or less seriously, crippled for life, then as we thought of the unspeakable joy that filled our hearts at the cessation of hostilities, there could not but come the thought of those who would not welcome their loved ones back again, those who have given their lives for the cause that took them over seas. And it is just at this point that such a word comes: "Wherefore comfort one another with these words."

"Shall we know one another in heaven?" someone says. Personally I never think we need trouble about that. The real thing is to try to get to know one another on earth. I do not question for a moment that in the light of this passage and many others, there will be reunion with those that have gone before as we are all together in the presence of our Lord. "Wherefore comfort one another with these words."

Then I pass on quickly to ask you to notice the Lord's coming in relation to *character*. Chapter v. I can only touch upon this very briefly, though there is much in it that will warrant closer study by individual readers and students of God's Word. The relation of God's coming to character. Verses 1 to 11. Verse 2: "You brethren, you know that the Lord's day is coming as a thief in the night; for when they shall say peace and safety, then will come sudden destruction. But you, brethren, are not in darkness that that day should overtake you as a thief. Ye are all the children of light." And then there are the two exhortations, verse 8 and also verse 10. "Let us, whether we wake or sleep, we should live together with Him. Wherefore exhort one another, comfort one another."

I just pause here to ask you to notice that the old English word "comfort" which is in our Bible means three things. It always means three things and never less nor fewer than three things. It means first of all that we are to be strong; that is seen in the word "fortress." Then we are to be brave or courageous; that is seen in the word "fortitude." And then because we are strong, and because we are brave, we are to console one another in the modern sense of comfort and cheer. And that is what you and I are to do in regard to this great event. It is not a subject of ignorance in our case. We know it. They do not know it, and because of that, we are to make others strong, make others brave, and to cheer and console those, as we are consoled of God. And then there comes this thought of preservation, in verses 12 to 24. From 12 to 22 there are various aspects of the Christian life. In verse 23 there is the anticipation of the great future. And in verse 24 there is the assurance that that future will be realized. Whenever we are reading verse

23, we ought never to omit verse 24 with it. "The God of peace sanctify you wholly; and I pray God your whole spirit and soul and body"—not body, soul and spirit; that is not God's order—"be preserved blameless unto the coming of our Lord Jesus Christ. Faithful is He that calleth you, who also will do it." The prayer of verse 23 will be answered, and God Himself will fulfil what the Apostle by guidance and inspiration has prayed may come to pass. Then I ask you to notice again very briefly the Lord's coming in relation to *vindication,* chapter 1 of ii Thessalonians. You will find in verses 6 and 7 there is to be rest after persecution. "It is a righteous thing with God to recompense tribulation to them that trouble you, and to you who are troubled, rest." And then in verse 10 there is glory after opposition. God, because of what has happened here and now, in that day when He shall come to be admired, you shall be glorified in Him as He is glorified in you. And so the people of God are going to be vindicated. Those who are today often persecuted and ostracised and boycotted and despised are going to stand out in that day, because they have been faithful to God and His Word; they are going to be honored and glorified in the presence of our Lord. And so we are to live day by day in the light of that coming, and feel sure that vindication will be ours. Meanwhile we are to take as our motto, or virtually as our motto, that which is the motto of a school in the north of Scotland: "They say. What do they say? Let them say," because we can afford to wait for our vindication. My last point is the Lord's coming in relation to *steadfastness.* You will find that all through chapter ii. I am not going to trouble you with any interpretation of that passage. That is not my subject this morning. But I want you to notice very briefly that first of all the

Apostle gives them information. Verses 1 and 12. Whatever may be the meaning, he intended that for their instruction. And then from verses 13 to 17 you will find that he goes on to exhortation. Because of the information they are to hold fast and they are to look forward with confidence and joy to the future, to that "everlasting consolation and good hope through grace" which will come to us in and through the Lord's coming Himself. And so as you look at these seven points,—the coming of the Lord in relation to holiness, in relation to comfort, in relation to character, in relation to vindication, in relation to steadfastness,—you see, I think, at least a little of the practical, definite, direct bearing of all this glorious teaching about the Lord's coming on our present day life and service. Christ has come. No one doubts that for a moment. As a matter of simple history Christ has come. Christ is coming here and now. As our loving Lord He is coming by His Spirit into every heart willing to receive Him. But Christ will come, and that coming will be as personal as the first coming. That coming will be as historic as the incarnation. And no one can read the New Testament without seeing at once that the Lord is coming just as certainly as He came to Bethlehem. You cannot give any theory, you cannot explain away the teaching, you cannot say that it was due to figures of speech or metaphors or anything at all. As literally as the first coming will be the coming again. According to the Word of the angel in Acts 1, according to the Word of Paul in I Thessalonians, 4; and still more according to the Word of Christ Himself in John 14: "I will come again and receive you unto myself." Meanwhile, you and I are to live in the light of this three-fold coming of the Lord. You know every one of you all about this in the light of that great passage in Hebrews ix:24, 26 and 28. Although the Greek words are different, the English has a very helpful association in the three appearings of Christ. In Hebrews ix:26, He appeared in the past; in verse 24, He now appears in the presence of God for us; and in verse 28, He will appear again the second time. And so we are to live, I repeat, in the light of this three-fold appearing; rejoicing in what Christ has done, rejoicing in what He is and is doing, but not forgetting to rejoice in hope of that glory when He shall come again. We are not now looking for signs. We are not now looking for great world catastrophes or convulsions. We are not looking for anything in the way of dates or signs or anything else, but we are looking for *Him*.

"It is not for a sign we are watching,
  For wonders above and below,
The pouring of vials of judgment
  The sounding of trumpets of woe.

It is not for a day we are looking,
  Nor even the time yet to be,
When the earth shall be filled with God's glory
  And the waters that cover the sea.

It is not for a King we are looking ,
  To make the world kingdom His own.
It is not for a judge who shall summon
  The nations of earth to His throne.

Not for these, though we know they are coming,
  For they are but adjuncts of Him
Before whom all glory is clouded,
  Beside whom all splendor grows dim.

We wait for the Lord, our Beloved,
  Our Saviour, Master and Friend,
The substance of all that we hope for,
  Beginning of faith and its end.

INFLUENCE OF THE STUDY OF PROPHECY

We watch for our Saviour and Bridegroom,
  Who loved us and made us His own;
For Him we are looking and longing,
  For Jesus, and Jesus alone.

Christ the Executor of All Future Judgments

JAMES M. GRAY, Dean of the Moody Bible Institute of Chicago.

The great classic on this theme is Christ's own words in John v:28.

He is meeting His enemies on the question of His equality with God, and after declaring such to be the fact, He confirms it by an argument drawn from His divine knowledge, power and authority.

As to the last-named, He says: "For the Father judgeth no man, but hath committed all judgment unto the Son, that all men should honor the Son even as they honor the Father" (22, 23).

As Dean Burgon puts it, there is an *original,* supreme, judicial power, and there is also a *derived* judicial power, i.e., a power given by commission. Christ considered as God, possesses the original power equally with the Father; but Christ considered as the son of man, possesses the derived power as having received it from the Father. In this sense judgment is the special, the peculiar work of the Second Person of the Trinity, and is not shared by the other Persons, the Father or the Holy Spirit. What a fitness there is in this, that He who was condemned by an unjust judgment, and who died for sinners, should have it as His peculiar office to judge the world! A corresponding passage is in Paul's words to the Athenians on Mars Hill, where in God's Name he commands men everywhere to repent, "Because He hath appointed a day in which He will judge the world in righteousness by that man Whom He hath ordained, whereof He hath given assurance in that He hath raised Him from the dead" (Acts xvii:30, 31). The "day" which God hath thus appointed is not one of twenty-four hours merely, but a long period, including as will appear, several distinct acts or scenes of judgment.

I.

The first of these is recorded in 2nd Corinthians v:9-11, and is a judgment of Christian believers and of them only, which takes place when Christ comes into the air, and the Church, which is His body, is caught up in clouds to meet Him.

Possibly it may surprise some to learn of a judgment of Christian believers, when we are so plainly taught in Romans viii:1 that "There is therefore now no condemnation (judgment) to them that are in Christ Jesus." But the explanation is that this is not a judgment unto condemnation, but rather to determine the question of rewards. It does not take place until believers are already glorified with Christ, and have been made like Him, hence it can in no wise be a judgment of their persons but only of their deeds.

It is referred to more specifically in Paul's first letter to the Corinthians, where at chapter iii:11-15, he says:

CHRIST THE JUDGE

"For other foundations can no man lay than that is laid, which is Jesus Christ.

"But if any man build on this foundation, gold, silver, precious stones, wood, hay stubble;

"Every man's work (i. e. every believer's work, every man who has built on the true foundation), shall be made manifest; for the day shall declare it, because it shall be revealed by fire; and the fire shall try every man's work of what sort it is.

"If any man's work abide which he hath built thereupon, he shall receive a reward.

"If any man's work (i.e., any believer's work) shall be burned, he shall suffer loss; but he himself shall be saved, yet so as by fire."

Recently my eye fell on an interesting comment on these verses which I should like to pass along. The author said; this is a judgment which assumes that we are God's sons, and only measures how far, in accordance with our standing and calling we have walked; like as a man now regards the behaviour of his own children because he is their father. And in that judgment by the Lord Jesus of all our works, we shall all heartily concur. We shall perceive where we failed, and what we allowed to hinder our full obedience to Him who saved us. And glad shall we be to see all those works of ours which He could not accept burned up, while all that He can reward He will. What a solemn warning it is however, and what an urgent motive for every believer to order his daily life and conduct in accordance with His will! It was stated that this judgment is scheduled for the time when we shall meet the Lord in the air, but this is not to say that He and we shall remain there in the air. That is our meeting-place with the Lord, but not necessarily our abiding place. It serves as the location of the judgment and for the adjudication of our rewards of our places in the coming Kingdom, but the meeting there is followed by the coming with Him to the earth. Dr. John Lillie, the Presbyterian Commentator, is to be credited with the discovery that there are only three other places in the New Testament where the phrase "to meet" is found as it is used in I Thessalonians iv; and in all of them, the party who is met continues after the meeting to advance in the same direction in which he was moving previously.

II.

This leads us naturally and easily to the second scene of judgment, which takes place on the earth and the object of which is the nation of Israel. To one unfamiliar with the Bible and with God's broad scheme of redemption for the world, it may seem strange that a single nation from all the other nations should be thus singled out for special judgment. And especially so when that nation is identical with a race so few in numbers as compared with other races, and when it is at present, and has been for many centuries, without any abiding place of its own.

But Israel has a great mission in God's plan of redemption for the world. He has not dealt with any other nation as with her. It is her disobedience and unfaithfulness heretofore which has prevented her from fulfilling that plan. But nevertheless, "the gifts and calling of God are without repentance" (Rom. xi:29). He has not changed His plan and will not change it. The prophets are a unit that Israel will be restored to her land again. Great Britain and her Allies are making this possible and even probable today. But this return will be in unbelief so far as her acceptance of the Lord Jesus as her Messiah is concerned. In that attitude towards God she will in some degree re-establish her former state and her former worship. But her hour of tribulation, which is her hour of judgment, will then appear. All the prophets speak of it from Genesis to Revelation, from Moses to John. "Alas! for that day is great, so that none is like it. It is the time of Jacob's trouble, but he shall be saved out of it" (xxx:7) says Jeremiah. Zechariah is very specific. "Behold the day of the Lord cometh, and thy spoil shall be divided in the midst of thee. For I will gather all nations against Jerusalem to battle; and the city shall be taken, and the houses rifled, and the women ravished; and half of the city shall go forth into captivity, and the residue of the people shall not be cut off from the city." We see also the Person of the Judge here as in the former case, for it is written further; "Then shall the Lord go forth and fight against those nations, as when He fought in the day of battle. And His feet shall stand in that day upon the Mount of Olives. . . . And the Lord my God shall come and all the saints with thee" (xiv:1-5).

It is of this day, and this judgment, that Christ speaks in the 24th of Matthew, where He says:

"Immediately after the tribulation of these days shall the sun be darkened, and the moon shall not give her light, and the stars shall fall from heaven, and the powers of the heavens shall be shaken.

"And then shall appear the sign of the Son of Man in heaven; and then shall the tribes of the earth mourn, and they shall see the Son of man coming in the clouds of heaven with power and great glory.

"And He shall send His angels with a great sound of a trumpet, and they shall gather together His elect from the four winds, from one end of heaven to the other." (29-31)

III.

The foregoing allusion to all the tribes of the earth suggests the third scene of judgment which also takes place upon the earth, its object being the Gentile nations. For its description we turn to the familiar prophecy of the sheep and the goats in Matthew xxv.

"When the Son of Man shall come in His glory, and all the holy angels with Him, then shall He sit upon the throne of His glory.

"And before Him shall be gathered all nations; and He shall separate them one from another, as a shepherd divideth his sheep from the goats." (31-46).

The prevalent idea is that this is a description of the last judgment of all the quick and dead and that it synchronizes with the text in Revelation xx. But this is a mistake. We have here a judgment of the living Gentile nations which takes place on the earth some time after the second coming of Christ; which means some time during the Millennial age or the Day of the Lord. The date doubtless is early in that period and following Israel's tribulation, but possibly, the judgment will cover considerable time and include several stages. As confirming this, observe (1), that the word "nations" in the text is one that occurs over 100 times in the New Testament, and always with reference to *living* nations, i. e., those that are upon the earth at the time to which the passage refers.

Observe (2), that the hypothesis of such a judgment agrees with many other parts of the Bible. Isaiah's words are familiar: "Come near, ye nations, to hear; and hearken, ye people, let the earth hear, and all that is therein, the world and all things that come forth of it. For the indignation of the Lord is upon all nations, and His fury upon all their armies. He hath utterly destroyed them; he hath delivered them to the slaughter" (xxxiv:1, 2). Similar predictions are found in Joel, in Ezekiel, Zechariah and the book of Revelation.

Observe (3), that there is not the slightest reference in this prophecy to a resurrection from the dead; and, as others have pointed out, this is an event of such importance as to most certainly be mentioned if our Lord had intended to include the dead as well as the living in this judgment.

Observe (4), that the decision between the two classes named, the sheep and the goats, leaves no room for doubt that all the dead as mentioned in Revelation xx, are not in mind here.

That decision rests on the kindness shown by the one class and not shown by the other class, to "these my brethren" as Jesus calls them.

"These my brethren" is a third class altogether distinct from the other two. Prof. J. T. Cooper, formerly of the Allegheny Seminary says, "It requires no words to show that, not to mention infants, there are millions upon millions who have died, to whom these reasons would have been wholly inapplicable. What multitudes in the ages of the past, have passed away who never heard of the Name of Jesus, or His brethren."

Observe (5), that the form in which this judgment is presented is altogether distinct from that in Revelation xx, in that case, as we shall see, there is a formal trial, an opening of books and a judging out of the things written therein; but here there is nothing of the kind. Here there is a King, sitting on the throne of His glory, and calling up subjects, rebellious or obedient. On these is pronounced the sentence of punishment or reward, and in such a way as to pre-suppose their previous innocence or guilt. All these features go to show that we are not dealing with the last judgment of Revelation xx, but that of the Gentile nations, especially with them among those nations which have shown kindness or failed to show kindness to the brethren of Jesus. And who are these brethren of Jesus? We remember that He once said, "My brethren are those who hear the Word of God and keep it"; but we are persuaded that here He is not using the word in that spiritual sense, but in the fleshly sense of Israel. We are persuaded that the words are to be taken in the light of Romans ix:5 where Paul says, that, as concerning the flesh, Christ came of the fathers, i.e., Abraham, Isaac and Jacob.

In other words, this judgment of the living Gentile nations at Christ's second coming has an intimate relation to, and in a sense, grows out of the tribulation of Israel previously referred to. The Gentile nations have been an instrument of her tribulation in all the centuries, and never will they have troubled her more sorely, than at the end time of this age. Then it is that the prince of Daniel ix, the beast of Revelation xiii will be at their head. And the beast was taken we are told, and with him the false prophet, and they two were cast alive into a lake of fire burning with brimstone. As to the nations you know the sequel. The sheep on the right hand of the king inherit the kingdom prepared for them from the foundation of the world, which is equivalent as we are told later, to their entering upon eternal life; while the goats on His left hand go away into eternal punishment.

This indicates by the way, that although it is with nations

we are here dealing, yet nevertheless, it is not simply in their collective or corporate capacity. The punishment on the one hand as well as the reward on the other seems to single out the individual.

IV.

This brings us to the fourth scene of judgment which is that of Gog and Magog and the devil who deceived them, at the end of the Millennium. The record is in Revelation xx:7-10:

> "And when the thousand years are expired, Satan shall be loosed out of his prison.
>
> "And shall go out to deceive the nations which are in the four quarters of the earth, Gog and Magog, to gather them together to battle; the number of them is as the sand of the sea.
>
> "And they went upon the breadth of the earth, and compassed the camp of the saints about, and the beloved city; and fire came down from God out of heaven and devoured them.
>
> "And the devil that received them was cast into the lake of fire and brimstone, where the beast and the false prophet are, and shall be tormented day and night forever and ever."

While this is spoken of as the fourth judgment, yet as intimated at the beginning, "Any one who desires a distinct view of the prophetic sequence of events, must grasp the thought that the whole millennial period is more or less a 'day of judgment,' because in one sense or another judgment characterizes it throughout. The Eternal Judge is in no haste. Leisurely, and with class after class, His irrevocable work proceeds." This loosing of Satan at the close of the thousand years, that he might tempt the millennial nations seems to be absolutely necessary in God's plan. During the millennial age men living on the earth will have every inducement to be godly, for everywhere evil will be repressed and righteousness rewarded. Still this favor shown to man must have its time of testing. As one interpreter remarks, if you have an employee who never robbed you, no praise is due to him if the reason be that he never had an opportunity. Therefore the question is, will the beautiful and perfect rule of the Righteous Judge be any exception to the ages that have preceded it? Will man be shown to be any better then, in his own nature, than he was before? The result shows that he will not.

Sir Edward Grey tells of a native African chief who protested to a British official against having to pay taxes. It was explained to him that they were used to keep order in the country so that men and women, and flocks and herds, and possessions of every tribe were safe, and that each could live in its own territory without fear. Thus the payment of taxes was for the good of all. But the effect on the chief was to make him angry. Before the British came, he said he could raid any neighbor as he pleased, and return with his captives and his captures of all sorts, and be received in triumph by the women and the rest of his tribe. To be sure his own tribe sometimes needed protection from such raids, but then he was willing to undertake that himself. "Now," he said, "you come here and tell me that I ought to like to pay taxes to be prevented from doing this, and that makes me mad." So will it appear to be with the millennial nations at the end. By many of them, if not by most of them, the reign of Christ will be regarded as intolerable, and when a vast rebellion is organized against it the exposure of unregenerate humanity will be complete.

The rebels in this case are termed Gog and Magog in obvious allusion to those designated in the same way, which at the beginning of the millennium are seen to swoop down upon Palestine after the destruction of the anti-Christ, as recorded in Ezekiel xxxvii and xxxviii. In that case the nation of Israel alone was the objective, but now it is the same plus the glorified Church of Christ, if so we may interpret the words, "The camp of the saints and the beloved city." Satan uses no agents in this last assembling of the enemies of God. There is no anti-Christ, no "beast" to be seen here. No subordinate is trusted, but he himself leads the attack against the heaven-appointed King. However, once more the battle is the Lord's. Nor is there any delay or any measure in their punishment. Fire comes down out of heaven and destroys them. And as for Satan who had been confined to the bottomless pit at the beginning of the Millennium, he is here cast into the lake of fire at his close, to be "tormented day and night forever and ever."

V.

This brings us to the last judgment, whose record is found in Revelation xx:11-15. It is sometimes called the judgment of the dead, for as only the living are before us in Matthew xxv:31, only the dead are before us here. "I saw the dead small and great stand before God." "The sea gave up the dead." "Death and hades delivered up the dead." And yet the dead, doubtless they stand before the Judge in resurrection bodies.

But of what nature or character are those bodies? In reply let me say that there will be none of the righteous among the dead. The righteous were all raised from the dead at the beginning of the millennial age, and it is probable that during the Millennium none of the righteous die. However that may be, the *results* of this judgment show that there are no righteous, no believers on the Lamb in this company.

It may be therefore, that just as the righteous dead are raised in glorified bodies like unto that of Christ Himself, so these will appear in all the hideousness of their sinful nature, and in bodies formed to endure torments which otherwise would dissolve them in a moment. Held up to view to expose what they are and what they had been, thus may the scripture be fulfilled which reads: "O Lord, when Thou awakest, Thou shalt despise their image" (Ps. lxxiii).

The location of the first scene of judgment was in the air, that of the next three is on the earth, but this is neither on the earth nor in the air.

> "And I saw a great white throne, and Him that sat on it, from whose face the earth and the heaven fled away; and there was found no place for them."

During the Millennium the full blaze of Christ's personal glory, while vouchsafed to His Church which is in the glory with Him, will not be the privilege of dwellers on the earth. That glory is only revealed to mortals as they are able to endure it. He is rebelled against and rejected in His lower glory by these millennial nations, and hence as His wont is, He retires into a higher glory (Lincoln).

But now when their rebellion has been judged, the veil drops from His face, and instantly, the earth and the heaven, terror stricken at the full refulgence of His Deity, flee away. There is no place for them wherein to hide from His awful gaze. The earth recedes and the dead are exposed to view. The bottomless pit which contained their souls, the graves which contained their bodies—both are gone. Even the fathomless ocean can no longer be a cover for its prey when God's time of judgment has arrrived. Yet, notwithstanding this, here we have an orderly assize, a strictly judicial accounting.

> "The books were opened, and another book which is the book of life. And they were judged out of those things which were written in the books according to their works."

All they have done is carefully examined. They had an opportunity to be judged in Christ, by faith in His blessed Name, but this they wickedly rejected. They chose to stand upon their own record rather than on His. They gloried in *their works*, they did not glory in Him. And God has kept an accurate record of that in which they gloried. This record is now exposed before their eyes in order that they may be convinced before they are condemned. Then will they condemn themselves, and as a result not one of them shall escape. Whoever is not found written in the book of life, is cast into the lake of fire, and not one of these is found written there—not one.

> That day of wrath, that dreadful day,
> When heaven and earth shall pass away,
> What power shall be the sinner's stay?
> How shall he meet that dreadful day?
>
> When, shriveling like a parched scroll
> The flaming heavens, together roll;
> When louder yet, and yet more dread,
> Swells the high trump that wakes the dead.
>
> —Sir Walter Scott.

There is but one answer to this question. Christ who is the executor of all future judgments, is in Himself the only hope of men. But He is an all-sufficient help, free, as He is accessible. In the very same breath almost in which He spake of Himself as the One to whom all judgment had been committed, He revealed the way in which the consequences of that judgment might be turned aside!

> "Verily, verily, I say unto you, he that heareth My words, and believeth Him that sent Me, hath everlasting life, and shall not come into condemnation, but is passed from death unto life."

Believest thou this?

The Hope of Russia in the Present Crisis

By H. PERTELEVITCH RAUD of Russia

Dr. Gray said in his address that the hope of the lost soul is Christ, and therefore this afternoon I feel very happy to talk to you on Russia, my native country, with its millions of souls whose only hope is Christ. We have heard much about Russia lately and about the conditions in that country, but we have heard little, very little, about the need of Russia—her spiritual need—evangelization. I will not try to speak to you of the many other needs in Russia, but I will seek to concentrate on one point, and that is—her evangelization. First of all, I desire to express my thanks to the American people for the kindness shown to Russia in the time of her need and great distress. I appreciate the attitude not only of this country, but also that of Great Britain, who has been standing with Russia and showing to her greatest kindness in these days. As this is not a political meeting, I am not going to touch on the political conditions of Russia, but allow me to say one thing—Russia is today in a chaotic condition and, by the mercy of God, she will have some day a stable government and some day she will hear the Gospel of the Lord Jesus Christ. My heart has never been so joyful as in this conference, seeing such a multitude of hungry children of God listening to the addresses of these men of God explaining the truth from the Word of God, but my heart has never been so sorrowful as in these days when I think that my beloved native country is in a state of chaos and she has not had these spiritual privileges. Millions are dying without the Lord Jesus, and for that purpose I am talking to you to show the need of Russia—her evangelization. The Allies are sending help to Russia—economic and commercial help which is generous—but there is one urgent need unmet and that is Russia's evangelization. Russia is a large country. If you look on the map, you see a very large piece of land in Europe and Asia—her population is about 185,000,000. Someone said some time ago in a lecture that Russia could sustain about one thousand million people, so large is her territory and so enormous are her resources. In Europe and Asia there are about 250,000,000 Slavs. Most of these Slavs have been untouched by the Gospel of the Lord Jesus. I envy you American people because you have had the open Bible for centuries, but the Slavs in Russia and elsewhere have not had that Book opened to them. We have not had the preaching of the Gospel in that way, but by the grace of God, the time will come when God in His mercy will give Russia and all Slavs a mighty spiritual awakening. Russia has a religion —the State religion—the Greek Orthodox church. This church is somewhat different from the Roman Catholic church. I am not going to speak to you about that church; suffice to say, it has about 120,000,000 members. There are also about 25,000,000 Mohammedans and six to seven million Jews, who have not heard the Gospel of Christ. Russia's need is the open Bible—the preaching of the Word of God. Until the recent revolution Russia has not had religious liberty, but she is going to have liberty—she is going to have the open Bible. The Word of God, the Gospel of the Lord Jesus has made this United States of America what she is.

Great Britain's greatness is also due to the Bible, the Word of God. Great Britain was among the first nations who sent the Bible to Russia. I myself personally read first the Word of God from a Bible which came from British sources, and I found the Lord Jesus through that Book. When Israel rejected the Word of God, she went to pieces. Germany as a nation had to go to pieces because she having had the Word of God rejected it as such. Therefore, friends, you have the open Bible—use it in the right way for the glory of God. Russia has need of the real Gospel. We do not want more religion in Russia—we have plenty of religion, but we want Christ and Him crucified—the risen and Glorified Christ—we want the Gospel of that Christ. We do not want religion because it does not give life to anybody, but as the Lord Jesus says, "I am come that they might have life and might have it more abundantly." That is the need of Russia. We do not need in Russia more denominations—we need the Bible. We need in Russia—not the "Christian Scientists"—keep them here. We do not need in Russia Russellites—nor do we need Unitarians—nor do we need or want in any of the Slavonic countries, higher critics—let them die here, and bury them here, too!

This conference ought to produce wonderful fruit for God. Children of God have a great responsibility—first to have the life of God to the overflow, and then to give it out to others. This conference ought to cause to overflow the heart of every Christian man and woman, to abound in prayer life. All the great spiritual movements have started through prayer. This conference started through prayer. Therefore, friends, let us let God have us at His disposal to pray for Russia. In the Word of God we find three special admonitions for prayer: Prayer for *all men* as we find in 1 Timothy ii. Christian men and women in this audience, we have come short of that. I hope we are going to pray for all men, including Russians, as never before. Russia has about six or seven million Jews—my heart is burning also for their salvation. The Apostle Paul said his heart was full of sorrow for Israel—let that sorrow for Jews enter into our hearts to pray for them. The Word of God says pray for all the saints. No matter where they are or what their spiritual condition, but pray for them. Pray for every saint. I want to emphasize prayer because it is a most important thing in the Christian life. A prayerless child of God is a powerless Christian in service, in home, in family life, in business life, everywhere.

I am glad to tell you that by the grace of God, there is already being formed in this country, a non-sectarian Russian Evangelization Movement in behalf of Russia and God has been working on that line in a wonderful way. Many Christian men of leading evangelical bodies are interested in this movement. This shows how God by His grace, has been putting Russia on the hearts of Christian men and women in this country. Now, the need of Russia, as I said before, is the pure Gospel of Christ. For that reason, we ought to have not a few men and women to send to Russia to preach the glad tidings of salvation. Those who know the truth and can rightly divine the word of God.

You may be surprised to hear that Russia has had very few Bibles and New Testaments. You have in this country the open Bible, and plenty of copies of the Scriptures. Therefore, pray for Russia, and pray in such a way that she soon may have the Word of God. You who have so much have a great responsibility in this matter. When this war started, the nations joined together in a wonderful way to defeat their foes, and let me tell you how much this war has cost:

Fifty-six million men in arms.

Eleven million were killed in the war.

The cost of the war in money to the Allies and also to the Teutonic countries, totals 221 billion dollars.

Think of this! That money has gone, and then eleven million men who have lost their lives in the cause of the war. How much have we given or done for the spreading of the Gospel of Christ, not only in Russia but the world over? Let us, Christian friends, learn from this war to stand together for the greatest cause for the calling out from Russia, and among the other nations, people for His Name and thus prepare the way for the speedy coming of our blessed Lord.

The Prince of Peace

PROFESSOR W. H. GRIFFITH THOMAS, Toronto, Canada

We are all rejoicing today in the cessation of hostilities and, as we hope and believe, in the near approach of peace. After four years of unutterable carnage, unutterable cruelty, unutterable craft, we are thankful tonight, as so many more are, that hostilities are at an end and that peace is in sight. But it is well for us to remember that the cessation of hostilities is not necessarily peace. There was no war before 1914, but no one could say that there was peace at that time. And when we ask why, I think the answer is, because there is something far deeper than political peace; and it is that something which brings us together tonight, and whilst we are rejoicing in this political condition, the cessation of hostilities, we cannot help remembering something infinitely more important. Not once or twice but something like seven or eight times God is called in the Bible the God of peace. In the Old Testament the Lord Jesus is called the Prince of Peace; in the New Testament He is called the Lord of Peace; and it is this deeper something that we want to consider tonight as we dwell upon the theme, the Prince of Peace.

What is the meaning of peace? There are few things more prominent in the Bible than peace. It is found in so many different aspects that it stands out, I was going to say, on almost every page of the Bible. Sometimes we read of the need of man, sometimes we read of the provision of God, sometimes we read of the believer's enjoyment of peace, and then again we read of the culmination in the future of the peace that is declared in Scripture. It is always I think somewhat significant—perhaps it was intended to be significant—that the Hebrew salutation, the greeting, was and still is "Peace"; "Shalom," peace. Palestine was a small country, and is still a small country, and in the old days it was between the great powers of Assyria and Egypt, between the upper and lower millstones. It was always in danger either from one side or the other, and we are not surprised that the cry of the people as expressed in that greeting is "Peace." And so it is not only in connection with national and political affairs; the cry of the heart and of the conscience is "Peace."

The word itself is full and deep and wonderful. The Greek word for "peace" implies that which binds, suggesting an agreement. The English and the Latin, from which the English comes, suggests a compact, an agreement; and we are told that the Hebrew word implies fullness, rest, security, quietness. So you see peace is wonderfully varied and complete, including this thought of union and agreement and of compact and fullness and rest and security and fellowship—practically everything. No wonder that man always craves for peace. But now comes the question, why does man need peace? If that is the meaning, what is the need of peace? And the answer at once is *sin*. The reason why man creaves peace is that which the Bible knows as sin. The old question,

> "Can'st thou not minister to a mind diseas'd,
> Pluck from the memory a rooted sorrow,
> Raze out the written troubles of the brain,

> And with some sweet oblivious antidote
> Cleanse the stuff'd bosom of that perilous stuff
> Which weighs upon the heart?"

That is the question in Macbeth, and that is the question tonight. That is the theme of all our novelists for the last fifty years, George Eliot, Nathaniel Hawthorne, and many more, all concerned with the nemesis of broken law, "Be sure your sin will find you out." Poets, even optimistic poets like Browning, not to say anything about men like Ibsen and Thomas Hardy, and even Tennyson, they are all concerned with this thought. And Huxley once said, "There is no forgiveness in nature." And Rudyard Kipling says,

> "The things ye do by two and two
> Ye must pay for one by one."

And this all bears testimony to the need of peace,—the peace of conscience in pardon, the peace of heart in fellowship, the burden removed and the barrier taken away. Peace is the unutterable craving, the constant desire and yearning of every man.

And it is just here that we need to remember the real meaning of our subject tonight; because it is not bearing false witness to say that politicians do not as a rule take any account of sin. It is because of this that we are here tonight with this subject, to remind not only politicians, but ourselves and all our fellow Christians, of that which is very much deeper than anything purely political or national. Now I want to be careful, and yet at the same time I want to be clear.

You know as well as I do that during the last few weeks

and months we have heard a great deal of the league of nations. Whether it came originally from President Wilson or not I do not know, but it has caught the ear and the mind and the heart of people in various countries. The London Times newspaper advocated it the other day and said: "A League of Nations is necessary to save civilization itself . . . to save the very conditions of human existence. It is a task for the best brains working together in all the Allied countries." Two weeks ago, just after the declaration of the armistice, Mr. Lloyd George, the British Premier, said these words:

"What are the principles on which this settlement is to be effected? Are we to lapse back into the old national rivalries, animosities and competitive armaments, or are we to initiate the reign on earth of the Prince of Peace?" And then he said: "It is the duty of Liberalism to use its influence to insure that it shall be a reign of peace."

Then our English paper, The Spectator, in discussing this subject said that there was only one thing that really could be effected by the league of nations just now, and that was the undertaking on the part of all the nations involved that treaties should henceforward not be regarded as scraps of paper; that was all that we could expect the league of nations to do, at any rate for the present.

We have in Canada a well known statesman and earnest Christian man, the Honorable N. W. Rowell, and this is what he said in Toronto two nights ago: "Unless democracy can be sanctified and controlled by Christian moral and spiritual ideals there is no hope for our race." One of our great British jurists, Sir Frederick Pollock, said the other day that the League of Nations should be called by its plainer American term, the "League to Enforce Peace."

And in Toronto we had two or three weeks ago a visit from Lord Charnwood, who has been over to the United States here as well, and he said that the deepest need at the present time—that was before the armistice—"The deepest need at the present time is not peace, but justice." All this I want you to notice bears upon our subject tonight. Sin must be taken into account, for if sin is not taken into account our politicians and statesmen will only touch symptoms; they don't touch the sores. It is easy, like Mr. Lloyd George, to speak of the Prince of Peace, but that title and the peace that is associated with it have never been possible apart from the Lord Jesus Christ Himself. International relationships may be set right for awhile—and there seems to be no doubt that from sheer exhaustion there will be peace and not war for some time to come—but as long as sin is in man's heart there is always the possibility of the flame bursting out afresh notwithstanding all that our politicians may do. There is one phrase that is quoted pretty often, from Tennyson, and it is thought to be almost the slogan of modern days. We are told to look forward to the time

> "When the war-drum beats no longer,
> And the battle flag is furled,
> In the parliament of man,
> In the federation of the world."

And yet we are here tonight to call attention to this, the way of peace. The meaning of peace, the need of peace, and the way of peace; and I want to say that the Lord Jesus Christ is the only way of peace. When you read, as you will read, in our papers and elsewhere in a few weeks, the Christmas message of peace on earth, it is important to remember that peace on earth is impossible apart from the

Lord Jesus Christ, and peace is only possible on the basis of righteousness, and God alone can deal with righteousness. You remember the message in Hebrew vii, "First righteousness, and then peace"; and it is only as there is righteousness that there can possibly be peace. And it is here that our message from this Conference should be sounded forth in this connection. We think of Christ in the past providing righteousness, and by that righteousness bringing peace. "He made peace by the blood of His cross." He made peace between Jew and Gentile through that cross. He sent forth His messengers preaching peace, and we know that the Gospel is called the Gospel of Peace. That is Christ in the past providing righteousness and guaranteeing peace. But then there is Christ in the present, Christ in the present bestowing righteousness and providing peace. Christ received into the heart as a living, loving Saviour and Friend is the Lord our righteousness, and not only is there peace with God, but the peace of God as the outcome of that righteousness.

But there is Christ in the future, who will usher in everlasting righteousness, and that in turn will bring about everlasting peace. The Lord Jesus Christ made peace and brought righteousness through the blood of His cross. The Lord Jesus Christ is providing righteousness and bestowing it and giving peace to the soul now. But bye and bye He is coming again, and in that coming there will be, according to the Psalm, "abundance of peace"; according to the prophet Micah, "when the swords shall be turned into ploughshares, and the spears into pruning hooks, and they shall learn war no more." That will be the day of everlasting righteousness.

Now I want you to notice that sin is dealt with by the

Lord Jesus Christ in two different ways. It is dealt with, first of all, now by His grace through the Gospel; and when we accept Him as our Saviour, being justified by faith we have peace. But it is also going to be dealt with bye and bye, not in grace, but in judgment. And we believe in both these. We believe in grace now, and judgment hereafter; and we believe that the one message of grace now is not and cannot be sufficient to deal with human sin. And we say this for three reasons.

In the first place, we appeal to past history, and we ask as we look over nineteen centuries, is there anything like, anything approaching a universal peace through the Gospel of the Lord Jesus Christ? Why, to ask that question is to answer it. And then we also justify this from the present condition of affairs, present experience. Just listen to this testimony. It comes from the editor of one of our leading theological and philosophical magazines, perhaps the most important of the present day. "Four years," he says, "is a short time to get so much evil done. Is there any power on earth which can do as much good to mankind in four years as the war has done harm?

"On earth there is certainly none. Take the powers of earth one by one; add them together; science, art, literature, education, social reform and the rest, and you will find that it is utterly beyond these to do in four years as much good as the war has done harm. Give them time enough, *give them centuries,* and no doubt they will have something to show for themselves. But evil has not taken centuries to inflict this war upon mankind. It has done the business in four years."

And because of that we believe that sin can only be dealt with in the final issue by judgment as well as grace here and now. And we say this for the third reason: the persistence of evil. If the Bible gave us any idea of a glorious time when sin should be no more as the outcome of the preaching of the Gospel, of course we would accept it and rejoice in it; but you remember the parable of the tares growing until the harvest, you remember the parable of the good and bad fish, until the angels come and separate, thereby showing that evil is not gradually to be done away, but that it will persist to the end. And yet you know those of us who say those things, are charged with being both pacifists and pessimists. Well, now, never mind these hard words; they are said to break no bones. They remind me very much of that British guardsman six feet tall who had a wife five feet nothing and a half, and she used to use the poker on him; and someone said to him, "Why don't you stop it?" "Oh," he says, "it pleases her and it doesn't hurt me." And so when we are called pacifists and pessimists, well, the moral is obvious; it doesn't hurt us in the least. But the point is are these things true? Pacifists? Why, we believe in national righteousness. Pacifists? We believe that this war was absolutely justifiable. Pacifists? We believe that nothing but the utter destruction of Prussianism will settle this affair. Pacifists? Why, I come from Canada; and if there are any pacifists in Canada they have been marvelously quiet the last four years. They knew very well they dare not say a word, otherwise, like the sniper at the front, they would have been done with and done for before very long. In another way they would have been compelled to silence for a long time, and they have found it wisdom if they believe in those things to keep quiet. Pacifism? Why, everyone knows that the Christians who believe in what we believe as represented by this Conference have been among the strongest and most determined advocates of this war from the very first. You in America here perhaps do not know as much about these things as some of us know. Why, there are people in England today who in the case of a war fifteen years ago were called, and perhaps rightly or wrongly—I am not now saying—little Englanders. But every one of them has been a big Englander during these four years, and there has been no pacifism among the vast majority of English speaking Christians in the old country. And yet you know the other day a leading American told us this. I must be careful to give you his words. He called those who held the premillenial view our Lord's coming "misguided," and he classes them with Millennial Dawnists, pro-Germans and Pacifists, and he says that in its practical bearings the views will smell the same by any name. Well, now, that is the head of what is called a school of religion in one of your states; and I want just to say this. I do not suppose my words will reach him, though I did venture to protest in the paper where the article occurred, and I have got the clipping here tonight. But I want to say this: If that man did not know that there is a difference between these whom he classes together, then it reflects upon his intelligence. And, secondly, if he said it and he did know, well then, I prefer not to follow that sentence to the conclusion, I will leave you to draw your own. I would say again that pacifism is absolutely intolerable. But when you look at facts we see at once, as Sherman said, that war is hell; and if there had been Christianity there would have been no war these last four years. We are perfectly certain that if the nations, especially the German nation, the aggressor, had been dominated by the Gospel of Martin Luther, we should have had no war at all.

But we are also said to be pessimists. Well, now, what is a pessimist? Someone says it is a man that has to live with an optimist. They tell us that the distinction between a pessimist and an optimist is this: A pessimist says, "Any milk in that jug?" And the optimist says, "Will you please pass the cream." The pessimist is said to look at the hole, and the optimist at the doughnut around the hole. Pessimism! Why, they tell us that we do not believe in progress. Well, I have only to ask you to notice the temperance movement, and the movement for social reform, and the great ethical and moral and social effects, to say nothing of the religious effect of missions. They tell us that the pre-millennial view cuts at the roots of modern missionary effort. Well, I think of men like Hudson Taylor, Arthur T. Pierson, D. L. Moody, and a score of others, and I ask were these men not keen, earnest, true-hearted missionary men, and yet they were pre-millennialists, every one of them. I think of those men who signed that paper in England a year or so ago, and I wonder if they are not interested in social reform, men like A. C. Dixon and Campbell Morgan, and three or four more. Are these men not interested in everything that makes for the betterment of the community? Why, to ask such a thing as this is to answer it. And yet we are said to be pessimists. Was the Lord Jesus Christ a pessimist when He said, "When the Son of Man cometh shall He find faith on the earth?" Was the Apostle Paul a pessimist when he said, "In the last days perilous times shall come?" Why then should we be regarded as pessimists? I will undertake this: I will challenge any of these who charge us with pessimism to give us a list of the social reformers and the missionary men who take the other view of prophecy, and see whether they can compare with the evangelists and the missionaries and the missionary workers of the premillennial view during the last twenty-five years. And I have no doubt whatever as to the result of that challenge.

But in particular we are charged with being unmindful of three great movements that are now dominating attention. We are said to be indifferent to the great movement for Church union which means co-operation. Well, I do not know that that is altogether accurate even in itself, because we believe that a divided church will never be a proper witness to the whole world, and that there is a great truth in our Lord's prayer "That they may be one, that the world may believe." But we ask this: If you are to have Church union, what is the basis of it? Is it to be founded on truth? That is the only true basis of unity; and it is because we believe that a great many of those who are now in favor of Church union and federation do not hold the truth of the Bible that we say we want unity, but never at the expense of truth. Then we are also told that we are indifferent to social service. Well, here again we have to be careful. We believe in reconstruction, but reconstruction based on regeneration. We would have reconstruction in every possible way, but pulling down the rookery and building the model dwelling will never destroy the fascination for crime. Pulling out the lion's teeth and claws will not destroy the lion's nature; it only prevents him from hurting *you*. And what we say about social reform is, we want it based upon that great principle of the New Testament, "Ye must be born again." And when you emphasize that, why, that will take care of social reform. Everyone knows that when a man is converted it not only affects himself and wife and family, but even his dog and cat. As someone has said,

"The soul of all improvement is the improvement of the soul." We are told that we are indifferent to religious education. Here again we want to know what kind of education is called religious? Is it an education that is based on evolution, or regeneration? Evolution, for which there is practically nothing in science and nothing at all in religion to justify it; evolution, which causes what has been lately called the paganising of our colleges and universities. Is that the religious education? Well, if so, we are glad to be as far away from it as we possible can. But, on the other hand, everything that ministers to a religious education that touches spirit, soul and body with the truth of the Gospel of the Lord Jesus Christ we welcome, and we say that this will make a man and a community which will glorify God and bring blessings everywhere. And so I say again, notwithstanding all that is charged against us, we are neither pessimists nor pacifists for calling attention to this great fact of sin. You have had here in America for the last few months—I think he has returned to England now—a well known member of Parliament and journalist, Mr. P. Whitwell Wilson, and in one of his addresses at Northfield last summer he said this, and though it is a little long I do not apologize for reading it to you. "I look," he says, "at this sorely stricken world, broken in twain, and I know of nothing in the political life of Europe which can heal the breach; it is irreparable. I heard every debate in the House of Commons for twelve years before I came to America, I knew every statesman personally; and I do not know what Lord Grey could have done by diplomacy that he did not do to save the world from this appalling calamity, and I know of nothing that any statesman can do today that will turn the heart of Germany at the present moment.

But I am not going to limit the power of God. 'Behold, He cometh with clouds.' In the time of the clear sky we did not see Him. But He cometh, and I wonder whether out of all this horrible calamity, this whirlwind of passion and hatred, we are not entitled to look for the great coming of Christ, not any longer to persuade, to plead, but in power to rule, to reign among the nations. As I see the development of the idea of a League of Nations,—one army, one navy, one system of finance, the whole world united by the telephone and telegraph and all the other means of communication, I think of 'Every eye shall see Him,' and I see looming above the League of Nations, guaranteeing the peace that is to come, the Prince of Peace." And so I say as I close tonight—I do not hesitate to say it; I do not hesitate to say this as plainly as possible—our word is not "The World for Christ," but "Christ for the World." And if this world is to be made safe for democracy, it must be made safe by the autocracy of Jesus Christ. Some years ago, Dr. Kilman, of Edinburgh, was travelling home to Scotland by one of the liners. One night he was talking to a leading American, and the discussion turned upon the slums of New York and other American cities, and the American was saying to Dr. Kilman what he thought about these great social problems, and he said: "You know there is only one way of settling these things, and that is by means of a king." "Oh," said Kilman, "I thought you Americans had done with kings long ago." "Oh, no," said the man; "no one but the King will settle these problems; and we know where He is and who He is." "Whom do you mean?" said Kilman. "The Lord Jesus," said the man.

And though we are not looking for that yet—we are looking for Him to come to take away His Church—yet we believe that afterward He will come again, put down all rule and all authority and power, take to Himself the kingdom, and reign and usher in everlasting peace. That is our meaning tonight of the Prince of Peace.

"Till o'er our ransomed nature
The Lamb for sinners slain,
Redeemer, King, Creator,
In bliss returns to reign."

When Will the Lord Come?

By W. B. Riley.

Prophecy long since anticipated the distractions and divisions that should finally come to the visible church. For some hundreds of years that prophecy has been increasingly converted into history, until to-day, the denominational bewilderment—the sectarian strife—is little less distracting than was yesterday's war of all nations. The one feature of the world-conflict that brought to men increasing amazement existed in the circumstance that when, in 1914, the long scabbarded sword, suddenly leaped into deadly action, there was a boasted unity on the part of the Teutonic forces that filled the world with fear, and an evident lack of unity on the part of the Allies that lost them the most important battles, and gave to neutral but friendly nations, the keenest conceivable alarm. Trusting to their evident unity in opinion and practice, the Teutons reasoned that they could make mastery of the earth by the way of "the mailed fist," and so hard were their blows and so loud was their boasting that timidity and fear took hold upon every man of opposing camp; and almost without exception, the Allied nations appointed days of fasting and prayer that the will of God might be known, and the way of the Lord adopted. The result, was, Teutonism increasingly divided and defeated, and the Allies increasingly unified and victorious.

A few years since every theologian who opposed the premillennarian position, called attention to the lack of unity among its representatives, and prophecied a speedy collapse of the premillennial camp. But when a company of honest men make honest appeal to God to show the way, and pledge themselves to walk in it, unity is ever the sure result, and to-day, in the visible church of Jesus Christ, the one section that speaks a definite shiboleth with the least hesitation of tongue, the one section that reveals a company wherein men most accurately keep step one with another, the one section in which divisions and distractions most seldom occur, is, beyond dispute, the premillenniarian section. Recently, however, there has risen a slight divergence of opinion over "the time element in our Lord's Return," and men have been found who insist upon employing different words, such for instance as "immediate," "imminent" and "remote," and debate has been the result. It is in the double hope of discovering the absolute truth, and thereby effecting a harmony among my beloved brethren, that I treat this subject and, in the light of Peter's words in the third chapter of his Second Epistle, I propose three questions concerning our Lord's return—Was it to have been immediate? If not, is it still remote? If neither be true, then is it imminent?

Was It to to Have Been Immediate?

Prof. Shailer Matthews, in his disscussion on "Will Christ

Come Again?" contends that the early Christian writers, believed that Christ would come "immediately."

That, doubtless, was the early impression of the disciples. Such an impression seems to have been voiced by the questions with which they immediately plied their risen Lord—"Wilt thou at this time restore again the kingdom to Israel?" That would be natural from the Lord's injunction to them "Therefore, be ye also ready, for in such an hour as ye think not, the Son of Man cometh" (Matt. xxiv:44), from the Lord's statement, also "Take ye heed, watch and pray, for ye know not when the time is" (Mark xiii:33). The language of the apostle Paul "The night is far spent the day is at hand" (Rom xiii:12), certainly has the suggestion of near approach. But that no man ever employed a term synonomous with "immediate," a word which means "without the lapse of intervening time," is significant in the last degree, and ought to be an end of controversy upon the subject, and should forever dispense with the employment of that word in premillennarian literature.

Since His return was not "immediate" it is logically certain that neither the Saviour, nor any apostle, ever promised it should be, for the double reason that such a promise would have been to have fixed the date, a thing against which the Lord solemnly inveighed; and also would have involved God's failure to keep His word, a thing which has never come to pass, and, in the nature of the case, in fact, by the nature of God, never can!

The impression was from the disciples wish rather than by the Divine Word. That wish was voiced in their question to the risen Christ,—"Lord, wilt Thou at this time"—immediately—"restore the kingdom to Israel?" That fact is somewhat fully discussed by the Apostle James from which some brethren have picked out a few words forgetting, and even ignoring the whole context. James writes—"Be patient therefore, brethren, unto the coming of the Lord; Behold, the husbandman waiteth for the precious fruit of the earth, and hath long patience for it, until he receive the early and latter rain. Be ye also patient; stablish your hearts: for the coming of the Lord draweth nigh" (5:7-8). That fact was further elaborated in the language of Peter (2 Pet. III:1-9).

That fact is also made still more clear by the words of the Lord Jesus, recorded in Matthew xxiv, and in answer to the three questions, "Tell us when these things shall be?" "What shall be the sign of Thy coming?" and "What of the end of the age?" If language means anything, our Lord's reply means history—history great, important, and far-reaching in its results, to be wrought in between His answer and the day when the end of this age should come; and there is not an instance to be found in the Scriptures when the time question was raised, without a reply that suggested some delay and consequent exercise of some patience on the part of ardent believers. The time element is suggested also in the parable of the nobleman, gone into a *far country,* to receive for himself a kingdom and return and in the phrase "Now, after *a long time* the Lord of those servants cometh." The disciples of our Lord, at the time to which these texts refer, were, the most of them, not inspired men; and, as yet, they were but poorly instructed men. Their questions were often crude, and their conceptions, mistaken. The answers to those questions by the Lord, and by the inspired apostles, were neither crude nor mistaken, but inerrant and dependable, and must forever provide the only basis for the Christian's belief.

WHEN WILL THE LORD COME

In the Divine Word, the doctrine of indefiniteness of time necessarily displaces immediateness. From time to time men have objected to the method of the Lord's answers to the three questions: "When will Jerusalem be destroyed?" "What will be the sign of Thy coming?" and "Of the end of the age?" on the ground that the Lord's reply seemed to make these events simultaneous or else following with such quick succession one upon another as to require no intervening space of time. It is a truth, however, that in the interpretation of prophecy, timelessness is a dominant element; and the sheet of the future is not outspread in such a way that the distinct time, point by point, could be measured upon it; but rather, is folded up in such a way that only a few successive events appear while the space of time that intervenes between them disappears." But better yet is the contention of Weiss that prophecy is always conditional. "God never says, through the lips of any prophet, what is to happen, whether in the form of weal or woe, without a reference either expressed or understood to human conduct. On the contrary, He even runs the risk of appearing to contradict Himself by leaving prophecies of good unfulfilled when men sin, and of evil unfulfilled, when they repent. The great purpose of Christ in all He says about the future is not to satisfy curiosity but to direct conduct, the sum of His teaching being an urgent admonition to watchfulness." And, it is evident to every reader of the New Testament that whatever might be the Father's delay in sending His Son in power and glory, the whole appeal of Scripture is to the expectant attitude on the part of the church—"waiting"—ready to receive Him at "any moment."

This declaration might seem to render unnecessary the

discussion of our second question with reference to the Lord's return—

Is It Still Remote?

But not so! There are too many men backing that contention to pass them over without further and fuller notice. The advocates of the Lord's "remote" return are to be found in three separate and distinct camps. First, in the camp of the critics, who in literal fulfillment of Peter's prophecy, scoffingly contend He will never come. Secondly, in the camp of the conservative postmillennialists, who fix His return at the close of the millennium; and thirdly, in the camp of certain premillennarians who defer His return to prophecy waiting to be converted into history. We are absolutely convinced that these respective companies are each and all without the backing of the Book, and we arraign each of them in turn as opposed to revelation.

The first interprets the Scripture concerning the second coming as figurative speech, destined to no literal fulfillment. To show that I do them no injustice whatever by such indictment, let me quote from an acceptable representative—Prof. Shirley Jackson Case, of the University of Chicago, He writes: "Undoubtedly the ancient Hebrew prophets announced the advent of a terrible day of Jehovah when the old order of things would suddenly pass away. Later prophets foretold a day of restoration for the exiles when all nature would be miraculously changed and an ideal kingdom of David established. The seers of subsequent times portrayed the coming of a truly heavenly rule of God when the faithful would participate in millennial blessings. Early Christians expected soon to behold Christ returning upon the clouds even as they had seen him in their visions literally ascending into heaven. In times of persecution, faith in the return of Christ shone with new luster, as afflicted believers confidently exclaimed, 'Behold, he cometh with the clouds; and every eye shall see Him, and the saints shall reign with Him a thousand years.' So far as the use of this type of imagery is concerned, millenarianism may quite properly claim to be biblical. Unquestionably certain biblical writers expected a catastrophic end of the world. They depicted the days of sore distress immediately to precede the visible return of the heavenly Christ, and they eagerly awaited the revelation of the New Jerusalem."

And yet, after having made such admissions concerning every claim that is made by the most ardent premillennialist, he turns deliberately about and asserts "Biblical forms of the millennial hope are not longer tenable," and further advises that "since biblical hopes are incapable of being literally produced, men should cease from every form of millennium speculation and "adopt outright a constructive policy of world betterment." In other words, the only hope for the final salvation of the world, presented by theological Moderns is not in "the Lord from heaven," but rests with "the man who is of the earth." Truly Peter's prophecy is finding literal fulfillment, and men of the Case and Mathew's type are agreeing wih their scoffing brethren, Dean Inge, for instance, that the "notion of the second coming is not now compatible with sanity" and with Dr. David Smith, "Millennialism has gone the common way of absurdities in a more or less sane world," or even with the further speech, "It was not the least of the blunders of the apostolic church that she regarded the second advent as imminent; this way madness lies!" For the comfort of believers, let it be remembered that one form of insanity is the opinion of its subject that sane people are out of mind. Christ and Paul were alike charged with madness! The scoffers have come.

Postmillennialists accept the certainty of the coming of the Lord; but at the close of the Millennium. To them the "Kingdom" and "Church" are convertible if not synonomous terms. In the language of one of their greatest exponents, George Dana Boardman, they believe "the Kingdom of God," viewed as an inception, has "already come"; "viewed as a process, is ever coming," "and viewed as a consummation," will have its end in the judgment.

In answer to this propaganda it is sufficient to say that such an opinion has no harmony whatever with Revelation! It leaves the opening sentences of the twentieth chapter of the Revelation meaningless; it converts "the thousand years" that follow the Lord's appearance, His overthrow of the Adversary, the first and final resurrections and the judgment of the wicked, at the close of the millennium into a senseless figure! It makes the "absent nobleman" a present reigning king; it makes that sentence of the Lord's prayer—'Thy kingdom come' a meaningless repetition of a petition long since answered; it makes the promise of His visible, glorious appearance, of His personal enthronement at Jerusalem, of the abdication of kings in His behalf, all a senseless verbiage; it makes the description of righteousness that shall obtain, under His reign, a travesty of terms; it makes the promise of prosperity, pledging every man "his own vine and fig tree," a hollow mockery; it makes the prophecy of "deserts" converted into "rose-beds" a tantalizing hyperbole; it contains about as much sound exegesis of Scripture as is in the now popular declaration—"Christ's second coming exists in the late present-world conflict!"

Great men and good are often the advocates of this theory, but it is doubtful if any open-minded and diligent student of the Scripture has ever been able to receive the same.

By certain premillennialists "that blessed hope" has recently been deferred for fulfilling prophecy. I need not call these, our beloved brethren, by name; they have made themselves sufficiently known. Not a man of us, but has been plied by their literature! Every mail piles it upon our desks. My love of them is such that I read most of it, but up to the present time, I remain absolutely unconvinced of their contention. We have been told that there is "not a passage in Scripture that teaches the imminent coming of Christ!" I have been unable to find one that did not teach it, for there is a difference and a distinction between the words "imminent" and "immediate." "Immediate"—is "without lapse of time!" "Imminent"—"possible to happen at any time."

We are told that"the death of Peter," the final "harvest," "the great tribulation," "the preaching of the gospel of the kingdom to all nations," "the rise of the anti-Christ," "the return of the Jews to Jerusalem"—all of this must come to pass and above all the rise of the ten nations and kings out of the old Roman empire, must occur before our Lord can come. I find myself unable to see how these brethren can plead necessary delay in the Lord's coming in view of the shifting scenes of history now in the making. The Lord is teaching us now, if He never taught us before, what marvelous changes may occur in a day. I cannot, therefore, consent that some considerable period must necessarily intervene before my Lord's appearance. The making of the period is with the Lord himself, and whether He will extend it or cut it short in righteousness, is as absolutely with Him as the very date of the return.

And now for my final question concerning the Lord's return. We have seen that it was never promised as an immediate certainty, we have seen that it cannot be certainly remote, IF NEITHER, THEN.

Is It Imminent?

With three remarks and their discussion I close. The plain words of all Scripture make it ever imminent; the converging lines of fulfilling prophecy mark its imminence; the expectant cry of the true church declares the soon-coming of that day.

The plain words of all Scripture make it ever imminent. If language is to have its original meaning, nothing can be made of the Lord's words—"Take ye heed, watch and pray, for ye know not when the time is" other than imminence. His illustration, "The Son of Man is as a man taking a journey into a far country, who left his house and gave authority to his servants, and to every man his work" followed by the injunction, "Watch, therefore, for ye know not the time" can mean nothing other than imminence. The language of Matthew xxiv:44 conveys the imminent coming of Christ; the parable of the five wise and the five foolish virgins loses its main point if "imminent" is not the word expressing the possibility of our Master's return. Paul's epistle to the Thessalonians, in which he says, "We who are alive and remain until the coming of the Lord" clearly expresses his hope that it might come to pass in his lifetime. It would be difficult to give any intelligent meaning to the injuncton to the Thessalonian church to wait for "God's Son from heaven" if he had known positively that their waiting would have been utterly in vain. Peter, in the Scripture that we made the starting point in this study, addresses the Christians of his day, calling them to a "separate" life, to "holy" conversation, and to the practice of "godliness" "unto the coming of the day of the Lord." James, while enjoining patience, expresses the hope "the coming of the Lord draweth nigh." There is no word in the English language that so well sums up the mind of the Lord and the Apostles, alike, as does the word "imminent."

The converging lines of fulfilling prophecy mark its imminence. If there ever was a time when the argument for unfilled prophecy was effective, that time is now past. "Peter" is long since dead; "false prophets" have been multiplied, pretending "christs" are common enough; "wars and rumors of wars" characterize every nation in the world; "famine" is sweeping its thousands and tens of thousands; "pestilence" is smiting in many countries; "earthquakes" are shaking continents; "evil men are waxing worse and worse"; "disobedience to parents" is the common observation; "unfaithfulness" and "unholiness" confront us at every turn; the governments of the earth are being "over-turned," and "over-turned" and "over-turned"; the professing church increases more and more in her apostasy in both faith and conduct; in spite of the roar of world-battles, the shrill piping of false prophets is heard above it all, crying "Peace!" "Peace!" The contending nations have consented that whatever the fortune of battle, "Judea shall go back to the Jew," and tens of thousands of Jews are already engaged in raising funds for the reoccupation of Palestine, and "the Zionist movement" in one of the most significant of the twentieth century." "The League to Enforce Peace" may succeed to make the temporary enthronement of the little horn (Daniel vii) possible. One thing, and one only remains to be enacted to demonstrate forever to believer and unbeliever, alike, our exact location in time, and that is the descent of the Lord into the heavens to receive His ascending saints—the entire company of risen and changed saints, whose spirits will attend Him in His descent (I Thess. iv:14), and whose bodies shall rise from earth "to meet Him in the air" (I Thess. iv:17). To be sure we are told that no Scriptures teach any such escape for the saints from the great tribulation that is to take place under the bloody hand of the anti-Christ, but if not, then what is the meaning of these words from the pen of the inspired Paul?

The converging lines of fulfilling prophecy mark its imminence, and how near the hour of that translation may be, who can tell? Deepening shadows, darkening clouds, roaring thunders, moaning winds have ever made the exact setting for the lightning's flash. Historically, the darkness deepens, the clouds blacken, war thunders in all the earth, every wind is laden with dying moans. The features of history face in one direction, and "as the lightning cometh out of the east and shineth even unto the west, so shall also the coming of the Son of Man be."

The increasing cry of the true Church suggests the imminent coming. When Christ was born in Bethlehem the faithful hearts in Israel were in expectant prayer, and for that matter, the world, in its blindness knew there was a portending something. Never since the day of Pentecost have the faithful of the earth stood on tip toe of expectation as they now stand! Their faces to-day are once more set heavenward like the faces of the early disciples.

I want to conclude this discourse with the words of the blind Bard of the English Commonwealth, John Milton, "Come forth out of thy royal chambers, O Prince of all the kings of the earth! Put on the visible robes of thy imperial majesty! Take up that unlimited sceptre which thy Almighty Father hath bequeathed thee! For now the voice of thy Bride calleth thee, and all creatures sigh to be renewed! Amen." Even so come, Lord Jesus.

TITLES IN THIS SERIES

The Evangelical Matrix 1875-1900

■ 1.William R. Moody
D. L. Moody,
New York, 1930

■ 2. Joel A. Carpenter, ed.
The Premillennial Second Coming: Two Early Champions
New York, 1988

■ 3. - 6. Donald W. Dayton, ed.
The Prophecy Conference Movement
New York, 1988

■ 7. Delavan Leonard Pierson
Arthur T. Pierson
New York, 1912

■ 8. Helen Cadbury Alexander Dixon
A. C. Dixon, A Romance of Preaching
New York, 1931

■ 9. Amzi C. Dixon
The Person and Ministry of the Holy Spirit
Baltimore, 1890

■ 10. Arthur T. Pierson, ed.
The Inspired Word: A Series of Papers and Addresses Delivered at the Bible Inspiration Conference, Philadelphia, 1887
London, 1888

■ 11. Moody Bible Institute Correspondence Dept. *First Course — Bible Doctrines, Instructor— R. A. Torrey; Eight Sections with Questions,*
Chicago, 1901

The Formation of A Fundamentalist Agenda 1900-1920

■ 12. Amzi C. Dixon,
Evangelism Old and New,
New York, 1905

■ 13. William Bell Riley
The Finality of the Higher Criticism; or, The Theory of Evolution and False Theology
Minneapolis, 1909

■ 14.-17 George M. Marsden, ed.
The Fundamentals: A Testimony to the Truth
New York, 1988

■ 18. Joel A. Carpenter, ed.
The Bible in Faith and Life,
as Taught by James M. Gray
New York, 1988

■ 19. Mark A. Noll, ed.
The Princeton Defense
of Plenary Verbal Inspiration
New York, 1988

■ 20. *The Victorious Life:*
Messages from the Summer Conferences
Philadelphia, 1918

■ 21. Joel A. Carpenter, ed.
Conservative Call to Arms
New York, 1988

■ 22. *God Hath Spoken: Twenty-five Addresses*
Delivered at the World Conference on
Christian Fundamentals, May 25- June 1, 1919
Philadelphia, 1919

Fundamentalism Versus Modernism 1920-1935

■ 23. Joel A. Carpenter, ed.
The Fundamentalist -Modernist Conflict:
Opposing Views on Three Major Issues
New York, 1988

■ 24. Joel A. Carpentar, ed.
Modernism and Foreign Missions:
Two Fundamentalist Protests
New York, 1988

■ 25. John Horsch
Modern Religious Liberalism: The Destructiveness
and Irrationality of Modernist Theology
Scottsdale, Pa., 1921

■ 26. Joel A. Carpenter,ed.
Fundamentalist vesus Modernist
The Debates Between
John Roach Stratton and Charles Francis Potter
New York, 1988

■ 27. Joel A. Carpenter, ed.
William Jennings Bryan on
Orthodoxy, Modernism, and Evolution
New York, 1988

■ 28. Edwin H. Rian
The Presbyterian Conflict
Grand Rapids, 1940

Sectarian Fundamentalism 1930-1950

■ 29. Arno C. Gaebelein
Half a Century: The Autobiography of a Servant
New York, 1930

■ 30. Charles G. Trumball
Prophecy's Light on Today
New York, 1937

■ 31. Joel A. Carpenter, ed.
Biblical Prophecy in an Apocalyptic Age: Selected Writings of Louis S. Bauman
New York, 1988

■ 32. Joel A. Carpenter, ed.
Fighting Fundamentalism: Polemical Thrusts of the 1930s and 1940s
New York, 1988

■ 33. *Inside History of First Baptist Church, Fort Worth, and Temple Baptist Church, Detroit: Life Story of Dr. J. Frank Norris*
Fort Worth, 1938

■ 34. John R. Rice
The Home — Courtship, Marriage, and Children: A Biblical Manual of Twenty -Two Chapters on the Christian Home.
Wheaton, 1945

■ 35. Joel A. Carpenter, ed.
Good Books and the Good Book: Reading Lists by Wilbur M. Smith, Fundamentalist Bibliophile
New York, 1988

■ 36. H. A. Ironside
Random Reminiscences from Fifty Years of Ministry
New York, 1939

■ 37 Joel A. Carpenter,ed.
Sacrificial Lives: Young Martyrs and Fundamentalist Idealism
New York, 1988.

Rebuilding, Regrouping, & Revival 1930-1950

■ 38. J. Elwin Wright
The Old Fashioned Revival Hour and the Broadcasters
Boston, 1940

■ 39. Joel A. Carpenter, ed.
Enterprising Fundamentalism: Two Second-Generation Leaders
New York, 1988

■ 40. Joel A. Carpenter, ed.
Missionary Innovation and Expansion
New York, 1988

■ 41. Joel A. Carpenter, ed.
A New Evangelical Coalition: Early Documents of the National Association of Evangelicals
New York, 1988

■ 42. Carl McIntire
Twentieth Century Reformation
Collingswood, N. J., 1944

■ 43. Joel A. Carpenter, ed.
The Youth for Christ Movement and Its Pioneers
New York, 1988

■ 44. Joel A. Carpenter, ed.
The Early Billy Graham:
Sermons and Revival Accounts
New York, 1988

■ 45. Joel A. Carpenter, ed.
Two Reformers of Fundamentalism:
Harold John Ockenga and Carl F. H. Henry
New York, 1988